"MORE... GOPHER HOCKEY BY THE HOCKEY GOPHER"

by
Ross Bernstein

"*MORE*...GOPHER HOCKEY BY THE HOCKEY GOPHER"
by Ross Bernstein

Published by BERNSTEINBOOKS.COM

ISBN#: 0-9634871-7-5

Distributed by Adventure Publications, Cambridge, MN (800) 678-7006

Printed by Printing Enterprises: New Brighton, MN

Photos courtesy of: the U of M Athletics Dept., USA Hockey & MN Historical Society

Ross Bernstein is extremely proud and honored to donate a portion of the proceeds from the sale of this book to the:

HERB BROOKS FOUNDATION

To learn more about the foundation or to make a donation, please contact Kelly Brooks at: (651) 206-4039 or kparadise@herbbrooksfoundation.com.

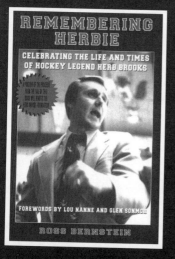

Thank You For Your Support!

The Herb Brooks Foundation is dedicated to providing more opportunities for kids to play the game of hockey. True to his words, the Foundation will assist in, "making hockey fun for kids and letting them learn to love the game the way we did." In keeping with this ideal, the Foundation will support programs that emphasize the development of youth hockey players and coaches throughout the country. The Foundation will also assist in providing more outdoor hockey facilities and programs, which directly impact the development of youth hockey players.

TABLE OF CONTENTS

Hey! Welcome back. Can you believe it has been 13 years since we last chatted? Wow, a lot has happened over that time and we have a lot of catching up to do. First, please allow me to explain what the heck you are holding in your hands right now and just what this new book is all about. For those of you loyal, bleed maroon & gold, die-hard Gopher Hockey fans, *"More...Gopher Hockey by the Hockey Gopher"* is simply the updated and expanded sequel to the original 1992 regional best-seller, *"Gopher Hockey by the Hockey Gopher."* It basically picks up where the old one left off, or sort of, going from 1990-2005. (I like round numbers, it's a rodent thing...)

OK, here is the original book jacket text which started it all, just in case you missed it: *A humorous, subjective, selective, and sometimes irreverent look at the history and heroes of Minnesota Gopher Hockey, past and present, as seen by, and told to, a large, furry rodent, better known as Goldy Gopher... Gopher Hockey fans have become accustomed to being entertained in high style by their favorite team, but also by Goldy Gopher who can usually be spotted going through his pranks and antics from his perch high above the ice in Mariucci Arena. While the view from that perch has given Goldy a unique perspective, Ross Bernstein decided that when his tenure as the "rodent" ended, he would try to provide the fans a unique perspective of their own on Gopher Hockey through the years. After spending the summer of '92 conducting hundreds of interviews with players, coaches, supporters, old-timers, fans and media-types, a unique book, "Gopher Hockey by the Hockey Gopher," was born. It will be treasured by anyone who might enjoy dozens of classic John Mariucci tales, the raucous times under Glen Sonmor, or to relive the championship years under Herb Brooks. A concise collection of quotes, innuendoes, facts and funny stories, including a comprehensive 100-year history of the program. It makes a great gift idea for any Minnesota hockey fan. Gopher fans past, present and future will find the book nostalgic, humorous, startling and historical — sometimes all at the same time."*

Now, for those of you who have no idea whatsoever what I am talking about, here is some background information that may help connect the dots on how I have come full-circle in my career. My name is Ross and I used to be "Goldy the Gopher," you know, the skating mascot at Gopher Hockey games back at old Mariucci Arena from 1990-92. Ring a bell? No? OK. I get that a lot. Let me go back a little further to tell you my crazy story. I am a former Gopher Hockey walk-on who, after a very brief "cup of coffee" as they say, as a practice pylon nonetheless, got cut from the team, but decided to stick around to take over as the team mascot. I will never forget, there were two basic criteria required for the job: One, you had to be a pretty good skater and know how to play hockey; and Two, you had to be a complete idiot. I apparently fit

A humorous, subjective, selective and sometimes irreverent look at the history and heroes of Minnesota Gopher Hockey, past and present, as seen by, and told to, a large, furry rodent, better known as Goldy Gopher.

Ross Bernstein

on both accounts. Needless to say, I got the job.

Well, after a couple of years of getting into trouble and causing a great deal of mischief as the lowest member of the food-chain, I was approached by a publisher one day after a game. He introduced himself to me and then proceeded to tell me that he wanted to write a book about all of the antics I had gotten into as Goldy. I told him I was flattered that he enjoyed my shtick and all, but really didn't think anybody would care to read about it. So, I politely said thanks but no thanks.

Now, at the time I was a senior and wasn't really sure what I wanted to be when I grew up. So, I got to thinking. What if I wrote a book about the history of Gopher Hockey, but with a twist — what if it featured interviews and stories from hundreds of former players, coaches and media personalities? And, most importantly, what if it was ghost-written with an inside slant from Goldy's perspective? Hey, that's not bad. I had never written a book before, but I thought this could be pretty fun. And, it would certainly help divert my attention away from the scary specter of entering the real world for at least one more year.

With that, I jumped in head first and started interviewing anybody and everybody who had ties to Gopher Hockey. I was buzzing around the Twin Cities in my little Plymouth Horizon, meeting up with the likes of everybody from Lou Nanne to Neal Broten to Stanley Hubbard to Glen Sonmor. It was a riot. If they had stories to tell, I was going to record them and put them in my book. What started as a "neat" project, completely took off. Soon, guys were looking me up and taking me to lunch, just to make sure that they got in the book. It was amazing. They were thrilled that Gopher Hockey was finally going to be chronicled, and were even more thrilled that if somebody was going to be doing it, that it was one of their own. That's right. Unbenounced to me, I had been secretly initiated into the Gopher Hockey fraternity. I was in, handshake and all.

Then, one day, I got THE call. *"Hello,"* I said. *"Ross, this is Herb Brooks."* Come on, I thought. No way this was THE Herb Brooks. Well, it was, and I couldn't believe my ears. Herb had heard about the book and wanted to call me to offer his support. I was literally speechless at that point, but just went with it. *"OK... What did you have in mmmmind Mr. Brooks?"*, I said nervously. *"Let's get together,"* he said. *"I'd like to discuss some ideas I have with you about your book."* Holy sh--! Herb Brooks, the former Gopher Coach and Miracle man himself just called me and wants to meet me. I was torn between worrying about getting fitted for a pair of cement shoes and a one-way ticket over the Washington Avenue Bridge into the Mississippi River, and acting like a giddy school girl worrying about what I was going to wear at our meeting. What did he want? Did I piss this guy off somehow by delving too far into the sacred covenant of Gopher Hockey?

So, we got together and we spent what seemed like an eternity talking about not just Gopher Hockey, but hockey in general. It was all good. Whew! I was in awe, hanging on his every word. It was like an outer body experience just sitting there with this guy who I figured to be larger than life. It turned out he loved the book idea and felt that the program's illustrious history was long overdue for something like this. Then, he told me something else that would have a profound effect on my life — even to this day. He told me that he loved the fact that even though I wasn't good enough to make the Gopher Hockey team, that he was proud of me for still wanting to be a part of the program. He knew that as the mascot I was still doing my part to provide entertainment to the fans, which, in turn, added to the home-ice advantage of playing at Mariucci Arena. He knew that the fans loved the antics I did and that in some small way, it may have enhanced their families' experience in a positive way.

Confused? I was a little bit too at that point, and then it hit me. Herb's dream was all about Minnesota hockey being the best it possibly could be, from top to bottom. He wanted kids to grow up in the Land of 10,000 Lakes with limitless hockey opportunities. He wanted to grow the base of the pyramid from the base up and get more kids interested in hockey. So, he saw what I was doing and he offered me his assistance because he appreciated the fact that my book was going to help "the cause." It was all a big-picture thing to him and he saw that I was doing my part. His goal was to get a whole bunch of other people doing their parts as well, particularly the younger guys. Because when that happened, he figured, hockey in Minnesota was going to really take off. That, was the big-picture. Anyway, we chatted for a while. He didn't tell me a bunch of wild stories or anything like that for the book, he just sort of wanted to tell me about his views on life and on hockey. In a way, he liked what I was doing and wanted to sort of pass the torch to a young guy who was full of energy and was in search of a cause. Hockey was Herb's cause, and that is what brought us together.

It was a real thrill, truly an Oprah *"Ah-Ha"* light bulb moment for me. I told him that it was ironic, but that he was actually the reason why I was sitting there across from him at that very moment. I told him that I grew up in the southern Minnesota town of Fairmont, down along the Iowa border, where hockey was almost non-existent. I explained to him that I grew up on a lake, but never played organized hockey until 1980, when I watched the *"Miracle on Ice."* Herb just smiled. I told him that I was an 11-year old kid that got completely sucked into the drama of watching a bunch of college kids, many of whom were former Gophers, beat the mighty Soviets and give our country a much-needed shot in the arm. I told him that the first thing I did after that was to beg my parents to let me go to the Herb Brooks' Hockey Camp in nearby Faribault. I told him that I actually met him all those years ago at the Shattuck School, during dry-land training one afternoon. It was a simple hello, how are you? But to me, it was like meeting a rock star. I never forgot it.

From there, I got utterly and completely hooked on hockey. I was a goalie at first, primarily because there was no place in town to buy any hockey equipment and the goalie got all his pads provided to him compliments of the Association. I lasted for about a year until I realized that you had to be completely insane to willingly let people shoot pucks at your head. Anyway, I played religiously with a group of neighborhood buddies, and we just loved it. We played out on Hall Lake, as well as at old Cardinal Park, where we used to stay out there all day on the weekends. We would order Jake's Pizza for dinner, and then help flood the rink at night so we could come back and do it all over again the next day.

We would travel around southern Minnesota playing teams like Luverne, Windom, Sleepy Eye and Worthington. All of the coaches were volunteers and none of them had any formal coaching experience whatsoever. They just did it for the love of the game and to give back to their communities. We didn't care. We weren't that good, but we just loved hockey. I remember having my mom order cases of White Castle cheese burgers for all my buddies so that we could watch the state high school tourney in my basement. We loved rooting for the underdogs, the Roseaus, the Warroads, the International Falls — that was what it was all about for us. We knew that we would never make it there in a million years, so we just ate Sliders and dreamed.

We played on outdoor ice all the way through my senior year, until when we finally convinced the city to build us an arena. Well, it was a hog barn, but you could put boards up in it and freeze the floor. Given our options at the time, we took it. It was old-school to the bone, and Herbie loved that. I didn't realize it at the time, but I was Herbie's target audience. I was not from Edina, or Bloomington, or White Bear Lake, or Hibbing, or Eveleth, where hockey was king. I was from down there, you know… wrestling and basketball country. Herbie knew that in order for the game to grow, we had to get the word out. We had to try to get new arenas built and start youth hockey associations so that these communities would embrace it. He needed more messengers. It was all part of his master plan.

As for me, I graduated from high school and followed my parents and two older brothers before me to the University of Minnesota. Not really knowing just how good or bad I really was, I took a shot in the dark and walked-on to the mighty Golden Gopher Hockey team. I had gotten to know some of the players like Benny Hankinson and Grant Bischoff and they encouraged me to come out, ensuring that they would put in a good word for me. At the time the program had a junior varsity. Most of the red-shirt freshman as well as the injured guys skated there and I figured that would be a great place to start.

I remember coming in for try-outs that first day, I was so nervous. Coach Woog was working with the players and the assistant coach, Bill Butters, a former NHL enforcer, was running practice. I showed up looking and acting like *"Rudy,"* you know the movie about the Notre Dame Football wannabe who spends four years busting his hump so that he can get into one stinking varsity game? Yeah, that was me. I was six-foot-nothing; weighed too much; and didn't have a lick of talent; but I had a heart the size of a major home appliance. My strategy was to basically fly under the radar with the hopes that they had a need for a big-hitting defenseman. That was my story, and I was sticking to it.

I will never forget being in practice one day, going through break-out drills. I had been pretty low-key for the first couple of weeks or so and finally decided to get myself noticed. So, on one particular play I saw Todd Richards line up at the other end of the ice. Richards, a star defenseman who was on the shelf at the time with an injury, was rehabbing with the JV in order to get some more ice time. Bingo. I was going to take this guy out and get noticed. I knew exactly which one he was too, because he was wearing a white jersey with a big red cross symbol on the front. "X marks the spot" I thought, as I moved in for the kill. Sure enough, he came in on me and I flattened him, best hit of my life. As I turned around, expecting to be greeted by hugs and high fives, I was instead met by Coach Butters' shoulder, which had just lodged itself deep into my spleen, and was now sending me flying across the ice. "Don't you know what the ?%$&! red cross is for, walk-on!?" Apparently, the red cross meant that you were injured and that in no way should anybody touch you out on the ice. Oops. Needless to say, my days in Gold Country were numbered shortly thereafter. In fact, my "cup of coffee" had just spilled all over my lap.

But, as luck would have it, fate caught up with me a little while later when I was asked to serve as the team mascot, Goldy. It was a blast. I got to hang out with the players; skate with them during practices once in a while; and be a complete idiot under total anonymity. What a gig! Officially, I was a cheerleader, which meant I was a "student-athlete," which meant I got perks, such as getting to hang out with a dozen beautiful cheerleaders all the time. Perks are good. We fast became friends and before long I was ready to hit the ice for my first game. I was nervous as hell, but rarin' to go. As soon as that zamboni got off the ice at old Mariucci Arena, we got the green light.

I will never forget racing out there all ready to strut my stuff. The cheerleaders went out first and then gave me a grand introduction by getting into two lines and then waving me through with their pom-poms. I was ready. The crowd was ready. They were anticipating some big-time comedic stunt and I didn't want to disappoint them on my first night. So, I flew out onto the ice waving a giant "M" flag, which I had been forbidden to take out onto the ice for fear that it would get ripped. No worries, I'm a hockey player, not a tuba player. (You see, prior to me, Goldy had always been a member of the marching band. But, because the higher-ups were tired of seeing Goldy get his ass kicked by Bucky the Badger and the Maroon Loon, they hired a ringer. I was that ringer.) OK, I am out of the gates. I am skating through the pom-poms and things are going great. The crowd is roaring as the band is playing the Rouser. Suddenly, as I reached center ice, I skated right over the flag, ripping it in half, and fell flat on my butt. My giant head then fell off and to add insult to injury, I looked down and saw that I had torn a huge gaping hole in the crotch of my furry outfit. Welcome to the *"Show,"* kid. So, there I was. The crowd loved it. Everybody thought it was hilarious. There's just one thing they didn't know, I didn't plan a bit of it. It took me about 30 seconds to realize that as long as nobody knew who the hell I was, I could act like an utter buffoon under the cloak of anonymity. I was like Bat Man, only I resembled a squirrel more so than a superhero. It didn't matter. I was in, and it was just the beginning to one of the greatest adventures of my life.

Being Goldy was a riot. I commandeered this TV platform, or perch, just under the scoreboard at the arena. In between periods, when I wasn't skating out on the ice with the cheerleaders, I climbed up there and had the best view in the house. I wound up doing this shtick where I would hold up signs all the time to get both sides of the crowd to basically yell stuff at each other, much like the old Miller Lite commercials: *"Tastes Great!"* vs. *"Less Filling!"* It was hilarious. Soon, I was branching out and making signs of people such as Larry Olimb, or Doug Woog, or even Frank & Wally, the TV announcers. The fans at it up: "Fraaaank!" "Waaaalllyyy" Eventually I started bringing toys up there with me, such as Gumby, Pokey, Fred Flintstone, Cookie Monster, Mr. Potato Head, Godzilla, Ken & Barbie, and even a three foot alligator — which I used to lower down onto the ice with a rope to taunt unsuspecting opposing players. It was affectionately called *"Goldy's Toy Box"* by various members of the media, and it brought out the kid in everybody I think.

What a rush though, to get eight thousand people screaming *"GUMBY!"* then *"POKEY!"* as loud as they could for no apparent reason whatsoever. I used to occasionally drop the toys on the ice too, which really pissed off the refs. One time Gumby wound up in the penalty box and I was threatened with a game misconduct penalty if it happened again. I behaved after that one. The crowd used to chant "MIN-NE-SO-TA," all around the four corners of the arena, but the student area was the NE-Section. It was also the loudest, rowdiest and drunkest — which always made for good comedy. Everything started in the NE section and before long I just had to point to my knee and the entire section would scream *"NEEEE!"* In fact, I could point to any body part and they would scream it out. My personal favorite was pointing to the opposing goalie and giving him the "Butt-Head." The best part of being at Gopher games during that era was being at old Mariucci, with all the die-hard fans who were having a ball. Gopher Hockey was in its heyday back then, and seldomly lost at home.

Now, I used to live in a frat house, just a half a block away, and would literally walk over to the arena all dressed in my costume, ready to go. Coincidentally, most Friday and Saturday afternoons, our fraternity had kegs tapped for all the brothers to get a jump-start on the evenings' festivities. So, once in a while I would partake in the social goings-on myself before a game, which sometimes made for some interesting fodder. Well, one time after a few cocktails, I came over to entertain the masses at the arena. No sooner than I got my skates off and climbed back up onto my perch, nature called and I had to relieve myself. So, I climbed down and went out into the hall to use the bathroom. Luckily, because the game was going on,

it was empty. The coast was clear, and I could now take off my head to take care of the business at hand. No pun intended. I had to be very careful that no little kids saw me though, otherwise it could mean big trouble. Little kids believe in Goldy the same way they believe in Santa Clause and the Easter Bunny, so Rule No. 1 of mascoting is and always will be: NEVER BE SEEN WITHOUT YOUR HEAD ON!

For those of you who may not remember the posh lavatory facilities at the Old Barn, let me refresh your memories, they were a dump! I had to choose between the ever-popular urinal trough, or the more private, luxurious stalls in the rear. I chose the stalls. Realizing

The Cast & Crew of the "Toybox..."

that my giant head would not fit in the stall with me, however, I took it off and put it on the toilet in the next stall over, closing the door behind me. I then went back into my stall and started to undo my breezers so that I could take care of business.

Then, I heard a sound. Someone had come in. I quickly jumped up on top of the stool so that I wouldn't blow my cover. That's when I heard it, a sound I will never forget. It was a horrifying, blood-curdling scream that could set off car alarms and drive dogs mad. As I peered through a crack in the stall door, I could see a little boy just standing there horrified, perplexed, and confused — pointing at the Gopher-less head which was sitting on the potty before him. Figuring that the rest of Goldy had been whooshed away like so many poo-poos before, he yelled out in sheer terror: *"Daddy, Daddy, help, quick! Goldy's flushed down the toilet!"*

I nearly fell off the can at this point, trying not to laugh. As dad came over and saw the situation, I knew that young junior had been emotionally traumatized. Daddy just shuttled his son away and tried to reason with the little fella, but to no avail. I could hear him screaming *"GOLDEEEEEEE!"* out the door and all the way down the hall. I only wish I could've heard the conversation that took place in the wagoneer family truckster on the way home from the game.

Other *"incidents"* during my tenure as Goldy included moments of temporary insanity. Look, it is extremely difficult to see anything while you were wearing a 60 gallon drum over your head with two tiny eye holes. I will never forget trying to slide on the ice between two parallel rows of Gopher cheerleaders and realizing that after building up a full-head of steam, I was going sideways. Tragically, I knocked them all over like bowling pins, which did not go over well at all after the intermission. Needless to say, I had to buy dinner after that one. That was not good. Nor was the time I came sliding across the ice out of control and knocked over the entire St. Cloud State cheerleading squad, which was in the midst of performing a pyramid at center ice. Let's just say I barely made it out of the arena alive after that one.

Well, I guess I just figured that I wasn't doing my job if I wasn't having fun and getting the crowd into it. I know that over the years countless people have told me, players included, that they enjoyed watching my antics up on the perch sometimes even more than the game itself. While I never intended to take away from the action on the ice, I will certainly take that as a huge compliment. I wanted to provide entertainment for the entire family up there, especially for kids, to make their event extra special.

This brings me back to my conversation with Herb Brooks. Again, Herbie loved the fact that I was able to make a positive out of a negative and do the right thing. My book went on to be a cult-best-seller back in 1992, and proved to be a wonderful experience for me. I got to meet so many great people and really found that I could actually make a difference. More importantly, I had figured out my true passion: sports and creative writing. Herb had always preached that you should figure out what you love first, and then figure out how to make a living doing it. That was the definition of happiness in his eyes.

Flash forward five years, and I am living in Chicago and then New York City with my wife. I had gotten involved in starting a children's entertainment company with some folks from Disney, and was working with several women who wrote children's books for a living. I thought back to what my true passion was and decided to take another leap of faith. With that, we moved home and I became a full-time sports author. I wound up interviewing Herbie for the next two books I wrote and we became friends. I continued to be a huge fan of his as well, as he went on to coach in the NHL and later with the 2002 U.S. Olympic team.

This is where the story comes full-circle for me. In 2003 I got a call from Herb one day. He had recently turned down a lucrative seven-figure contract to coach the New York Rangers. He had previously coached the team for five seasons after the *"Miracle on Ice,"* but didn't want to go back to the Big Apple. So, he turned it down. He wanted to spend more time with his family and also do more motivational speaking around the country. So, when he told me that he wanted me to write a series of motivational/self-help books with him to compliment his public speaking business, I was completely floored. I agreed, and we spent the next six months working on his new books. It was an incredible experience to be a part of the inner circle of a man I had worshipped for so long. Herbie had told me that he considered using some other writers from ESPN, but that he wanted to work with me because he knew me and could trust me. I was as humbled as I was flattered.

Flash forward again to the afternoon of August 11, 2003. I had been up at the U.S. Hockey Hall of Fame Golf Tournament on the Iron Range that weekend and had fun catching up with Herbie, talking about our book project among with other things. Herb had to leave early that afternoon though, to get home for a speaking engagement in Chicago that night. Well, later that day I heard the awful news, Herbie had been tragically killed in an automobile accident just outside the Twin Cities on his way home. I, like so many others, was absolutely devastated. I remember driving home from Duluth with my wife, daughter and dog, who is named Herbie in his honor, just wondering what I could do. We ultimately drove down I-35 past Forest

Lake and came right up onto the crash site. Just then, I looked over and saw a cross that somebody had erected out of two hockey sticks with a Gopher jersey draped over it. I just lost it.

So, I decided right then and there to turn our project into a living memorial. I wanted to honor the legacy of my friend and mentor, so I turned our book project into a different project altogether, entitled *"Remembering Herbie"* — with proceeds benefiting the newly created Herb Brooks Foundation. The book was much like my Gopher Hockey book, in that it was full of quotes and stories from all spectrums of Herbie's life, including friends, family, former teammates and players. Some laughed, some cried, but they all... remembered Herbie.

Herbie had recently written a foreword for a book I had just done before he died about Minnesota's greatest coaches. Ironically, I had asked him how he would want his epitaph to read. *"You know, I have always felt strongly about the name on the front of the sweater being much more important than the name on the back. They'll forget about individuals in this world, but they'll always remember the teams. That is how I want to be remembered."*

That was Herbie, the ultimate team player. His message wasn't always what others wanted to hear, and that is what made him so unique. He was tough, controversial and said whatever was on his mind, whenever he wanted. He was so principled, so passionate and so determined that once he committed himself to a goal, he was going to succeed — no matter what it took. In fact, looking back at famed television announcer Al Michael's notorious last second call from the 1980 Olympic semifinal game against the mighty Soviets, "Do you believe in miracles?... Yes!" — one can only assume that Herb probably didn't. Sure, he was a dreamer, but there were no short-cuts or divine interventions for this guy — it was all about hard work, commitment and passion.

That was it for me. Here I am, a walk-on wannabe, but I had found my passion. Thirty books later I am proud to be doing my part to grow the pyramid from the base up. So, for me, yes, miracles really can come true. I am so proud to be able to say that a portion of the proceeds from the sale of this book will benefit the Herb Brooks Foundation. That is what this is all about — keeping it all going for the next generation of kids who love hockey.

With that, I give you *"More...Gopher Hockey by the Hockey Gopher."* Back by popular demand, I can't even tell you how many people have begged me to write a sequel to the first one over the years. That book was described as the "ultimate bathroom book," which, as a sports writer, you have to take as a compliment I suppose. I vowed never to do it though, unless they won a national championship. All I can say there is thank you Don Lucia! I wound up interviewing over 100 current and former Gophers for the book, and also included the entire history of the two-time defending national champion Lady Gophers as well.

As for the down-and-dirty about the book, here is the deal. I picked a good sampling of players to interview. The history is up front and then it goes into quotes, stories and questions about the players. Look, I am not winning any Pulitzer Prizes for this stuff, people. This is just fun, light reading. Don't get bent out of shape if you can't find anything about your best friend's brother's uncle who scored a goal against Alaska-Anchorage back in 1992. This is not that kind of book. It features history, fun quotes, a where-are-they-now? and a whole bunch of hilarious stories. Just enjoy it for what it is and then wait patiently for the sequel in the year 2020.

You know, I can still remember sitting at the old Civic Center in St. Paul with my buddy Lindy, watching the Gophers lose in overtime to Harvard in the NCAA Finals. It was devastating. "Skarda hit the pipe!" became like Paul Bunyan folklore, which die-hard Gopher fans struggled with for so many years. How appropriate that the ladies have beaten those very Harvard Crimson two straight years in a row in the NCAA Finals to really avenge that loss. Now, fans will remember where they were when Grant Potulny lit the lamp against Maine in 2002 to finally get the monkey off the program's back. As for me, I was at the semifinal game against Maine with Lindy, yet again, but decided to watch the Finals on TV at home. Too much pressure for this guy. And do you know what? When Grant scored the game-winner I literally fell to my knees and cried like a baby. We finally did it.

It was amazing, and hopefully you will be able to relive moments like that plus many, many more in the book. Gopher Hockey is all about fathers and sons; mothers and daughters; and about hanging banners... lots of banners. Four national championships between the men and the women over the past four years, that's a pretty good start. What do you think? See you in the NE section. Thanks, enjoy!

M-I-N-N-E-S-O-T-A......Heyyyy Gophers.... Rah!

FOREWORD BY
DARBY HENDRICKSON

When it comes to hockey royalty in Minnesota, you needn't look any further than Darby Hendrickson — one of the all-time fan-favorites in the Land of 10,000 Lakes who has proven that with hard work and dedication, dreams really can come true. Darby grew up in Richfield loving hockey and loving life. He learned the game at a very early age from one of the best hockey minds in the business, his dad Larry.

"My dad taught me so much about the game," said Darby. "As a high school coach he led Richfield to a second place finish at the state tourney in 1976 and later guided Apple Valley to a state title in the mid-90s as well. He is just a great dad and a great coach, I think the world of him. He was always positive with his kids and knew that there was a fine line as to how much to push them and when to back off. I know that he is a big reason as to why I have been fortunate enough to play the game for as long as I have."

Darby went on to star at Richfield High School, where he led his team to the state tourney in 1991, en route to being named as "Mr. Hockey" that same year.

"Growing up that was all I wanted to do, to be able to say that I played in the state high school hockey tournament," he said. "So many good teams and so many good players got to play in the tourney: teams like Willard Ikola's Edina Hornets, the Bloomingtons, the Roseaus and Warroads. The tourney is what it is all about. I mean you play all year with the buddies who you grew up with and hope that your team has a shot to make it in the end. Being there, at the old Civic Center, was something I will never forget. We got knocked out by Duluth East in our quarterfinal opener, but those memories are still so vivid even to this day."

From there, Darby got to live out his dream by playing for the University of Minnesota. As a Gopher, Darby wasted little time in making a name for himself, garnering WCHA Rookie of the Year honors right out of the gates. Known for his speed and work ethic, Darby went on to play for two seasons in Gold Country, scoring 82 points in just 75 collegiate games.

"For me to be a Gopher was really a dream of a lifetime," he said. "That was it for me. Growing up as a kid in Minnesota I wanted to wear that big maroon 'M' and luckily I was able to have that dream become a reality. I will never forget going to old Mariucci Arena as a kid and watching the team, it was just bigger than life for me. Then, when I got to step out onto that ice, it was everything I could have ever hoped for and more. The program has so much history and so many great, legendary names who played there. So, for me to be able to look back and realize that I was a small part of that, it is something I will never forget."

In 1994 Darby got to live out another dream, to represent his country at the Winter Olympics in Lillehammer, Norway, as a member of Team USA.

"That was a really special time for me," said Darby. "I mean as a kid the 'Miracle on

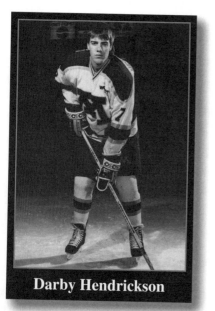

Darby Hendrickson

Ice' was such a big deal for me and my family. So, to be able to represent my country like that and have that opportunity meant the world to me. From the Opening Ceremonies to the National Anthem to living in the Olympic Village, it was all sort of surreal. Even thought we didn't win a medal it was still the thrill of a lifetime."

Following the Olympics, Darby had a tough choice to make: return to Minnesota or turn pro. He ultimately decided to make a leap of faith and take his game to the next level.

"I was dead-set on returning to the Gophers after the Olympics to try and win a national championship, but I ultimately decided to turn pro," he said. "It was so hard to not come back, it really was. My brother, Danny, was there and I still had two years of eligibility left. But, Toronto made me an offer I couldn't refuse and I decided to take my game to the next level. It was a smart business decision for me and in that regard I have no regrets. I have been fortunate in my career, no question. I have been playing professional hockey for a long time and certainly count my blessings for everything I have accomplished.

"I have certainly gone through my share of ups and downs though, but I have always enjoyed the challenge of persevering and to be my best. The challenge to be the best professional that I can be, both on and off the ice, is what I have always strived for. It takes a huge focus to be ready to play this game every single day and that can be tough. I am so lucky to have been able to make my career playing a game that I love and the bottom line for me is that it has been fun. That is what this is all about and I am very proud to say that. I have met and played with so many great people along the way too, which has been such a thrill. Another thing that has always driven me is the fact that you are never as good as you believe you can be. Playing well and helping your team to win is what it is all about and I have always tried to do those things to be the best team player that I can be. That is what drives me everyday."

Over his illustrious NHL career Darby has played in 12 NHL seasons with Toronto, New York, Colorado, Vancouver and Minnesota, scoring 65 goals and 64 assists for 129 points in 518 career games. So, what's the secret to this guy's success? "It's all about how you approach the game and how you dedicate yourself in order to achieve success," said Darby. "First, you have to stay in great shape physically and really take care of your body in order to withstand the grind of an 80-90 game season. My dad was the strength coach for the North Stars back in the day, so I learned a lot from him on how to train and stay healthy. It is all about how you approach the game, win or lose, in my opinion. For me, I was always trying to improve and get better. If you are lucky enough to play in the National Hockey League for as long as I have, you definitely go through a maturation process in which you grow up both as a player as well as a person. I have always tried to learn as much I could from my teammates, especially the veterans, in order to be successful. The stretching, the practice time, the nutrition, the sleep and relaxation time, how they spend their days off — it is all a part of it. You have to study how they approach the game and emulate what they do both on and off the ice. There is a reason that they have been in the league for so long.

"You can control those things, but you can't control injuries or politics. So, focus on the things that you can control and

Darby with the Wild

you will be OK in the long run. Beyond that I have always tried to be a good team-mate and have always tried to mix in well with my team's chemistry. I have always tried to find a balance between hockey and family too, which is so important. I always wanted to be able to leave the game at the rink, so that when I came home I was just a dad and husband. You need to be able to turn that on and off in order to have a normal, healthy life outside of the game. It is tough sometimes to juggle your family life with the business and pressures of hockey, but you just have to stay strong. Beyond that you need to stay positive and you need to keep your spirit up or this game will get the best of you. Being a true professional is about working hard, being consistent and about making the right choices both in and out of the rink. It is like somebody once said, 'the prize is worth the price,' and I couldn't agree more."

Perhaps the greatest thrill of Darby's professional career came when he found out that the NHL's newest expansion franchise, the Minnesota Wild, had sought him out to lead the new team in its inaugural campaign back in 2000.

"I grew up worshipping Neal Broten and wanting to play for the North Stars," said Darby. "Then, when they moved to Dallas, I was devastated. So, to be able to finally play pro hockey for my hometown team, that is about as good as it gets in this business. Those three years with the Wild were amazing, the fans were so good to me. I couldn't even begin to thank them enough for all their support. Hey, I even got to make a little history by scoring the first ever goal at the Xcel Energy Center. I got a great pass from Maxim Sushinsky to set up one of many great memories I was fortunate to have there. That was a huge thrill and something I will never forget."

As for the state of the state of hockey in Minnesota today, Darby is optimistic about the future but knows that we need to work hard in order to avoid complacency. "As kids growing up in Richfield all my brother and I ever wanted to do was play hockey," he said. "We practically grew up at Fairwood Park, our neighborhood rink. We used to literally skate down our icy road to the rink and play out there all day. It was awesome. There was a group of kids who all played down there together and we were like family. We all played other sports too, but hockey was the thing that kept us together — even in the Summer when we played roller hockey out on the tennis courts.

"We learned so much out there in that unstructured environment with no coaches around, telling us what to do and what not to do. I think kids today need a lot more of that to tell you the truth. There are still a lot of die-hard rink rat kids out there, but not nearly as many as when I was a kid. There are so many arenas nowadays and frankly a lot of kids don't like to play outside in the cold. That is too bad. Sure, warm weather is always an issue, but for the most part I just don't see the numbers of kids outdoors playing all day and all night. I see a lot of them at the local rink by my house in Inver Grove Heights, but it doesn't feel like it used to be back in my day. We used to be out there playing three-on-three or ten-on-ten, however many kids came out — we were there playing all day and all night. We loved it. So, hopefully that will change in the future.

"Overall though, I think the state of the game in Minnesota is great. To see so many guys who played either at the collegiate level or in the pros come back and get into coaching, that is just fantastic. They are passing on so much to the next generations of boys and girls here and that is really neat to see. As for the youth levels, I think we are strong and only getting stronger — for both the boys and the girls. The high school tournament is still very special, although it has lost a bit of its luster due to the fact that so many of the top kids are opting to play junior hockey nowadays instead. But, we are definitely doing something right. I mean we had four Minnesota kids get drafted in 2005, two of them coming out of Class 'A,' in T.J. Oshie and Matt Niskanen. So, there is a lot of talent out there and the fact that we are getting kids onto the next level is a testament to the jobs our coaches are doing at the youth levels on up."

While Darby is extremely proud and humbled by all of his success, he has never forgotten where he came from and knows where to give credit where credit is due.

"Minnesota hockey fans are so amazing," he said. "They are so smart and so educated about the game and they really know what is going on both on and off the ice. I have also always felt that Minnesotans are pretty simple people who live by the golden rule of 'treat people the way you want to be treated,' and that is how I have always wanted to live my life as well. As a player I respected that so much and was so lucky to have played here at so many stops along my career. They were wonderful to me every step of the way, especially when I came home to play with the Wild, and I will never forget their generosity and kindness to me and my family. They are just first class fans and I could never begin to thank them enough for their support.

"You know, I always loved what Herbie Brooks said: 'The name on the front of the jersey is always more important than the one on the back.' I couldn't agree more. So, when it is all said and done, I just want to be known as a good teammate, both on and off the ice, and someone who thought about the team first. Hey, all I can say is thanks, it's been a great ride and, yes, a real-life dream come true."

FOREWORD BY
JORDAN LEOPOLD

Jordan Leopold grew up in Golden Valley loving sports and went on to graduate from Armstrong High School, where he earned all-conference honors in both hockey and baseball. Despite the fact that Jordan had to overcome a serious asthmatic respiratory condition, he always worked hard and played for the love of the game.

"As a kid I just loved to skate," said Jordan. "I'd go to the park to skate on the ice in the winters and when the weather was warm, I'd be on roller blades skating in my driveway or playing street hockey somewhere in the neighborhood. No one pushed me to play this game, it's just something I always wanted to do, and my parents still have a few holes and dents in the garage to prove how much I wanted to improve my shot. We weren't supposed to use real pucks in the driveway, but, you know, kids will be kids, even if my dad wasn't too happy when he learned about what we had done to the garage."

After spending his senior prep season with the U.S. National Under-18 Team in Ann Arbor, Mich., he came home to wear the maroon and gold sweater that he had always dreamt of.

"When I was a little kid I was a huge Larry Olimb fan," he said. "I remember watching the Gophers play on TV on the old channel 23 down in my basement, the signal would barely come in. But, I sat down there religiously, watching them, and then I remember trying to emulate all of Larry's moves down there. I put a lot of holes in those walls with pucks too, but hey, it was all worth it."

Jordan Leopold

As a Gopher Jordan went on to become a two-time All-American, earn All-WCHA and WCHA Defensive Player of the Year honors, and was even named as the 2002 Hobey Baker Memorial Award Winner — emblematic of the nation's top collegiate player. In 164 career games at Minnesota, Leopold registered 45 goals and 99 assists for 144 points. The coaches and scouts alike both agreed that this guy had what it took to succeed at the next level.

"He was the best defenseman I've ever coached, and I've coached four All-Americans," said Coach Don Lucia. "He was better than all of them because he was so good on both ends of the ice."

Following his graduation that year, Jordan went on join the NHL's Calgary Flames. In his three years with the Flames, the sturdy blue liner has tallied 13 goals and 34 assists for 47 points in 146 career games. The highlights there have been many, including an improbably Stanley Cup Finals run in 2004, among others. That same year Jordan was the only under-30 defenseman named to the Team USA roster for the 2004 World Cup of Hockey. It didn't take long for the NHL's best to take notice of this kid.

"He's got the hands of a scoring forward," said Calgary All-Star Jerome Iginla. "And the important part of his makeup is he never looks rushed in practice. One of these days, he's just going to emerge and everyone will wonder where this kid came from."

All in all, Jordan Leopold is one of those special kids who comes along once in a great while. It was not just his ability to find the back of the net that made him so unique either. Jordan leads by example, epitomizes class and helped to resurrect a Gopher program that was on the verge of slumping towards mediocrity before he got there. He is also as humble as he is talented, a quality that has endeared him to the Golden Gopher faithful. No one has patrolled the blue line like him before and no one will be able to match his exploits in the future. He is a one of a kind player who has certainly made Minnesota proud.

"It was much fun being at the U of M and I had just had a great time there," said Jordan. "I grew up watching the Gophers and dreamt of one day playing for them, so it was a real life dream-come-true for me. I would have to say that it was the best four years of my life by far. Then, to be able to win a national championship, that was the perfect ending to a perfect college experience. I will always be grateful to the coaching staff for giving me the chance to play there and to have that opportunity to play with some of the best players in the country. Overall, being a Gopher meant everything to me and it always will. I really don't know what my life would be like without it to tell you the truth. I made so many great friends and so many wonderful relationships there, it was amazing.

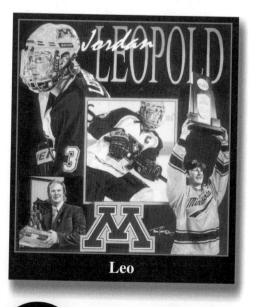

Leo

"The highlight of it all for sure was winning the national championship in 2002 over in St. Paul. That was one of the most exciting games I have ever been a part of and it will go down as a true classic. It was just an amazing moment for everybody that has been involved in Gopher Hockey and it is certainly something that I will never forget. All the emotion that came out on the ice following that incredible ending was indescribable. To be out there with my teammates and friends was so special. It was really a day I will always look back on and cherish forever.

"Then, to come back the next year and watch all my old teammates do it again, that was really neat too. I was playing in Calgary at the time but I flew out to Buffalo to watch them play in the Frozen Four. I wouldn't have missed it for the world. I sat in the press box and just kind of soaked it all in. It was so different from the year before when it was in St. Paul, I mean that atmosphere was so insane with all of the Minnesota fans there. Anyway, I told the guys that if they won another national championship that I would be throwing them a serious party afterward. All I can say is that I kept my word, and it was awesome.

"The Gopher Hockey program is just first class from top to bottom. I was so lucky to have been able to be a part of it. The program has seen a lot of changes over the years and as long as the coaches can adapt to those things, then they will stay on top. A lot of people had differing opinions after Coach Lucia came in about whether or not the roster should still be all Minnesota kids. Well, for me, I think you need to recruit the best players when they present themselves. Period. Nowadays with five Division One programs in Minnesota alone, there are a lot of options for kids to play hockey out there. So, we need to try to get the best kids who can help us win and not worry about the other stuff. As for myself, I was lucky. I grew up watching the Gophers and wanted to come there more than ever. It may not be that way for other kids in different parts of the country though, and we need to reach out to some of those kids and welcome them here if we think that they can make a contribution. Sure, having all Minnesota kids was a great tradition, but times have changed and the program needed to adapt. Looking back, I am really glad that they went in that direction. It makes our program so much stronger now.

"I would tell kids who are thinking of coming to the U of M that it would be the best decision that they could ever make. I mean it doesn't get any better than playing hockey right here in the Twin Cities. For starters, if their hockey careers don't work out, then there are plenty of networking opportunities for them to take advantage of afterwards. Other schools that are not in big metropolitan areas don't have that, and as a result they will have a lot fewer career contacts down the road. Beyond that, they will get so much national exposure playing here. College hockey is a really big deal here and the media covers it very well. So, that will only help their chances both in hockey as well as in business down the road.

"As for the state-of-the-state of hockey in Minnesota right now, I think it is great to tell you the truth. I think it is growing from the youth levels on up and we are getting a lot of guys on to the next levels, and that is what it is all about. When you have older kids having success and getting a lot of exposure, then that trickles down to the younger kids who see that and want to emulate it. It is good for the kids to dream because sometimes dreams can come true and become reality. I was one of those kids who wanted to shoot for the stars and luckily I got a lot of opportunities along the way. I made the most of them and I am proof that sometimes good things can happen to guys who work hard.

"My dreams did come true here and sometimes I have to just pinch myself when I think about it. The fans in Minnesota are second to none and were so good to me, they really were. I was so fortunate to have had so many people support me over my career and that has been wonderful. I just want them to know how much I appreciate it. So many people had a role in my success and for that I just want to say thank you. Those are the people I got pumped up to play for and they need to hear that.

"You know, when it's all said and done, I would hope to be remembered as a champion. That was my goal when I first got to the University of Minnesota and I finally got to experience it four years later. It was an honor to help rebuild that program and I hope that our NCAA title will be the first of many, many more down the road. My teammates and I went through a lot, but we came together under a new coaching staff and got it done. It was a thrill of a lifetime being a Gopher and I will always look back with so much pride on my Minnesota heritage. That is who I am and I am so proud of that."

The 1990-91 Season...

While the University of Minnesota's Golden Gopher Hockey program has roots which extend all the way back to the 1880s, the program's official inception began in 1922. Over the ensuing years the Maroon and Gold would dominate the college hockey landscape, right up through the final decade of the 20th century. By 1990, some 68 years after its humble beginnings, just 10 coaches had stood behind the Gopher bench: I.D. McDonald, Emil Iverson, Frank Pond, Larry Armstrong, Doc Romnes, John Mariucci, Glen Sonmor, Herb Brooks, Brad Buetow and lastly, Doug Woog — who had taken over the reigns in 1985.

Woog, a former All-American under John Mariucci back in the 1960s, would make the most of his opportunity in Gold Country. While he would never achieve the success that Herbie Brooks had done, winning three NCAA championships during the 1970s, he would leave his mark as one of the program's best ever. And, like Brooks had done before him, Woog was determined to get it done exclusively with kids from the Land of 10,000 Lakes.

By 1990 the Gophers had won 17 WCHA/WIHL Championships since the league's inception back in 1951 and Woog would add to that number considerably during his tenure. Minnesota had also made 14 appearances in the NCAA Final Four by now, tying them for the all-time lead with Boston University. Perhaps the most exciting title run in Gopher history came just a year earlier, in 1989, when the Gophers lost an overtime heart breaker to Harvard right in their own backyard at the St. Paul Civic Center. They followed that up with an NCAA quarterfinal loss to Boston College in 1989-90, and were eager to make it back to the promised land.

In Woog's first five years behind the bench he achieved the highest winning percentage of any collegiate coach in the country at .715%. In addition to winning back-to-back WCHA league titles in 1987-88 and 1988-89, his teams had also made it to the NCAA Final Four in four of the last five years as well.

With that, Minnesota entered the 1990-91 season with a nice mix of veterans and talented newcomers, including 15 returning lettermen. Among them were goalies Tom Newman (19-13-2, 3.84 GAA) and Jeff Stolp (5-1-0, 4.75 GAA), both solid netminders. A gaping hole had been left by those who had graduated and moved on, however, including the team's top two scorers in captain Peter Hankinson and Scott Bloom, who each tallied 66 and 52 points, respectively. The other key players absent from this season's lineup were Jon Anderson, Dean Williamson, Brett Strot and Lance Pitlick — who would go on to have a very successful career in the NHL.

Replacing all of that firepower would not be easy. Filling in would be an outstand-

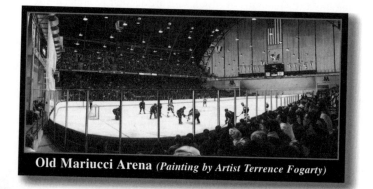

Old Mariucci Arena *(Painting by Artist Terrence Fogarty)*

ing trio of forwards, headlined by captain Ben Hankinson and alternate captains Ken Gernander and Grant Bischoff. Others expected to provide scoring punch that season were Jason Miller, Trent Klatt, Cory Laylin, Joe Dziedzic, Jeff Nielson, Andy Mills and Craig Johnson. The blue line corps included the likes of Travis Richards, Doug Zmolek, Tom Pederson, Larry Olimb and Luke Johnson, as well as outstanding newcomer Chris McAlpine.

Coach Woog

"We need to find roles for some of our veterans," said Woog. "If they are going to score goals, they will be on the power play. If not, then maybe we will put them on the penalty-killing unit. Either way, I feel it is important to find a role for them so they can feel involved in the game."

Minnesota started the season on fire, not losing a single game in its first 12 WCHA contests. The team finally came back to earth on November 30th when they lost to UND up in Grand Forks, but remained ranked at the top of the national polls at the midway mark of the season with an impressive 14-1-3 record. The second half of the season was up and down, producing some big wins as well as humbling defeats. A big turning point came when two of the team's top scorers, Trent Klatt and Craig Johnson, left to compete for Team USA in the World Junior Championships in Canada.

The Gophers played solid into the New Year, sweeping both Denver and then St. Cloud State, which joined the WCHA after competing for a few seasons as a Division One independent. Minnesota hung in there and looked good entering the home stretch after beating defending national champion Wisconsin by the scores of 5-3 and 8-1. From there the Minnesota-Duluth Bulldogs played spoiler by beating the Gophers on their home ice in the first game of a weekend series and then gained an overtime tie in Game Two. Northern Michigan then took three of four points that next weekend in a pair of overtime thrillers to really throw a monkey wrench into their plans.

Minnesota rebounded with a pair of sweeps over both North Dakota and Michigan Tech at home, and kept it going into the WCHA tourney, where, after sweeping Michigan Tech and then beating Wisconsin, they came up short against the eventual national champions from Northern Michigan in the tournament championship game, 4-2.

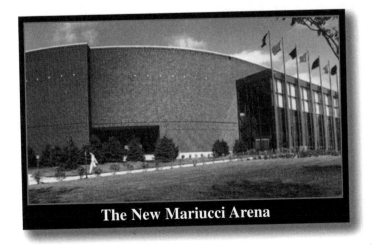

The New Mariucci Arena

Peter Hankinson

The Gophs went on to sweep Providence in the first round of the NCAA tourney and then headed east, to Orono, Maine, where they faced the Black Bears for the right to advance to the NCAA Championship Tournament. Motivating the Maroon and Gold was the fact that if they beat the Bears, they would get to home to play the NCAA Finals in their own backyard at the St. Paul Civic Center. Eager to avenge their NCAA Finals overtime loss to Harvard just two years earlier at the Civic Center, there was plenty of incentive for the Gophers to play hard. Maine wasn't about to roll over though and promptly handed them their first shutout of the season, 4-0, in Game One. They then followed that up with a 5-3 nail-biter the next night to end Minnesota's season on a sour note.

The team finished with an impressive 30-10-5 overall record along with a second place WCHA finish, marking the seventh straight year that they had finished no lower than second in the league. Larry Olimb led the squad in scoring with 19 goals and 38 assists in just 45 games, and Grant Bischoff and Trent Klatt added 47 and 44 points of their own, respectively. With regards to post-season honors and accolades that season, Center Larry Olimb, who led the team in scoring with 19 goals and 38 assists, was named as a second-team All-WCHA selection. In addition, Chris McAlpine and Craig Johnson were named to the WCHA All-Rookie Team as well.

The 1991-92 Season...

The University of Minnesota hockey team knew that they had their work cut out for them right out of the gates in 1991-92. In fact, the team had one of its toughest schedules ever that sea-

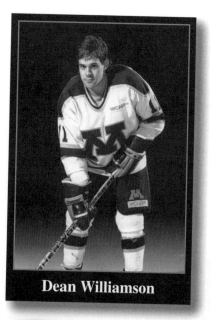

Dean Williamson

son, playing 15 games against opponents which had qualified for the NCAA Tournament the year before. The Gophers started out their campaign pretty rough, going 4-5 through their first nine games before finally getting back on track against Wisconsin. The Gophers won a 5-4 nail-biter in the opener at Mariucci Arena on Trent Klatt's game-winner, and then completed the sweep with a 4-1 win behind Jeff Stolp's 26 saves in front of nearly 16,000 fans in the "Border Battle" game at the Met Center.

"That Wisconsin series really got us going, said Head Coach Doug Woog. "After that, we played consistently strong hockey for the remainder of the season."

From there, Minnesota got hot and rattled off sweeps over Alaska-Anchorage and North Dakota to end the month of November. In all, they won 19 of their next 21 games, including a league-high 11-game win streak that ended at the hands of the Badgers in Madison. Over the next three months the Gophers climbed to the top of the national polls and finished the season fully 12 points ahead of their nearest competitor. In all there were 11 weekend sweeps for the Gophers and an impressive 30 wins in the final 36 games. The team capped off the season by winning the WCHA's MacNaughton Cup at home on February 22, with a 7-3 win over Denver, in front of 7,503 ecstatic fans. It was the program's ninth title and the third in the seven-year tenure of Coach Woog.

Minnesota then went on to win two out of three games from the Fighting Sioux in the first round of the WCHA Playoffs, followed by a 5-1 win over Colorado College in the WCHA Final Four at the St. Paul Civic Center. They then lost a 4-2 heartbreaker to Northern Michigan in the Final Four. From there, the team headed to the "Joe," where they got thumped, 8-3, by the eventual national champions from Lake Superior State in the NCAA Quarterfinals at Joe Louis Arena in Detroit to end their season.

For the record, senior goaltender Jeff Stolp, who finished with a 26-9 record and a 2.91 GAA, led the WCHA in almost every category and was the backbone of the team's league-leading defense which held its opponents' to a stingy 2.75 goals per game. The defensemen were led by All-American Doug Zmolek, a No. 1 draft choice of the North Stars whose rights were later obtained by the San Jose Sharks. Joining him on the blue line were Travis Richards, Sean Fabian, Eric Means and Chris McAlpine, an All-WCHA freshman who was never afraid to mix it up out there.

The offensive charge was led by Hobey Baker finalist Larry Olimb. The Warroad native led all scorers that season with 80 points, becoming just the seventh Gopher to score 200 career points to date. He also set the program's career assist mark with 159 as well. Forward Trent Klatt notched 30 goals and 36 assists, while Craig Johnson tallied 58 points of his own. In addition, Richfield's Darby Hendrickson garnered WCHA Freshman of the Year honors as a result of his 55 point season.

Lance Pitlick

The 1992-93 Season...

The defending WCHA champion Golden Gophers came into the 1992-93 season knowing that they were going to have to rebuild and reload with the next wave of talent, but were determined to get back to the post-season festivities. Coach Woog was optimistic heading into the season.

"Our team has suffered some tremendous losses in the past year due to graduation and professional signings," said Woog. "The first big question is who will replace Jeff Stolp. the top goalie in the WCHA last year; Larry Olimb, a Hobey Baker Finalist and arguably one of the top playmakers in the country; Trent Klatt one of the top scoring forwards in the country; three veteran defensemen, including All-American Doug Zmolek. Throw in the versatile Cory Laylin and you have seven players who were veterans of the WCHA and four who were legitimate stars. You just don't replace those kind of losses overnight.

Ken Gernander

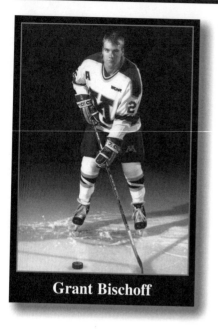

Grant Bischoff

"Last year we scored over five goals per game in the WCHA and that obviously played a big part in our success. The loss of Olimb, Klatt and Laylin up front will reduce our firepower initially, but those spots will be filled by our up-and coming veterans. We feel that we have a nucleus of very fine group of forwards returning, with Craig Johnson (19-39=58), Darby Hendrickson (25-30=55), Steve Magnusson (9-24=33), Jeff Nielsen (15-15=30), Justin McHugh (14-9=23), Scott Bell (15-7=22), Joe Dziedzic (9-10=19) and John Brill (8-9=17) all back. We look at it as more of a reloading year, because we feel the returning players, along with the talented new-comers could give us an even more explosive attack."

Behind goalies Tom Newman and Jeff Callinan, the Gophers opened the season with a split at home with North Dakota, followed by a split at Colorado College. The latter game of that series, a 6-7 loss, wound up being the first of four consecutive overtime games for the Gophers, of which they tied the next three against Northern Michigan and Wisconsin. They managed to take three points from Denver, then swept Michigan Tech and St. Cloud State before heading into the Christmas break. It was a tough January, however, with one of the top highlights coming at Duluth on January 9th, where freshman phenom Brian Bonin got the game-winner in a thrilling 6-5 overtime victory.

The team showed tremendous resolve though and regrouped from their mid-season slump by winning 12 of their last 14 games. Down the stretch they even swept hated North Dakota, 6-4, and 5-4 in overtime, in the first round of the WCHA Playoffs. After beating Wisconsin in the WCHA Final Four, thanks to Jeff Nielsen's overtime game-winner, they dug deep and came up with a 5-3 victory over Northern Michigan for the WCHA Tournament title.

From there, they wound up beating Clarkson in the NCAA Quarterfinals in Worcester, Mass., only to get beat the next night by Maine, 6-2, to end their season.

The Maroon and Gold finished with a 22-12-8 overall record, good for second place in the WCHA with a 16-9-7 mark. More importantly though, they battled back into the post-season picture by garnering the program's ninth consecutive NCAA Tournament appearance.

Leading the charge offensively was junior center Craig Johnson, who tallied 22 goals and 24 assists en route to earning All-WCHA Honorable Mention honors. Junior forward Jeff Nielsen followed Johnson with 21 goals and 20 assists, while All-WCHA Second Team defenseman Travis Richards was third in scoring with 12 goals and 26 assists. (Nielsen also took home the coveted WCHA Student-Athlete Of The Year Award that year as well.) Richards finished his illustrious career in Gold Country as the second leading goal scorer from the blue line in school history and second on the all-time assist charts for defensemen, behind his older brother Todd,

Ben Hankinson

who tallied 128 from 1985-89.

In addition, Senior Goalie Tom Newman started out slow but came on strong, finishing the season with a WCHA-leading 3.12 GAA and a 14-4-2 record. Another great senior campaign was had by versatile winger John Brill, who finished with 12 goals and 13 assists, and meant a great deal to the team's overall chemistry. Freshman center Brian Bonin also contributed right away with 10 goals and 18 assists en route to earning All-WCHA Rookie Team honors.

The 1993-94 Season…

Big changes hit Gold Country in 1993 and none was bigger than the brand spanking new Mariucci Arena, which was built across the street from the old one. While many fans were sad to be leaving behind one of college hockey's greatest old shrines, most were excited to be moving into what was considered to be the premier college hockey facility in the country. The new arena opened on August 21st with the Alumni Legends Game, followed two months later by the regular season home opener vs. St. Cloud, where Brian Bonin's two goals and an assist gave the Gophers a 4-4 tie against the Huskies.

Jason Miller

The 1993-94 Gophers were young but had a lot of promising young talent. Gone were Craig Johnson and Darby Hendrickson to the U.S. Olympic Team, as were Travis Richards, John Brill and Tom Newman to graduation. Add in the season ending back injury to Scott Bell and it was readily apparent that there were going to be some holes to fill. Leading the charge, however, was pre-season All-American defenseman Chris McAlpine, who was known not only for his toughness in the defensive zone, but also for his a knock-out punch scoring ability inside the opponents' blue line. Up front, the Gophers also had their second leading scorer back from a year ago in All-American candidate Jeff Nielsen, as well as Joe Dziedzic, Jed Fiebelkorn, Justin McHugh, Tony Bianchi, Steve Magnusson, Brian Bonin, Brandon Steege, Andy Brink and Bobby Dustin. In goal this year were a pair of talented underclassmen in Junior Jeff Callinan and sophomore Jeff Moen.

"This team is kind of an unknown because of the turnover in players," said Woog. "But if we get the kind of solid defensive play that we had a year ago and the goaltenders are solid, then we won't give up a lot of goals. On offense, we need our veteran forwards to lead the way, names like Nielsen, Dziedzic, Fiebelkorn, McHugh and Bonin have to appear in the scoring summary every night or we will struggle. I think if the veterans do their part, the younger players will fill in the gaps and we'll really add some excitement to our offense."

The 1993-94 schedule was brutal, as the team played seven of its first eight regular season games on the road. The young Gophers started 0-5-1, the second-worst start in program history, but then rattled off a 6-2-2 record head-

Larry Olimb

Chris McAlpine

ing into the new year. The Gophers then posted a 14-4-1 second-half record in the conference, finishing just a half game away from winning the WCHA title. They then rattled off four straight WCHA playoff wins over Denver (twice), followed by Michigan Tech and St. Cloud State, to notch their second straight WCHA Tournament Championship. Nick Checco scored a pair in the title game, including the game-winner, while Jeff Moen made 25 saves en route to the big win.

From there, the Gophers were NCAA bound, and headed to East Lansing, Mich., to face Lowell. There, Goalie Jeff Callinan, who rattled off 12 victories in his last 15 starts, was huge. Behind Nick Checco's third period game-tying goal, and Jeff Nielsen's dramatic game-winner in double over-time, Minnesota advanced back to the NCAA Final Four — which was being held at the St. Paul Civic Center.

With the bad memories of the 1989 NCAA Finals overtime loss to Harvard still fresh in their minds, the Gophers hit the ice against Boston University with high hopes that March 31st. Callinan came up with 29 saves that evening, but the more than 16,000 fans in attendance were crushed, yet again. wound up on the wrong side of a 4-1 loss.

The team finished the season with a 25-13-4 record though, recording one of the most remarkable turnarounds in NCAA hockey history along the way. While All-WCHA co-captains Jeff Nielsen and Chris McAlpine led the way individually, with 45 and 30 points, respectively, this was clearly a team effort. All-WCHA honorable mention honoree Brian Bonin tallied 44 points; Justin McHugh finished third on the team with 36 points; Tony Bianchi came out of nowhere to score eight goals and a team-high 27 assists; Eric Means tallied 16 points while playing great defense; and Joe Dziedzic scored nearly a point a game in a frustrating season that saw him miss 26 of 44 games with two separate fractures of his right arm.

The 1993-94 season will go down as a memorable one as this group of over-achievers battled back from a lot of adversity and thanks to a dramatic late-season rush, wound up back in the Final Four for the fifth time in the last nine years.

"We certainly started off on a rocky note," said Woog of the season. "But our players never got down on themselves and they picked each other up. The team battled and clawed its way into the Final Four and that's what the Minnesota tradition of 'Pride On Ice' is all about."

The 1994-95 Season...

With 18 returning letter winners and the highest-rated recruiting class in more than a decade coming in, the state of the state of Gopher hockey looked very bright indeed heading into the 1994-95 campaign. Jeff Callinan and Jeff Moen both had solid seasons between the pipes in 1993-94, and were joined that season by sophomore Steve DeBus — giving the team a trio of quality net-

Cory Laylin

minders. Among the frosh who were expected to contribute right out of the gates were Casey Hankinson, the youngest brother of former Gophers Peter and Ben, and the highly touted Mike Crowley, who earned "Mr. Hockey" honors after leading Bloomington Jefferson to its third consecutive state high school hockey title. Add to that the fact that Scott Bell was returning after missing an entire year due to a back injury, and there were high hopes in Gold Country this year.

Minnesota sprinted out to a 6-0 start on its way to the No. 1 ranking in college hockey by sweeping their perennial intra-state rivals from Minnesota-Duluth, followed by the cheese-heads from Wisconsin and then the Huskies from St. Cloud State. From there things got a bit dicey, earning just one point from UND and then split-ting with Michigan Tech at home. After beating Michigan State and Michigan to capture the College Hockey Showcase over the Thanksgiving weekend at the Civic Center, the Maroon and Gold struggled through December and January. First place Colorado College had jumped up to the top of the pack and everybody

Scott Bell

else was chasing them in the standings. The Gophers' once potent power play was on the fritz and the team needed to regroup.

In February the team came back to life, taking three of four points from Tech and then sweeping Duluth and Denver on back-to-back weekends thanks in large part to the efforts of Bonin and Bell, who were lighting the lamp early and often. Then, after garnering a pair of ties with North Dakota, the team swept St. Cloud State and Duluth yet again, to head into the WCHA Playoffs. In the Duluth Series, Casey Hankinson scored the overtime game-winner in Game One, while Crowley tallied the third period game-winner in Game Two. At the WCHA Playoffs the Gophers came out swinging and upended the Fighting Sioux thanks to more

Hankinson heroics, with this game-winner com-ing in the third period. After losing to CC, 5-4 in overtime, Minnesota rallied back to beat Denver, 5-4, on Bell's overtime winner at 17:14 of the extra session. Things were looking up.

Woog's crew had come on down the stretch and found themselves back in the NCAA Tournament for the 11th straight year, and 10th under Woog. The team opened up the quarterfi-nals at the Dane County Coliseum in Madison by blanking RPI, 3-0, thanks to a pair of Nick Checco goals and a perfect 22 for 22 saves by Goalie Jeff Callinan. From there, Minnesota beat CC, 5-2, behind a pair of Dave Larson goals, to advance on to the NCAA championships for the second year in a row. Making it even more special was the fact that the victory was Woog's 300th as the Gopher's head coach.

Eager to finally bring home the hard-ware, the team headed east to the Providence Civic Center, where they faced off against Boston University in the Final Four. Despite first period goals by Crowley and Jesse Bertogliat, the team allowed four unanswered

Trent Klatt

Jeff Nielsen

goals in the third period to wind up on the wrong end of a 7-3 contest to end their season on a downer.

When it was all said and done, Minnesota ended the year with a solid 25-14-5 record, finishing third in the WCHA standings, the WCHA Final Five, and the NCAA tournament. Incredibly, Woog had now led his teams to the NCAA tournament in each of his 10 years behind the Gopher bench, reaching the Final Four six of those times.

As for individual accolades, it was all about Center Brian Bonin, who finished with 63 points (32 goals, 31 assists) to lead the team in scoring. For his efforts, he was selected as a first-team All-American, was named one of 10 finalists for the Hobey Baker Award, won the WCHA Player of the Year award, and was the WCHA scoring champion. Other top players included Junior Dan Trebil who not only led all WCHA defensemen in scoring with 43 points (10 goals, 33 assists), but was also named to the Academic all-Big Ten team. Joining him on that elite squad was Justin McHugh, who, along with scoring 40 points, was also named as the WCHA Student-Athlete of the Year.

In addition, Goaltender Jeff Callinan finished as the WCHA goaltending champion, posting the lowest goals-against average in the league at 2.73. Callinan earned all-WCHA honorable mention honors and placed himself among the leaders in career and single-season goaltending records at Minnesota. As for the freshman, Minnesota placed two members on the All-Rookie squad. In fact, Mike Crowley was named the WCHA Freshman of the Year and earned All-WCHA honorable mention honors for his 38 point (11 goals, 27 assists) performance. Joining him was Center Ryan Kraft, who recorded 46 points (13 goals, 33 assists) to finish second on the team in scoring.

Eric Means

The 1995-96 Season...

Minnesota hit the ice in 1995-96 with yet another outstanding crop of freshman, including the 1995 recipient of the state's "Mr. Hockey" award, Erik Rasmussen from St. Louis Park, as well as Bloomington's Mike Anderson, Warroad's Wyatt Smith and Anoka's Reggie Berg.

The Gophers struggled out of the gates, going 1-2-1 over their first four games on the road at Michigan Tech and eventual WCHA champion Colorado College. The friendly confines of Mariucci Arena were a welcome sight as the team took out their frustration on Alaska-Anchorage by outscoring the Seawolves 13-3 en route to a weekend sweep. Kraft, Crowley, Berg and Bonin tallied eight of the goals in the shellacking. This was just the beginning of one of the greatest stretch runs in Gopher hockey history as the team took off from there. After sweeping St. Cloud State, the Gophers split with Denver. From there, the team went up 35W and did what no other team in WCHA history had ever done before, pull off a shut-out road sweep at Duluth. The pucks kept bouncing Minnesota's way after that as the team ended the month by claiming the College Hockey Showcase title in Milwaukee with wins over both Michigan and Michigan State.

While November was utterly fantastic for the Maroon and Gold, December and January proved to be even better as the team went 13-0-1 over the next two months. After sweeping North Dakota at home, the team took three of four points on the trip to Alaska-Anchorage — always a tough task to pull off with the long travel time and lack of sleep. Reggie Berg tallied a hat trick and Jeff Moen stopped all 20 pucks he faced in the second game, a 5-0 shut-out. The team said good bye to 1995 with its first Mariucci Classic title in four seasons by beating Harvard and Bowling Green, thanks to outstanding goaltending from both Moen and DeBus, who let in just four goals between them during the tourney.

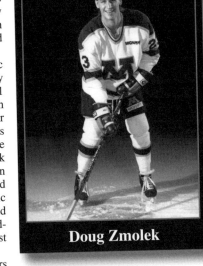

Doug Zmolek

The new year was good to the Gophers as they enjoyed their first unbeaten and untied January in school history. With sweeps over Denver, UMD, Wisconsin, and Northern Michigan, the team found itself riding a school record 19-game unbeaten streak into February. The wheels came off shortly after that, however, as the team won just two of their next eight games. In fact, in between sweeps by North Dakota and Wisconsin, the team managed a couple of really tough splits with first place Colorado College and then St. Cloud State. Incidentally, the first game of the home-and-home with St. Cloud State saw the team pummel the huskies, 8-3, behind Rasmussen's hat trick and a pair of goals from Brian Bonin — his 200th career point as a Gopher.

In March the team got it figured out. After sweeping Alaska-Anchorage in the first-round of the a WCHA Playoffs, Minnesota ended Wisconsin's season at the WCHA Final Five thanks to Berg and Bonins' third period goals, followed by Nick Checco's overtime game-winner. From there, the team beat Michigan Tech in the title game to clinch their 12th consecutive bid to the NCAA Tournament.

In the opener the Gopher beat Providence, 5-1, behind a pair of Wyatt Smith goals to set up a rematch with Michigan in the quarterfinals. There, ironically, for the third consecutive time in as many years, the eventual national champion would knock out the Gophers and send them packing. This time it was the Wolverines as they rallied late in the game to come up with a pair of third period goals to win the game, 4-3, in East Lansing, Mich. Casey Hankinson tied it up at three apiece with five minutes to go, but DeBus got beat just a few minutes later to seal the deal. It was a bitter loss to an otherwise brilliant season.

The honors and accolades that season started and stopped with Center Brian Bonin (81 points) and Defenseman Mike Crowley (63

Joe Dziedzic

Travis Richards

points), who were both named as Hobey Baker Finalists. Both players were also named as first team All-Americans, marking the first time since 1981 (Neal Broten and Steve Ulseth) that two Gophers were honored as such in the same season. Bonin, who became just the fifth player in league history to win back-to-back league scoring titles, also took home both the WCHA regular-season and tournament MVP honors. Crowley, meanwhile, broke the single-season point record with his four-assist effort in the WCHA Final Five championship game against Michigan Tech, giving him 46 helpers on the year — three better than previous record-holder Todd Richards, who set the record back in 1987.

In addition, senior defenseman and co-captain Dan Trebil (46 points) was named as a second team All-American as well as a second-team Academic All-American. For his efforts he was given the prestigious WCHA Student-Athlete Of The Year Award. Trebil also became just the second blue-liner in Gopher history to tally 100 or more assists in his career. Other Gophers honored by the WCHA included goaltender Steve DeBus and freshman Erik Rasmussen, who were named to the All-WCHA first team and All-Rookie team, respectively.

On a side note, Minnesota's "Pride On Ice" was the subject of national media attention when it was featured on ESPN's "NCAA Today" show that year, highlighting the unique fact that every player on the roster was home grown from Minnesota.

The 1996-97 Season...

The festivities celebrating the 75th anniversary of Gopher hockey kicked off by honoring all of their past All-Americans in a weekend series against three-time defending WCHA champion Colorado College. Erik Rasmussen's pair of goals led the Gophers to a 4-2 victory in the opener, but the team came up a goal short the next night, 2-1, to split the series with the Tigers. From there, Minnesota split a pair of series with both Duluth and Wisconsin, but rebounded in November by sweeping North Dakota, Michigan Tech and Northern Michigan to catapult to the top of the WCHA standings. In the second game with North Dakota, Casey Hankinson scored four goals and added a pair of assists as Minnesota crushed the eventual national champions, 10-6. Then, against Michigan Tech, Freshman Goalie Erik Day made history when he debuted with back-to-back shut-outs, becoming the first Gopher netminder in school history to accomplish the feat in his first two collegiate starts.

Minnesota then lost their opener against Michigan at the College Hockey Showcase in Detroit, but rallied back behind Wyatt Smith's third period goal to beat Michigan State, 4-3, for

Darby Hendrickson

third place. From there, the Gophs came up with an impressive 4-1 win at SCSU, highlighted by senior Dan Hendrickson's four assist effort, but lost the back end of the series in overtime, 4-3, despite a pair of Rico Pagel goals. The team rounded out the year by winning the Mariucci Classic, defeating Boston College, 4-2, and Miami University, 7-4.

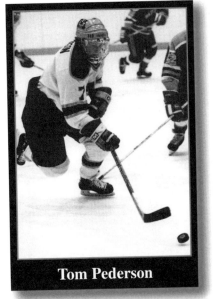

Tom Pederson

January kicked off with a bang as the team garnered a tough road sweep over Alaska-Anchorage behind junior Ryan Kraft's hat trick in the Saturday game, giving him WCHA Player of the Week honors. Minnesota then split with Denver, winning the opener, 3-2, on Nick Checco's thrilling overtime goal at 1:35 of the extra session. After splitting with St. Cloud State in a tough home-and-home series, the Gophers rebounded to sweep Michigan Tech, outscoring the Huskies 13-6. Freshman Ben Clymer had a goal and an assist in the opener and then notched his first career hat trick in the Saturday game.

Things got ugly when the Gophers headed up to Grand Forks though, as the Sioux swept the Maroon and Gold to open up a three-point lead in the WCHA standings. Determined, Minnesota rebounded to sweep Northern Michigan, 4-3 and 2-1, on Billy Kohn's game-winner in Game One and Ryan Kraft's two goals in Game Two. UMD crushed the Gophers that next weekend in the opener, 8-4, only to get hammered right back the next night, 7-1, behind Duluth East grad Dave Spehar's two goals and Ryan Kraft's four assists. Minnesota then captured three out of four points on the road against Colorado College and then swept rival Wisconsin at home thanks in large part to the efforts of Kraft, who played out of his head, tallying five goals in the series. For their efforts, the team finished as co-WCHA champs with a record of 21-10-1 in league action.

After sweeping Alaska-Anchorage in a first round WCHA playoff series at Mariucci Arena, Brian LaFleur scored a pair and then Mike Crowley clinched it in over-time to lift the Gophers to a dramatic come-from-behind 5-4 win over St. Cloud State at the WCHA Final Five in St. Paul. The next night, however, North Dakota eked out an overtime win of their own over the Gophers, winning 4-3, despite goals from Hendrickson, Spehar and Checco. With the Broadmoor Trophy in hand, UND got the higher seed and forced the Gophers to Grand Rapids, Mich., to face Michigan State. There, they dominated the Spartans, 6-3, behind Casey Hankinson's two goals and two assists.

With that, the Gophers now found themselves in hostile territory, facing rival Michigan for the second consecutive season in an NCAA quarterfinal showdown. The defending NCAA champs didn't disappoint either, jumping out to a 4-0 lead and beating Minnesota convincingly, 7-4, despite a pair of unassisted goals from Erik Rasmussen. The team finished with a very respectable 28-13-1 overall record,

Craig Johnson

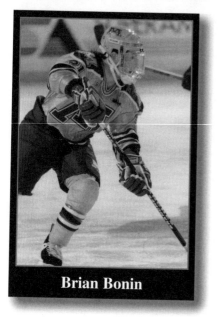

Brian Bonin

but simply could not get the 900 pound gorilla otherwise known as Michigan off of their backs.

When the smoke had finally cleared Mike Crowley (56 points) was named as the WCHA Player Of The Year, a Hobey Baker Finalist, and earned first-team All-American honors for the second year in a row — just the third player ever to do so in back-to-back seasons. In addition, Goalie Steve DeBus, a Rochester native, was named to his second straight All-WCHA first team. DeBus led the league in wins (18) and was among the top four netminders in the league in goals-against average (3.081) saves (705), shutout periods (32) and minutes played (1,675:23). The other top scorers from that season included Ryan Kraft who tallied 46 points; Casey Hankinson, who added 41 points; and Dave Spehar and Reggie Berg, who each notched 37 points apiece as well.

The 1997-98 Season...

The Gopher's 1997-98 campaign was all about splits early on, and ultimately ended in frustration as the team wound up bowing out in the first round of the WCHA playoffs. Minnesota began the year by splitting the season-opening series with Hockey East power Maine at Mariucci Arena, 1-6 and 3-2. From there they headed to Duluth, where Junior Center Wyatt Smith scored four goals in the weekend series split against the Dogs. The team then earned splits with both North Dakota and Wisconsin, in four tight games that were each decided by a goal. Erik Westrum and freshman Aaron Miskovich each tallied two goals in the 6-5 win over the defending national champs from North Dakota in the Friday game, while Reggie Berg's two goals capped a great comeback in the 4-2 Friday win at Wisconsin.

To say that November and December were tough on the Maroon and Gold would be

Reggie Berg

an understatement to say the least. The Gophers embarked on a rough nine-game losing streak which included sweeps at the hands of Alaska-Anchorage, Colorado College, and both games of the College Hockey Showcase against Michigan and Michigan State. The only silver lining was the fact that six of the seven losses during that stretch were by only one goal. Following a pair of losses to St. Cloud State, Minnesota finally got a "W" with a 6-3 win over Brown at the Mariucci Classic thanks to Wyatt Smith's four points and Dave Spehar's two goals. They lost to Northeastern that next night, but rebounded to sweep Mankato State the next weekend, 6-2 and 4-3, in their first ever meeting. Wyatt Smith scored six points in the series while Dylan Mills added three of his own.

January would prove to be much better for the Gophers. After a home split with Denver, they went on to sweep the UMD Bulldogs behind hometown hero Dave Spehar's four goals in the series. In addition, Defenseman Brett Abrahamson notched the game-winner on Saturday, earning him WCHA Defensive Player of the Week honors in the process. The team closed out the month on a downer, getting swept up in Houghton, Mich., by Michigan Tech. One bright spot, however, was the play of Junior Forward Mike Anderson, who notched six goals and four assists while scoring a point in seven of the eight games during the month.

From there, the team got it together by sweeping Wisconsin, 4-1 and 7-0. The Gophers snapped the Badger's 13-game unbeaten streak in Game One thanks to a pair of Ryan Kraft goals. Then, in Game two, Wyatt Smith scored a hat trick; Ryan Kraft scored four points; Stuart Sendin scored a pair of his own, and Steve DeBus stood on his lips by turning aside all 34 shots that came his way in front of nearly 15,000 fans at the Target Center.

Jeff Callinan

Minnesota then lost to UND, 4-2, in Game One, and then blew a 3-0 third period lead to the defending NCAA champions in the finale. The team headed to Alaska-Anchorage that following weekend and won Game One, 3-0, behind Steve DeBus' 14 saves, and Wyatt Smith's two goals. Kraft, Sendin, Spehar and Berg all tallied in the 4-2 Saturday win to complete the sweep.

Despite Wyatt Smith's five goals against CC that next weekend, which resulted in him earning WCHA Offensive Player of the Week honors, Minnesota got swept by the Tigers, 4-3 and 9-6. Minnesota rallied to sweep St. Cloud State that next week though, 6-2 and 5-3, behind Reggie Berg's hat trick in Game One and Casey Hankinson's game-winner late in the third in Game Two.

Hoping to make a splash in the post-season, Minnesota got trounced by UMD, 7-3, in the first round of the WCHA playoffs, but came back behind DeBus' 5-0 shutout at the DECC in Game Two. The third and final game, however, saw UMD score four unanswered goals in the third period to send the game to overtime. There, Mike Peluso scored the 5-4 heart-breaking game-winner, giving the Dogs a 2-1 series win. With that, an otherwise marginal season by Gopher standards was over courtesy of an ugly first-round exit.

The Golden Gophers ended the season with a 17-22-0 overall record and a 12-16-0 mark in conference action. Despite the team's average season, Minnesota did manage to set the NCAA Attendance Record with a total home attendance of 201,126 for 20 home dates. In fact, Minnesota became the first school in NCAA hockey history to average over 10,000 per game in a single season with 10,056.

Among the honors and accolades that year, Reggie Berg was named to the all-WCHA second team as he tied for the conference lead in scoring with 17 goals and 17 assists in 28 games. Berg, who was +19 with 28 points in Minnesota's 17 wins, led the team with 179 shots on goal and finished with 39 points — good for a share of the WCHA Scoring Crown. In addition, Wyatt Smith was named to the all-WCHA

Ryan Kraft

Dave Spehar

third team after leading the Gophers in overall points with 47 and tying for the WCHA lead with 17 tallies in league games.

The 1998-99 Season...

Coming off of one of the worst seasons in recent memory, the Gophers were anxious to get the ship turned in the right direction. Among the positives heading in: the league's scoring co-champion in Reggie Berg and the league leader in goals in all games in Wyatt Smith were back. Add to the mix several proven veterans in Dave Spehar, Mike Anderson, Nate Miller, Bill Kohn, Mike Lyons, Ryan Trebil, Dylan Mills, Aaron Miskovich and Erik Westrum. Then, toss in freshman sensation Johnny Pohl of Red Wing, the all-time Minnesota state high school scoring record holder, and things looked promising. But, the team lost Ben Clymer that summer when he opted to pursue a pro career, as well as goalie Steve DeBus, to graduation. Freshman Adam Hauser was going to be thrown to the wolves and nobody knew how well the kid was going to do.

Despite all of the this, Coach Woog learned a lot from the year before and was optimistic.

"In some ways, we all probably benefitted from last season," said Woog. "We all learned that you can't take things for granted, and that you've always got to work hard. There were many times when I was pleased with the effort I was seeing last season, but everything from the injuries to the bad bounces just made every mistake we committed magnified more than normal. I'm really looking forward to getting this season going more than any other in recent memory. This team has some very talented, hard working players who I feel can be good examples to some of our younger players. If we can get some answers in the nets and on the blueline, this has the potential to be a good team."

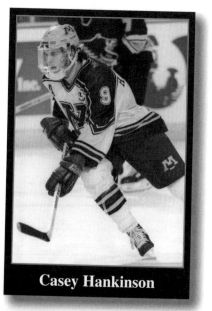

Casey Hankinson

Minnesota opened the year on a positive note, beating St. Lawrence and Ohio State before taking three out of four points from UMD at home. Aaron Miskovich scored a pair of goals in the 3-1 win against Duluth. Hauser then proved he was the real deal when he blanked St. Cloud State in Game Five, turning away all 26 shots he faced that night. The Gophers then lost the back end of the series at the National Hockey Center in St. Cloud the next night, as the Huskies scored with just 16 seconds to go for a 6-5 win. From there, Minnesota pulled off a pair of 3-2 victories to earn a hard fought sweep over the Wisconsin Badgers at the new Kohl Center in Madison. Erik Westrum and Dave Spehar each tallied a pair of goals in both games to seal the deal.

Things got tough from there, however, as back-to-back series' against Colorado College and North Dakota yielded just one point for the Gophers, a 4-4 tie against the Sioux. One bright spot though was the outstanding play of fresh-man Defenseman Jordan Leopold, from Robbinsdale, who went on to score five goals in the next five games.

The Gophers earned a split up at Alaska-Anchorage before returning home for the College Hockey Showcase. A 3-2 loss to Michigan was followed with a 2-1 win over Michigan State, thanks to Wyatt Smith's third period power-play game-winner from Dave Spehar. From there, Minnesota stumbled with rare losses to both Princeton and Ohio State at the Mariucci Classic. The new year kicked off with an embarrassing 8-4 loss to Boston College, followed by a 3-3 tie, which saw the Gophers rally to score a pair of third period goals from Anderson and Pagel to secure a point in the standings. They tied Denver by that same score the following weekend, only to get blanked, 5-0, in Game Two.

Wyatt Smith

A pair of ties to Minnesota State-Mankato were then followed up with a pair of crushing defeats at the hands of the top ranked Fighting Sioux, 5-4 and 6-5. The Gophers ended the month on a positive note though, returning home for a pair of 4-2 wins over Michigan Tech thanks to sophomore Matt Leimbek's two goals and three assists which earned him WCHA Offensive Player of the Week honors. Minnesota's ensuing trip to Colorado College saw the team score just two goals in what turned out to be a pair of blowout losses.

After earning just a split with Alaska Anchorage at home, Minnesota posted a pair of ties with St. Cloud State, 4-4 and 2-2. The high point of February came in a road sweep of UMD at the DECC in Duluth. There, the Gophers put on an offensive show, taking the opener, 10-7, on Wyatt Smith's hat trick. They then took Game two, 4-1, on Reggie Berg's four-goal masterpiece. Next up was Wisconsin, where despite a pair of goals from sophomore Erik Westrum, the Badgers took Game One, 6-4. Minnesota earned a 2-2 tie in the finale, however, thanks to goals from Berg and Leopold. Hauser played big in that game too, kicking away 33 of 35 shots.

Hauser kept it going the next series as well, blanking Alaska-Anchorage, 4-0, in Game One and 1-0 in Game Two. Rico Pagel had the game-winner in the second game as Minnesota headed into the WCHA Final Five at the Target Center with some solid momentum behind them. There, Minnesota got a pair of goals each from Berg and Spehar to open the post-season with a 5-3 win over St. Cloud State. The team's bid for an invitation to the Big Dance, the NCAA Championships, then died the following evening when top-ranked North Dakota skated past the Gophers, 6-2, thus ending Minnesota's season. To make matters worse, the team lost the third-place game to Colorado College the following afternoon, 7-4, putting an exclamation point on an otherwise mediocre season.

The Golden Gophers ended the season with a 15-19-9 overall record and a mark of 10-12-6 in WCHA regular season action. Leading the way for the Maroon and Gold was Senior Forward Reggie Berg, who, in addition to becoming the 23rd member of the Gopher 150-

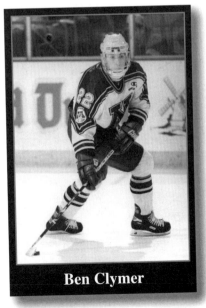

Ben Clymer

Steve DeBus

Point Club, led the team in total scoring with 20 goals and 28 assists for 48 points. Senior Forward Wyatt Smith was named to the all-WCHA third team after leading the team with 23 goals, ultimately finishing his career with 129 points in 152 career games. In addition, freshman Jordan Leopold, who led all Golden Gopher rookies in scoring with seven goals and 16 assists on the season, was named to the all-WCHA third team as well as the league's all-rookie team.

The 1999-2000 Season...

That off-season, big changes hit the program hard as Doug Woog stepped down as the team's head coach. In his 14 seasons behind the Gopher bench Woog posted an outstanding 390-187-40 record, good for a .665 winning percentage. Woog didn't go far though, as he was named as an assistant Athletic Director with U of M's Athletics Dept. working with fundraising and corporate sales.

Woog's replacement was another Minnesota boy, Don Lucia, a Grand Rapids native who played college hockey at Notre Dame. Lucia's resume was solid. A former head coach at Alaska-Fairbanks, Lucia came to the Gophers via Colorado College, where he had guided the program from 1993-99. There, he led his teams to a pair of Frozen Fours in 1996 and 1997 and was a two-time WCHA Coach of the Year as well. Expectations were high under the new coach, but he came in ready to make his mark.

"I am really looking forward to getting things going this season and getting back on the ice," said Lucia. "I told the guys when I took the job that I was not going to look at any tape of them last year and make any judgments, positive or negative about their performances based on that alone. Everyone starts this year with a clean slate, and is going to have to prove themselves once practice starts in the Fall. I like the attitude and comments I've heard from the players as I have come in contact with them this summer. Most of all, I'm just excited about the opportunity to be coaching back in my home state, and to be a part of a tradition like Golden Gopher hockey."

The new coach was also optimistic about the talent he inherited on his new roster.

"We have some nice depth and talent at this position," he said. "I've seen more of the veteran guys than some of the others, but I like the reports I've heard on the younger players. Obviously, we'll need some more goal scoring production out of guys like Spehar, Westrum, and Miskovich to help offset the loss of (Reggie) Berg and (Wyatt) Smith. And as an opposing coach, I always respected the work ethic and effort of guys like Westrum and Miller. Last year seemed to be kind of a break-out type season individually for Westrum, and he definitely possesses the type of makeup to be one of the best in the league this season. I know players like Pagel, Leimbek, and Senden have been on the shelf for

Coach Lucia

quite a few games over the last few years, and hopefully our luck will change in that department this season so we can all see what these players can do given a full season without interruption."

The new-look Gophers hit the ice under Coach Lucia on October 16th, 1999, on the road at Maine. There, despite four goals from Erik Westrum, the Gophers got swept by the Black Bears, 5-3 and 5-4, to start the season on a real downer. Minnesota came back that next weekend, however, to gain a hard earned 2-2 tie at home against North Dakota, thanks to goals by Leopold and Spehar, not to mention a career-high 44 saves from sophomore Goalie Adam Hauser. They came up short that next night though, dropping Game Two, 3-2. The team's lone victory of the month came that next week-end against top-ranked Boston College, where they got an overtime goal from senior captain Nate Miller for a 6-5 win. (Incidentally, those three teams: Maine, North Dakota and Boston College, would all advance to the NCAA Frozen Four that year.)

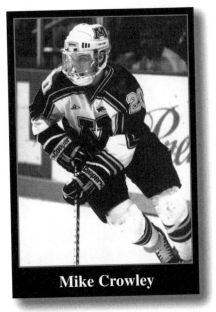

Mike Crowley

Coach Lucia had a homecoming of sorts when he faced his old squad from Colorado College that next week. After dropping the first game, Minnesota broke a 10 game losing streak to the Tigers as Nate Miller notched both Gopher goals in a 2-1 win. A trip to Wisconsin the following weekend resulted in two bitter losses to the hated Badgers, with both contests being decided on the final shots of the game. Incidentally, Erik Westrum tallied his first career hat trick in the second game, a 5-4 loss. The Gophs rebounded and got their first sweep of the season against Minnesota-Duluth, beating the Bulldogs 5-3 and 4-0. Sophomore Forward Johnny Pohl had a hand in four of five goals in Game One, as the team capitalized on six power-play goals that weekend. The team then rounded out November with a solid 6-1 win over Michigan on the road.

December began with a series split with the Seawolves up at Alaska. From there, the team managed just one conference point out of a home-and-home confrontation with St. Cloud State. Game Two was particularly frustrating as the team squandered a two goal lead with less than five minutes to play in the game. By now the team was sporting a 6-10-2 record heading into the Mariucci Classic. There, the Gophers pulled it together and posted convincing wins over Harvard, 5-2, and Northern Michigan, 6-2, to lay claim to the tourney title. Fully nine different Gophers scored goals in the two games and Adam Hauser stopped 40 of 42 shots in the Northern Michigan win.

Into January the Gophers came out swinging, sweeping Denver, 7-6 in overtime, and 7-3. Johnny Pohl made his presence felt in the series as he assisted on four goals in the overtime victory and then netted his first career hat trick in Game Two against the Pioneers. They kept it going that next weekend too, earning a hard-fought split with the eventual national champions from North Dakota. Goalie Adam Hauser was

Dan Trebil

Erik Rasmussen

outstanding in goal, outplaying UND first-team All-American Karl Goehring by stopping 67 of 70 shots on the weekend. Mankato was next and thanks to Pohl's two goals the Gophers took the opener, 3-2. But, the second game was a heartbreaker as the Mavericks rallied for a 6-5 overtime win to even the series at one apiece.

February began with a sweep on the road at the expense of the Minnesota-Duluth Bulldogs. Junior Forward Stuart Senden notched the 3-2 game-winner in Game One, while Nate Miller's two-goals paced the Gophers in the 4-1 sweeper victory. Minnesota pummeled Colorado College, 6-2, in the opener of the following weekend series behind Aaron Miskovich's four point night, only to see the Tigers answer back with a 5-1 decision of their own on the following evening. The Gophers then swept Michigan Tech on the road, 9-2 and 4-2, thanks to Dave Spehar's first career hat trick. Also getting in on the action were freshman Jeff Taffe, who had four assists, and Dan Welch, who scored a pair of goals as well.

Minnesota got some bad news that next week when it was learned Goalie Adam Hauser would be sidelined for two weeks with mononucleosis. Walk-on freshman Goalie Erik Young filled in admirably against the visiting Badgers, stopping 57 of 65 shots, but came up short as Wisconsin prevailed, 4-2 and 5-4. The slide continued from there as St. Cloud State swept the Gophers in a home-and-home to end the regular season on a sour note. As a result, the Gophers had to play the first round of the WCHA playoffs on the road at Colorado College. There, the team came up huge behind a now healthy Adam Hauser, sweeping the Tigers, 4-2 and 3-2, to catapult into the WCHA Final Five quarterfinals against Mankato at the Target Center.

Against the Mavericks the Gophers got a pair of goals from Erik Westrum and rallied to win, 6-4, setting up a highly anticipated fifth meeting against top-ranked Wisconsin. Would Minnesota rise to the challenge? Nope. They got goals from Westrum, Pohl and Leopold, but came up on the wrong end of a 5-3 contest. Down but not out, they tried to rally in the third-place game against St. Cloud State, which in essence was an NCAA tournament game to the players. There, Minnesota got a pair of goals from Nate Miller, but could not rally back from a 3-1 first period deficit, losing 6-4. With that, the season was over.

Nate Miller

The team, which played by far the toughest schedule of any program in the nation, finished with a respectable 20-19-2 overall record, good for 13-13-2 in the WCHA. Sophomore Johnny Pohl led the team in scoring that season with 18 goals and 41 assists for 59 points. Erik Westrum was second with 53 points, while Nate Miller finished third with 35.

The 2000-01 Season...

The Gophers opened their season with Coach

Lucia taking on his alma mater, Notre Dame, in the Hall of Fame Game at the Xcel Energy Center in St. Paul. Highlighting the 7-3 victory was freshman Matt Koalska netting his first career goal on his very first shift. The Gophers then traveled north for a first-ever meeting against Bemidji State and thanks to Erik Westrum's career-high five point effort, Minnesota won easily, 9-3. From there, the Gophers swept Duluth and then took three of four points against Alaska Anchorage.

The festivities continued into November as the team swept previously unbeaten Wisconsin at Mariucci Arena behind Adam Hauser's shutout in the series-opening 4-0 win. With that, the team found itself with a gaudy 7-0-1 record and ranked No. 1 in the nation. Minnesota then traveled to North Dakota where they got a little humble pie, taking just one point from the Sioux with a 7-5 loss and 5-5 tie. They rebounded to sweep the Huskies of St. Cloud State as Hauser registered his second shutout of the season with a 2-0 victory in Game One.

Mike Anderson

Game Two was much closer, winning 4-3 on goals from Pohl, Anthony, Westrum and Taffe. Their No. 1 ranking was lost that next week, however, when the Gophs dropped a pair of home games in the College Hockey Showcase to Michigan State, 3-2, and Michigan, 4-1.

The slump continued into December with the Maroon and Gold getting swept on the road at Denver. Scoring just one goal in the series, the team had now managed to score just four goals in four games — the fewest in program history in nearly a half century. Minnesota rebounded with a convincing 11-2 victory over Quinnipiac behind Stuart Senden's first career hat trick. Following a three-week holiday break, the team returned well rested and rejuvenated, winning the Mariucci Classic by upending Union and Lake Superior State.

The new year was ushered in with a sweep at Alaska-Anchorage behind Johnny Pohl's five-point weekend. From there the team split with top-ranked UND, taking the second game by scoring five unanswered goals in a 5-1 victory. Another split ensued at Wisconsin as the Badgers won the opener 4-2, only to see Minnesota come back behind Grant Potulny's first career hat trick and win 8-2. Into February the team kept rolling with sweeps of Michigan Tech and at MSU, Mankato. Erik Westrum posted a six-point weekend against the Mavericks and as a result was named as the WCHA Player of the Week. The next week things got even better as the Gophers swept Colorado College. Goalie Adam Hauser picked up his third WCHA Player of the Week honor after holding the Tigers to just a pair of goals in the series.

With that, the red hot Gophers headed up 35W to face Duluth. They were not welcomed with open arms, however, as they got upset by the last place Bulldogs, 5-4, in overtime. They came back the next night behind goals from Koalska, Leopold, Westrum and

Ryan Trebil

35

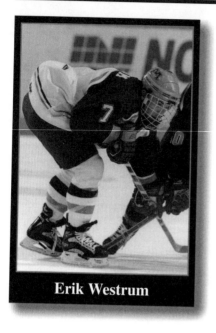

Erik Westrum

Taffe, though to win 4-0. Despite more than 100 penalty minutes, Hauser was able to hang on for his third shut-out of the year.

March rolled in with Minnesota needing a sweep over St. Cloud State in its regular-season finale to claim a share of the MacNaughton Cup. What they got, however, were a pair of ugly 5-2 and 6-1 losses. The Gophers wound up finishing third in the conference, their first top-three finish in four seasons. As such, they hosted Michigan Tech in a first-round WCHA Playoff series, beating the Huskies 7-2 and 3-1 to advance on to the WCHA's Final Five. Nick Anthony and Stuart Senden each tallied a pair of goals in the series. Next up was St Cloud State, who beat the Gophers like a drum, 3-0. The Gophers then lost to CC, 5-4, in the third-place game.

Despite the two setbacks in the Final Five, the Gophers finally got back to the NCAA Tournament. Incredibly, it was their first trip in four years. There, they faced Maine in the opener out in Worcester, Mass. The two teams needed overtime to settle this one, and in the end it was not pretty for the Gophers. Pohl and Potulny scored in the first and second periods, respectively, to make it 2-2. Potulny then notched his second goal of the game which was then followed by Erik Westrum's go ahead goal in the third to make it 4-3. Maine hung in there though and wound up scoring a power-play goal on penalty by Paul Martin with less than a minute to play. With Maine's goaltender pulled for an extra attacker, the Black Bears got the equalizer with just three seconds to play to send it to overtime. There, the game roared back and forth with both teams getting several quality scoring chances. Finally, at 13:04 of the extra session, Maine's Robert Liscak beat Hauser to give his team the thrilling 5-4 victory. Season over.

The University of Minnesota posted a much improved 27-13-2 overall record and 18-8-2 mark in the WCHA that year — good for third place. The Gophers also served notice that they were back among college hockey's elite. Minnesota was led by the efforts of senior Erik Westrum, who led the team in scoring with 26 goals and 35 assists for 61 points. Junior Defenseman Jordan Leopold was second with 49 points and for his efforts earned first-team All-American honors and was named as a Hobey Baker Finalist as well. In addition, freshman Grant Potulny paced the nation with 16 power-play goals, while Johnny Pohl finished second with 13. Grant Potulny, Troy Riddle and Paul Martin all earned All-WCHA Rookie Team honors to boot.

The 2001-02 Season...

Minnesota opened the 2001-02 season against North Dakota in the Hall of Fame Game as UND christened its brand new Engelstad Arena in Grand Forks. The Golden Gophers spoiled the party though as they rallied from a 5-3 deficit and came up with four unanswered third-period

Jeff Taffe

goals. The momentum carried over after that as the team went on to destroy Bemidji State and Colgate at home by the insane margin of 31-3. Johnny Pohl tallied four goals against the Beavers, while Goalies Adam Hauser and freshman Justin Johnson each notched back-to-back shut-outs against the Raiders. Riddle, Anthony, Martin, Pohl, Tallackson, Erickson, Leopold, Ballard and Martin all had multiple points in that series as well.

Minnesota opened their WCHA schedule at Michigan Tech over the first weekend in November and managed to rally for a win and a tie against the Huskies. Six unanswered goals were the big story in the opener, while Jordan Leopold's power-play equalizer with 1:09 to play in the game was the difference in the 5-5 Game Two. Back at home the Gophs swept both MSU, Mankato and UM-Duluth to improve their record to an impressive 10-0-1. Jeff Taffe then tallied his first career hat trick in a 5-2 win over Michigan at the College Hockey Showcase. Two days later against Michigan State the Gophers rallied from a 3-2 deficit in the third period on

Johnny Pohl

goals from Potulny, Wendell, and Tallackson to salvage a 4-4 tie. The undefeated Gophers got their first loss on November 30th at home against St. Cloud State, 3-2.

The team began the month of December with a rematch against St. Cloud, this time rallying back from a 2-0 lead on goals from Barry Tallackson and Jordan Leopold to salvage a 2-2 tie. The next week Adam Hauser stopped 30 of 31 shots in a 2-1 opening win against Denver, but the team got upended, 4-3, in the second game. Minnesota went on to win the Mariucci Classic after Christmas Break, beating Ferris State, 3-2, in the opener, followed by a 6-1 shellacking of Providence in the championship game thanks to Johnny Pohl's two goals and two assists.

January was all about the second game of the weekend series as the team went 0-3-1 in the openers, but rebounded to go 4-0-0 in the rematches. UND was next on the docket for the Gophs as they saw the Sioux rally back from a 3-0 third period deficit to take the opener, 4-3. Then, in the rematch game the following night, All-American Jordan Leopold became the school's all-time leader in goals by a defenseman when he netted a pair of lamp-lighters in the third period to rally his squad back for a 2-1 victory. Against the Badgers in Madison, Wisconsin pounded Minnesota, 8-3, in Game One, only to see the Gophers take the rematch, 6-2, behind Adam Hauser's 34 saves. The following week was tough as the Maroon and Gold allowed Anchorage to score with one second remaining in the game to steal a point and a 3-3 tie. The team rallied in Game Two, however, behind a pair of Jeff Taffe goals to earn a 5-2 win. The month came to a close with a rematch against then-No. 1 Denver. The Pioneers took the opener, 3-1, only to see the Gophers erupt for a 6-1 rout in Game Two behind Ballard's two goals

Adam Hauser

Grant Potulny

and Pohl's goal and two assists.

The team got back on track in February despite its opening 5-2 loss at UMD. After rebounding to take the revenge game, 2-1, to earn a split, the Gophers swept UND in Grand Forks. Jon Waibel's Game Two game-winner with 10 seconds left was the highlight of the series as the team rallied from a 3-1 deficit for a 4-3 win. After a tough 6-5 loss at home against Colorado College the next week, the team came back to earn the split by defeating the Tigers 7-3. From there, Minnesota beat rival Wisconsin, 6-3, at Mariucci Arena in Game One, and then completed the 4-3 sweep the next night courtesy of Jordan Leopold's overtime goal at 2:01 of the extra session.

March was magical as the team went 6-1 into the post-season with a lot of momentum behind them. They closed out the regular season with a St. Cloud sweep, winning the opener, 5-4, and then the rematch, 3-1, behind Adam Hauser's 25 saves on Senior Night at Mariucci Arena. The team kept rolling into the WCHA Playoffs, where Johnny Pohl's four points led Minnesota past rival North Dakota in Game One at Mariucci, 7-2. Game Two was a thriller and was ultimately decided on Keith Ballard's game-winner in overtime with less than two minutes to play in the first extra session.

That next week the Gophers took on St. Cloud State in the Final Five at the Xcel Energy Center. Leopold, Riddle, Taffe and Koalska all lit the lamp in this one as the team cruised to a 4-1 win. Lady luck ran out on our boys in the championship game against Denver, however, as Pioneer goaltender Wade Dubielewicz stopped 38 shots to lead his team in a 5-2 win. Minnesota earned an NCAA Tournament bye though and used their rest wisely, coming refreshed against Colorado College in the West Regional in Ann Arbor, Mich. There, Minnesota rallied with goals from Grant Potulny, Nick Angell and Jeff Taffe, and then sat back and relaxed after Johnny Pohl's shorthanded breakaway goal in the third to seal the 4-2 win. With that, the team had earned themselves a trip to the Frozen Four, which, ironically, was right back in St. Paul at the Xcel Center.

Finally, the Gophers were back in the final four of college hockey. Sure, they were no strangers to the pinnacle of March Madness, but it had been nearly a quarter century since they had won it all. Things were looking good for the Gophs though. After all, the NCAA's Frozen Four was being held at the posh Xcel Energy Center in St. Paul, right in their very own backyard. West Seventh Street was overflowing with maroon and gold that afternoon as a record crowd of 19,234 showed up at the "X" to watch the team do battle in the opening semifinal round against Michigan.

The Gophers drew first blood in this one when Jeff Taffe, who was forechecking in to the offensive zone, deflected a clearing attempt towards the net. There, Grant Potulny grabbed

Matt Koalska

the deflection and, while on his knees, flipped it past Michigan Goaltender Josh Blackburn to make it 1-0 midway through the first period.

Minnesota then made it 2-0 at the 4:33 of the second period when Potulny netted his second tally of the evening — this one coming on the power play. Potulny redirected a Jordan Leopold slapper from the point to beat Blackburn through the five-hole on this one as All-American Johnny Pohl gathered the second assist of the evening to boot. Hauser played tough through this point and particularly stood on his head with just over 30 seconds to go in the second when he made a leaping glove save across the crease to stop Jed Ortmeyer's scoring bid.

The third period was eerily similar to the previous two in that the Gophers wound up tallying an early goal. This time it was junior Jeff Taffe, scoring his team-best 34th of the season on a thrilling breakaway just over a minute into it. Taffe took a sweet pass from his Hastings High School teammate, Dan Welch, to burn up the ice and deposit the biscuit between Blackburn's legs on a backhander. It was now 3-0 and things were looking good.

Keith Ballard

But, as in all good stories, this one would have its share of drama as well. The Wolverines were not about to lie down in this one and roared back midway through the third, finally scoring at the 13:55 mark on a shorthanded goal by J.J. Swistak which beat Hauser through the five hole. Then, with just under a minute and a half to go in the game, Michigan, playing with six skaters and their goalie pulled, made it 3-2 when Jed Ortmeyer beat Hauser on that very same five-hole on a tough angled shot from the goal line.

The drama was thick in the X at this point as the Gophers then hung on for their dear lives to stop the Wolverines in the games' final moments. Hauser, who stopped 25 of 27 shots that night, came up huge in the last minute and when the buzzer finally blew, the Maroon and Gold suddenly found themselves back in their first national championship game since 1989.

"Losing to Denver in the Final Five probably made our playoffs to tell you the truth, because that humbled us and we needed that," said Jordan Leopold. "We were not focused going into that and that forced us to get back to the basics and not get too overconfident. We then got a first round bye, and that was huge. From there we faced a very good Colorado College in the opener, and wound up coming out on top. Then, to come home to St. Paul was awesome. It was really magic in that Final Four opener with Michigan. We felt confident going in, but didn't actually play our best game at all. We did enough to win though and that was all that mattered."

The Finals would go down as one of the greatest ever as Minnesota took the ice that next night against the University of Maine. The Gophers opened the scoring at 7:18 of the first period on the power play when a streaking Keith

Troy Riddle

Barry Tallackson

Ballard slammed home a beautiful one-timer courtesy of Troy Riddle that beat Maine Goalie Matt Yeats through the five-hole.

The Black Bears rallied to tie it up at the 4:47 mark of the second period, however, when Michael Schutte tallied on a power play goal that saw Adam Hauser get screened big-time in front. The Gophs jumped back on top less than a minute later though on an awesome wrister by Johnny Pohl which beat Yeats top-shelf glove side. And, with that timely 27th goal of the season, Pohl was able to clinch the national point-scoring race, pulling ahead of New Hampshire's Darren Haydar with 77 points.

Maine tied it up early in the third as Schutte tallied his second goal of the game, this one coming on a one-timer from the point which beat Hauser low to the glove side. With everything tied up at two apiece, the action was fierce. Things stayed that way for another 14 minutes too, until Maine's Robert Liscak banked a floater off of Hauser's leg pad from behind the net with under five minutes to go to give the Black Bears their first lead of the game. The fans were crushed.

Minnesota, which had played conservatively throughout the third period, now rallied fiercely in the game's final moments. Maine hung in there though and it appeared to be all but over. Shortly after a time-out, Coach Lucia pulled Hauser with 58 seconds remaining in the game and put an extra attacker out on the ice. Then, in one of the greatest goals in Gopher history, Matt Koalska tied it up with 54 seconds on the clock to knot the game at three apiece and send the home crowd into hysterics. Johnny Pohl, who won the face-off in the Maine zone, dropped the bouncing puck back to Troy Riddle. Riddle then deflected it over to Koalska in the high slot, where he pounded home a low liner between Yeats' legs to light the lamp.

G.W. & Grant Potulny

So, it was now off to overtime, where the collective breath of every Minnesota hockey fan was being held. The other two times that the Gophers had lost NCAA championship overtime games were back in 1954, when John Mariucci's club was upset by RPI, and then again in 1989, when Wooger's club was beaten by Harvard. This, however, was not going to have the same outcome.

In the extra session the two teams battled mercilessly up and down the ice for nearly 17 agonizing minutes. The fans were beside themselves as the tension mounted with every face-off. Then, at the 16:58 mark of overtime, history was made when North Dakota native Grant Potulny, the Maroon and Gold's lone non-Minnesotan, ended it all. Here's how it went down: Maine, playing on the short side of a controversial power-play for tripping, was trying to ice the puck out of their own end. A face-off in the Black Bear's end wound up going right to Jordan Leopold at the point. Leo then shot the puck into traffic in front of the net with the rebound bouncing to Pohl. Pohl then slid it to

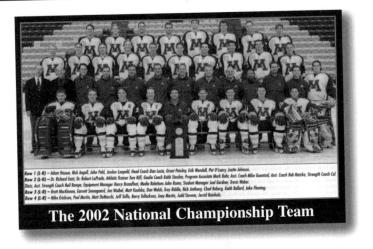

Row 1 (L-R) – Adam Hauser, Nick Angell, John Pohl, Jordan Leopold, Head Coach Don Lucia, Grant Potulny, Erik Wendell, Pat O'Leary, Justin Johnson.
Row 2 (L-R) – Dr. Richard Feist, Dr. Robert LaPrade, Athletic Trainer Tom Kiff, Goalie Coach Robb Stauber, Program Associate Mark Bahr, Asst. Coach Mike Guentzel, Asst. Coach Bob Motzko, Strength Coach Cal Dietz, Asst. Strength Coach Neil Rampe, Equipment Manager Harry Broadfoot, Media Relations John Ramo, Student Manager Joel Gardner, Travis Weber.
Row 3 (L-R) – Brett MacKinnon, Garrett Smaagaard, Jon Waibel, Matt Koalska, Dan Welch, Troy Riddle, Nick Anthony, Chad Roberg, Keith Ballard, Jake Fleming.
Row 4 (L-R) – Mike Erickson, Paul Martin, Matt DeMarchi, Jeff Taffe, Barry Tallackson, Joey Martin, Judd Stevens, Jerrid Reinholz.

The 2002 National Championship Team

Potulny, who slapped the puck under Yeats' pads for the thrill of a lifetime. Minnesota had won the game, 4-3. Utter bedlam ensued throughout the Land of 10,000 Lakes.

Absolute insanity erupted not only at the Xcel Energy Center, but throughout Minnesota as the fans rejoiced. A friendly riot even took place back in Dinkytown just for good measure. That 23-year-old monkey was now off their backs and the Gophers were NCAA champions for the fourth time in team history. The team, coaches and staff stormed the ice and celebrated amidst a sea of sticks, gloves and helmets which now littered the rink. Minnesota was finally back on top of the hockey world.

"That was one of the most exciting games I have ever been a part of and it will go down as a classic," said Leopold, who finished with 48 points that season — tops in the nation among defenseman. "It was just an amazing moment for everybody that has been involved in Gopher Hockey and it is certainly something that I will never forget. All the emotion that came out on the ice following that incredible ending was indescribable. To be out there with my teammates and friends was so special. It was really a day I will always look back on and cherish forever."

When it was all said and done Jordan Leopold and Johnny Pohl, who led the nation in scoring with 79 points, were named as first team All-Americans. In addition, Leo, a two-time WCHA Defensive Player of the Year, was given the ultimate prize in college hockey, the Hobey Baker Award. Other Gophers getting in on the action included Sophomore defenseman Paul Martin, who was named to the second-team All-WCHA team, while junior Jeff Taffe was a third-team honoree. Keith Ballard was also named to the WCHA's All-Rookie Team as well.

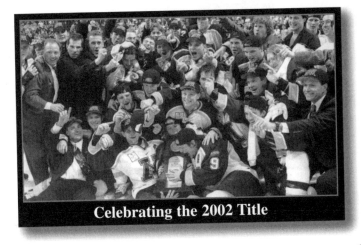

Celebrating the 2002 Title

Thomas Vanek

Furthermore, Potulny, Pohl and Adam Hauser, who stopped 42 shots in the title game and 69 of 74 shots in the tourney, were named to the Frozen Four All-Tournament Team. Incidentally, with the win, Adam Hauser become the WCHA's all-time leader in wins with 83.

The 2002-03 Season...

The defending National Champion Golden Gophers opened their 2002-03 campaign right back at the Xcel Energy Center, where they pummeled Ohio State in the Hall of Fame Game, 7-2. Keith Ballard had four points in the game but the bad news came when it was determined that junior captain Grant Potulny got injured and would be on the shelf for several months. From there, the team headed east to play New Hampshire in a battle between No. 1 and No. 3 in the country. The Gophers managed to capture just one point against the Wildcats though, as they tied 5-5 in Game One behind a pair of goals each from Riddle and Martin, but then lost the rematch, 3-1. October came to a close on the road at Michigan Tech, where freshmen Thomas Vanek and Gino Guyer scored two goals apiece in a 5-4 win. Minnesota had to settle for a 3-3 tie in Game two, however, when Goalie Justin Johnson let in the Husky equalizer at 16:44 of the third.

The month of November was christened in style as the Gophers raised their 2002 NCAA Championship banner just prior to their game with Alabama-Huntsville and then proceeded to pound the Chargers, 12-1, behind hat tricks from Troy Riddle, Jon Waibel and Thomas Vanek. After taking the follow-up game, 4-2, the team hit the road to play Minnesota State, Mankato. There, the Gophers watched the Mavericks score three unanswered third period goals in a span of just over seven minutes for a shocking 3-2 win. Troy Riddle, who was still suffering from a separated shoulder, contributed two goals and two assists in the 7-4 revenge victory the next night. Things got scary the next weekend as CC came to town and spanked the Gophers, 7-3, in the opener and then salvaged a 2-2 tie in Game Two to take three of four points in the series. The home-stand continued with a 4-2 win over Michigan Tech in Game One, followed by a dramatic come from behind 2-1 win in Game Two, which featured third period goals from Paul Martin and Dan Welch. The month came to a close at the College Hockey Showcase where Thomas Vanek posted a hat trick in a 5-5 tie versus Michigan State. The team then dropped its next game against Michigan by the final score of 3-1.

The first half of the season came to a close on a positive note when Minnesota swept rival Wisconsin. Goalie Travis Weber posted 31 saves in securing his first career shut-out in 3-0 Game One, while Matt DeMarchi was the hero of Game Two when he got the game-winner late in the third to seal a 3-2 victory. Following a three-week holiday hiatus, the team resumed play by

Mike Vannelli

winning its fourth straight Dodge Holiday Classic title. After a big 7-3 win over Yale, the team beat Boston College in the title game thanks to Troy Riddle's over-time goal at 2:30 of the extra session to secure the 2-1 victory.

The new year was up and down for the Gophers as they got off to a rocky start by earning just one point in a home-and-home series with St. Cloud State. The team's woes continued that next weekend as they suffered a 4-2 home loss North Dakota in the opener but then rebounded behind Matt Koalska's four assists to take Game Two, 6-3. The Gophers were down 3-2 in this one but rallied back with four third-period goals to seal the deal. Following a bye week, the Gophers hosted Minnesota State, Mankato, and wound up with a couple of 2-2 and 4-4 ties. The next week they hit the road for Anchorage, where Troy Riddle scored two goals and Travis Weber recorded his second shutout of the season, blanking the Seawolves with 18 saves in a 4-0 Game One win. The team then completed the sweep with a 4-1 win in Game Two as Justin Johnson stopped 20 of 21 shots and Thomas Vanek added two goals and an assist.

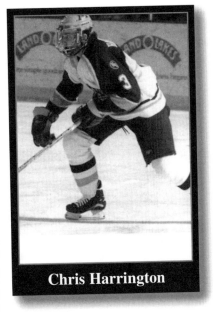

Chris Harrington

Top-ranked Colorado College was next on the schedule and the Tigers came out swinging in Game One, pouncing on the Gophers, 6-2. The next night was much different though as the Maroon and Gold rallied in the third period to win 3-2 behind goals from Thomas Vanek and Jake Fleming to earn a hard-fought split. Minnesota pounded on Wisconsin that next weekend at Mariucci Arena, outscoring the cheese heads, 13-3, in a two-game sweep. Highlighting the festivities were Koalska and Tallackson, who each netted a pair in Game Two. They kept rolling the next week up in Duluth, where Thomas Vanek's two goals in the third period helped seal a 5-4 Game One victory. Game Two was a heartbreaker though as UMD's Jon Francisco tied the game with 11 seconds to go on the clock and then scored the game-winner just minute into overtime to secure a 5-4 Bulldog win. Denver was next for the Gophers and they came to town ready to roll, jumping out to a quick 3-0 lead at Mariucci Arena. Minnesota hung in there though and got a pair of goals late from Grant Potulny to secure a 3-3 tie. The exact same scenario happened the next night too, but this time the three goal deficit was not only matched, but surpassed when Minnesota scored four goals in a span of 3:54 against All-American Goalie Wade Dubielewicz, en route to a huge 8-5 win.

The Gophers closed out their regular season at St. Cloud State with a 5-3 win over the Huskies in Game One, followed by a 1-1 tie thanks to Troy Riddle's second period tally from Koalska and Martin. With those three points, the team finished tied for second-place in the WCHA. From there, Grant Potulny put the Gophers on his back as the team opened the post-season at home with a pair of wins over Michigan Tech. Potulny scored three goals in the

Kellen Briggs

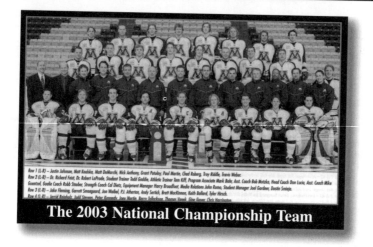

Row 1 (L-R) – Justin Johnson, Matt Koalska, Matt DeMarchi, Nick Anthony, Grant Potulny, Paul Martin, Chad Roberg, Troy Riddle, Travis Weber.
Row 2 (L-R) – Dr. Richard Feist, Dr. Robert LaPrade, Student Trainer Todd Gaddie, Athletic Trainer Tom Kiff, Program Associate Mark Bahr, Asst. Coach Bob Motzko, Head Coach Don Lucia, Asst. Coach Mike Guentzel, Goalie Coach Robb Stauber, Strength Coach Cal Dietz, Equipment Manager Harry Broadfoot, Media Relations John Rome, Student Manager Joel Gardner, Dustin Smieja.
Row 3 (L-R) – Jake Fleming, Garrett Smaagaard, Jon Waibel, P.J. Atherton, Andy Sertich, Brett MacKinnon, Keith Ballard, Tyler Hirsch.
Row 4 (L-R) – Jerrid Reinholz, Judd Stevens, Peter Kennedy, Joey Martin, Barry Tallackson, Thomas Vanek, Gino Guyer, Chris Harrington.

The 2003 National Championship Team

3-1 and 5-2 victories, giving his squad a ticket to the WCHA Final Five in St. Paul. There, the eventual tournament MVP came up huge again, this time notching the game-tying goal late in the third period against the Mavericks. Vanek then took over down the stretch, scoring the overtime game-winner at 3:57 of the extra session. In the Finals against top-ranked Colorado College it was all Potulny yet again as he this time scored two goals and added an assist in the first six minutes of the game en route to leading his team to a 4-2 victory, and its first Broadmoor Trophy since 1996.

With that, the Gophers earned the top seed in the NCAA West Regional at Mariucci Arena. There, the Gophers took care of business, pounding on Mercyhurst in the first round, 9-2, on Potulny's three goals and Guyer's five assists. The next day CCHA Champion Ferris State came to town and thanks to Vanek's two goals, Minnesota hung on to beat the Bulldogs, 7-4, and advance on to the Frozen Four for the second straight year. Determined to make it a repeat, the Gophers wound up meeting their old foes the Michigan Wolverines in the national semifinals in Buffalo, N.Y. Michigan came out firing on all cylinders in this one, out-shooting Minnesota, 15-5, in the first period. Travis Weber played big though, allowing just one goal during that frame, and kept his squad in it. Minnesota roared back in the second, out-shooting the Wolverines, 15-6, but found themselves down 2-0 late in the period. Troy Riddle finally got Minnesota on the board at 17:45, on a couple of sweet passes from Vanek and Koalska. They rolled from there as Guyer took a centering pass from Tallackson and buried it at 1:35 of the third to tie it up at two apiece. Both teams played well down the stretch and the game ultimately went into overtime. There, Vanek proved to be the hero yet again as he scored on an unas-

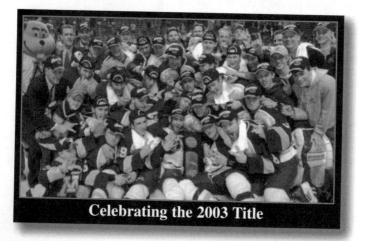

Celebrating the 2003 Title

sisted goal at 8:55 of the extra session to complete the comeback and send his club back to the NCAA championship game.

The title tilt had the Gophers facing off against New Hampshire, a team which had beaten them earlier in the season. Minnesota came out fired up in this one and controlled the puck for most of the game. DeMarchi got the Gophers on the board first at 10:58, only to see the Wildcats even it up on a power play with just 19 seconds to play in the first period. The Gophers had plenty of chances in the second but could not find the back of the net. Luckily for Minnesota fans, neither could New Hampshire, as Weber played solid between the pipes. Then, at 8:14 of the third frame, Thomas Vanek lit the lamp for his 31st tally of the year on a gorgeous goal set up by Koalska and Riddle to give his club a 2-1 lead. From there the boys smelled blood and dominated. Jon Waibel scored on a nice centering pass from Vanek just three minutes later, and Tallackson put the final nail in the coffin when he scored a pair of goals down the stretch to give the Golden Gophers back-to-back NCAA titles in as

Danny Irmen

many years. Travis Weber turned away 26 of 27 shots as the Gophers cruised to a 5-1 victory. Again, the team went crazy at center ice, celebrating every second of their magical moment.

When it was all said and done, Minnesota had become the first team in more than 30 years to repeat as NCAA Champions, when Boston University last accomplished the feat in 1972. It was the school's fifth NCAA Championship, with the other three coming in 1974, 1976 and 1979 under legendary coach Herbie Brooks. As for individual accolades, Thomas Vanek became just the fourth freshman since 1948 to be named Most Outstanding Player of the NCAA Frozen Four. Joining Vanek on the All-Tournament Team were Matt DeMarchi, Paul Martin and Travis Weber. In addition, Junior Defenseman Paul Martin, who finished with a career-high

39 points, was named as a second-team All-American. Martin, Vanek, who led the team with 62 points, and Keith Ballard, who tallied 41 of his own, were all named to the All-WCHA second-team as well. Troy Riddle, who wound up finishing second on the team in scoring with 51 points, was selected to the third-team. Riddle, along with Harrington and Vanek were also named to the league's all-rookie team, with Vanek being named as the WCHA Rookie of the Year to boot.

The 2003-04 Season...

As back-to-back national champions, the Gophers knew that they were going to be marked men in 2003-04. And, with the return of all but three regulars from the previous year's title team, including Potulny, Riddle, Koalska, Tallackson and Vanek — who was drafted fifth over-all by the NHL's Buffalo Sabres that Summer, the Gophers were gunning to become just the second team to ever win three NCAA Championships in a row. Gone were blue-liners Paul Martin and

Gino Guyer

Ryan Potulny

Matt DeMarchi, as well as goaltender Travis Weber, but they reloaded with prized recruits, Ryan Potulny and Danny Irmen. It was not going to be easy, that was for sure. Coach Lucia was optimistic but very realistic about his team's chances.

"Our sights are set on becoming the best team that we can possibly be when the end of the year rolls around," said Lucia. "Our goal is to get to the NCAA Tournament and then take our swings at it like every other team. That's what we've done in the past and I don't think our charge will be any different this season. We're not going to change our routine or our thought process on what we're trying to do. We're going to worry about us and be the best hockey team this group is capable of becoming. Every time you lose some pieces of the puzzle, you have to start over. Just because we won it last year doesn't guarantee us anything this year."

The Gophers opened the season as the consensus No. 1 team in the nation. That apparently did not impress Maine in the least, however, as the Black Bears shut-out the two-time defending champs in the opener, 4-0, snapping a 91-game streak of games without being shut out. They rebounded in a big way in their second game though by coming from behind, 3-0, to score seven unanswered goals and beat Nebraska-Omaha, 7-3. From there, things got ugly as the Gophers returned home only to get swept by rival Duluth 4-3, in overtime, and 4-2. Aside from the raising of the 2003 NCAA Championship banner and the ceremony which honored the late Herb Brooks, it was a total disaster. To add insult to injury, defenseman Keith Ballard suffered a knee injury which resulted in him missing seven games. By no coincidence the team went 1-5-1 over that same stretch which included a split with Denver and a sweep by North Dakota. Their lone win came on October 31st, when they beat Denver, 6-2, behind Grant Potulny's two goals and Matt Koalska's goal and two assists.

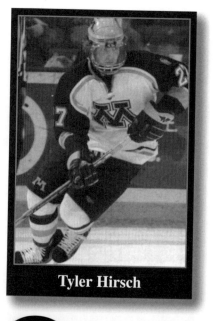

Tyler Hirsch

November was pretty rough for the Maroon and Gold. Following the debacle at Grand Forks, Minnesota headed to Madison where they managed just one point in the standings against rival Wisconsin. To make matters worse, the Badgers rallied from two-goal deficits each night to tie 3-3 and win 4-3. Maybe that was the breaking point for the Gophers because from there on out they were a changed team with a whole new attitude. From there, Minnesota swept Michigan Tech, 6-2 and 3-0, as freshmen Danny Irmen and Jake Taylor notched goals and rookie goaltender Kellen Briggs posted his first career shut-out. Next up was the College Hockey Showcase, where Minnesota posted 52 shots on goal and cruised to a 5-1 win over Michigan State on their home ice in East Lansing. The Gophers then won the title the next night by rallying from a 2-1 deficit on a shorthanded goal by Troy Riddle, followed by a pair of even-strength tallies by Andy Sertich and Barry Tallackson to bring home the hardware for the first time in eight years.

The Gophers had a solid December by going 3-1 and getting back on track. Kellen Briggs made it a December to remember by posting his second shut-out of the year in a 4-0 win at Alaska Anchorage. Game Two was another story though as UAA rallied back in the third period to win, 6-4. The team then returned home where they proceeded to capture their fifth straight Dodge Holiday Classic title with a pair of big wins. The first was a 9-0 blow-out over Princeton, and the second was a rematch of the 2003 NCAA Championship game against New Hampshire. And, just like the last time the two teams met, the Gophers came out on top. With two points each from Matt Koalska, Keith Ballard and Chris Harrington, they beat UNH, 4-2. With that, Minnesota was above the .500 mark for the first time on the season.

The Maroon and Gold opened the new year in style by going on a six-game unbeaten streak. Chris Harrington, Keith Ballard and Troy Riddle each had four-point weekends to lead the U to a pair of 5-5 ties against Boston University. From there the team swept Colorado College, 2-1 and 3-0, followed by Minnesota State, where they out-scored the Mavericks by the whopping margin of 16-3. Vanek had a seven-point weekend, while Briggs earned both wins, including a shut-out to set a new Minnesota rookie-record with four shut-outs on the year. Next up was No. 1 ranked North Dakota at home. The Gophers went up 2-1 in the opener, only to see the Sioux rally back behind three third period goals to win, 4-2. Game Two saw the Gophers break the team's 14-game unbeaten streak thanks to goals from Danny Irmen and Matt Koalska which made it 2-1. Riding the wave of momentum the Gophers rolled over Wisconsin that next weekend, sweeping the Badgers 4-2 and 3-2. Ballard was the difference in the series, earning Player of the Week honors after having a hand in three of the team's seven goals.

Blake Wheeler

The Gophers came back to Earth in February, going 4-4-0. They opened the month on a strong note, however, sweeping Bemidji State, 2-1 and 5-1. Keith Ballard, Troy Riddle and Brett MacKinnon each had three-point weekends for the Maroon and Gold. From there things got ugly as the Duluth Bulldogs crushed the Gophers at the DECC, 6-1 and 4-1 to extend the nation's-longest unbeaten streak to 12 games. The season sweep was UMD's first-ever over the Gophers and it couldn't have come at a worse time. Gino Guyer and Danny Irmen both had three-point outings en route to a sweep over Alaska Anchorage that next week. With the good came the bad though, as Minnesota followed its winning sweep with a losing one on the road that next week at Denver, getting spanked, 6-2 and 6-3. Kellen Briggs struggled and was ultimately relieved in favor of Justin Johnson on both nights.

Things got turned around in a big way in March as the team went 7-1-0 during the month. With WCHA playoff implications on the line, the Gophers, behind four point outings each

Phil Kessel

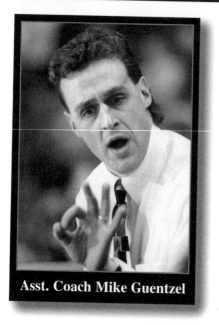

Asst. Coach Mike Guentzel

from Thomas Vanek and Barry Tallackson, went out and swept St. Cloud State, 7-4 and 4-2, to clinch a tie for fourth place with Denver. With that, Minnesota opened the WCHA Playoffs against St. Cloud State for the second straight week. And, just like the week before, the Golden Gophers swept the Huskies, 6-1 and 7-3, to move their record to 20-0-0 all-time in first-round play-off games at home and advance to their sixth straight WCHA Final Five. Troy Riddle had an amazing nine point weekend, while Ryan Potulny added six of his own.

Minnesota then went on to successfully defend its WCHA Final Five title by downing third-ranked UMD, 7-4, and top-ranked North Dakota, 5-4, to claim yet another Broadmoor Trophy. Minnesota had 12 different players score at least one point against UMD with Danny Irmen leading the attack by scoring two goals. Duluth led 3-1 in the first period, but the Gophers rallied back to advance to the Finals. There, the Gophers got goals from Irmen, Waibel, Vanek and Riddle to make it 4-4 midway through the third. The game roared back and forth and featured no less than two lead changes and four ties. Then, at the 13:58 mark of the final frame, Grant Potulny scored to give Minnesota a thrilling 5-4 victory. Kellen Briggs, who turned away 35 shots that night, was named as the WCHA Final Five MVP.

With that, Minnesota earned a No. 1 seed for the NCAA Midwest Regional in Grand Rapids, Mich., where they then proceeded to come from behind to defeat Notre Dame, 5-2, in the regional semifinal. Matt Koalska, who finished with a goal and an assist, got things started for the Gophers by scoring off a nice pass from Vanek just 24 seconds into the second period, slicing Notre Dame's lead to 2-1. After Danny Irmen deflected in a shot by Chris Harrington midway through the period to make it 2-2, Vanek took over. Minnesota out-shot Notre Dame 21-7 in the second period, and an Irish turnover allowed the awesome Austrian to grab the puck and put it in the back of the net for what would prove to be the game-winning goal at 16:34. Vanek scored again midway through the third, while Riddle added an empty netter for good measure.

Next up for the Gophers were their longtime nemesis, Minnesota-Duluth. The Dogs came out smoking in this one and held a two goal lead into the third period. Grant Potulny finally got Minnesota on the scoreboard at 5:25 of the final frame when he tallied on a short-handed goal from Guyer and Tallackson. Duluth was too tough down the stretch though and wound up winning the game, 3-1, behind Goalie Isaac Reichmuth's 22 saves, to end the Gopher's chances of an NCAA Championship three-peat. UMD wound up beating Minnesota in five of six meetings that season and made it count when it matter most, moving on to their first Frozen Four appearance since 1985.

The Golden Gophers posted a 27-14-3 overall record and a 15-12-1 mark in the WCHA that

Goalie Coach Robb Stauber

year to finish tied for fourth in the final conference standings with eventual national champion Denver. Considering their shaky start, it was a major accomplishment for them to win the WCHA Final Five and to come within one game of advancing back to the Final Four. Among those earning honors and accolades that year were Keith Ballard and Thomas Vanek, who were both named to 2003-04 All-WCHA Team. Ballard, who tallied 36 points that season, earned first team honors, while Vanek, who led the team with 26 goals and 25 assists for 51 points, was named to the second team. In addition, Ballard was also one of 10 finalists for the 2004 Hobey Baker Memorial Award, presented to the best Division I college hockey player in the nation. Incidentally, Troy Riddle finished third on the team in scoring with 49 points, while Matt Koalska came in fourth with 39 of his own.

Harry Broadfoot
Equipment Manager

The 2004-05 Season...

Minnesota started out their 2004-05 campaign on a high note, downing the defending NCAA champs from Denver in the Hall of Fame Game at St. Paul's Xcel Center. Grant Potulny was the hero in this one, tallying a hat trick right out of the gates to lead the Gophers past the Pioneers, 5-2. The team headed north to Alaska that next week, where Potulny lit the lamp yet again and Goalie Kellen Briggs turned away all 17 shots he faced to blank Massachusetts, 1-0, at the Nye Frontier Classic tournament. After losing to Alaska-Anchorage in the tourney finals, the team returned to the Lower 48 where they faced off against rival North Dakota up in Grand Forks. There, the Gophers lost to UND in Game One, 4-2, but came back in a big way the next night behind Briggs' second shut-out of the season to crush the Sioux, 6-0. Leading the charge yet again was Potulny, who had a pair of goals and an assist in the big win. Minnesota kept it going that next week too, beating up on Minnesota State, 9-2, back at Mariucci Arena. Eight different Gophers found the back of the net in this one while Mike Howe scored his first two of the year. The next night was much more interesting, however, as the Gophers rallied behind Kris Chucko's overtime winner at 1:48 of the extra session to make it 3-2 and take the series.

The Gophers opened the month of November with a series sweep over Wisconsin, 3-2 and 4-2. Gino Guyer and Danny Irmen each notched third period goals to secure the come-from-behind win in Game One, while each had two points apiece in Game Two as well. From there, the Gophers hit the road to take on Denver. Potulny had a pair of goals in the opener as the team fended off a four-goal barrage in the third period to hang on to a 5-4 win. Denver then took the night-cap, 5-2, to earn the split. Back at home that next weekend it was all about Potulny yet again as his two goals paced the Maroon and Gold past Michigan, 5-1. Then, the following night, Kellen Briggs stopped all 23 shots he faced as the Gophers blanked Michigan State, 5-

Patty Bjorklund
"Team Mom ..."

Pride on Ice...

0. After getting swept that next week by CC out in Colorado, the Gophs returned home to face St. Cloud State in a home-and-home series. Game One was a thriller up in the Granite City as Jake Flemming got the overtime game-winner at 2:21 of the extra session to give his squad a 2-1 victory. Irmen, Potulny, Sertich and Guyer each then scored that next night back home to secure the 4-2 sweep. The annual Dodge Holiday Classic was next up on the docket as the Gophers pounded on Merrimack, 6-2, and then rolled past Northern Michigan, 4-1, behind a pair of Tyler Hirsch goals to secure the title.

Minnesota ushered in the new year by beating Boston University, 2-1, thanks to goals by Guyer and Irmen in Game One. The roles were reversed that next night, however, as BU beat the Gophers by that same 2-1 margin. The next weekend was tough as the team got swept by CC, which included a heart-breaking 3-2 overtime loss in the opener. The Maroon and Gold got back on track from there though, taking both games from Minnesota State that following week, 9-6 and 2-1. Danny Irmen notched a hat trick in Game One, while Kris Chucko got both goals for the Gophers in Game Two. Following a tough home sweep at the hands of the Michigan Tech Huskies that next weekend, the Gophers could only manage a split with UMD on the last series of the month.

February was ushered in with yet another split, this one with rival Wisconsin in Madison. After dropping the opener, 3-1, the team rebounded to take Game Two, 5-3, on goals by Irmen, Hirsch, Potulny, Tallackson and Sertich. Then, the team managed to earn just one point at home against Alaska-Anchorage that following weekend. After dropping the opener, 3-2, they wound up with a 5-5 overtime tie which saw them squander a 5-4 lead with just over

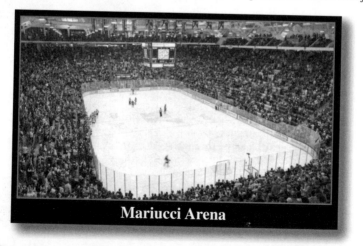

Mariucci Arena

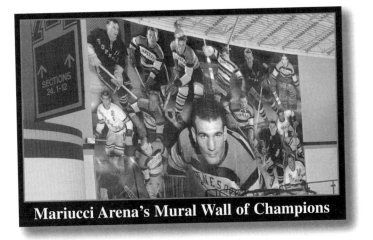

Mariucci Arena's Mural Wall of Champions

a minute to go in the game. Minnesota went on to win the front-end of the home-and-home with St. Cloud State that next weekend behind of pair of Alex Goligoski goals which resulted in a 5-4 victory. After dropping the revenge match, 4-1, the team went on to sweep Michigan tech on the road. Hirsch, Irmen, Stevens and Sertich each tallied in the 4-2 Game One win, while Game Two was all about Goalie Justin Johnson, who stopped all 26 shots he faced that night to earn a tough 5-0 shut-out.

Minnesota kept it going that next week, sweeping Minnesota State back at Mariucci Arena, 7-2 and 5-3, in the first round of the WCHA Playoffs at the Xcel Center in St. Paul. Tallackson and Irmen each had a pair in the opener, while Johnson stopped 25 of 28 shots in Game Two. The team hit the wall after that though, getting shut-out by Colorado College in the semifinal game, 3-0, and then dropping the third place game as well, 4-2, to North Dakota. As luck would have it, the Gophers got an invite to play in the NCAA West Regional Final that next weekend, which was being held at Mariucci Arena. There, with their home crowd behind them, the Maroon and Gold beat Maine, 1-0, on Evan Kaufmann's overtime game-winner at 1:46 of the extra session. The Gophers, who out-shot the Black Bears 38-25, were unable to capitalize on nine power-play opportunities during the game, but hung in there thanks to some outstanding goaltending from Kellen Briggs, who turned aside all 25 shots he faced that night.

From there, the team went on to upset Cornell that next night, 2-1, in overtime, to advance back to the Frozen Four. The Big Red got on the board first in this one when Mitch Carefoot beat Briggs on a shorthanded three-on-one midway through the second period. But the Gophers quickly responded with Andy Sertich tying the score just over a minute later on a

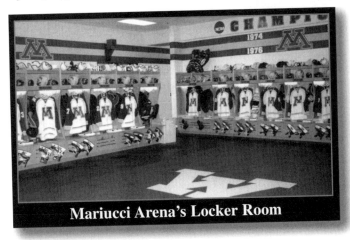

Mariucci Arena's Locker Room

backhander from Smaagaard out front. After a scoreless third period, "Mr. March," Barry Tallackson took over in overtime, as he took a pass out of the corner from Mike Howe and beat Cornell Goaltender David McKee, five-hole, on his own rebound. Tallackson was then mobbed by his teammates, just a few feet from where Evan Kaufmann was the center of attention the night before. With that, Tallackson and fellow seniors Garrett Smaagaard, Jake Fleming, Jerrid Reinholz, Justin Johnson and Judd Stevens were going to their third Frozen Four in four years.

With the hopes of making it three NCAA titles in four years, the Gophers headed to Columbus, Ohio, where they faced off against hated North Dakota in an all-WCHA NCAA Frozen Four semifinal. (Denver and Colorado College were the other two teams and Denver would ultimately win its second straight title.) Expectations were high going in, but this one was all UND as the Sioux led from start to finish and came away with a big 4-2 win. Erik Fabian, a fourth-line winger from Roseau, scored two early goals while Travis Zajac added two third-period scores of his own to put the Sioux up 4-0 in the third. Goaltender Jordan Parise, from Faribault, stopped 26 shots and was almost unbeatable in net, making a number of acrobatic saves and frustrating the Gophers all night. He faltered briefly in the third period when Mike Howe and Guyer each scored power-play goals just 90 seconds apart to make it interesting, but he hung on down the stretch to come up with the win and end Minnesota's season.

Kellen Briggs and Ryan Potulny were named to the All-WCHA team that year, while defenseman Alex Gologiski earned All-WCHA Rookie honors. Tyler Hirsch led the team in scoring with 44 points, with Irmen and Potulny adding 43 and 41, respectively.

The 2005-06 Season and Beyond...

The future has never looked brighter in Gold Country than it has heading into the 2005-06 season. With the top-ranked freshman class that nobody can stop talking about, expectations are running high for the Golden Gophers. Among them include: Phil Kessel (Madison, Wis.), Blake Wheeler (Plymouth), R.J. Anderson (Lino Lakes), Justin Bostrom (Vadnais Heights), Ryan Stoa (Bloomington) and goalie Jeff Frazee (Burnsville). And, while the freshman class looks outstanding, the rest of the team looks pretty solid from top to bottom as well. In fact, the Gophers have six players — Kris Chucko, Ryan Stoa, Jeff Frazee, Nate Hagemo, Alex Goligoski and Blake Wheeler — who have all been picked in the first two rounds of the NHL draft.

Wheeler, a six-foot-four, 185-pound forward, even became the highest drafted high

school player since 1983 when the Phoenix Coyotes selected him fifth overall in 2004. Add to that perhaps the biggest prize of all, the fact that Minnesota landed Phil Kessel, who could be the No. 1 overall pick in the 2006 NHL draft. Kessel spent the last two seasons playing with the USA Hockey National Team Development Program in Ann Arbor, Mich., where he shattered nearly all of the all-time NTDP career and single-season records. Perhaps never in Gopher hockey history has any single player come in with so much hype and high expectations.

Only time will tell, but things are definitely looking up for the Gophers as they head into the future. With Coach Lucia steering the ship, things have never looked better. One thing is for sure... somewhere, somehow, the patriarchs of Minnesota hockey, John Mariucci and Herbie Brooks, are looking down and feeling pretty good about what they started so many years ago here in Gold Country. With a group of kids like this making us proud, it is obvious that their legacies are alive and well.

Looking to the Future...

THE HOBEY BAKER AWARD

Each April the nation's best collegiate hockey player receives the Hobey Baker Memorial Award, college hockey's equivalent to the Heisman Trophy. The recipient is the player who best exemplifies the qualities that Hobey Baker himself demonstrated as an athlete at Princeton University in the early 1900s. Baker was considered to be the ultimate sportsman who despised foul play — picking up only two penalties in his entire college hockey career. With his speed and superior stick handling, Baker opened up the game of hockey and set new standards for the way the game was played. A true gentleman, his habit of insisting upon visiting each opponent's locker room after every game to shake their hands became a model for today's players. An American hero, Baker gave his life as a decorated pilot in W.W.I. In 1981

Leopold

Bloomington's Decathlon Club founded the Hobey Baker Award and each year the coveted honor is presented to the nation's top skater. The top hockey coaches, players, media and fans from around the country, as well as the finalists themselves, fly in to attend the gala event each year in Minneapolis. The balloting for the award is voted on by the nearly 50 NCAA D-I coaches who are asked to pick the top three players in their league as well as the top three in the nation.

Broten, Bonin & Stauber

PAST HOBEY WINNERS:

Year	Recipient	School
2005	Marty Sertich	Colorado College
2004	Junior Lessard	University of Minnesota-Duluth
2003	Peter Sejna	Colorado College
2002	**Jordan Leopold**	**University of Minnesota**
2001	Ryan Miller	Michigan State
2000	Mike Mottau	Boston College
1999	Jason Krog	New Hampshire
1998	Chris Drury	Boston University
1997	Brendan Morrison	University of Michigan
1996	**Brian Bonin**	**University of Minnesota**
1995	Brian Holzinger	Bowling Green University
1994	Chris Marinucci	University of Minnesota-Duluth
1993	Paul Kariya	University of Maine
1992	Scott Pellerin	University of Maine
1991	David Emma	Boston College
1990	Kip Miller	Michigan State University
1989	Lane MacDonald	Harvard University
1988	**Robb Stauber**	**University of Minnesota**
1987	Tony Hrkac	University of North Dakota
1986	Scott Fusco	Harvard University
1985	Bill Watson	University of Minnesota-Duluth
1984	Tom Kurvers	University of Minnesota-Duluth
1983	Mark Fusco	Harvard University
1982	George McPhee	Bowling Green University
1981	**Neal Broten**	**University of Minnesota**

TOTAL CAREER POINTS (100 POINT CLUB)

	Player	Years	GP	G	A	Pts
1.	John Mayasich	1951-55	111	144	154	298
2.	Pat Micheletti	1982-86	162	120	149	269
3.	Corey Millen	1982-87	149	119	122	241
4.	Butsy Erickson	1979-83	144	109	129	238
5.	Larry Olimb	1988-92	182	59	159	218
6.	Brian Bonin	1992-96	166	100	116	216
7.	Steve Ulseth	1977-81	148	84	118	202
8.	Tim Harrer	1976-80	157	117	84	201
9.	John Pohl	1998-02	165	72	128	200
10.	Dick Dougherty	1951-54	81	109	78	187
11.	Peter Hankinson	1986-90	176	82	100	182
12.	Tom Vannelli	1973-77	138	69	111	180
13.	Troy Riddle	2000-04	171	82	96	178
	Aaron Broten	1979-81	86	72	106	178
14.	Erik Westrum	1997-01	161	69	99	168
	Richard Erdall	1981-85	123	55	113	168
15.	Ryan Kraft	1994-98	159	62	104	166
16.	Scott Bjugstad	1979-83	133	86	77	163
17.	Grant Bischoff	1987-91	180	80	81	161
	Tom Rothstein	1980-85	158	67	94	161
18.	Steve Christoff	1976-79	119	77	82	159
	Mike Polich	1971-75	148	70	89	159
19.	Reggie Berg	1995-99	160	74	84	158
	Todd Richards	1985-89	167	30	128	158
20.	Mike Crowley	1994-97	125	37	120	157
21.	Jason Miller	1987-91	173	53	102	155
22.	Ken Yackel Sr.	1952-56	112	70	78	148
	Don Micheletti	1976-80	127	64	84	148
23.	Steve MacSwain	1983-87	139	68	79	147
24.	Trent Klatt	1989-92	121	68	78	146
25.	Jordan Leopold	1998-02	164	45	99	144
26.	Neal Broten	1978-81	76	38	104	142
27.	Jeff Nielsen	1990-94	172	76	65	141
	Jay Cates	1985-88	136	55	86	141
28.	Dave Snuggerud	1985-89	126	73	67	140
	Ken Gernander	1987-91	176	78	62	140
29.	Dean Blais	1969-73	124	56	83	139
30.	Matt Koalska	2000-04	171	42	94	136
31.	Craig Johnson	1990-93	119	54	81	135
32.	Kevin Hartzell	1978-82	140	54	80	134
33.	Travis Richards	1989-93	176	35	98	133
34.	Pat Phippen	1973-76	123	46	85	131
35.	Todd Okerlund	1983-87	133	44	86	130
36.	Dave Spehar	1996-00	160	61	68	129
	Wyatt Smith	1995-99	152	67	62	129
	Warren Miller	1972-76	157	58	71	129
37.	Justin McHugh	1990-95	160	66	60	126
38.	Dan Trebil	1992-96	164	24	100	124
39.	Paul Broten	1984-88	172	50	72	122
40.	Wally Chapman	1982-86	144	67	54	121
41.	Phil Verchota	1975-79	161	59	61	120

42.	Gene Campbell	1951-54	80	52	67	119
43.	Bill Baker	1975-79	154	30	88	118
44.	Gary Shopek	1983-87	173	24	93	117
45.	Grant Potulny	2000-04	146	68	48	116
46.	Thomas Vanek	2002-04	83	57	56	113
	Jeff Taffe	1999-02	120	56	57	113
47.	Tony Kellin	1982-86	165	37	75	112
48.	Robb McClanahan	1976-79	121	45	63	108
	Gary Gambucci	1965-68	88	52	56	108
49.	Cory Laylin	1988-92	170	58	49	107
	Mark Lambert	1974-78	160	42	65	107
	Bill Klatt	1966-69	89	52	55	107
50.	Eric Strobel	1976-79	120	52	54	106
	Joe Micheletti	1973-77	135	25	81	106
	Casey Hankinson	1994-98	149	50	56	106
51.	Les Auge	1971-75	134	19	85	104
52.	Dick Meredith	1951-55	110	43	59	102
53.	Doug Woog	1963-66	80	48	53	101
	Tom Chorske	1985-89	123	51	50	101
	Peter Fichuk	1966-69	92	43	58	101
54.	Keith Ballard	2001-04	123	33	67	100
	Ben Hankinson	1987-91	155	49	51	100

Nearest Current Gophers:

Gino Guyer	2001-	129	36	57	93
Tyler Hirsch	2001-	127	27	66	93

TOTAL CAREER GOALS

1 John Mayasich, 1951-55	144
2 Pat Micheletti, 1982-86	120
3 Corey Millen, 1983-87	119
4 Tim Harrer, 1976-80	117
5 Butsy Erickson, 1979-83	109
Dick Dougherty, 1950-54	109
7 Brian Bonin, 1992-96	100
8 Scott Bjugstad, 1979-83	86
9 Steve Ulseth, 1977-81	84
10 Troy Riddle, 2000-04	82
Peter Hankinson, 1986-90	82
12 Grant Bischoff, 1987-91	80
13 Ken Gernander, 1987-91	78
14 Steve Christoff, 1976-79	77
15 Jeff Nielsen, 1990-94	76
16 Reggie Berg, 1995-99	74
17 Dave Snuggerud, 1985-89	73
18 Aaron Broten, 1979-81	72
19 Johnny Pohl, 1998-2002	71
20 Ken Yackel, Sr., 1974-77	70
Mike Polich, 1971-75	70

TOTAL CAREER ASSISTS

1	Larry Olimb, 1988-92	159
2	John Mayasich, 1951-55	154
3	Pat Micheletti, 1982-86	149
4	Butsy Erickson, 1979-83	129
5	John Pohl, 1998-2002	128
	Todd Richards, 1985-89	128
7	Corey Miller, 1983-87	122
8	Mike Crowley, 1994-97	120
9	Steve Ulseth, 1977-81	118
10	Brian Bonin, 1992-96	116

TOTAL CAREER POINTS BY A DEFENSEMEN

Player	G	A	Pts
1 Todd Richards, 1985-89	30	128	158
2 Mike Crowley, 1994-97,	37	120	157
3 Jordan Leopold, 1998-2002	45	99	144
4 Travis Richards, 1989-93	35	98	133
5 Dan Trebil, 1991-96	24	100	124
6 Bill Baker, 1975-79	30	88	118
7 Gary Shopek, 1983-87	24	93	117
8 Tony Kellin, 1982-86	37	75	112
9 Joe Micheletti, 1973-77	25	81	106
10 Les Auge, 1971-75	19	85	104

TOTAL CAREER GAMES PLAYED

1	Larry Olimb, 1988-92	182
2	Grant Bischoff, 1987-91	180
3	Ken Gernander, 1987-91	176
	Peter Hankinson, 1986-90	176
	Travis Richards, 1989-93	176
6	Jason Miller, 1987-91	173
	Gary Shopek, 1984-88	173
8	Judd Stevens, 2001-05	172
	Jeff Nielsen, 1990-94	172
	Paul Broten, 1984-88	172
10	Matt Koalska, 2000-04	171

TOTAL CAREER PENALTY MINUTES

1	Matt DeMarchi, 1999-03	473
2	Chris McAlpine, 1990-94	453
3	Pat Micheletti, 1982-86	403
4	Ben Hankinson, 1987-91	400
5	Casey Hankinson, 1994-98	347
6	Dave Larson, 1992-96	314
7	Erik Westrum, 1997-01	307
8	Jeff Nielsen, 1990-94	292
9	Lance Pitlick, 1986-90	285
10	Bill Kohn, 1995-99	274

YEAR BY YEAR SCORING LEADERS (1990-2005)

Year	Player	Pos	Gm	G	A	Pts
1989-90	Peter Hankinson	W	46	25	41	66
1990-91	Larry Olimb	D/C	45	19	38	57
1991-92	Larry Olimb	C	44	24	56	80
1992-93	Craig Johnson	C	42	22	24	46
1993-94	Jeff Nielsen	W	41	29	16	45
1994-95	Brian Bonin	C	44	32	31	63
1995-96	Brian Bonin	C	42	34	47	81
1996-97	Mike Crowley	D	42	9	47	56
1997-98	Wyatt Smith	C	39	24	23	47
1998-99	Reggie Berg	F	43	20	28	48
1999-00	Johnny Pohl	F	41	18	41	59
2000-01	Erik Westrum	C	42	26	35	61
2001-02	Johnny Pohl	C	44	27	52	79
2002-03	Thomas Vanek	F	45	31	31	62
2002-03	Thomas Vanek	F	45	31	31	62
2004-05	Tyler Hirsch	F	41	11	33	44

YEAR BY YEAR RECORDS (1990-2005)

Season	Gms	W	L	T	.Pct	Coach
1990-91	45	30	10	5	.722	Doug Woog
1991-92	44	33	11	0	.750	Doug Woog
1992-93	42	22	12	8	.619	Doug Woog
1993-94	42	25	13	4	.619	Doug Woog
1994-95	44	25	14	5	.625	Doug Woog
1995-96	42	30	10	2	.738	Doug Woog
1996-97	42	28	13	1	.679	Doug Woog
1997-98	39	17	22	0	.436	Doug Woog
1998-99	43	15	19	9	.453	Doug Woog
1999-00	41	20	19	2	.512	Don Lucia
2000-01	42	27	13	2	.667	Don Lucia
2001-02	44	32	8	4	.773	Don Lucia
2002-03	45	28	8	9	.722	Don Lucia
2003-04	44	27	14	3	.648	Don Lucia
2004-05	44	28	15	1	.648	Don Lucia

GOPHER ALL-AMERICANS (1990-2005)

1995	Brian Bonin	C
1996	Brian Bonin	C
1996	Mike Crowley	D
1997	Mike Crowley	D
2001	Jordan Leopold	D
2002	Jordan Leopold	D
2001	Johnny Pohl	C
2004	Keith Ballard	D

GOPHER CAPTAINS (1990-2005)

1989-90	Peter Hankinson
	Lance Pitlick
1990-91	Ben Hankinson
1991-92	Larry Olimb
1992-93	Travis Richards
1993-94	Chris McAlpine
	Jeff Nielsen
1994-95	Scott Bell
	Justin McHugh
1995-96	Brian Bonin
	Dan Trebil
1996-97	Mike Crowley
	Casey Hankinson
1997-98	Casey Hankinson
	Ryan Kraft
1998-99	Wyatt Smith
1999-00	Nate Miller
	Dylan Mills
	Erik Westrum
2000-01	Dylan Mills
	John Pohl
	Erik Westrum
2001-02	Jordan Leopold
	John Pohl
	Grant Potulny
2002-03	Grant Potulny
	Nick Anthony
	Paul Martin
2003-04	Grant Potulny
	Troy Riddle
	Keith Ballard
2004-05	Judd Stevens
	Jake Fleming
	Barry Tallackson
	Chris Harrington
2005-06	Gino Guyer
	Chris Harrington
	Danny Irmen

SINGLE SEASON STATS

SINGLE SEASON TOTAL POINTS

Player	G	A	Pts
1 Aaron Broten, 1980-81	47	59	106
2 Pat Micheletti, 1984-85	48	46	96
3 Steve Ulseth, 1980-81	41	52	93
4 Scott Bjugstad, 1982-83	43	48	91
5 Butsy Erickson, 1980-81	39	47	86
6 Corey Millen, 1985-86	41	42	83
7 Butsy Erickson, 1982-83	35	47	82
Tim Harrer, 1979-80	53	29	82
9 Brian Bonin, 1995-96	34	47	81
10 Larry Olimb, 1991-92	24	56	80
Pat Micheletti, 1985-86	32	48	80
John Mayasich, 1954-55	41	39	80
13 John Pohl, 2001-02	27	52	79
14 John Mayasich, 1953-54	29	49	78
John Mayasich, 1952-53	42	36	78
16 Steve Christoff, 1978-79	38	39	77
17 Richard Erdall, 1984-85	25	51	76

SINGLE SEASON TOTAL GOALS

1 Tim Harrer, 1979-80	53
2 Pat Micheletti, 1984-85	48
3 Aaron Broten, 1980-81	47
4 Scott Bjugstad, 1982-83	43
5 Dick Dougherty, 1953-54	42
John Mayasich, 1952-53	42

SINGLE SEASON TOTAL ASSISTS

1 Aaron Broten, 1980-81	59
2 Larry Olimb, 1991-92	56
3 Neal Broten, 1980-81	54
4 John Pohl, 2001-02	52
Steve Ulseth 1980-81	52
6 Neal Broten, 1978-79	50
7 John Mayasich, 1953-54	49

ALL-TIME GOALTENDING STATS

GAMES PLAYED

151	Adam Hauser	1998-02
98	Robb Stauber	1986-89
96	Steve DeBus	1995-98
96	Jeff Callinan	1991-95
96	John Blue	1984-87
94	Jeff Stolp	1988-92
91	Steve Janaszak	1975-79
91	Tom Newman	1989-93

WINS

83	Adam Hauser	1998-02
73	Robb Stauber	1986-89
64	John Blue	1984-87
56	Jeff Stolp	1988-92
54	Steve DeBus	1995-98
51	Frank Pietrangelo	1982-86
50	Steve Janaszak	1975-79
50	Jim Mattson	1951-54
50	Tom Newman	1989-93

SHUT-OUTS

8	Kellen Briggs	2003-
8	Adam Hauser	1998-02
7	Steve DeBus	1995-98
7	John Blue	1984-87
7	Jim Mattson	1951-54
5	Robb Stauber	1986-89
5	Murray McLachlan	1967-70
5	Tom Newman	1989-93

GOALS-AGAINST AVERAGE

2.48	Jim Mattson	1951-54	(61 GP)
2.53	Kellen Briggs	2003-	(74 GP)
2.64	Travis Weber	2001-03	(44 GP)
2.77	Robb Stauber	1986-89	(98 GP)
2.86	Adam Hauser	1998-02	(151 GP)
2.88	Justin Johnson	2001-05	(46 GP)
3.08	Steve DeBus	1995-98	(96 GP)
3.13	Jeff Stolp	1988-92	(94 GP)

SAVE PERCENTAGE

906	Jim Mattson	1951-54	(61 GP)
906	Robb Stauber	1986-89	(98 GP)
903	Kellen Briggs	2003-	(74 GP)
902	Murray McLachlan	1967-70	(82 GP)
899	Adam Hauser	1998-02	(151 GP)
896	Brad Shelstad	1970-74	(78 GP)
896	Travis Weber	2001-03	(44 GP)
891	Steve DeBus	1995-98	(96 GP)
890	Justin Johnson	2001-05	(46 GP)
890	Jeff Tscherne	1973-77	(51 GP)

NCAA TOURNAMENT APPEARANCES

▶ **29 Appearances**
1953-54-61-71-74-75-76-79-80-81-83-85-86-87-88-89-90-91-92-93-94-95-96-97-2001-02-03-04-05
(record of 49-30 .620)

▶ **19 Frozen Four Appearances**
(1953-54-61-71-74-75-76-79-81-83-86-87-88-89-94-95-2002-03-05)
(record of 19-16, .543)

Five NCAA Championships	**(1974-76-79-2002-03)**
Six Runner-Up Finishes	**(1953-54-71-75-81-89)**
Six Third-Place Finishes	**(1961-89-87-94-95-2005)**
Two Fourth-Place Finishes	**(1983-88)**

NCAA RECORD VS. OPPONENTS

TEAM	SERIES	LAST MEETING
Boston College	4-4	3/22/86, BC 6, MN 1
Boston University	4-3	3/30/95, BU 7, MN 3
Bowling Green	1-0	3/18/79, MN 6, BG 3
Clarkson	3-0	3/26/93, MN 2, CU 1
Colgate	2-0	3/21/81, MN 5, Col 4
Colorado College	2-0	3/23/02, MN 4, CC 2
Cornell	1-0	3/27/05, MN 2, CU 1 (ot)
Denver	1-1	3/28/86, MN 6, DU 4
Ferris State	1-0	3/28/03, MN 7, FSU 4
Harvard	3-2	4/1/89, HU 4, MN 3 (ot)
Lake Superior State	0-1	3/29/92, LSSU 8, MN 3
Maine	3-5	3/26/05, MN 1, ME 0 (ot)
Mercyhurst	1-0	3/27/03, MN 9, MCY 2
Michigan	2-3	4/10/03, MN 3, MI 2 (ot)
Michigan State	3-2	3/22/97, MN 6, MSU 3
Michigan Tech	3-1	3/26/81, MN 7, MTU 2
Minnesota Duluth	0-1	3/28/04, UMD 3, MN 1
New Hampshire	4-0	4/12/03, MN 5, UNH 1
North Dakota	1-1	4/7/05, UND 4, MN 2
Northern Michigan	0-1	3/22/80, NMU 4, MN 3
Notre Dame	1-0	3/27/04, MN 5, ND 2
Providence	3-2	3/23/96, MN 5, PC 1
Rensselaer	3-1	3/24/95, MN 3, RPI 0
St. Lawrence	0-1	4/1/88, SLU 3, MN 2
Wisconsin	2-1	3/10/82, UW 6, MN 2
UMass-Lowell	1-0	3/27/94, MN 2, UML 1 (ot)
Total	**49-30**	

ALL-TIME NCAA TOURNAMENT FINISHES BY SCHOOL

CHAMPION		RUNNER-UP		THIRD PLACE*		FOURTH PLACE	
Michigan	9	**Minnesota**	**6**	Michigan	11	Boston College	6
Denver	7	Boston University	5	Boston University	8	Harvard	6
North Dakota	7	North Dakota	5	**Minnesota**	**6**	St. Lawrence	5
Minnesota	**5**	Boston College	4	Boston College	6	Boston Univ.	3
Wisconsin	5	Michigan Tech	4	Michigan State	5	New Hampshire	3
Boston University	4	Clarkson	3	Clarkson	4	**Minnesota**	**2**
Lake Superior St.	3	Colorado College	3	Maine	4	Colorado College	2
Michigan Tech	3	Maine	3	Colorado College	3	Cornell	2
Boston College	2	Cornell	2	Harvard	3	Denver	2
Colorado College	2	Dartmouth	2	Dartmouth	2	Michigan Tech	2
Cornell	2	Denver	2	Denver	2	Brown	1
Maine	2	Harvard	2	Minnesota-Duluth	2	Maine	1
Michigan State	2	Michigan	2	New Hampshire	2	Michigan State	1
RPI	2	Michigan State	2	North Dakota	2	North Dakota	1
Bowling Green	1	New Hampshire	2	RPI	2	Northern Michigan	1
Harvard	1	St. Lawrence	2	St. Lawrence	2	Providence	1
Northern Michigan	1	Brown	1	Wisconsin	2	RPI	1
		Colgate	1	Bowling Green	1	Wisconsin	1
		Lake Superior St.	1	Brown	1		
		Minnesota-Duluth	1	Cornell	1		
		Northern Michigan	1	Michigan Tech	1		
		Providence	1	Northeastern	1		
		Wisconsin	1	Ohio State	1		
				Providence	1		
				Vermont	1		
				Yale	1		

*Note: In championships without a third-place game (after 1989), both teams are awarded third place. Denver's participation in 1973 tournament and Wisconsin's participation in 1992 tournament vacated.

NCAA TOURNAMENT RECORD BOOK (TEAM)

NCAA CHAMPIONSHIPS

9	Michigan
7	Denver
	North Dakota
5	**Minnesota**
	Wisconsin

FROZEN FOUR APPEARANCES

22	Michigan
20	Boston University
19	**Minnesota**
18	Boston College
15	North Dakota

FROZEN FOUR WINS

24	Michigan
21	North Dakota
19	**Minnesota**
18	Denver
	Boston University

CONSECUTIVE FROZEN FOUR APPEARANCES

10	Michigan, 1948-57
5	Colorado College, 1948-52
	Boston University, 1974-78, 1993-97
4	**Minnesota, 1986-89**
	St. Lawrence, 1959-62
	Cornell, 1967-70
	Michigan, 1995-98
	Boston College, 1948-50

TOURNAMENT APPEARANCES

29	**Minnesota, 1953-2005**
28	Boston University, 1950-2005
28	Michigan, 1948-2005
25	Boston College, 1948-2005
23	Michigan State, 1959-2005
20	Wisconsin, 1970-2005
20	Harvard, 1955-2005
20	North Dakota, 1958-2005

CONSECUTIVE TOURNAMENT APPEARANCES

15	Michigan, 1991-2005
13	**Minnesota, 1985-97**
10	Michigan, 1948-57
9	Michigan State, 1982-90
9	Lake Superior State, 1988-96
9	Boston University, 1990-98
9	Michigan State, 1994-2002
7	Maine, 1999-2005
7	Maine, 1987-93

CURRENT CONSECUTIVE TOURNAMENT APPEARANCES

15	Michigan, 1991-2005
7	Maine, 1999-2005
5	**Minnesota, 2001-05**
4	Harvard, 2002-05
	New Hampshire, 2002-05

TOURNAMENT WINS

49	**Minnesota, 1953-2005**
44	Michigan, 1948-2005
34	North Dakota, 1958-2005
33	Boston University, 1950-2005
29	Wisconsin, 1970-2005
27	Boston College, 1948-2005
26	Maine, 1987-2005
25	Denver, 1958-2005
24	Michigan State, 1959-2002

TOURNAMENT WINNING PERCENTAGE

.694	North Dakota, 1958-2005 (34-15)
.677	Michigan, 1948-2005 (44-21)
.641	Lake Superior State, 1985-96 (20-11-1)
.620	**Minnesota, 1953-2005 (49-30)**
.612	Wisconsin, 1970-2005 (29-18-2)
.605	Maine, 1987-2005 (26-17)

Source: Gopher Media Guide 2005

ALL-TIME NHL ENTRY DRAFT PICKS (1986-2005)

Player	Team	Year	Rd	Pick
Ryan Stoa	Colorado Avalanche	2005	2	34
Jeff Frazee	New Jersey Devils	2005	2	38
Nate Hagemo	Carolina Hurricanes	2005	2	58
Blake Wheeler	Phoenix Coyotes	2004	1	5
Kris Chucko	Calgary Flames	2004	1	24
Alex Goligoski	Pittsburgh Penguins	2004	2	61
R J Anderson	Philadelphia Flyers	2004	4	101
Derek Peltier	Colorado Avalanche	2004	6	184
Thomas Vanek	Buffalo Sabres	2003	1	5
Danny Irmen	Minnesota Wild	2003	3	78
Ryan Potulny	Philadelphia Flyers	2003	3	87
Mike Vannelli	Atlanta Thrashers	2003	4	136
Gino Guyer	Dallas Stars	2003	5	165
Keith Ballard	Buffalo Sabres	2002	1	11
Barry Tallackson	New Jersey Devils	2002	2	53
Mike Erickson	Minnesota Wild	2002	3	72
Andy Sertich	Pittsburgh Penguins	2002	5	136
P J Atherton	Tampa Bay Lightning	2002	6	170
Jake Taylor	New York Rangers	2002	6	177
Jeff Taffe	St. Louis Blues	2000	1	30
Matt DeMarchi	New Jersey Devils	2000	2	57
Paul Martin	New Jersey Devils	2000	2	62
Troy Riddle	St Louis Blues	2000	4	129
Matt Koalska	Nashville Predators	2000	5	154
Grant Potulny	Ottawa Senators	2000	5	157
Joey Martin	Chicago Blackhawks	2000	6	193
Dan Welch	Los Angeles Kings	2000	8	245
Jordan Leopold	Anaheim Mighty Ducks	1999	2	44
Adam Hauser	Edmonton Oilers	1999	3	81
Doug Meyer	Pittsburgh Penguins	1999	6	176
Pat O'Leary	Phoenix Coyotes	1998	3	73
Erik Wendell	Washington Capitals	1998	5	125
Erik Westrum	Phoenix Coyotes	1998	7	187
John Pohl	St. Louis Blues	1998	9	255
Ben Clymer	Boston Bruins	1997	2	27
Aaron Miskovich	Colorado Avalanche	1997	5	133
Wyatt Smith	Phoenix Coyotes	1997	9	233
Erik Rasmussen	Buffalo Sabres	1996	1	7
Reggie Berg	Toronto Maple Leafs	1996	7	178
Mike Anderson	Washington Capitals	1996	7	180
Ryan Kraft	San Jose Sharks	1995	8	194
Casey Hankinson	Chicago Blackhawks	1995	8	201
Jason Godbout	Pittsburgh Penguins	1994	9	232
Nick Checco	Quebec Nordiques	1993	6	137
Mike Crowley	Philadelphia Flyers	1993	6	140
Dan Hendrickson	Washington Capitals	1993	7	173
John Hillman	Quebec Nordiques	1993	11	283
Charlie Wasley	Quebec Nordiques	1992	5	100
Dan Trebil	New Jersey Devils	1992	6	138
Greg Zwakman	Hartford Whalers	1992	9	201
Brian Bonin	Pittsburgh Penguins	1992	9	211

Jeff Moen	Minnesota North Stars	1992	11	250
Steve Magnusson	Calgary Flames	1991	4	85
Jeff Callinan	St. Louis Blues	1991	5	109
Jay Moser	Boston Bruins	1991	8	172
Jed Fiebelkorn	St. Louis Blues	1991	9	197
Craig Johnson	St. Louis Blues	1990	2	33
Mike Muller	Winnipeg Jets	1990	2	35
Joe Dziedzic	Pittsburgh Penguins	1990	3	61
Jeff Nielsen	New York Rangers	1990	4	69
Darby Hendrickson	Toronto Maple Leafs	1990	4	73
Chris McAlpine	New Jersey Devils	1990	7	137
Doug Zmolek	Minnesota North Stars	1989	1	7
John Brill	Pittsburgh Penguins	1989	3	58
Trent Klatt	Washington Capitals	1989	4	82
Tom Nevers	Pittsburgh Penguins	1989	5	100
Tom Newman	Los Angeles Kings	1989	5	103
Peter Hankinson	Winnipeg Jets	1989	-	4
Jon Anderson	Winnipeg Jets	1989	-	9
Jeff Stolp	Minnesota North Stars	1988	4	64
Travis Richards	Minnesota North Stars	1988	9	169
Grant Bischoff	Minnesota North Stars	1988	11	211
Cory Laylin	Pittsburgh Penguins	1988	11	214
Sean Fabian	Vancouver Canucks	1987	5	87
Ken Gernander	Winnipeg Jets	1987	5	96
Ben Hankinson	New Jersey Devils	1987	6	107
Jake Enebak	Quebec Nordiques	1987	8	156
Lance Werness	Chicago Blackhawks	1987	9	176
Larry Olimb	Minnesota North Stars	1987	10	193
Jeff Pauletti	Edmonton Oilers	1987	11	231
Dave Snuggerud	Buffalo Sabres	1987	2	2
Scott Bloom	Calgary Flames	1986	5	100
Robb Stauber	Los Angeles Kings	1986	6	107
Randy Skarda	St. Louis Blues	1986	8	157
Marty Nanne	Chicago Blackhawks	1986	8	161
Lance Pitlick	Minnesota North Stars	1986	9	180
John Blue	Winnipeg Jets	1986	10	197
Steve MacSwain	Calgary Flames	1986	-	4

1989-90 SEASON SCORING STATS

Name	GP	G	A	Pts
Peter Hankinson	46	25	41	66
Scott Bloom	43	24	28	52
Ken Gernander	44	32	17	49
Larry Olimb	46	6	36	42
Grant Bischoff	45	21	19	40
Tom Pederson	43	8	30	38
Trent Klatt	38	22	14	36
Jason Miller	41	10	26	36
Luke Johnson	44	4	31	35
Ben Hankinson	45	19	12	31
Jon Anderson	42	15	14	29
Travis Richards	45	4	24	28
Cory Laylin	39	13	14	27
Dean Williamson	46	10	11	21
Brett Strot	42	8	8	16
Doug Zmolek	40	1	10	11
John Brill	34	2	8	10
Sean Fabian	40	0	10	10
Lance Pitlick	14	3	2	5
Eric Means	22	0	4	4
Jake Enebak	20	0	3	3
Tom Newman (G)	35	0	2	2
Lance Werness	2	0	1	1
Nick Gerebi	4	0	0	0
Jeff Stolp (G)	10	0	0	0
Scott Nelson (G)	11	0	0	0

1990-91 SEASON SCORING STATS

Name	GP	G	A	Pts
Larry Olimb	45	19	38	57
Grant Bischoff	44	23	24	47
Trent Klatt	39	16	28	44
Ken Gernander	44	23	20	43
Ben Hankinson	43	19	21	40
Jason Miller	43	15	25	40
Travis Richards	45	9	25	34
Tom Pederson	36	12	20	32
Luke Johnson	43	8	24	32
Craig Johnson	33	13	18	31
Cory Laylin	40	12	13	25
Jeff Nielsen	45	11	14	25
John Brill	44	6	13	19
Doug Zmolek	42	3	15	18
Chris McAlpine	38	7	9	16
Joe Dziedzic	20	6	4	10
Mike Muller	33	4	4	8
Sean Fabian	41	0	7	7
Scott Bell	24	3	1	4
Nick Gerebi	19	3	0	3
Lance Werness	13	2	1	3
Jake Enebak	20	1	2	3
Paul Schwab	2	0	1	1
Tom Newman (G)	22	0	1	1
Todd Westlund	1	0	0	0
Andy Mills	3	0	0	0
Jim Anderson	6	0	0	0
Jeff Stolp (G)	32	0	0	0

1991-92 SEASON SCORING STATS

Name	GP	G	A	Pts
Larry Olimb	44	24	56	80
Trent Klatt	44	30	36	66
Craig Johnson	44	19	39	58
Darby Hendrickson	44	25	30	55
Travis Richards	44	10	23	33
Steve Magnusson	41	9	24	33
Cory Laylin	44	19	12	31
Jeff Nielsen	44	15	15	30
Doug Zmolek	44	6	21	27
Justin McHugh	41	14	9	23
Scott Bell	44	15	7	22
Joe Dziedzic	37	9	10	19
John Brill	38	8	9	17
Mike Muller	44	4	12	16
Chris McAlpine	42	3	9	12
Eric Means	43	1	11	12
Tony Bianchi	24	1	4	5
Sean Fabian	35	1	4	5
Todd Westlund	22	1	3	4
Brandon Steege	13	1	1	2
Jeff Stolp (G)	36	0	1	1
Nick Gerebi	4	0	0	0
John O'Connell	4	0	0	0
Jeff Callinan (G)	6	0	0	0
Jed Fiebelkorn	7	0	0	0
Tom Newman (G)	12	0	0	0

1992-93 SEASON SCORING STATS

Name	GP	G	A	Pts
Craig Johnson	42	22	24	46
Jeff Nielsen	42	21	20	41
Travis Richards	42	12	26	38
Justin McHugh	42	13	15	28
Brian Bonin	38	10	18	28
Darby Hendrickson	31	12	15	27
John Brill	41	12	13	25
Joe Dziedzic	41	11	14	25
Chris McAlpine	41	14	9	23
Scott Bell	37	5	11	16
Andy Brink	20	5	9	14
Jed Fiebelkorn	34	8	5	13
Dan Trebil	36	2	11	13
Brandon Steege	40	4	8	12
Steve Magnusson	21	1	10	11
Tony Bianchi	22	3	6	9
Dave Larson	25	4	3	7
Bobby Dustin	19	3	4	7
Charlie Wasley	35	2	5	7
Eric Means	22	2	2	4
Mike McAlpine	26	0	3	3
Jesse Bertogliat	16	1	0	1
Dan Woog	3	0	1	1
Greg Zwakman	36	0	1	1
Dave Norqual	2	0	0	0
Todd Westlund	2	0	0	0
Jeff Moen (G)	6	0	0	0
Jeff Callinan (G)	21	0	0	0
Tom Newman (G)	22	0	0	0

1993-94 SEASON SCORING STATS

Name	GP	G	A	Pts
Jeff Nielsen	41	29	16	45
Brian Bonin	42	24	20	44
Justin McHugh	42	15	20	35
Tony Bianchi	36	8	27	35
Chris McAlpine	36	12	18	30
Dan Trebil	42	1	21	22
Dan Woog	38	5	14	19
Bobby Dustin	39	10	7	17
Joe Dziedzic	18	7	10	17
Andy Brink	40	7	10	17
Dave Larson	31	6	11	17
Eric Means	36	5	11	16
Charlie Wasley	36	1	14	15
Steve Magnusson	16	2	12	14
Nick Checco	41	7	5	12
Jed Fiebelkorn	39	5	6	11
Brian LaFleur	40	0	9	9
Greg Zwakman	42	2	6	8
Dan Hendrickson	39	3	2	5
Jesse Bertogliat	17	2	2	4
Jeff Moen (G)	20	0	1	1
Steve Green (G)	1	0	0	0
Jim Hillman	6	0	0	0
Mike McAlpine	7	0	0	0
Brent Godbout	12	0	0	0
John Hillman	20	0	0	0
Jeff Callinan (G)	26	0	0	0

1994-95 SEASON SCORING STATS

Name	GP	G	A	Pts
Brian Bonin	44	32	31	63
Ryan Kraft	44	13	33	46
Dan Trebil	44	10	33	43
Justin McHugh	35	24	16	40
Scott Bell	41	18	21	39
Mike Crowley	41	11	27	38
Nick Checco	43	14	11	25
Dan Woog	44	5	16	21
Andy Brink	43	3	15	18
Dave Larson	42	9	7	16
Dan Hendrickson	40	4	12	16
Jed Fiebelkorn	41	4	9	13
Brian LaFleur	34	0	10	10
Casey Hankinson	33	7	1	8
Bobby Dustin	24	4	2	6
Charlie Wasley	36	2	4	6
Greg Zwakman	43	0	6	6
Joe Pankratz	18	3	2	5
Jesse Bertogliat	22	2	3	5
Jay Moser	13	1	4	5
Jason Godbout	32	1	4	5
Brandon Steege	15	1	3	4
Jeff Callinan (G)	43	0	2	2
Jason Seils	15	1	0	1
Will Anderson	1	0	0	0
Brent Godbout	2	0	0	0
Jeff Moen (G)	6	0	0	0

1995-96 SEASON SCORING STATS

Name	GP	G	A	Pts
Brian Bonin	42	34	47	81
Mike Crowley	42	17	46	63
Erik Rasmussen	40	16	32	48
Dan Trebil	42	11	35	46
Ryan Kraft	41	13	24	37
Casey Hankinson	39	16	19	35
Reggie Berg	40	23	11	34
Dave Larson	38	13	13	26
Dan Woog	39	6	16	22
Jay Moser	21	10	9	19
Nick Checco	41	8	11	19
Brian LaFleur	40	6	12	18
Andy Brink	33	5	13	18
Jason Godbout	39	6	7	13
Jesse Bertogliat	22	5	5	10
Wyatt Smith	32	4	5	9
Mike Anderson	28	3	6	9
Greg Zwakman	42	1	6	7
Bobby Dustin	18	3	3	6
Charlie Wasley	41	1	5	6
Dan Hendrickson	23	2	3	5
Bill Kohn	7	0	2	2
Brett Abrahamson	3	1	0	1
Steve Debus (G)	24	0	1	1
Clint Johnson	1	0	0	0
Jeff Moen (G)	21	0	0	0

1996-97 SEASON SCORING STATS

Name	GP	G	A	Pts
Mike Crowley	42	9	47	56
Ryan Kraft	42	25	21	46
Casey Hankinson	42	17	24	41
Dave Spehar	40	20	17	37
Reggie Berg	38	11	26	37
Brian LaFleur	30	12	21	33
Wyatt Smith	38	16	14	30
Erik Rasmussen	34	15	12	27
Mike Anderson	42	9	11	20
Ben Clymer	29	7	13	20
Dan Woog	41	4	13	17
Dan Hendrickson	42	5	11	16
Bill Kohn	42	5	10	15
Nate Miller	40	5	9	14
Nick Checco	41	5	9	14
Brett Abrahamson	35	5	8	13
Jason Godbout	42	2	9	11
Rico Pagel	29	5	5	10
Mike Lyons	32	1	5	6
Brent Godbout	15	0	2	2
Cory Miller	11	1	0	1
Steve Debus (G)	38	0	1	1
Tom Nevers	1	0	0	0
Willy Marvin (G)	4	0	0	0
Erik Day (G)	5	0	0	0
Ryan Trebil	8	0	0	0

1997-98 SEASON SCORING STATS

Name	GP	G	A	Pts
Wyatt Smith	39	24	23	47
Reggie Berg	39	20	19	39
Dave Spehar	39	19	18	37
Ryan Kraft	32	11	26	37
Mike Anderson	31	12	13	25
Casey Hankinson	35	10	12	22
Bill Kohn	36	4	16	20
Rico Pagel	39	8	11	19
Erik Westrum	39	6	12	18
Nate Miller	39	8	6	14
Brett Abrahamson	39	3	10	13
Mike Lyons	38	1	12	13
Aaron Miskovich	28	4	8	12
Dylan Mills	39	1	10	11
Stuart Senden	32	5	3	8
Ryan Trebil	39	2	3	5
Matt Leimbeck	34	0	5	5
Jason Godbout	24	2	1	3
Ben Clymer	1	0	0	0
Willy Marvin (G)	3	0	0	0
Erik Day (G)	9	0	0	0
Cory Miller	22	0	0	0
Steve Debus (G)	34	0	0	0

1998-99 SEASON SCORING STATS

Name	GP	G	A	Pts
Reggie Berg	43	20	28	48
Wyatt Smith	43	23	20	43
Dave Spehar	42	13	23	36
Erik Westrum	41	10	26	36
Jordan Leopold	39	7	16	23
Aaron Miskovich	42	11	11	22
Mike Anderson	43	10	7	17
Johnny Pohl	42	7	10	17
Rico Pagel	32	4	11	15
Erik Wendell	41	7	7	14
Nate Miller	43	6	8	14
Dylan Mills	39	2	12	14
Matt Leimbeck	28	4	8	12
Stuart Senden	34	4	5	9
Bill Kohn	43	3	6	9
Nick Angell	37	1	8	9
Doug Meyer	36	4	4	8
Mike Lyons	42	1	4	5
Brad Timmons	11	1	2	3
Ryan Trebil	21	1	2	3
Pat O'Leary	17	0	2	2
Cory Miller	2	0	0	0
Willy Marvin (G)	4	0	0	0
Rob LaRue (G)	5	0	0	0
Mark Nenovich	13	0	0	0
Adam Hauser (G)	40	0	0	0

1999-2000 SEASON SCORING STATS

Name	GP	G	A	Pts
Johnny Pohl	41	18	41	59
Erik Westrum	39	27	26	53
Nate Miller	41	16	19	35
Aaron Miskovich	41	16	16	32
Dylan Mills	40	8	21	29
Jordan Leopold	39	6	18	24
Jeff Taffe	39	10	10	20
Dave Spehar	39	9	10	19
Dan Welch	36	6	8	14
Stuart Senden	40	7	5	12
Ben Tharp	32	0	12	12
Shawn Roed	12	3	6	9
Nick Angell	37	3	6	9
Nick Anthony	34	4	4	8
Pat O'Leary	25	6	1	7
Matt DeMarchi	39	1	6	7
Erik Wendell	32	4	2	6
Matt Leimbeck	23	1	4	5
Mark Nenovich	29	2	2	4
Doug Meyer	26	1	3	4
Rico Pagel	17	0	2	2
Mike Lyons	25	0	2	2
Ryan Trebil	11	0	1	1
Erik Young (G)	3	0	0	0
Pete Samargia (G)	6	0	0	0
Adam Hauser (G)	36	0	0	0

2000-01 SEASON SCORING STATS

Name	GP	G	A	Pts
Erik Westrum	42	26	35	61
Jordan Leopold	42	12	37	49
Johnny Pohl	38	19	26	45
Jeff Taffe	38	12	23	35
Grant Potulny	42	22	11	33
Troy Riddle	38	16	14	30
Aaron Miskovich	41	12	12	24
Matt Koalska	42	10	14	24
Dylan Mills	42	2	21	23
Paul Martin	38	3	17	20
Nick Anthony	34	5	12	17
Stuart Senden	34	7	6	13
Matt DeMarchi	39	4	9	13
Pat O'Leary	38	5	4	9
Ben Tharp	38	4	4	8
Nick Angell	38	3	5	8
Jon Waibel	42	1	7	8
Erik Wendell	33	5	2	7
Matt Leimbeck	23	3	2	5
Joey Martin	18	0	2	2
Pete Samargia (G)	5	0	1	1
Erik Young (G)	1	0	0	0
Chad Roberg	6	0	0	0
Mark Nenovich	9	0	0	0
Adam Hauser (G)	40	0	0	0

2001-02 SEASON SCORING STATS

Name	GP	G	A	Pts
Johnny Pohl	44	27	52	79
Jeff Taffe	43	34	24	58
Jordan Leopold	44	20	28	48
Troy Riddle	44	16	31	47
Paul Martin	44	8	30	38
Grant Potulny	43	15	19	34
Matt Koalska	44	10	23	33
Barry Tallackson	44	13	10	23
Keith Ballard	41	10	13	23
Nick Anthony	25	9	9	18
Erik Wendell	44	8	9	17
Judd Stevens	41	1	15	16
Nick Angell	44	4	11	15
Jake Fleming	43	3	9	12
Dan Welch	19	4	7	11
Matt DeMarchi	36	3	8	11
Jon Waibel	44	5	4	9
Pat O'Leary	40	4	2	6
Brett MacKinnon	20	1	3	4
Joey Martin	11	0	4	4
Mike Erickson	9	1	2	3
Garrett Smaagaard	18	1	2	3
Adam Hauser (G)	35	0	2	2
Mark Nenovich	5	0	1	1
Chad Roberg	2	0	0	0
Justin Johnson (G)	6	0	0	0

2002-03 SEASON SCORING STATS

Name	GP	G	A	Pts
Thomas Vanek	45	31	31	62
Troy Riddle	45	26	25	51
Keith Ballard	45	12	29	41
Matt Koalska	41	9	31	40
Paul Martin	45	9	30	39
Gino Guyer	41	13	16	29
Tyler Hirsch	43	9	15	24
Grant Potulny	23	15	8	23
Barry Tallackson	32	9	14	23
Jake Fleming	41	10	9	19
Chris Harrington	45	4	14	18
Jon Waibel	40	9	8	17
Matt DeMarchi	44	8	9	17
Andy Sertich	44	5	8	13
Jerrid Reinholz	33	3	10	13
Dan Welch	18	5	5	10
Judd Stevens	44	3	6	9
Garrett Smaagaard	21	2	7	9
Joey Martin	24	3	4	7
Nick Anthony	34	1	4	5
P J Atherton	20	2	2	4
Brett MacKinnon	16	1	3	4
Mike Erickson	16	0	2	2
Peter Kennedy	10	0	1	1
Justin Johnson (G)	14	0	1	1
Travis Weber (G)	34	0	1	1

2003-04 SEASON SCORING STATS

Name	GP	G	A	Pts
Thomas Vanek	38	26	25	51
Troy Riddle	44	24	25	49
Matt Koalska	44	13	26	39
Keith Ballard	37	11	25	36
Gino Guyer	44	11	21	32
Chris Harrington	41	5	24	29
Grant Potulny	38	16	10	26
Barry Tallackson	44	10	15	25
Tyler Hirsch	43	7	18	25
Dan Irmen	44	14	8	22
Andy Sertich	43	8	14	22
Jake Fleming	41	7	13	20
Garrett Smaagaard	33	3	14	17
Ryan Potulny	15	6	8	14
Jon Waibel	42	5	9	14
Mike Vannelli	27	2	9	11
Jake Taylor	39	2	6	8
Judd Stevens	43	3	4	7
Jerrid Reinholz	12	3	3	6
Peter Kennedy	34	1	4	5
Brett MacKinnon	7	1	2	3
Kellen Briggs (G)	40	0	3	3
Joey Martin	11	0	2	2
P J Atherton	28	0	2	2

2004-05 SEASON SCORING STATS

Name	GP	G	A	Pts
Tyler Hirsch	41	11	33	44
Danny Irmen	44	24	19	43
Ryan Potulny	44	24	17	41
Gino Guyer	44	12	20	32
Chris Harrington	44	2	24	26
Kris Chucko	44	10	11	21
Alex Goligoski	33	5	15	20
Barry Tallackson	36	11	8	19
Derek Peltier	43	6	13	19
Garrett Smaagaard	44	8	8	16
Mike Vannelli	40	4	12	16
Mike Howe	35	7	8	15
Andy Sertich	44	6	9	15
Jake Fleming	43	4	10	14
Evan Kaufmann	30	7	6	13
Judd Stevens	44	4	8	12
Nate Hagemo	30	2	8	10
Ben Gordon	24	0	9	9
Jerrid Reinholz	33	2	5	7
Brent Borgen	17	2	3	5
P J Atherton	17	2	2	4
Tom Pohl	12	2	0	2
Justin Johnson (G)	13	0	1	1
Peter Kennedy	6	0	1	1
Kellen Briggs (G)	34	0	0	0

CHAPTER 2

WHAT DOES IT MEAN FOR YOU TO BE A GOPHER, OR TO BE A PART OF THE GOPHER FAMILY?

"I grew up in Bloomington playing with guys like Mike Crowley and Dan Trebil, so when they went to the U of M it just made me want to follow in their footsteps too. It was just an amazing experience going there and to be a part of that tradition. Hey, I live in Chicago but still have season tickets, so I always plan on being a part of it." — *Mike Anderson, Gopher 1995-99*

"Like most kids in Minnesota, I grew up dreaming of one day becoming a Gopher. You know, I blew out my knee my senior year and Wooger let me take over the video-taping duties. Then, with the departure of Billy Butters, I took over the travel arrangements. My job description has just kind of grown from there into bigger and better things. Now, I deal with the booster clubs, the alumni, the Williams Fund, the fundraising efforts, and team operations issues. So, I have been lucky. Wooger gave me a shot and it turned out to be a real dream come true. Now, that I have made it my career, it is more than I ever thought possible. I just feel really fortunate to be a part of this great tradition." — *Mark Bahr, Gopher 1991-94, Current Director of Hockey Operations*

"Growing up in Northern Minnesota I watched the Gophers on TV every week. I just fell in love with the program and dreamed about playing for them one day. So, when I had the opportunity to come here, I jumped at it. To be a part of a school with so much tradition is just incredible. The program is just synonymous with success. The three years that I had there were unbelievable. So, it was very special to me, those were some of the best years of my life. In fact, the best memories and friendships that I have are from my days at the University of Minnesota." — *Keith Ballard, Gopher 2001-04*

"For me it was the realization of a goal that I had set for myself way back in ninth grade. It just meant everything for me to be a Gopher. I even turned down a full-ride from Colorado College to play there on just a quarter scholarship, that was how badly I wanted it. I will never forget how it happened, I was playing junior hockey with Sioux City and after a game one night Coach Woog came up to me and offered me the partial quarter scholarship. I was so excited, I accepted it right there on the spot. Right after that Brad Buetow, the head coach at Colorado College, came up to me and offered me a full-ride. I told him thanks but no thanks, it had been a dream of mine to play for the Gophers and that it wasn't about money. I told him I appreciated his offer and that I was going to look forward to playing against him. He just sort of smiled. He was a Gopher too, so he knew what that dream was all about.

"Looking back, it was the best decision of my life. I made so many lifelong friends at the University of Minnesota and we remain close to this very day. I mean it is so great to get together with old teammates and have our kids play together, that is what it is all about. Even my parents remain friends with some of the other player's parents who they met back when we were playing, which says so much about the entire program I think.

"When I reflect about what it meant to be a Gopher, I think that was my NHL. That was the pinnacle for me. So many of my hopes and dreams came true there and I got to be a part of a team that was second to none. I had such a great time there and created so many relationships that I know will be with me forever. The entire experience was just super, I wouldn't change a thing." — *Scott Bell, Gopher 1991-95*

"It meant everything. As a kid growing up in Minnesota there was one thing I wanted to do, play hockey for the Gophers. I remember going to games at the old Barn when I was a kid, it was amazing. Just to be around that atmosphere was so special and it just made me want to be a part of that incredible tradition. So, to be able to finally do that was really a dream come true. It is the best college hockey program in the nation and I am just proud to be a part of it." — *Reggie Berg, Gopher 1995-99*

"I grew up in Northern Minnesota following the team, so when I got the opportunity to go there I considered it to be a huge honor. I just felt very lucky to be one of the few high school kids in the state of Minnesota to get a scholarship to go there. So, it means a great deal to me and it is something I look back on very proudly. Even today, to be able to bring my kids to games and to let them see all of that is just priceless. They love coming down and watching Goldy and dancing to the band, it just means so much to me." — *Grant Bischoff, Gopher 1987-91*

"Working with kids keeps me young. I love getting to know the kids and watching them grow up over their four years here. This is a great program which has had a lot of success over the years, and it was nice to see that they finally got some rewards in the last couple years for all of their hard work. You know, it is a family here and I have been fortunate to be a part of it for so long. If you have a 40-hour a week job, I have always felt that you better like what you are doing. I love what I do. I like the coaches, I like the friends who I have made here — it has kind of become my life. Wait, I just got married. Let me rephrase that... next to my HUS-BAND, it is my life! How's that?" — *Patty Bjorklund, Longtime Gopher Hockey Administrative Assistant*

"I had always followed the Gophers ever since I was a kid but never dreamt in my wildest dreams that I would ever have the opportunity to play for them. So, when that finally happened it really was a dream come true for me. To be a part of such a first class organization was just awesome. The tradition, the fans, the arena — it was all a part of it. I mean to play with all of the top kids from around the state of Minnesota was such a special thing, I made so many great friends and just feel blessed to have had the chance to play there. I am very proud to say that I was a Gopher, it means a great deal to me." — *Brian Bonin, Gopher 1992-96*

"For me it is different from the guys who grew up in Minnesota watching the Gophers and dreaming of one day wearing the 'M.' I grew up in Colorado as a Colorado College fan, but got to know the Gophers by virtue of being a college hockey fan. I was always really impressed whenever I saw them play and then really began following them when I was playing junior hockey in Sioux Falls. It is such an amazing program with so much history. Plus, they have had so many great players come through here, which was really a huge draw for me. From what I understand I am the first non-Minnesota goalie to play here since John Blue, almost 20 years ago. That means a lot to me. So, for me I am just proud to be a part of it and to hopefully add to that great history." — *Kellen Briggs, Gopher 2003-Present*

"When you are a part of the Gopher Hockey family there is a certain responsibility and tradition to uphold. When you hear players say that they have to bring their 'A' game, I feel the same way when I do my job. I take a lot of pride in that. One of the great things about college hockey is that there is always a turn-over of new players, which always makes it interesting. You get to know these kids and you become like a big family. You watch them grow up, make mistakes, learn from those mistakes and mature. When they come in as freshmen, they are not men, they are still kids. Hopefully, by the time they graduate and move on, then they are men. That is neat to watch from behind the scenes. I will say though that while most of the young men mature, others simply grow taller. That is all I will say about that! I have been lucky though in that I have made a lot of great friends here over the years and that is something I have never taken for granted." — *Harry Broadfoot, Gopher Equipment Manager 1986-Present*

"I never really appreciated what it meant while I was there. Later on though, it made a lot more sense and took on a very special meaning in my life. I made a lot of great friendships and had a great time there. I had three wonderful coaches too, in Glen Sonmor, Ken Yackel and Herb

Brooks. To know those guys as men and to watch them coach and learn from them was very special. My desire to become a coach and to have an impact on young men's lives came from those guys. Beyond that, it was just the memories. I think back to listening to the band play the rouser as I was walking up those old wooden stairs out onto the ice at Mariucci Arena, or Williams Arena back when I played. It was a thrill, it really was." — *Bill Butters, Gopher Player 1971-73; Assistant Coach 1985-95*

"I don't think it really hit me until I got into the room with the guys. I was a little apprehensive at first, because I knew it had always been an all-Minnesota team, but they couldn't have been nicer. I knew that the program had a lot of history and tradition, but seeing it first hand totally blew me away. The love of the team that the fans here have is just huge. There is just so much pride and effort and excitement that surrounds each and every game here. So, to be a part of the program is very special. Then, to be one of first kids from Canada to come here in many, many years, that means a great deal to me too. I looked at that as an extreme honor, to be asked to play here. Sure, there was some pressure at first, but I have been welcomed by the fans with open arms. Peter Kennedy is the other token Canadian on the team and it has been nice to have him around as well. One of the guys who has really helped me is Glen Sonmor, who is also Canadian. He just told me to work hard and good things would happen. He was right. We all realize that kids are kids, wherever they come from. Hey, I am from Canada, not from Mars, people! So, it's all good." — *Kris Chucko, Gopher 2003-Present*

"It was such a great experience. My family had season tickets 25 rows up right on the red line. So, I grew up as a huge Gopher fan. I worshiped those players as Gods, I was just in awe of them. When they would come on to the ice with the band playing the Rouser, I still get goose bumps thinking about that. The tradition and pride there was so amazing, it meant just a great deal to me to have the opportunity to be a part of all that. My only regret is that I should have stayed longer than I did. It was too bad it didn't work out that way, but I had other goals in hockey that I wanted to achieve. You see, I had surgery on my shoulder at the beginning of my second year, so I opted to use a little known loophole that said if you left school and went to go play junior hockey, then you could be free of the NHL team which drafted you. Well, Boston drafted me and I knew that it was going to be an uphill battle to get the kind of money I was looking for out there, so I opted out. It was a financial business decision more than anything. Sometimes you have to take advantage of those unique situations when they present themselves. Believe me though, I definitely missed out on things by leaving early." — *Ben Clymer, Gopher 1996-98*

"Growing up my family had season tickets, so for me it was truly a dream come true to play for the Gophers. In fact, my parents shared tickets with the Checco's, which is pretty ironic. I was lucky, I got to play hockey with a ton of my high school buddies from Bloomington, where we had just won three state tourney titles, and we just had a ball. To play at Mariucci Arena in front of your friends and family was just the best. So, to be a part of that incredible tradition was a real honor." — *Mike Crowley, Gopher 1994-97*

"Looking back it was an amazing feeling to be a Gopher. Knowing that you were going to be a part of that tradition and would be following in the footsteps of so many outstanding players before you, was just incredible. I was so lucky to have the opportunity. I came up through the Minnesota youth hockey system and felt like that was the pinnacle of success. So, it meant a lot then and it still means a lot now." — *Steve DeBus, Gopher 1995-98*

"I just grew up loving Gopher Hockey. It was a love affair that started when I was a little kid. We used to love watching them on TV, but it wasn't like today when they are on FOX every single week, or even before when they were on MSC. Back then it was hit or miss. It was a big deal when you could watch them because they were only on a handful of times throughout the season in those days. So, when they were on I was just glued to it. Heck, that was the highlight of my weekend!

"From there, I can remember going to games at old Mariucci Arena and sitting in those crappy general admission seats. We would have to get there early and sit around the lobby until they opened the doors. They would ring this bell and then everybody would run up to get seats, it was hilarious. All of the regulars had their favorite seats which gave them the best site-lines and it was a race to see who could get up there first. I remember my buddies and I would split up and go to different doors on all sides of the building in hopes of one of us getting up there first so we could all sit together. We were just really into it. Finally, in the late '80s we said enough was enough and got season tickets. We were big-time, we had officially arrived.

"You know, I dreamed of being a Gopher when I was a little kid, but unfortunately I was notoriously soft, just a real baby. I played hockey up until junior high school, but playing outside just killed me. It pains me to even say that. So, I wound up playing basketball, which was punishment enough I suppose." — *Jeff Dubay, KFAN Radio Host & Longtime Gopher Fanatic*

"It was everything. You know, as a kid my buddies and I used to sneak into the Old Barn and watch games. We would always go down to that one corner under the overhang and stand down there, it was awesome. I used to be in awe of Corey Millen and Tom Chorske. You know, I work with kids now and it is so neat to see how they look up to certain guys on the team now the same way we did. That is all a part of the tradition there, that you get to look up to 'your guy,' so to speak, when you are a kid. That cycle of new kids is what keeps it all going. I just always dreamed of one day being able to wear the Maroon and Gold, so when it finally came true it was almost surreal. Growing up in Northeast Minneapolis was a far cry from growing up in Edina or Wayzata, with regards to having opportunities in hockey. I was really proud to come from Edison High School though and to represent my community at the U of M. A lot of kids transfer out of there to go to private schools, but for me it was about playing with the guys I grew up with. So I took a ton of pride in the fact that I stayed and was able to make it to the big-time. I just loved playing on the weekends against our rivals like Duluth, Wisconsin and North Dakota. You really got up for those games and the fans did too. It was all such an amazing experience, I really miss it." — *Joe Dziedzic, Gopher 1990-94*

"At the time you are playing you aren't really aware of everything that it entails. It was a great time while you were there, but you don't realize how special it really was until you are gone. So, it meant a great deal to be a Gopher. A couple players from Greenway, Mike Antonovich and Mike Guentzel, who I really respected and looked up to as a kid, went there and that made a big difference in me wanting to go there too." — *Ken Gernander, Gopher 1988-91*

"Get this. My mom was a member of the first ever on-ice cheerleading squad up at Eveleth High School back in the late 1940s and early '50's, when the team was in the midst of winning four straight undefeated state championships. So, the fact that my mom got to be out on the ice with the legendary Johnny Mayasich made me an instant Gopher fan. Beyond that, covering hockey for me has always been just a real passion. I love hockey; I played hockey; and I am a fan of the game at all levels. I have always loved the Gophers though and it was a thrill to be a part of that program as a broadcaster." — *Eric Gislason, Former Gopher Radio & Television Commentator*

"Growing up in Northern Minnesota I followed the Gophers as a kid. So, when I got the opportunity to come there, I jumped at it. It was a thrill to be able to be a part of this great tradition and something I am very proud of. It is amazing to think that it has been 24 years since I was a freshman, and I am thrilled to be able to still be a part of the program all these years later as an assistant coach. Being a coach, it is very gratifying to work with these kids and to watch them grow and mature into men. The program that we have here is second to none in college hockey and just keeps getting better and better. So, I have over 16 years of my life invested in Gopher Hockey now, and I feel as much a part of this program as anybody. It is like family to me." — *Mike Guentzel, Gopher Player 1981-85; Assistant Coach 1994-Present*

"Growing up in Minnesota it is every kid's dream to be a Gopher, so it is very special to me. It is also the culmination of a lot of hard work too. I mean when other kids were out playing on their dirt bikes, I was out back shooting pucks. I set a goal for myself at a very young age that this was what I wanted to do and I have stuck to that. It was a real dream come true for me to be a Gopher and it is something I am really proud of. The best thing about being a Gopher to me though, is being able to have so many great teammates. I have made so many wonderful friendships here and it is really like a big family. It's awesome." — *Gino Guyer, Gopher 2003-Present*

"It was an honor and a privilege to play for the Gophers. It was one those things that you didn't really appreciate until it was over. I grew up going to games and had always loved the tradition over there. For Doug Woog to give me a shot, I will always be grateful. I am also grateful to my older brother Peter, who basically handed me to them on a silver platter. If not for that I would have definitely been overlooked. So, it was a real dream come true, no question. Later, to be named as the team captain, that was really special too. So many great leaders have worn the 'C' over the years and that was such a privilege to be able to represent the team like that. Being the captain was a double-edged sword though because that meant I couldn't get into as much trouble as I was normally accustomed to. Overall though, it was one of the best experiences of my life, and something I will never take for granted." — *Ben Hankinson, Gopher 1987-91*

"It meant everything to me. I was in a unique situation in that I grew up watching my two older brothers, Peter and Ben, play for the team back in the '80's. I played hockey on a my backyard rink every day in the Winter just dreaming of wearing that big 'M' and when it finally came true it was one of the greatest moments of my life. It was just so amazing to be a part of a program with such history and such tradition. To think that I am now a small part of that is so humbling. So, I guess you could say that I viewed Gopher Hockey just behind God in the grand scheme of things in my life." — *Casey Hankinson, Gopher 1994-98*

"Like most kids growing up in Minnesota, it was a childhood dream. To put on that maroon and gold jersey for the first time was one of the highlights of my life. So, it means the world to me. My dad was a Gopher quarterback on the football team and my mom was a cheerleader, so it is wonderful that my two brothers and I got to all be a part of this amazing tradition in Gold Country as well." — *Peter Hankinson, Gopher 1986-90*

"It was interesting growing up for sure. I mean my dad played at UMD and he later went on to coach at both St. Cloud State and Denver, so the Gophers were always the hated enemy. But, I just grew up watching them on TV and somehow fell in love with them. So, it means a great deal to me now to say that I am a part of this program and that I am a Gopher. It is just a great tradition and it is really a second to none school in terms of getting a great education while also being able to play hockey. It is a first class school and it has definitely been an honor to play here." — *Chris Harrington, Gopher 2002-Present*

"I learned a lot about life while I was there. I went through a lot of good times as well as a lot of bad times, but that just made me a stronger person. You see, I came in as an 18 year-old freshman straight out of high school and started playing right away. You don't see that anymore. Almost every kid who comes in now spent time in junior hockey for at least one season and typically for two. For me, that was an extremely difficult transition. Being on TV twice a week and living under the constant media scrutiny was tough. The pressure is hard enough for goaltenders, but to add a lot of what I had to go through on top of that was very trying to say the least. I learned some tough lessons along the way though, like never read the newspapers; never watch commentary about yourself on TV; never listen to the radio when they are talking about you; and just never believe what the media says about you. So, you have to be ready for that and prepare yourself mentally in order to be successful. Looking back, I wish I had been able to deal with that a little differently. Having said that, I would never want to trade my four years for anything because it has gotten me to where I am today. I am glad that I was able to win a national championship, however, and leave on my own terms with a great education. To be honest, after four years I was ready to get out." — *Adam Hauser, Gopher 1998-2002*

"It was always something I had hoped to aspire to, like so many other kids in Minnesota. I grew up watching them on TV and couldn't wait to wear that big 'M.' So, it was a real blessing when

I finally got the opportunity to play here." — *Tyler Hirsch, Gopher 2002-Present*

"I grew up in Fargo as a huge Gopher Hockey fan. The pride and tradition there are just amazing. I watched them on TV ever since I was a little kid and even used to wear a Gopher jacket and hat around town. It was great. It's funny, because when I was a kid and playing hockey, people used to tease me because they knew that Coach Woog only took Minnesota kids. So, when Coach Lucia came in, it was like a dream come true for me. I went up to the University of North Dakota on a recruiting visit, out of respect, and they basically said to me 'Here's the rink; you're from North Dakota; we expect you to come here...'. Needless to say, I committed to the Gophers shortly after that during the Summer of my junior year during the early signing period. Hey, UND loved Woog, they never had to worry about local kids like me leaving. Well, not any more!" — *Danny Irmen, Gopher 2003-Present*

"It meant a lot. I remember watching them when I was growing up and it was always such a thrill when my dad took me to a game. Being a Gopher was just something I always wanted to be. So, when I got the opportunity to finally walk up those old wooden stairs at Mariucci Arena, it was a thrill of a lifetime. It was just so much fun playing with all of your buddies, going to school together, living together and hanging out. It was a really special atmosphere, I miss it." — *Craig Johnson, Gopher 1990-93*

"I am so excited. We are going to have a great team this year and I can't wait to be a part of this amazing tradition. You know, I got recruited pretty hard from some other schools, but the biggest factor in me deciding to come to Minnesota was their style of play. I really liked their offensive system. Plus, I played on the U.S. development team in Ann Arbor with Ryan Stoa and Jeff Frazee, and we became good friends, so that certainly helped too. I am proud to be the first player from Wisconsin to play here in a long, long time. Hey, I have never been a big Packers fan if that helps! Really though, Minnesota was the best school for me and for my needs, so I am happy to be here and to help them try to win a national championship." — *Phil Kessel, Gopher 2005-Present*

"It meant everything. When I was a kid growing up that is all I wanted to do, to play for the Gophers. It was the biggest dream come true in my life, it really was." — *Trent Klatt, Gopher 1989-92*

"It meant everything. I used to go to the *'Skate with the Gophers'* when I was a kid and was just in awe of being out on the ice at Mariucci Arena. I remember watching the games on TV every weekend with a couple of my neighborhood buddies and we would play knee hockey while the game was going on. I had Mike Crowley's name written on my stick, so when we played — I WAS Mike Crowley! Then, between periods, my dad would make us frozen pizzas and Polish malts. Those were the best times. You know, just being from Minnesota and growing up watching the Gophers and then to finally being able to be a part of that was more than a dream come true. Being so close to home was great too, knowing that my family was going to be at all my games meant the world to me. The pride, the tradition, the history — it was such an honor to be a small part of that." — *Matt Koalska, Gopher 2000-04*

"Believe it or not, it was a childhood dream come true. This, coming from a guy who grew up in Moorhead about 75 miles from the University of North Dakota. My dad went to school there too, so we would go to hockey games up there all the time. So, I started out as a huge Sioux fan, but when I got a little older and started watching the Gophers on MSC (TV), I just fell in love with them. Every Friday and Saturday night I would follow them and from there I just wanted to be a Gopher. The Sioux even offered me a full-ride, but I took a partial scholarship from Woog instead. That was where my heart was and it was one of the best decisions of my life." — *Ryan Kraft, Gopher 1994-98*

"Being a Gopher was all I ever wanted when I was a kid. I will never forget the first game my dad took me to when I was a kid. It was amazing. From there on out I used to love watching the games on TV and rooting for them. I was obsessed with them, that was all I wanted to do, to become a Gopher. It was really a driving force for my work ethic growing up. It literally drove me to work hard so that I could one day make the team. Then, when I made it, it was everything I had ever hoped for and more. So, being a Gopher means the world to me, and it will forever." — *Cory Laylin, Gopher 1988-92*

"It is a tremendous honor when you look at the coaches are who have been here. We are talking about some great, great hockey people who devoted their lives to the sport. So, I feel very fortunate to have gotten the opportunity to be a part of this program. It is a real honor to be the head coach of the Minnesota Gophers. There is also a tremendous amount of responsibility that goes along with it to do your best and to maintain the level of excellence that is expected here." — *Don Lucia, Current Gopher Head Coach*

"Growing up in Minnesota it was a dream of mine to wear that big 'M' on my chest. I grew up watching the team on TV and you never really think that you could ever possibly be a part of that. Then, when it happens it is almost surreal. I was just fortunate to get the opportunity to go there. I didn't even visit any other schools because that is where I wanted to go. So, it means everything for me to be a Gopher." — *Paul Martin, Gopher 2000-03*

"It means an awful lot because people really care about Gopher Hockey. They care about the sport and they care about the players. It goes to their soul. So, to be able to convey information to them, that just means everything to me. For me, I have a real passion for what I do. I also have a real passion for Gopher Hockey. So, it would be hard for me to do TV work on a national basis where I would be doing a 'game of the week' or something like that. I would rather be tied to a local team like the Gophers where you can watch them week in and week out. It has just been so much fun and I am very lucky to be doing what I am doing." — *Frank Mazzocco, Longtime Gopher TV Analyst*

"It was a real honor to be a Gopher, it was something that I am very proud of. To be a part of that program means a lot to me and I have so many great memories from my time there. Now, to see the success that they are having as of late with the two national championships makes it even better. You know, I was fortunate enough to get my name on the Stanley Cup, but being a Gopher means more to me than just about anything." — *Chris McAlpine, Gopher 1990-94*

"It was always a dream of mine growing up to one day play hockey for the Gophers. So, when it happened it really was a dream come true. To be a part of that tradition and to play in the old Barn, it was awesome. I made so many great friends there and just had such a wonderful time. To be a part of that big family was just the thrill of a lifetime." — *Jason Miller, Gopher 1987-91*

"It meant so much to me. I grew up wanting to be a Gopher so badly. I remember going to games at old Mariucci Arena with my family. I was so in awe of all the players and just dreamt about one day playing there myself. So, when it finally happened it was almost surreal. It was such a neat and unique experience to play there. I just feel so lucky and honored to have been a part of such an amazing program." — *Nate Miller, Gopher 1996-00*

"I had followed the team ever since I was a kid and had seen the pipeline of great players who had gone to school there, so I wanted to be a part of that. I watched them on TV a lot and just fell in love with them. So, when I got the opportunity to be a part of that great tradition I jumped at it. It was one of the best decisions I ever made." — *Jeff Nielsen, Gopher 1990-94*

"It was really special. Coming from Warroad I had always been a fan of Gopher Hockey, but it wasn't until I got down here that I really learned about the tradition and the history. Then, to get to know my teammates was just fantastic. Being all Minnesota guys we obviously had a lot in common and wound up becoming great friends. That was the biggest thing I think that I took out of it. Sure, the hockey was great and so was the degree, but the friendships and the memories are what I will carry with me for the rest of my life." — *Larry Olimb, Gopher 1988-92*

"Being a Gopher was something I always wanted to do. My father competed on the Gopher Track & Field team back in the '50s, so I grew up loving the University of Minnesota. I followed the hockey team as a kid and made up my mind pretty early that I was going to skate for them. I don't know what I would have done if I wasn't good enough to play for them. So, for me it was everything. It was also a springboard to my career in the National Hockey League as well." — *Tom Pederson, Gopher 1988-91*

"It meant everything. I wasn't recruited very much coming out of Cooper High School. We didn't have a super strong team, so I didn't get a ton of exposure there. I got letters from several college coaches but I actually never went on a single recruiting trip. So, when the Gophers officered me a half-scholarship I thought it was about the greatest thing in the world. I never dreamed I would get the opportunity to play there, so when it finally happened I just worked hard and tried to make the most of it. You know, I wasn't the best student coming out of high school. So, being in the structured environment at the University of Minnesota really helped me to stay focused and do well both in the classroom as well as out on the ice. The work ethic I had to learn in school really carried over and was a big part of why I was able to play for eight seasons in the National Hockey League. My parents always told me that the odds of playing hockey were so small that I had better get my degree. I was grateful to get that scholarship and wanted to make the most of it. So, for me it was about being a part of the school pride, winning, working hard, having fun, making friends and playing together as a team." — *Lance Pitlick, Gopher 1986-90*

"It was awesome. It was everything I could ever ask for and more; playing at home for a great university with a great tradition; a phenomenal rink; a great coach; great teammates; and great memories. Every aspect of my entire college experience was just amazing. I just loved every minute that I was there. Looking back, it means even more to me now than it did at the time. So, being a Gopher to me means everything." — *Johnny Pohl, Gopher 1998-2002*

"Being a Gopher was amazing. To be the first non-Minnesota kid to be asked to be a part of the program in so many years was such an honor. When I was in high school up in Grand Forks I remember telling my dad that I would love to go to a Division One school where I could not only play hockey, but also watch big-time college football and basketball. I mean those were things I couldn't do at the University of North Dakota. My dad said 'It's too bad that the Gophers only take Minnesota kids, that would be a perfect fit for you.' Then, I wound up talking to a Gopher assistant while I was up in Canada for a junior tournament. There were rumors that they were going to start taking non-Minnesota kids under Coach Lucia, but I didn't believe it. Lucia was from Minnesota so I figured he would keep it going. Well, they invited me in for an official visit. I had already taken my other official visits and was undecided between Wisconsin and Michigan State, actually. So, Lucia finally sat me down and told me that he wanted me to become a part of the program. I was floored. I was also a little bit nervous because I knew that being the first non-Minnesota kid meant that I would be front page news. I loved that pressure though, it really motivated me. I also knew that if they were going to bring me in then that meant that they were going to have to play me as a freshman. I signed up and the rest, they say, is history. And do you know what? North Dakota finally called my dad at the very end of the recruiting process and told them that they would offer me a 20% scholarship, enough to buy my books. It was an absolute insult. Now, I later talked to Coach Blais, a former Gopher, and he apologized. He is a class guy, so, it was cool. But I was thrilled to be a Gopher and it worked out just awesome. I fit in with all the guys and had the time of my life. I loved the fact that being a Gopher meant that you had a target on your chest. I loved how wherever we played at, teams played us like it was do-or-die. I guess I would equate it to the Yankees in baseball, everybody wants to beat them because they are the best. It was almost a 'love to be hated' feeling, and I loved that. So, to be a part of this amazing tradition is something I will never forget." — *Grant Potulny, Gopher 2000-04*

"It's pretty special to be able to wear the same 'M' that so many great players in the past have worn. To be a part of the tradition that has been built here in Minnesota over the years just means the world to me. What an honor. It was such a privilege to follow my big brother, Grant, here too. He is such a great person and was a really respected player. I am his No. 1 fan. He accomplished a lot in Gold Country, so if I can do half of what he did here I would be happy. Even though I was injured for most of the year, we did get to play together for one season as Gophers and that was incredible. As North Dakota kids I know that we both feel really honored to be a part of this program." — *Ryan Potulny, Gopher 2003-Present*

"My dad and my uncle were a part of the program, so for me it has been a part of my life since I could ever remember. Being a Gopher though, it's kind of hard to explain. You show up for that first practice and you know all of the familiar faces sitting next to you in that locker-room because you grew grow up playing against them. It was such a welcoming situation and it felt like you were at home. All of us became great friends and those are my best friends even to this day. Whenever I see any of them it is like nothing ever changed. You don't really realize how special it is when you are there until you leave. You also don't realize how much you are looked up to by little kids when you are there either. I think back to when I was a little kid and dreaming of being a Gopher, those guys were in the same situation as role models. So, we tried to be good players and good people too, so that the next group of kids behind us would feel that way and want to keep the whole tradition going. Overall, it was just an amazing experience and something that I was very proud to be a part of." — *Erik Rasmussen, Gopher 1995-97*

"I covered the Gophers for a lot of years and just had a ball over there. I started out with Doug McLeod and later worked with Bob Kurtz and Frank Mazzocco, among others. College hockey is so much fun because the players are pretty pure. They haven't got dancing fairies in their heads yet about playing in the pros, and so on. For most kids it is about having a great season and enjoying the moment. As an announcer you have to squeeze the pro guys to get anything out of them, whereas the college kids just love to be on TV or on the radio and that is very refreshing to see." — *Tommy Reid, Former Gopher TV & Radio Announcer*

"Looking back, it was the greatest thing ever. Growing up in Minnesota it is every kid's dream to be a Gopher. You know, I wasn't the blue-chip recruit coming out of high school. Heck, I only took a half-scholarship to go there and even wound up red-shirting my freshman year. I had full-ride offers elsewhere, but I wanted to be a Gopher. So, I sacrificed a lot to go there, but it was the greatest experience of my life. It is something I look back on all the time and just think about how lucky I was to play there." — *Travis Richards, Gopher 1989-93*

"It meant being a part of a great tradition. It was just a real sense of pride to be a Gopher. As a kid I watched the team every Friday and Saturday night with my dad down on the basement couch. Since then, it was a dream of mine to put on the maroon and gold sweater. When it came true, it was like 'pinch me,' I couldn't believe it was really happening. So, it meant the world to me to be a part of that." — *Troy Riddle, Gopher 2000-04*

"It means the world to me. It is an absolute dream job. I have been a part of the Gopher Hockey family for a long time now. I first started out doing TV with Frank Mazzocco back in the mid-1980s and later moved on to do St. Cloud State games. Then, I moved over to the radio side, which I have been doing alongside Glen Sonmor for the past five years now. It is a lot of fun to get to know these kids and spend time with them on the road. To watch them grow up over their four years in college is pretty special. So, it has been a big part of my life and certainly something I have really enjoyed doing. You know, I have been in this business for 32 years now and it is like I always say 'I am just a big kid with a toy called hockey.' " — *Wally Shaver, Longtime Gopher Radio & TV Announcer*

"I grew up always wanting to be a Gopher, which was unique considering the fact that I came from Warroad, where it was all about the University of North Dakota. I couldn't wait to get to school and begin my career there, it was all so exciting coming to a new place and starting fresh. I had such a great time there too, I made so many great friends and just had the time of my life. It was a decision I will never regret one bit." — *Wyatt Smith, Gopher 1995-99*

"Even though I never played at the University, I am a graduate of the school, and of course I coached there as well. So, being a Gopher means the world to me. You know, I wouldn't be here today if it weren't for one guy, John Mariucci. A lot of these kids today play in Mariucci Arena, but they have no idea who John Mariucci was. He was the Godfather of Minnesota hockey, and a true legend in every sense of the word. John helped me get started in this business; he got me to go to school and get my degree; and he took me under his wing during my career. It all began when we were teammates on the old Minneapolis Millers together back in 1949. I will never forget what he told me after that season, he said 'Glen, I have played pro hockey now for 10 years and nearly every one of my teammates was Canadian. You are the first one I have met that actually graduated from high school, so you are going to college. Period!' So, he took me down to the University of Minnesota and got me enrolled. I was just a kid, but I listened and started going to summer school. Then, that changed my life later on when I lost my eye in 1955 when I was just 25 years old and playing pro hockey with Cleveland. I will never forget laying in a hospital in Pittsburgh scared to death. My wife and I had just had our first baby four days earlier and she was still in the hospital back in Cleveland. I honestly didn't what I was going to do. I knew that my playing career was over and was terrified.

"Just then, John Mariucci called me and said, 'Hey kid,' he used to always call me kid, 'don't you worry about a thing, I have arranged for you to come to Minnesota where you can finish your degree and be my freshman coach for the Gophers.' Wow, it was like God had spoken directly to me. Then, to come back to the University, that was such a great time. Herbie (Brooks) was on that freshman team and it was just a ball. John really almost adopted me because he was just so good to me and my family. He was truly my guardian angel. Then, a few years later, in 1966, when John left to go to the North Stars, he was the one who got me the head coaching job with the Gophers. I had been at Ohio State coaching and getting my masters degree, but was elated to come back to Minnesota. I have been here ever since. And do you know what? I graduated from the 'U' with high distinction, which is something I am very proud of. John went to all that work to get me in there and I wasn't going to let him down. I studied hard and worked my tail off. John and I were friends for so long and he was really a father figure to me as well as my mentor and best friend.

"I say even to this day that every kid in Minnesota who plays college hockey anywhere in this country should say a little prayer to John Mariucci to thank him for all the work he did. So, what does it mean for me to be a Gopher? It has meant literally everything to me."
— *Glen Sonmor, Former Gopher, North Stars & Fighting Saints Coach; Current Gopher Radio Broadcaster*

"It meant everything in the world to me. You know, I grew up watching the Duluth Bulldogs, guys like Brett Hull, Bill Watson and Tom Kurvers, but every time the Gophers would come to town to play I was just mesmerized by them. That is no disrespect towards UMD, they have a wonderful hockey program, I just happened to fall in love with the Gophers at a very young age." — *Dave Spehar, Gopher 1996-2000*

"It meant everything to me. When I pulled on that jersey it wasn't for my teammates, it wasn't just for me, it was for the fans. When you stepped out onto that ice at Mariucci Arena it was for them. I was just so honored and humbled to have been a part of this amazing program, and to have brought joy to the fans who came out and supported us. With that came a lot of pressure, but also a great sense of pride and purpose. I grew up dreaming of wearing that big 'M' and when it came true I was so excited. I made so many amazing friendships here and had such a great time as a Gopher. It just meant the world to me. My only regret is that I wasn't able to help bring the program a national championship. I wanted that so badly for not only myself and my teammates, but especially for the fans who have followed us so loyally." — *Robb Stauber, Gopher 1986-89; Current Gopher Goalie Coach*

"Ever since I was a kid I wanted to be a Gopher. It was such an honor to be a part of that great tradition and history. It means so much more now that I am gone and playing professional hockey. The memories and friendships that I made there will be with me forever." — *Jeff Taffe, Gopher 1999-02*

"It is something that I always dreamt about as a kid. To be able to play for your home state and play for such great fans was really an honor. I just have a huge sense of pride about it and am very proud to be a Gopher. It was the best four years of my life and the friendships and memories will last forever." — *Barry Tallackson, Gopher 2001-05*

"I spent about six seasons doing Gopher Hockey broadcasts and really had a ball doing it. I grew up playing hockey and watching hockey, so to be able to be a part of the Gopher Hockey program was really special. It was just the culmination of a lot of goals and dreams. And to be able to follow in the footsteps of my hero, Al Shaver, was just really special." — *Dan Terhaar, Former Gopher Radio Announcer*

"It was awesome. You grow up and they are the team that you watch and the team that you dream of playing for. That was me." — *Dan Trebil, Gopher 1992-96*

"It was unbelievable. I enjoyed my time here in Minnesota so much, the fans were so great to me and I really appreciated that. We did a lot while I was there, which I am obviously very proud of. We won a pair of WCHA Playoff titles and, of course, we won the 2003 national championship, which was absolutely amazing. Being a Gopher was so much fun. I was only there for two seasons but was fortunate to have made so many great friends. Those memories will last for a lifetime. The people there are just so nice and that is why I intend to spend my off-seasons there from here on out.

"My only regret is that I wasn't able to stay for more than two years, because it would have been so much fun to try and win a couple more national championships. But, playing in the NHL was always a dream of mine ever since I was a little boy and I was excited to get the opportunity to be able to do that. I felt like I was ready to make that transition at that point and was anxious to begin the next chapter of my hockey career.

"As for being the first foreign kid to come into the program? I knew coming in that I was going to be under the microscope a little bit because I am from Austria, but the players really welcomed me and made me feel at home. While I looked at it as a real honor to come there, I also know that the biggest reason why they recruited me was because I could play hockey. I don't think it mattered much where I was from, it mattered that I could score goals and help the team win a national championship. Fortunately for all of us, that is exactly what happened. So, looking back I hope people don't look at me as an Austrian, I hope that they look at me as a Gopher." — *Thomas Vanek, Gopher 2002-04*

"It is so much fun to play here, it is just great. I grew up watching the team and couldn't wait to get the opportunity to play here. The pride and tradition here is amazing and it is a real honor to be a part of it. My dad was on two Gopher National Championships, so to follow him here is really special." — *Mike Vannelli, Gopher 2003-Present*

"For me it was really special. I was in a unique situation where I truly did grow up dreaming of being a Gopher because my dad was a former player and captain back in the late 1960s. So, when I got the chance to wear the 'M' it was just a huge honor. The tradition and history is so amazing there. From John Mariucci to Herb Brooks to Neal Broten — there have just been so many legendary hockey figures who have played there. I idolized the players ever since I could walk and used to love going to games. It was just a thrill to be there and something I will always look back on fondly." — *Erik Westrum, Gopher 1997-2001*

"To me it is really a dream come true. I have dreamt about wearing the 'M' ever since I was a little kid. I have always looked up to the players so much. So, now, to be able to be a part of this program just means everything to me." — *Blake Wheeler, Gopher 2005-Present*

"You know, it kind of defines your life when you think about it. For me it is almost 20 years after the fact, but it is still a huge part of my life. Whether it is work, or home, or church or my kids' school, or wherever, your tie is to the Gophers and that is a very special feeling. That bond with the other guys is just really neat. I still keep in touch with a lot of the guys from those days and the memories of playing there will be with me forever. So, being a Gopher meant a great deal to me and I am extremely honored to have been a part of it. I grew up watching the team as a kid and when I got to put on that sweater for the first time and step onto the ice at Mariucci Arena, it was a real dream come true. My dad was a Gopher too and I am so proud to be able to share that bond with him." — *Dean Williamson, Gopher 1987-90*

"It means everything to me. To think about my journey just to get there, starting out on figure skates at the old 'Mud Hole' in my neighborhood, to South St. Paul High School — to the University of Minnesota. It was just an amazing opportunity to be a part of that tradition under legendary coach John Mariucci. You know, back then there weren't that many opportunities for college kids after college as far as hockey was concerned, with only six NHL teams and all. So, we played for the love of the game and were happy to get our educations so that we were able to make a living. My time there as a player was incredible though, and then, to come back years later to serve as the head coach — that was more than I had ever imagined.

"It never would have happened though it if weren't for John and Herbie (Brooks), who went to Paul Giel (athletic director) and lobbied for me. Herbie had actually been offered the job but turned it down. A lot of people don't know this, but before Herbie said no he had actually lined me up to be his assistant. I never knew it at the time, but he had actually gone to my superintendent at South St. Paul High School, where I was coaching at the time, and found out my salary. Well, Herbie ultimately wound up going on to coach back in the NHL from there, and then Mike Sertich (UMD's head coach) was offered the job. But he too turned it down and then Herbie pulled for me to get it. So, it's funny how things wind up in life, and luckily for me I was in the right place at the right time and had some former Gophers working for me behind the scenes.

"Then, to be able to coach so many great kids for so many years here, the whole thing was a real dream come true, it really was. And hey, being a television analyst now, that is just the best. I absolutely love it, I really do. Working alongside Frank (Mazzocco) is a real joy, he is one of the best in the business, without a doubt. To still be a part of this program in a small way, I am so lucky. Maroon and Gold is in my blood, so I hope to always be a part of it in some way." — *Doug Woog, Former Gopher Player & Coach; current Gopher Hockey TV Analyst*

"Growing up in Rochester I didn't grow up watching the Gophers on TV every weekend like the Twin Cities kids did. So, it meant a lot more to me once I was up there and could learn what the program was all about. In fact, the first time I ever stepped foot in Mariucci Arena was on my recruiting trip up there. I was just in awe of the Old Barn and from that moment on I knew that I wanted to play there. It was a little bit stressful coming into the program after being drafted No. 1 by the North Stars, but the guys were great to me and I didn't feel that much pressure about it to tell you the truth. To play there though, that was just amazing. The atmosphere, the fans, the tradition — it was all so much fun to be around. So, being a Gopher meant a lot to me and it still does to this day." — *Doug Zmolek, Gopher 1989-92*

DID YOU KNOW THAT 42% OF THE PLAYERS IN THE 2005 FROZEN FOUR HAILED FROM MINNESOTA?

That's right, 42% of the players who participated in the 2005 Frozen Four NCAA Division I Hockey Championships hailed from Minnesota. Of the 107 players on the four teams 45, or 42%, came through Minnesota's hockey system. (Frozen Four Player Breakdown: Colorado College – 13/28 players, Denver – 4/28 players, Minnesota – 21/26 players, North Dakota – 7/25 players.) Including the Minnesota players in the Frozen Four, the Land of 10,000 Lakes provided a total of 205 men to all Division I hockey teams in North America (12.9% of all D-1 men's players). In addition, Minnesota also provided 98 women to Division 1 hockey teams (14.3% of all D-1 women's players) as well. Both of those numbers led the nation in providing players to Division 1 college hockey teams.

— *(March 2005 Stops and Starts AHCA Newsletter)*

CHAPTER 3
HOW HAS GOPHER HOCKEY CHANGED OVER THE YEARS?

"Moving from the old Mariucci to the new Mariucci was a huge change. We left a lot of history and tradition back in the Old Barn and felt it was really important to start a new tradition across the street at the new one. Over the years we have done so pretty well I think, especially after winning the two national championships." — *Mark Bahr, Gopher 1991-94, Current Director of Hockey Operations*

"I think the biggest thing has been the media coverage. Gopher Hockey was always well known in Minnesota and in the Midwest, but now I think it is getting a lot more national attention, particularly after the two national championships. So, I think that recognition is great for not only the players, but for the program as a whole." — *Keith Ballard, Gopher 2001-04*

"I was lucky, I got to play over in old Mariucci. There was so much tradition and history in there, I really miss that. That old barn had so much character and that was sort of a reflection of the entire program I think. It was so unique. I can remember coming up those old wooden steps from the locker room and racing out onto the ice as the band was playing the Rouser. I get goose bumps just thinking about it. I always stood next to Sean Fabian during the National Anthem, that was our own little tradition. Nowadays, I think Gopher Hockey has gotten very corporate, it is much more of a business. They have to compete with the Wild a little bit I think too. Don't get me wrong, the new arena is great and the program is doing fantastic. But, with the new facility you have other things such as high ticket prices and $9 parking and that type of thing. The players have to pay that much to park too, believe it or not. So, we lost a little bit when we moved across the street into the new building, but the memories are certainly still there. I think all of college sports has gotten that way to tell you the truth, it's all big business these days and that is just the way it is." — *Scott Bell, Gopher 1991-95*

"College sports in general has become such a big business and Gopher Hockey is no different. I mean look at all the new arenas just in the WCHA, it's incredible. Beyond that, the players over the years have gotten bigger, faster and stronger, and they hit harder, shoot better and skate faster. So, it has changed a lot I think. The overall product is better though and that is great to see. I think college hockey is much more exciting now, for sure." — *Reggie Berg, Gopher 1995-99*

"Recruiting has changed drastically. When I first started there was really no early-signing of athletes. You watched them all year in high school and then you signed them in the Spring. That changed a lot because now you are signing younger kids much earlier. So, we recruit a lot more in the Summer now than we ever did before. Beyond that, the program is a lot more visible thanks to our television deal. We are definitely in the spot-light a lot more because of that, which is good. The kids have a lot more focus on them now with all the media attention surrounding them. One of the biggest changes is money. The NCAA pays a lot more attention to college hockey as a whole than they did years ago because the programs are generating a lot more revenue for their schools nowadays. You know, it went from being a college sport to a big business, and that is just the way it has evolved. Add in the new arena, of course, and yes, there have been a lot of big changes around here over the years." — *Patty Bjorklund, Longtime Gopher Hockey Administrative Assistant*

"They go all year pretty hard, playing and training all year round, so I don't even know if I could even play there nowadays. I wasn't brought up that way. It is a totally new atmosphere now. I mean we didn't lift weights or ride stationary bikes or anything like that when I was there. Times have changed and the athletes are in unbelievable shape all year round. It is very cut-throat and there is more and more pressure on these guys to win. Almost all of them come out of the junior ranks now, where they are playing for a year or two to get better before they even play college hockey. They come in so much more mature now too. Back when we were in high school if the coaches would have told us to go play juniors for two years before we could get a scholarship, we probably would have laughed at them. It was just a completely different time, whereas now it is the norm. So, college hockey has changed a great deal over the past 10-15 years and it is just a very different environment." — *Brian Bonin, Gopher 1992-96*

"Well, as far as equipment goes, it has really changed a great deal. The technology nowadays is amazing. From the lightweight, protective padding, to the skates, to the new composite sticks — it all gives the players a real edge. It's certainly not very inexpensive either." — *Harry Broadfoot, Gopher Equipment Manager 1986-Present*

"I think that the recruiting of junior players and the recruiting of non-Minnesota kids are the biggest changes. Most players came right out of high school up until recently, but now kids are playing juniors for a year or two to get some seasoning. As a result, the teams are a little older and a little more experienced, so it only makes sense that they would be better. I also think it is tough when kids have to give up their senior year of hockey and leave their buddies in order to play on a junior team. Along those same lines, I think it is too bad that most of the elite kids nowadays are one-sport athletes. Sure, there are exceptions to the rule with guys like Paul Martin, but for the most part these kids have to specialize very early on and that is too bad. Kids today are in Summer leagues and developmental camps all year long, traveling all over the place, which isn't necessarily always a good thing. These guys are missing out on a lot. When I was a kid I played all kinds of sports and was able to do so right up through high school. So, that has changed.

"Now, as for the non-Minnesota kids, that has been an evolution. When I grew up watching Gopher hockey there had guys like Lou Nanne and Murray Williamson, who were both from Canada. Herbie Brooks recruited mostly Minnesota kids, but he had a few guys who weren't from here either. Then when I was on Doug's (Woog) staff as an assistant, we all agreed that we were going to go exclusively with Minnesota kids. It wasn't that we were against kids from outside of the state, we just wanted to give the opportunities to the local kids, the same way we got the opportunities when we played. Now, under Lucia, they have gone away from that, which is fine. They obviously have done pretty well given the fact that they won a couple of national championships along the way. So, change is good and the program looks like it is in great shape now and well into the future.

"The one negative thing I would add is that the University has to be careful that they don't wind up like the football program in that they cater too much to the corporate crowd and forget about the students. We have to be careful or we too could wind up with a white-haired fan-base that doesn't make a lot of noise. We are not there yet, but I hope they always make students welcome at the games. We need them there, they make a big difference in my opinion." — *Bill Butters, Gopher Player 1971-73; Assistant Coach 1985-95*

"I think we are definitely developing players. It just seems so different now where as before we used to know the kids who were coming to the 'U' because we saw them play in the state tournament. Now, they all play junior hockey or play in Ann Arbor on the U.S. Developmental team for two years before coming in. So, that has certainly changed in my eyes." — *Mike Crowley, Gopher 1994-97*

"It is much more of a global game now. We have different players from not only different states, but from different countries, which is all new and different. The program has had to evolve and adapt over the years though, and that is why they continue to stay on top as the premier program in the country." — *Steve DeBus, Gopher 1995-98*

"To me it has gone from almost a little cottage industry private club atmosphere to being really big-time. You know, back in the day guys just begged to come here and recruiting was never an issue. They would pick the top kids from the state tournament every year and had success playing in this old, run-down, lousy arena. It didn't matter that they didn't have a big sexy TV deal, or that there were no luxury boxes — it was just old school hockey. Now, it is totally different. Now they have to scout and recruit kids from all over the country and in Canada, and you have to recruit them much earlier in the game too. The best players from Minnesota aren't necessarily playing high school hockey anymore, they are playing juniors and Triple-A and coming out of the national developmental program. Now the top kids have a lot of choices too, as in five Division One schools in Minnesota alone. On top of all of that, to be successful in college hockey today, you simply must have a state-of-the-art facility and a regional cable contract to boot. Luckily for us we have those things, and that is a big part of why we are doing so well. I mean it should be no coincidence as to whey the WCHA has been dominating college hockey these past few years: new arenas in Minnesota, North Dakota, Wisconsin, Denver and Colorado College. It is a no-brainer. Tradition and pride are great, but in the end kids want to play in front of 10,000 fans in fancy arenas with luxury boxes and state-of-the-art weight rooms, and oh by the way, they want to be on TV. That's just the reality of college hockey today. The top kids want to make it to the NHL and will choose the programs that offer them the best chance of achieving that. Minnesota has been way ahead of the curve on this and that is part of the reason that they have had so much success." — *Jeff Dubay, KFAN Radio Host & Longtime Gopher Fanatic*

"Well, certainly taking non-Minnesota kids has been a big change. Aside from that, I would have to say that I just miss the Old Barn, it had such character. You know the new arena is fabulous, don't get me wrong, but the old one had an atmosphere that you just don't see in sports anymore. I used to love everything about that old place; the wooden steps down to the locker room; the smell; and even how the lights hung down from the ceiling and lit up the ice like it was center-stage at a theater. It was so intimate, whereas the new arena is lit up like a bathroom. There was just so much tradition in there and so much history. But hey, it is hard to argue with progress and they have already created a bunch of new history in the new place." — *Joe Dziedzic, Gopher 1990-94*

"Certainly the new building would have to be the biggest thing. It is great to see them playing in such a nice place, but I am a nostalgia guy. I miss old Mariucci, the Old Barn was the best. I am the type of person who enjoys Yankee Stadium and Fenway Park. I appreciate the history and old stuff. But, times change and obviously it is for the better." — *Ken Gernander, Gopher 1988-91*

"I am not so sure that it has that much. With that big sheet of ice Minnesota hockey has always been synonymous with skating and speed. I always thought of the Gophers as the Edmonton Oiler teams of the '80s — they did a lot of coast-to-coast coasting and a lot of wide-open play. I think that has always been a constant in my eyes. Gopher Hockey is a constant; the same people who watched it every Friday and Saturday night back then are the same people watching it today. The only difference is that there are a lot more people watching them today." — *Eric Gislason, Former Gopher Radio & Television Commentator*

"I don't know if it has ever changed to tell you the truth. I still think we have our own little niche within the hockey community. People are passionate about Gopher Hockey. It is a different kind of an atmosphere and always has been. It is a very knowledgeable crowd; a very enthusiast crowd and a very loyal crowd. Certainly when pro hockey came back to town a few years ago we all wondered if that was going to cut into our following, but it hasn't. If you look at our television ratings and the amount of press we get in the papers, it is amazing. Gopher Hockey is big in this state and the coverage we get is just tremendous. That affords us a lot of recognition and notoriety, which is great for recruiting and great for our program as a whole." — *Mike Guentzel, Gopher Player 1981-85; Assistant Coach 1994-Present*

"I think it has become much more corporate, and is definitely a big business now. Not only is it a business to make money, it is also a business to move these players onto the next level too.

When we played it was all about being Minnesota kids; having fun; and trying to win. Now, the game has changed and the stakes are much higher. Players also have a lot more choices of where to play, which has changed the game a lot. I mean back when I was playing guys would walk-on and play on the junior varsity, or take half-scholarships like me, just to be a part of the program and to be a Gopher. Now, those same kids who were walk-ons can get full scholarships at Bemidji and Mankato, or elsewhere, so times have certainly changed." — *Ben Hankinson, Gopher 1987-91*

"Certainly, the fact that non-Minnesota kids are playing there now is the big thing. Beyond that, it is really different for the fans in that they don't recognize who the incoming freshmen are. I mean, back in the day you knew who the top kids were because you saw them in the high school tournament. Now, with so many kids playing junior hockey for two years after high school, and then coming to college, I think we lost some of that. The landscape is entirely different now and I think for a lot of people, that is enough for them to maybe not follow it as closely as they would have under the old system." — *Peter Hankinson, Gopher 1986-90*

"You know, when I was a kid and grew up watching the team, even from the vantage point of being on the bench with my dad when his teams were playing against the Gophers, I think the style of play has really changed. It seems like back then the players focused more on the skill stuff, where they really didn't emphasize working hard in the corners or on things like that. I don't mean that negatively, I just think that they had so much talent and so many skill players that they didn't need to do a lot of that. They were able to dominate doing what they were doing. Well, now, under Coach Lucia, I think that is totally different. He started recruiting guys who really want to dig out the puck and want to go into the corners so that they can show what they can do. He has gone after a lot of kids who are bigger and stronger, but most of them can handle the puck as well. In order to be successful in college hockey nowadays, you have to recruit the older players too, who have played juniors and have been around the block. Those are the biggest differences in my eyes." — *Chris Harrington, Gopher 2002-Present*

"When I was a kid growing up watching the team they never wore face masks, which is a huge change from today's game. That era was totally a totally different style of hockey, really old school and much, much more physical. I think that is probably the biggest thing." — *Darby Hendrickson, Gopher 1991-93*

"Obviously, being from North Dakota, I am thrilled that Coach Lucia decided to bring in kids from out-state. That is the biggest and best change that they ever could have made." — *Danny Irmen, Gopher 2003-Present*

"From what I have seen, I don't think it has changed very much at all. They still play the same open system where guys have the freedom to use their offensive abilities, while also being responsible defensively." — *Ryan Kraft, Gopher 1994-98*

"All you have to do is contrast the old Mariucci Arena with the new Mariucci Arena. Before, it was much more low-key. Nowadays it is very high profile and really big business. And it is not just in Minnesota either, look at the arenas in North Dakota and Wisconsin, they have all had to keep up with the Jones'. So, the game has evolved at that level, and that is probably for the better." — *Bob Kurtz, former Gopher Broadcaster*

"I think it has grown, especially with the attention of the FOX television network. The exposure that the program gets is really second to none as far as college hockey is concerned. With all of the games on TV everybody knows who you are. That caught me off guard when I first got here. I remember going to watch my kids' youth hockey games and everybody there recognized me and wanted to talk to me about the games that past weekend. It was amazing. Even if people aren't there in the stands, they follow it either on TV or the radio, which is so great to see. I have had a lot of people tell me that watching Gopher Hockey is what they do on the weekends in Minnesota. They gather around and make a night of it. So, the fact that the team is woven into the fabric of life around here the way it is just speaks volumes I think." — *Don*

"With the big sheet of ice there they have always had fast skaters. Lately though, they have brought in bigger guys, role players, who can put the puck into the back of the net from out front. Then, obviously, the kids are from out-state now. So, some things have changed but I think the team's tradition and philosophy have remained the same." — *Paul Martin, Gopher 2000-03*

"The facilities have certainly changed for starters, which is a good thing. Another thing that has changed is coverage. I mean back when I started in 1986 we did less than a dozen games and now we are broadcasting 31 games this year. So, the availability is much greater. I think the fan-base has remained the same through it all though. I mean if we had cable television back in 1986 or even 1976, I think the viewership and interest would have been as obvious as it is today. This program just has very loyal fans who have been with them forever." — *Frank Mazzocco, Longtime Gopher TV Analyst*

"I don't know if it has really changed that much. I think kids still grow up dreaming of being Gophers, that certainly hasn't changed. What has changed though is the amount of media coverage that they get. From the TV deal on FOX to P.A. & Dubay on KFAN bringing a lot of attention to the program, that stuff all makes a positive difference. It keeps growing and getting better, year in and year out, and that is what it is all about." — *Chris McAlpine, Gopher 1990-94*

"I think the biggest change has to be how all of the kids are coming out of the junior ranks nowadays. Back in my era we all came straight out of high school. As a result, the talent is a lot more polished and the kids are a lot bigger too." — *Jason Miller, Gopher 1987-91*

"I don't know that it has changed that much. It is still about Minnesota people; about Minnesota fans; and about Minnesota tradition. Certainly the business side of it has changed, with the new arena and the television coverage. But, while the fans may be more comfortable in their new arena, I think that the old Mariucci had a lot more nostalgia as well as a lot more students who could afford to be there. So, the program may be more corporate now, but the game itself has stayed the same. It is still all about young kids with a dream; wanting to have fun and play hockey." — *Larry Olimb, Gopher 1988-92*

"It seems to me that it is more of a business nowadays. Back when I played it was lunch pail hockey, where you punched in to go to work and you punched out to go work-out down in the dungeon — our old weight room under the building. Now, it has a much different feel to it. Don't get me wrong, I love the new arena and couldn't be happier for the program's success. In fact, I am a little jealous that we didn't get to play in the new Mariucci, it is an amazing place.
    "You know, I think another big thing that changed since my era was when the NHL opened up its salary disclosure information. Now, everybody knew how much money you could make playing pro hockey, which in some sense made college hockey a sort of stepping stone on the way to bigger and better things. When I was there, college was all we thought about. I mean until you were a senior, you didn't worry about any of that stuff. It was all about winning, the camaraderie and about the team. Again, I don't want to sound like none of us ever dreamed about playing in the NHL or anything like that, I am just saying that a lot of that has changed over the past 15 years for both good and bad." — *Lance Pitlick, Gopher 1986-90*

"I am obviously biased, but I think that the Gophers are the hockey team that people care most about in the state of Minnesota, including the Wild. In my opinion, fans go to Gopher games not as entertainment or as just something to do, but because they want to see good hockey and they want to see the Gophers win. When that happens, that is entertaining to them. So, I just think that the program continues to get bigger and better each and every year." — *Johnny Pohl, Gopher 1998-2002*

"If anything, I think Gopher Hockey has gotten more popular. It is still the No. 1 hockey ticket in town, in my opinion. The two national championships just enhanced that too. Aside from that, the program has pretty much stayed the same. It is cyclical in that even when Minnesota is bad, they are still pretty good. Other teams, when they are bad, that might be a four or five year cycle of being bad. We are able to re-load each year with the top talent and that is what keeps us on top." — *Erik Rasmussen, Gopher 1995-97*

"For many years the junior A leagues in Canada were the premier developmental league for the NHL. By the 1970s, however, college hockey started to make a name for itself. More and more players were electing to go to the college ranks versus going to Canada. A big part of that was due to the fact that guys wanted to get a college education too, because back then there were only half as many pro teams as there are today. Since then, the quality of college hockey has grown tremendously and the Gophers have certainly led the way in that regard." — *Tommy Reid, Former Gopher TV & Radio Announcer*

"The biggest change by far is how all of the high school kids are playing juniors for a couple years before heading to school. It is a lot different from my era, but if that is what it takes to be competitive and to get a scholarship, then that is what you have to do." — *Travis Richards, Gopher 1989-93*

"Certainly with Coach Lucia the program has really turned around and gotten back on track, so that is great to see. To see them back to being the No. 1 program in the country is just fabulous. So, the changes as of late are all positive in my eyes." — *Wyatt Smith, Gopher 1995-99*

"I think it has become more physical and less of a wide open skating game. You don't see guys flying all over the ice the way you did when you had guys like Neal Broten and Tim Harrer out there. You just don't see that style of play anymore, and that is one of the negatives I think on how the game has changed. Obviously, a big change as of late is Coach Lucia's decision to recruit kids outside of Minnesota. I think that changed because of the number of kids playing junior hockey these days. They come in two years older and that much more polished. Then they are recruited by schools all over the country, which is great for them. I think the bottom line is that you just can't get it done with high school seniors anymore. So, times change and you move on. Hey, you can't argue with the results." — *Dan Terhaar, Former Gopher Radio Announcer*

"I am not sure that it has changed that much over the years. It is still the heart and soul of this community, and the excitement of the games is just as great today as it ever was. I enjoyed watching it as a kid and my kids watching it today. So, to me the allure and thrill of it all is still intact." — *Dean Williamson, Gopher 1987-90*

"So much has changed over the years, it is incredible. The tradition and pride have stayed the same, but so much else has evolved. One thing that I don't particularly care for is how commercial and corporate it has become. Once we moved into the new building and got the big TV deal, all bets were off. It is a big business today and it is almost treated like a pro sports franchise. You know, because Gopher Football doesn't necessarily make the revenue that perhaps it could, the University really leans on hockey to generate extra income. That's the corporate influence. Gopher Hockey is a cash cow, and does very, very well. It gets great television and radio ratings and the fans enjoy watching these kids play outstanding hockey. It is a just great product. Hey, with progress comes change, and the program has never been in better shape. Donny (Lucia) has done a tremendous job and I couldn't be happier for the program's success." — *Doug Woog, Former Gopher Player & Coach; current Gopher Hockey TV Analyst*

"The biggest thing in my eyes is the fact that they are recruiting kids from all over now, versus just Minnesota. I think it is a good idea. I mean not only do they get the best players from right here in Minnesota, but they also get the best players from everywhere else. It can only be good for the program in the long run as far as I am concerned." — *Doug Zmolek, Gopher 1989-92*

"My first emotion was jealousy, but in a good way. I was really happy for the guys and for the team as a whole. To be an alumni, you just take a lot of pride in that and have to feel good about the direction the program is heading in now." — *Mike Anderson, Gopher 1995-99*

"To be a part of a program that was able to win back-to-back national championships was truly unbelievable. The first one was so special. I mean to host it, and to be in it, and to win it, was almost unthinkable. So, it meant a great deal to me personally, as well as professionally. It really put the program back up on top of the college hockey world where it belongs." — *Mark Bahr, Gopher 1991-94, Current Director of Hockey Operations*

"They were very special. Particularly the first one, coming in St. Paul in front of all of our fans, that was just amazing. You could tell that it was sort of a collective big relief for all Minnesota hockey fans. They had waited for that for so long and I was just thrilled to able to be a part of that. That 23 year wait was tough for a school with such high standards of excellence I think. Then, the second one was neat because we had to go that whole season with a target on our backs. The challenge of going back-to-back was a thrill and to be able to pull that off when no one expected us to, was something I will never forget. We had lost Leopold, Taffe, Pohl and Hauser, and it was supposed to be a re-building year, but we stepped up huge that year. It was more of a team effort that year. And it was our statement too, that we weren't re-building, we were re-loading. Our young guys came through for us too, especially Thomas Vanek, he was unbelievable. So, it was just an honor to be a part of those teams and to play with so many great players." — *Keith Ballard, Gopher 2001-04*

"I was so happy when that finally happened. It was really nice for the older players who worked so hard over the years to get there, I think we all shared in that a little bit. I was also happy for Wooger, who had recruited that senior class which won the first one. I was most happy for the fans who have been there and supported this team for so long. Overall, it was just a fantastic boost for the entire program. Gopher Hockey was back on top and that was really nice to see." — *Scott Bell, Gopher 1991-95*

"It was great. I would have loved to have won one myself, but unfortunately that wasn't in the cards during my four years in Gold Country. So, if you can't win it yourself, the next best thing is to see the following group of guys get it done. Watching both of them brought back so many great memories and made me feel very proud to be a part of that program. We all shared it in though because essentially we are all one big Gopher Hockey family." — *Reggie Berg, Gopher 1995-99*

"I still have season tickets and follow them pretty closely. The first one was awesome. I was so happy for those guys. It was a long time coming, that was for sure. It was also eerily similar to our overtime game to Harvard back in 1989 at the Civic Center. I relived that horror a little bit that night too, only this time it had the right ending. Then, to see them repeat the next year just validated it even more. So, their recent success means a lot to me, as well as all of the other former Gophers as well." — *Grant Bischoff, Gopher 1987-91*

"They meant a lot, it was a very special time. I have watched so many games over the years, from Brad's (Buetow) teams to Doug's (Woog) team's, which have had the same kind of talent but were never able to win the big one. People don't understand that you can get there, but winning it is another story. It is such a hard thing to do. A lot of teams get there, but it is still just one game and one goal. We saw that. It is a break here or there and maybe a lucky bounce. A lot of things have to happen to be able to win it. So, to finally see the success come back around to the program was wonderful. For all of the years that they went there, to the Frozen Four, and lost — those two titles more than made up for it." — *Patty Bjorklund, Longtime Gopher Hockey Administrative Assistant*

"It's weird, but I was actually very jealous at first. Then, I was super happy about it. I even wound up calling a bunch of guys over the next couple of weeks to congratulate them and thank them. I wanted to thank them because I felt a part of that championship. I just felt like it was part mine. It is something I worked towards and something I have been waiting for, for a long time. I didn't get to win one of my own, but I still felt like I was a part of this one. I hope all of the alumni players feel a part of it, we are all part of the same Gopher family." — *Brian Bonin, Gopher 1992-96*

"They meant a lot. I committed to the program not too long after they won the first title. To watch the guys celebrate like that after working so hard that season, I just knew that I wanted to be a part of that." — *Kellen Briggs, Gopher 2003-Present*

"You know, when Don (Lucia) asked me how I felt about finally winning a championship, I told him I would have to get back to him. So, that night, after the game, it dawned on me. It was like having sex and then having the biggest orgasm you could ever have. That is the best way to describe it. It was amazing. It was so fun to be able to meet the President and do all of that stuff that you never dreamed you would ever do. I have seen a lot over the past 20 years, but nothing was as sweet as that first one. Then, to win the second one, that was a real thrill too. To me, it was totally unexpected. It really came out of nowhere. When we wound up in the Frozen Four, then it became real. At that point it was like 'Well, somebody has got to win it, it might as well be us…'. The attitude of the kids was so much different that second time too. All they wanted to do was defend that title. I had never seen that before and that was really neat to be a part of." — *Harry Broadfoot, Gopher Equipment Manager 1986-Present*

"I was happy for Donny (Lucia) and his staff at the University. They finally got the monkey off their back, which was great to see. It was a very exciting thing to have happen. You know, to me they have always had one of the top two or three programs in the country anyway, whether they won a national championship or not. But, it is nice to see, no question. As a former Gopher I am proud of their accomplishments and feel very good about that." — *Bill Butters, Gopher Player 1971-73; Assistant Coach 1985-95*

"The championships were huge, and really a big factor in me coming here. They were absolutely a big selling-point for me, no question. I had other opportunities, but being able to win a championship with my teammates, that would just be the ultimate honor. You know, I have always said that I would much rather be a fourth line player on a championship team than a first line player on a mediocre team. Minnesota is in the hunt each and every year and I wanted to come to a place where I knew that I would be surrounded by winners." — *Kris Chucko, Gopher 2003-Present*

"I was extremely proud of those guys and for the program. The players did a great job and really represented us well." — *Ben Clymer, Gopher 1996-98*

"It was so great to see the guys be able to do that. Obviously I would have loved to had the opportunity to do the same when I was there, but that wasn't in the cards for us. The first one was so thrilling too, the way they won over in St. Paul. That was a really special moment. Then, to do it again, that put us at dynasty status as far as I was concerned. It was just wonderful not only for those guys, but for everybody involved with the program — from the alumni to the coaches to the fans. It put us back up on top, where we always belonged." — *Mike Crowley, Gopher 1994-97*

"There is a small part of you that is jealous, but at the same time you are happy just to be associated with the program. I was thrilled that they did it and that they finally got the monkey off of their back. I was most happy for Adam Hauser, a fellow goaltender, because he was a huge part of the team's success for a lot of years there. So, to see him get to go out on top like that was really neat. It was just a huge source of pride for all of us, we all shared in that a little bit. The two titles also did a lot for all of Minnesota hockey. We may not even see the results of that for many years down the road either, because a whole new crop of Gopher fans was born after watching that and maybe they too will grow up wanting to wear the 'M' like we did." — *Steve DeBus, Gopher 1995-98*

"It has been so much fun following this team, especially the past five years or so. I mean Gopher fans who have been following this program over the long haul have sort of been college hockey's equivalent to being a Cub's fan, in terms of dealing with heartbreak. It had been a seemingly endless array of disappointment for this team. I mean the first NCAA Finals I ever went to was back in 1987 at Joe Louis Arena in Detroit. Even though they completely outplayed Michigan State, they wound up losing a totally bogus one-goal game. I still remember it vividly. Tied at three apiece, John Blue went behind the net to get the puck and it wound up hitting a seam in the zamboni door and popped right out front where a Spartan tapped in what turned out to be the game-winner. That just totally sucked. The next year, 1988, they lost to St. Lawrence in the final 30 seconds; and in 1989 they lost in overtime to Harvard right here at the old St. Paul Civic Center. The list went on and on until 2002, when they finally exorcised the demons. Up until that time it had gotten to be so gut-wrenchingly painful to watch them late in the post-season that you almost couldn't take it at times.

"So, when they beat Maine for that first title, it was one of the greatest moments in the history of Minnesota sports. I remember being at one of the pre-game rallies before the game just thinking to myself, 'If they don't win it now are they ever going to?' I mean the game was at home; they had just beaten a very good Michigan team; they were better than Maine; and they were so long overdue it was sick. The planets had aligned for them, and luckily, they came through in the clutch. Just prior to Koalska tying it up I thought we were doomed yet again. I almost couldn't even bear to watch it at that point. Then, when he tallied, I just knew that we were going to somehow win. When Potulny scored, it was so unbelievable. Watching the guys pile onto each other as they were celebrating on the ice was so much fun. It was so emotional for the fans too, so many of them were just weeping, it was amazing to see. It was almost surreal because that was a scene we had seen so many other teams get to partake in, but never us. Every year you see that end-of-the-season pile with all of the gloves and sticks littering the ice, but that was never our guys in that pile. I remember standing next to my brother and just enjoying that moment. I had no idea how long it would be before that might happen again, so I wanted to take it all in.

"Then, to follow them to Buffalo that next year and watch them completely out-class New Hampshire in a laugher from beginning to end, was oh-so-sweet. I never thought I would be referring to my Gophers as the two-time back-to-back national champions, but I loved saying it. I remember going out to the bars after the game in Buffalo and this guy wearing a Michigan State jersey came over to us and raised his glass and said 'Back-to-back, man, that is big-time...' Yeah, it was big-time, and I was so proud of those guys. It was an amazing run and I was just lucky to be around to see it all." — *Jeff Dubay, KFAN Radio Host & Longtime Gopher Fanatic*

"It certainly brought back the luster to the program, which was awesome to see. It is great as an alum to see the guys having success and taking care of business. Even though we weren't able to do it ourselves, I am thrilled for that group of guys who was able to get it done. We were all a part of it I think." — *Joe Dziedzic, Gopher 1990-94*

"I think it was awesome for the program and really for the entire state. I was most happy for the fans, they had been waiting for that for a long time." — *Ken Gernander, Gopher 1988-91*

"I covered both of them and to me it was a bridging of the gap of what Herbie Brooks had done; and what Woogie had tried so valiantly to do; to what was hoped and expected for so long, alas, finally came true under Donny Lucia. To me it really galvanized the fact that Minnesota was still hockey country. The 23 years in between national championships were tough, because we came so close so many times, but the way that team was able to win it over in St. Paul the way that they did sort of made up for all of it. Then, to win another one and go back-to-back the next year, that just validated it. It was a culmination of history; a culmination of dedication; and a culmination of accomplishment — all wrapped into one. The true hockey people have always known that this was a premier program and those two titles certainly reinforced that. It was such a statement and I couldn't have been happier for Donny (Lucia) and everybody over there in that program." — *Eric Gislason, Former Gopher Radio & Television Commentator*

"It meant a lot of satisfaction from the standpoint of knowing how hard it is to win one, let alone two. So, when we won it I felt great for not only the current players, but for all the past players who tried but came up short in their day. It was a big relief to everybody in the program to finally get that 23 year old monkey off of our backs. It was a long time between titles, but what a thrill to finally get it. I was also really happy for the fans, because they have remained so loyal over the years and they really deserved it." — *Mike Guentzel, Gopher Player 1981-85; Assistant Coach 1994-Present*

"I was on the second one and it was by far the greatest experience of my entire life. It is something I will never forget, it was just amazing. To be able to share that experience with all of those guys was really the thrill of a lifetime. I am very proud of that and would love nothing more than to win another one." — *Gino Guyer, Gopher 2003-Present*

"It was just great closure. A lot of guys were jealous, for sure. But we were all super proud and we all felt like we were a part of it. To get that big, fat monkey off of all of our backs was so sweet. Finally! I mean we came so close on several different occasions, but couldn't get it done. So, I am just thrilled that they did it. Then, to win it again just validated it and made it even better. That was a dynasty team and it put Minnesota hockey back up on top where it belongs." — *Ben Hankinson, Gopher 1987-91*

"The pressure had been building for so long and it was just a relief. During my four years there we went to the Final Four three times, coming up short each time. There have been so many Gopher teams over the past 15 years or so that have been right on the doorstep, but couldn't get in. So, to see them finally win it was just amazing." — *Peter Hankinson, Gopher 1986-90*

"I was a freshman on the team that won the second title. The entire experience was just unbelievable. Watching the first one just made me excited to get there and to have a chance to win one of my own. Then, when it happened, it was just the thrill of a lifetime." — *Chris Harrington, Gopher 2002-Present*

"It was so amazing to see those guys win it back-to-back, I was so proud of them. I mean that is why you went to the U of M, to win a national championship. For me, and so many other guys who weren't able to achieve that, I think it represented a great deal. I played on some great teams when I was there, but obviously we never got it done. So, I was very happy for not only the guys but also for the coaches and everybody associated with the program. It put us back up on top, like we were under Herbie Brooks, and that was just fantastic. The bottom line is that you just have to tip your hat to Coach Lucia and those players, they got it done. And, the fact that they did it here, in St. Paul, made it even that much more sweeter." — *Darby Hendrickson, Gopher 1991-93*

"I played on the second one and it was amazing. That entire season was something I will never forget. We worked really hard and it was just great to be rewarded for that in the end. Overall, it is great for the state of hockey and it is great to see the program back on top where it belongs." — *Tyler Hirsch, Gopher 2002-Present*

"It just made me want to be a Gopher just that much more. It also raised the bar, because I want to be able to say that I too am a national champion before I leave here." — *Danny Irmen, Gopher 2003-Present*

"It meant a lot. I was playing with the L.A. Kings at the time and finally had some bragging rights with the guys in the locker room, which was pretty sweet. For the program to finally get the recognition that it deserves was just great. It just made me really proud to be a Gopher." — *Craig Johnson, Gopher 1990-93*

"They meant a ton to me. They meant that we were back on top of the college hockey world again, where we should be. Speaking for all the old Gophers, thank you." — *Trent Klatt, Gopher 1989-92*

"Just to be a part of not only one, but two titles, is almost beyond words. A lot of people were saying that we were the best class of all-time, but we were like NO WAY. There have been so many great Gophers who have played here and we were not about to go down that road. We just worked hard and were fortunate to have made an impact. Hopefully our legacy will be that we inspired a new crop of kids to grow up as Gopher fans and that they will want to keep the tradition going when they get old enough. As for the games themselves, what can I say? They were incredible. The first one was so special because it was so new and the fans were so into it. Then, the next one was amazing too because we were so determined to defend that title at all costs. When that happened I was just elated, we all were. I will never forget them for as long as I live, that is for sure." — *Matt Koalska, Gopher 2000-04*

"I will admit at first I was very jealous. No question. But, at the same time I was just thrilled that they had finally broken their 20+ year draught. We were finally champions again and that made me feel really good. I just thought about how proud and honored I was to be a part of the program. You know, it really hit me when I saw Jordan Leopold being interviewed on TV after the game and he said that the win was for all the Gophers who never got to win a national championship. That was such a classy thing to say and that is what made it so special to me." — *Ryan Kraft, Gopher 1994-98*

"I think that the two titles sort of validated the program. Lucia came in with his own agenda and really stuck to his plan. The titles elevated the team's stature to the top of the college hockey ranks and that is great for Minnesota hockey in general. It is especially good for our young kids, who will hopefully be inspired by that and want to go out and play more hockey." — *Bob Kurtz, former Gopher Broadcaster*

"I got to know a lot of those guys and they are such good guys, just great people. I am grateful to them, I mean they got the monkey off our backs, so to speak, which was great. It was sad that such a great program like that hadn't been able to win one for so long, but that was all forgotten when those guys came through for us." — *Cory Laylin, Gopher 1988-92*

"They mean I get to coach longer! No, really, they mean an awful lot. The first one was special because it was so new and unique for all of us. I mean to have it happen in St. Paul with 19,000 Gopher fans there, I mean that was amazing. The second one was special too, but different. We had to defend our title and repeat with a target on our backs. So, both were unique and I will cherish those memories for as long as I live. I was most happy for the players. They put so much hard work into it and it was great to see that reward at the end of the season. That wasn't just something that happened in one year. Most of the players have put in the time their whole life to get to that point. So, it was a tremendous achievement for all of us and something we all take a lot of pride in. When we won the first one I could feel a collective exhale from across the state. It was a big deal to a lot of people and I am just proud to have been a part of it. You know, there were a lot of great teams, maybe even better teams, over the years that didn't win it. So, that win was for all of those guys too. You have to get a little bit lucky and things have to go your way to win it and that is what happened for us. It was a total team effort though, from the assistant coaches to the strength coaches to the trainers to the managers — everybody played a part in it." — *Don Lucia, Current Gopher Head Coach*

"At the time it was almost indescribable. The first one, in St. Paul, was like a fairy tale. It was so emotional and so incredible to be able to do that in your own backyard in front of all your fans. That was by far the greatest moment of my hockey career. Then, to repeat, that was just so validating to all of us. We had the proverbial targets on our backs, which made it a lot tougher, but we dug in and just found a way to win it. We lost a lot of guys that off-season and nobody predicted us to win it, which made it even more gratifying. So, to be a part of one national championship was amazing, but to be a part of two, that was more than I ever could have hoped for. So, looking back I think that it was just the culmination of a lot of hard work and determination of a group of guys who came together as a team. It had been so long since the program had won a title too, so I was most happy for the loyal fans who have stuck with us through thick and thin." — *Paul Martin, Gopher 2000-03*

"I felt a great sense of relief for the University, for the Athletics Department and the Gopher Hockey program. Finally, after 23 years, we got the trophy that went along with how we have always felt about the team. We finally got that national stamp of approval, that recognition, that validation, which they had really longed for. Whether they won it or not wasn't going to make this program any greater than it already was. Winning it was just a great sense of relief for everybody, especially the fans." — *Frank Mazzocco, Longtime Gopher TV Analyst*

"I thought it was great. I felt a real sense of pride when it happened as did most alumni I think. We all felt a part of it. It was like when the Twins won the World Series back in 1987, it was that big and meant that much to the community. I was playing with the Chicago Blackhawks that year and got a lot of bragging rights after that with the other college guys on the team, like Tony Amonte. He used to always refer to us the 'Golden Chokers,' and it was great to finally shut that S.O.B. up once and for all! So, it was wonderful. It still makes the hairs stand up on the back of my neck when I think about it." — *Chris McAlpine, Gopher 1990-94*

"They meant a lot to us. We came so close back in 1989, when we lost to Harvard in the Finals at the Civic Center. So, this was sort of closure for a lot of us alumni." — *Jason Miller, Gopher 1987-91*

"It meant a lot. I was happy for the whole state, actually. I know how much people from all corners of the state support the program, and I am glad that they were finally able to enjoy that. Then, you know, being a former player, I was obviously thrilled for the guys and for Coach Lucia. It was fun to see so many guys that I had an opportunity to play with achieve that, guys like Johnny Pohl, Jordan Leopold, Matt DeMarchi and Nick Anthony, to name a few. The fact that it happened right here at home was pretty amazing too." — *Nate Miller, Gopher 1996-00*

"As a spectator it ranks right up there with my biggest thrills. I am really, really proud of the team and the coaching staff for what they have accomplished over there. It was so enjoyable to watch and I just can't say enough good things about this program. Lucia has done a marvelous job first of all. He has a plan and sticks to it and I respect that so much. He has been just sensational for the University of Minnesota. He really brought those kids along, especially in 2003, and allowed them to mature. It was great to see. All of those great kids from Leopold to Potulny to Taffe to Martin to Pohl to Ballard to Tallackson to Vanek, they just stepped it up those two seasons and really come through. Then, they got some great goaltending from Hauser and Weber too, and that was a big, big part of it. Overall, I am just proud to be a Gopher and to see my alma mater doing well. They are recruiting well and the entire program just looks to be in great shape. If they can keep some of these guys from turning pro early, there might even be a few more titles for them. — *Lou Nanne, Gopher 1961-63*

"It was great. It made me realize how disappointing it was to realize how much I would have loved to have won one myself when I was there. We had great teams but lost in the semifinals once and the quarterfinals three straight times. So, we never were able to get it done, but those two titles certainly helped to ease the pain — that is for sure. It was just super for the program to achieve that and I couldn't be happier for the guys and for Coach Lucia. They are finally back on top of the college hockey world and that was long overdue." — *Jeff Nielsen, Gopher 1990-94*

"They meant a lot. I sure wish that I could have been a part of it, but I was really happy for the guys. I was especially happy for the University though, it was just so long overdue. You know, for me it was so eerie to watch the team win the first one over Maine. I mean, that was us back in 1989, when we lost to Harvard in sudden-death on that exact spot in those exact same circumstances. So, to see the outcome be so much different this time around was just fantastic. I can't even imagine how I would feel if they would have lost that game. I am just thrilled that they were able to get it done and put the program back up on top. I really felt like I was a part of it. To get that big monkey off our back was wonderful." — *Larry Olimb, Gopher 1988-92*

"I was pretty proud of them. I make sure to rub it in to my Wisconsin buddies out here, or anybody else that wants to hear about it. It was just great to see Minnesota kicking ass again." — *Tom Pederson, Gopher 1988-91*

"It was such a thrill to see them finally win it. It was such a sense of satisfaction and validation to all of us that yes, Minnesota was and is one of the best college hockey programs in the country, and it always will be. Then, to go back-to-back, that was just awesome. Those guys really put Minnesota back on the map as far as being the elite program that we all knew that we were." — *Lance Pitlick, Gopher 1986-90*

"Well, I was a part of the first title in 2002 and honestly, I can't even put into words what that meant to me. To win it at home the way we did, it was just amazing. I have never been prouder of anything in my life. I can vividly remember standing out on the ice with like 50 seconds or so on the clock when Coach Lucia called a time-out. We all huddled and I am a pretty positive person, but remember thinking to myself, 'I can't believe we came this far and are going to let down all of these people...'. Then, Keith Ballard skated up and said 'Let's get this together,' which was sort of our rallying cry that whole season. That just flipped a switch for some reason. Koalska tied it up and then we got into overtime, where we just got a lucky bounce. It was so incredible when Grant scored to win it. Our team really came together that last minute and it is something I will never forget for as long as I live. Looking back, it is just a blur. I actually remember very little from that point on because it was just so insane after that. We partied hard that night too, none of us slept a wink. I had to watch the replay on TV to really see what happened, I was completely out of it. Wow, what a memory though, it was so special.

"Then, to watch them win the next year, that was so gratifying too. I know that guys like Erik Westrum, Nate Miller and Dylan Mills, who had graduated just before we won it in 2002, were proud of us when we won it. I felt the same way the year after I left and was able to see all my buddies make it two in a row. I know that myself, Jordan Leopold, Erik Wendell and Pat O'Leary, who were all seniors in 2002, all felt a part of that second title the next year too. I was so happy for the guys and was just excited for the program. The long-term effect of the two titles will mean that a whole new generation of kids will grow up just like we did, wanting to be Gophers. So, that is the legacy of those titles in my eyes." — *Johnny Pohl, Gopher 1998-2002*

"The first one still gives me chills. We focused on that date two years prior. We knew that the Frozen Four was going to be at the Xcel Center in St. Paul in 2002 and we were so determined to get there. Everything just built up to that and when we finally made it, we just knew that it was going to be destiny. We were so on a mission. We marched into Grand Forks and beat them on the first game of the year. From that moment on, I knew we had something really special. The whole season was magical, right up through beating Michigan in the opening round of the NCAA Finals.

"Then, to beat Maine the way that we did, was absolutely the biggest thrill of my life. When Matty Koalska got the equalizer to send it to overtime, I just had a feeling that it was our time. The overtime was so stressful, you could just feel the pressure and tension in the air. The fans were beside themselves. My legs were dead and I was drained, but I when we got the penalty and went on the power-play, we all got a boost of energy. Johnny (Pohl) won the draw over to Jeff (Taffe) and he shot it. It hit Johnny and then it bounced towards me, so I just sort of swung at it. When I saw the red light go off it was like a slow motion movie. To be honest I didn't even know I scored. From there, everything is just a blur. We all just started piling on each other and it was a total yard sale with all of our equipment littering the ice. I remember looking up into the crowd and seeing grown men crying and hugging each other. It was incredible. I mean to score the overtime game-winner to win the NCAA Championship in front of your home fans — you just can't make that stuff up. I have goose bumps even talking about it right now.

"The next year was different, but just as gratifying. I remember hearing Sid Hartman say 'They lost Leopold, Taffe, Pohl and Hauser, they got no chance…'. That motivated us like crazy. Our young guys, like Thomas Vanek, really stepped up and came through for us that year. Even though we had the targets on our backs as national champs, we just played loose and had fun. We didn't have any sort of master plan this year, it was just go-with-the-flow hockey all the way around. Nobody expected us to do anything. So, we just grinded it out and wound up back in the Frozen Four, where we knew it was anybody's game. We wound up beating Michigan again, in overtime this time, and then played so strong against New Hampshire to win it. It was like, wow! We were back-to-back NCAA Champions. So, what did the two titles mean to me? Everything." — *Grant Potulny, Gopher 2000-04*

"As a high school player that was all I wanted, to play at the U of M. So, to see them now doing so well is just fabulous. It was long overdue. They have had some teams that have been close through the years, but this was long overdue. It is crazy to think that I was on the last national championship team, back in 1979, and it has taken this long. But it was worth the wait. They looked poised to keep on winning too, they are tough. It was just amazing that they were able to win two in a row, that is really impressive." — *Mike Ramsey, Gopher 1979; Current Wild Assistant Coach*

"I was extremely jealous that I never got to win one if you want to know the truth. Really though, I was thrilled. It was kind of like redemption. We had gotten so close for so long and we were just due. It was such a long time coming. As for me personally, I won a lot of bets on them. I mean you always bet your alma mater, and I was finally able to cash in!" — *Erik Rasmussen, Gopher 1995-97*

"It was just fantastic. You know, I have been playing minor league hockey in Grand Rapids now for about 10 years and over that time I have talked a lot of smack about the Gophers to my teammates and opponents. So, all I can say is thank you! It was about time!" — *Travis Richards, Gopher 1989-93*

"When I think back, I just can't believe that it really happened. To win one was amazing, but to win two is almost indescribable. You don't really appreciate it until you are away from it and can look back and reflect. To do that with my teammates, who also happen to be my best friends, was so special. Now, to talk to old Gophers who say thanks and congratulate you, that is really neat too. So, for me, it was the thrill of a lifetime to be a part of that." — *Troy Riddle, Gopher 2000-04*

"Honest to God, those were the most thrilling moments of my lifetime in hockey, especially the first one. To get that win was so exciting, I mean it had been 23 years between national championships, so it was long overdue. That last minute was the longest minute of my life. For whatever reason, I hadn't given up on the them even with a minute to go. I just knew somehow they were going to rally, and they did. Then, when they pulled it off, I was just beside myself. I remember when Matty Koalska scored the equalizer leaning over and saying to Glen (Sonmor) 'Now we have a chance…'. Finally, in overtime, Leopold's goal just about brought the house down. The crowd absolutely exploded. I mean we were just fans at that point, we had no objectivity whatsoever, it was great. We were total homers, just giddy. That was by far the most thrilling moment I have ever experienced in hockey. I get goose bumps even thinking about it today." — *Wally Shaver, Longtime Gopher Radio & TV Announcer*

"That was so great to be a part of, just wonderful. I have been doing Gopher hockey broadcasts for a long time now and could see the frustration building within the program for so long. So, when they finally did it, it was so incredible. And to do it in such dramatic fashion, winning that first one in St. Paul — just marvelous. I thought back to how close they had come in years past, under Doug (Woog), and was very happy for everybody associated with the team. You know, it really had an impact on all of the Gopher alumni too, they all got to share in those victories as well. To see the absolute joy of those kids out on the ice after the game was what it was all about. That is why we play this game and to see that raw emotion out there afterwards was very special." — *Glen Sonmor, Former Gopher, North Stars & Fighting Saints Coach; Current Gopher Radio Broadcaster*

"They meant so much. I played on some really good teams but we could never get going at the right time in the end to make a run. So, to see these guys win it all like that was just great. Lucia is a great coach. I could tell right when he came in, my senior year, that things were going to be different. That is no disrespect to Coach Woog, he is a tremendous coach and a great guy, but Lucia had a plan and you could tell good things were going to happen with him." — *Dave Spehar, Gopher 1996-2000*

"I think it put us back on the map. It had been a long time between titles in Minnesota and I was just thrilled to be a part of that. The Gophers had so many great teams in the '80s and '90s but just couldn't get it done. There were so many teams that came so close over the years and I think we all felt that pain. I mean to be able to give the fans what they have been wanting for so long was really gratifying. Then, to see the team win it again that next year was just incredible. I think the biggest thing that will come out of it is the fact that more and more kids will grow up wanting to become Gophers the same way so many of us did. So, from a recruiting standpoint it was invaluable." — *Jeff Taffe, Gopher 1999-02*

"It was pretty special. Not many people can say that they won a national championship, let alone two. So I am very proud of that and I will always have those two rings to remind me what those magical seasons meant. The first one was so amazing, winning it at home in front of our fans. The second one was totally different, because we had such a young team, and we didn't really have high expectations. It was more of an internal thing between the players to win that second one because nobody thought we could do it. To go back-to-back was just amazing though and I will never forget it." — *Barry Tallackson, Gopher 2001-05*

"I was thrilled for the program, it was long overdue. Personally, it was frustrating in the sense that when they won it in 2002, which was my first year removed as the radio play-by-play guy. I would have loved to have been a part of it because it was an amazing accomplishment. Then, to win it again the next year, that was just as impressive, especially from a coaching standpoint. It really put them into an elite handful of college hockey teams and hopefully they will stay there for a long time." — *Dan Terhaar, Former Gopher Radio Announcer*

"I was jealous, I mean I wish like heck that I could have won two national championships when I was there. We came close, but couldn't get it done. So, I think in a small way those two titles are for all of us guys who didn't get it done. It was great, I couldn't be happier for the players and for the program. It is fun to see them back on top, where they belong. Plus, I was sick and tired of hearing it from my friends from North Dakota. This definitely shut them up, which is always nice." — *Dan Trebil, Gopher 1992-96*

"Well, the first one definitely made me want to come here to win one of my own. Then, to be able to actually do that, was almost indescribable. It was an experience that I will never forget for as long as I live. To share those memories with my 25 teammates is absolutely priceless." — *Thomas Vanek, Gopher 2002-04*

"Once a Gopher, always a Gopher. It is always 'your team,' even when you're done playing.

All of us who played are all members of that exclusive fraternity, and we all shared in the excitement and pride of it. It was amazing. That is what you play for, championships, and I am sure that each and every one of us wishes that he was able to hoist up that trophy the way those guys did. So, back-to-back, that's more than special, it's historic." — *Erik Westrum, Gopher 1997-2001*

"I was so happy for those guys. It felt great to finally see the program back up on top, where it should be. You know, I work with the youth hockey association here in Rochester now and it was really neat to see how much the kids followed it. Hopefully, a whole new crop of Gopher fans was born when that all happened. That to me is another big benefit that will come out of it as well." — *Doug Zmolek, Gopher 1989-92*

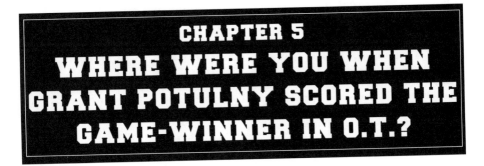

CHAPTER 5

WHERE WERE YOU WHEN GRANT POTULNY SCORED THE GAME-WINNER IN O.T.?

"I was in London on business and listened to it on the internet. It was awesome." — *Mike Anderson, Gopher 1995-99*

"I was so close I could taste it!" — *Keith Ballard, Gopher 2001-04*

"I was coaching in Rockford, Illinois, at the time and was at home watching the game on TV. My family was all sleeping at the time and I was out on the couch by myself. When Grant scored that goal I jumped straight up in the air and screamed so loud that I woke up my wife and kid. My kid was crying and my dog even went nuts. I didn't care, it was worth it. That was so amazing, I will never forget that moment." — *Scott Bell, Gopher 1991-95*

"I had a game that night but got to see the replay afterwards. It was amazing to see. I will never forget just getting a flurry of phone calls from old teammates, we were all celebrating the moment together from all over the country. It was really emotional for all of us." — *Reggie Berg, Gopher 1995-99*

"We had a big party at my house here in Grand Rapids. Everybody just went crazy when he scored. It was really cool." — *Grant Bischoff, Gopher 1987-91*

"Ha! (laughing) There is a great story behind that. I was so nervous for the first title in 2002 that I couldn't even sit in my seat. I was just a mess. So, I abandoned my family and was out walking the halls. What's so funny is that you can't get away from it at the Xcel Center — I mean they have TV's and radio broadcasts going everywhere, even in the bathrooms for goodness sakes! Finally, in the overtime, I wound up watching it out in the hallway with Assistant Coach John Hill, who had left the program at that time but had recruited a lot of those kids, and Brad Arnett, our former strength coach, who had worked with a lot of those kids as well. John had his arm around me so tightly and when Grant scored I thought he was going to squeeze my head off. His words to me at that exact moment were: 'Now what do you think about out-of-state players?!'. It was amazing and something I will never forget. I was just a bundle of emotions that night, a real puddle. I bawled, I laughed — I had just wanted to see that team succeed for so many years that when it finally happened I just lost it. The second one was great too, but nothing can compare to the first one because it was at home and happened in such a dramatic manner." — *Patty Bjorklund, Longtime Gopher Hockey Administrative Assistant*

"I was playing with Tampa Bay at the time and I got to watch the game down there in my apartment. It was so exciting and just a really classic game." — *Ben Clymer, Gopher 1996-98*

"I was in Chicago at a buddy of mine's wedding. The game was on in the bar, so we were all running back and forth to watch it. The best part about that night was razzing my buddy at his own wedding…you see he played hockey at Wisconsin. It was awesome." — *Mike Crowley, Gopher 1994-97*

"I was at home watching it and I about went nuts. I was so nervous. It was amazing, that is all I can say." — *Steve DeBus, Gopher 1995-98*

"I got to catch the last bit of it in the locker room after a game I had just played in Hartford. I definitely had some bragging rights for a while with the other college players, that was for sure." — *Ken Gernander, Gopher 1988-91*

"I was standing in front of the Plexiglas in the zamboni lane right behind the net, waiting to go out onto the ice for post-game interviews. So, I was literally just 10 feet away from 'the goal.' The hair stood up on the back of my neck and I just said 'Finally!'. — *Eric Gislason, Former Gopher Radio & Television Commentator*

"I was playing junior hockey down in Lincoln, Neb., and it was during the last game of the season. I remember sitting on the bench with Ryan Potulny and Danny Irmen, and watching the game through the glass on a tiny TV that was out in the lobby of the arena. We were all committed to the Gophers at that point, so we were really rooting for them to win. Well, eventually we saw all the players throw their gloves up in the air and we knew that they had won. Later, our coach told us that Ryan's brother, Grant, had scored the overtime game-winner, and we were all just really pumped. It was pretty cool." — *Gino Guyer, Gopher 2003-Present*

"I was at the Xcel Center and I think I jumped up about three feet into the air when Grant scored that goal. It was amazing, just amazing." — *Ben Hankinson, Gopher 1987-91*

"I was playing for the Norfolk Admirals at the time, in the minors, and wound up watching the game on a bus ride back to Virginia from Philadelphia. We had a satellite on the bus so we were able to watch the entire game on the way home, it was awesome. I remember when Grant scored in overtime I just jumped up and screamed 'Yes!!' I think I woke up half the team. Here I am with a bus load of Canadians and they are all like 'big deal, a college team won…' I didn't care, I was so unbelievably happy for those guys. I would have loved to have been there and better yet, I would have loved to have been out on the ice. It meant so much to the alumni and we were all just thrilled to finally get one." — *Casey Hankinson, Gopher 1994-98*

"I was there with my boss, Bruce Telander, who has a long history with the program. So, we got to enjoy it together. It was just shocking when he scored it. You know, after losing to Harvard at that very same spot back in 1989 in such a similar situation, I was thinking 'Oh no, here we go again…'. But, they came out on top this time and I couldn't have been happier." — *Peter Hankinson, Gopher 1986-90*

"I was in Omaha at the time. I had played junior hockey down there along with Keith Ballard, Jake Flemming and Dan Welch the year before. They were a year ahead of me, but I got to know those guys pretty well. So, I remember calling them right after they won to congratulate them. It was pretty amazing." — *Chris Harrington, Gopher 2002-Present*

"I was standing in the crease, bracing myself for all of my teammates to pile on me." — *Adam Hauser, Gopher 1998-2002*

"I was actually sitting at home in my living room at the time because I was recovering from an eye injury I had suffered when I was playing with the Wild. So, I watched it with one eye, literally. I was on bed rest for two weeks because of the injury, and was under specific orders from my doctor to not elevate my blood pressure. Yeah right! I am so glad they won because I couldn't even imagine how much it would have hurt if they lost and I started crying!" — *Darby Hendrickson, Gopher from 1991-93*

"I remember watching it on the bus ride home from playing in the national AAA midget tournament. I was playing for Shattuck at the time and had already committed to the program, so I was very interested in the outcome. Seeing them win was amazing and it just made me want to be a Gopher even more." — *Tyler Hirsch, Gopher 2002-Present*

"I was on the bench playing a junior game in Des Moines at the time. I was with Ryan Potulny and we were watching the game between shifts through the glass on a big-screen TV out in the lobby area. It was amazing. When Grant scored it was like the greatest feeling in the world. I was so happy for Ryan, but I was also happy that a kid from North Dakota got the game-winner." — *Danny Irmen, Gopher 2003-Present*

"I was playing a game with the L.A. Kings that night, but one of the trainers came running over to tell me the good news while I was on the bench. It was pretty cool." — *Craig Johnson, Gopher 1990-93*

"I had a game that night, but I did get to watch the Michigan game the night before. I was actually playing up in Vancouver at the time with Brendan Morrison, a Michigan guy, and we had been going toe to toe with each other for bragging rights that whole week. So, to see the Gophers beat the Wolverines in the opening game of the Frozen Four was awesome. I rubbed that in hard, which felt great. Then, to see them win it that next night was just amazing. I was so happy for the guys and for the whole program in general. It was long overdue and something that we, as former Gophers, all shared in a little bit." — *Trent Klatt, Gopher 1989-92*

"I was playing a game in Cincinnati at the time, but was trying to keep tabs on the game while it was going on. As soon as our game was over I looked at my cell phone and I had 14 messages from old teammates, which was really cool. Everybody was just ecstatic. We all sort of shared in that moment, and that's what it's all about." — *Ryan Kraft, Gopher 1994-98*

"I was in a hotel bar out in Fresno, Calif., all by myself. I had come back to the States to play for the San Diego Gulls in their play-off run, but was on the shelf due to a concussion I had just gotten. So, I was out there all alone screaming at the TV as I was watching the game. It was awesome!" — *Cory Laylin, Gopher 1988-92*

"I was right there baby!" — *Paul Martin, Gopher 2000-03*

"I was in the press box at the Xcel Center. As the crowd was roaring, I just sat there and soaked it in. For me, that was the first national championship that I had been involved in since I started broadcasting hockey way back in 1977. So, I just sat back and watched and listened. It was amazing. I wanted to feel what it was like from a fan's perspective. The emotion was running so high, it was just something I will never forget. To make it even sweeter, I was sitting next to a photographer buddy of mine who actually shot the game-winning goal. He was so excited, it was just unbelievable. That picture is now hanging in Tommy Reid's bar right now. So, whenever I see that picture I have a great story to go along with my great memory. The whole thing was just too good to believe." — *Frank Mazzocco, Longtime Gopher TV Analyst*

"I was in my living room watching the game on TV with my wife. It was pretty sweet." — *Jason Miller, Gopher 1987-91*

"I was out in Manchester, N.H., playing in the minors at the time. We had a game that night and I was able to watch the overtime on a stationary bike in our training room. When Grant scored I just about went through the roof. It was ironic too, because I was in there watching the game with Ted Donato, who was on the 1989 Harvard team that had beaten the Gophers right on that same spot when it was the Civic Center. So, he was rooting for us this time around and we both celebrated afterwards. It was amazing." — *Nate Miller, Gopher 1996-00*

"I was at the game, it was amazing." — *Jeff Nielsen, Gopher 1990-94*

"I was at my nephew's hockey tournament in St. Cloud. My brother and I wound up watching the game in the hotel. It was a pretty memorable family moment for us." — *Larry Olimb, Gopher 1988-92*

"I remember the Maine kid shooshing the crowd by holding his finger up to his lips after he scored the go-ahead goal early on. So, to see the Gophers rally back and beat those guys in overtime was just incredible. We were so due to win one and it happened is such dramatic fash-ion. I was watching the game but actually had to get in my car and just drive around for a while because I was so nervous. I knew deep down that if I was watching at the end that they would somehow be jinxed and wouldn't win. So, they can thank me for that! Really though, it was a huge win not only for them, but for all of us guys who could never get it done when they were there." — *Tom Pederson, Gopher 1988-91*

"I was playing with Florida at the time and we were up in Toronto that night playing the Leafs. Our video guy kept coming over and giving me updates between periods, I was so nervous. Finally, he came over and told me it was in overtime, so I quickly called my parents after our game and they told me the good news. I was so excited. I got to enjoy it with Mark Parrish, who was probably the only other American with me at the time." — *Lance Pitlick, Gopher 1986-90*

"I was so close I could taste it!" — *Johnny Pohl, Gopher 1998-2002*

"Believe me, I was right there baby!" — *Grant Potulny, Gopher 2000-04*

"I was playing junior hockey with Lincoln, and we had a game in Des Moines that night. We had already wrapped up second place in the league and it was our last game of the year. So, I was just dying to watch the game, and I remember being able to sit at a certain spot on the bench where I could see the game being shown on a big-screen TV out in the arena lobby. It was hard to see it though, because it was really far away and because I had to keep taking shifts. Anyway, I came back to the bench at one point and my coach told me that the game was in overtime. Finally, I saw a commotion and I saw all the guys piling on each other out on the ice. I knew that Minnesota had won it, but didn't find out until after our game that it was Grant who had actually scored the game-winner. My coach announced it to everybody in the locker room and everybody congratulated me like I had just had a baby or something. It was pretty special. The first thing I did was to call him, it was just insane — I will never forget it." — *Ryan Potulny, Gopher 2003-Present*

"I had a game that night but I rushed back to the locker room to catch the highlights on ESPN. It was awesome. Plus, we had an assistant coach on our team from Maine, so I really got to rub it in." — *Travis Richards, Gopher 1989-93*

"You know, I had assisted on Koalska's goal to tie it up and send it to overtime, but I was so exhausted by that point — both mentally and physically. Believe it or not, when Grant scored I had just come off a long shift and I had my head down between my legs gasping for air on the bench. So, I missed the whole thing. I actually wound up seeing the replay on TV. I remem-ber staying up all night that night with the guys and just partying like we were rock stars. My hand hurt from high-fiving so much, it was insane. We skipped class the next day and just savored every minute of it. I will never forget it." — *Troy Riddle, Gopher 2000-04*

"I was playing for the Phoenix Coyotes minor league team in Springfield, Mass., at the time and we had just finished playing a game. Erik Westrum and I were teammates out there and after the game we went straight to the player's lounge to watch the third period. We didn't even take our equipment off or anything, we were just glued to the TV. It was great having a fellow Gopher to watch it with and to share that moment with. When they won it we were so pumped. It was pretty special. As a member of the Gopher family I felt a part of it, I really did. I think all of the former players do, so that was really neat." — *Wyatt Smith, Gopher 1995-99*

"I was broadcasting the game up in the booth and I can honestly say that I lost all journalistic objectivity as soon as Grant scored the goal. At that moment I was not a broadcaster, I was a Gopher. Hey, I am a homer and damn proud of it!" — *Glen Sonmor, Former Gopher, North Stars & Fighting Saints Coach; Current Gopher Radio Broadcaster*

"I was at the game and it was unbelievable. I have never, ever seen anything like it. The place erupted, it was one of the most awesome things I have ever witnessed." — *Dave Spehar, Gopher 1996-2000*

"It was like time stood still. We all went nuts and just jumped over the boards to go out and celebrate. For as long as I live I will never forget that moment." — *Jeff Taffe, Gopher 1999-02*

"I was playing junior hockey in Sioux Falls at the time and our whole team watched it. It was fun because there were a bunch of kids on the team from Michigan, so when the Gophers beat them in the semis, the Minnesota recruits all got bragging rights for the rest of the year. It was pretty sweet." — *Mike Vannelli, Gopher 2003-Present*

"I had actually just finished playing a minor league game out in Springfield. I wound up watching the third period and overtime with my teammate, Wyatt Smith, and we still had our equipment on and everything in the team lounge. It was so exciting, I was just on pins and needles. It was weird, that was our team's last game of the year and we got so caught up in the Gopher game that by the time it was over we were the last guys in the locker room. I was like 'Hello, anybody out there...?' After I showered up I got a bunch of phone calls from all my old teammates, it was really cool. I knew all of those guys because I had just graduated the year before, so it was fantastic to see them get it done. I only wish that I could have been a part of it. I was so pumped for those guys that I actually drove straight home that next day and met up with the team at to celebrate." — *Erik Westrum, Gopher 1997-2001*

"I got to watch it out in Colorado Springs at a restaurant with my bantam team which had just won the national tournament. All of the guys were so excited, it was amazing." — *Blake Wheeler, Gopher 2005-Present*

"I was on the red line, row 20, with my wife. When we scored that goal, and I say 'we' because I felt as part of it as everybody out on the ice, it was almost surreal. I was totally lost in the moment and while I was celebrating it really felt like I was out there with my teammates. I was so proud of the team, it was so well deserved — just a true team effort all the way around. I was very appreciative of the players too, because they were so respectful of how they treated it. They made it very clear that the win was for all of Gopher Hockey, and not just for them. That was great because that is exactly how all of us guys felt too. I will never forget the days following the big win, I was just on cloud nine. Guys were calling each other and congratulating each other, it really was a special moment." — *Dean Williamson, Gopher 1987-90*

"I watched it here in Rochester in my living room with my family. It was incredible to watch Potulny knock it in to end it. My heart was just racing." — *Doug Zmolek, Gopher 1989-92*

CHAPTER 6
WHO WAS YOUR HOCKEY HERO GROWING UP?

"Growing up in Bloomington it would have to be Tom Kurvers." — *Mike Anderson, Gopher 1995-99*

"I was a big fan of both Bobby Smith and Dino Ciccarelli." — *Mark Bahr, Gopher 1991-94, Current Director of Hockey Operations*

"When I was little I loved Corey Millen, he was so fast. Then, I really admired guys like Randy Skarda and Lance Pitlick, who were so physical and dominant." — *Scott Bell, Gopher 1991-95*

"Neal Broten was certainly someone I admired as a kid." — *Reggie Berg, Gopher 1995-99*

"Being from Grand Rapids I would have to say Billy Baker. I really looked up to him as a kid, especially after he was on the 1980 'Miracle on Ice' team." — *Grant Bischoff, Gopher 1987-91*

"Wayne Gretzky was my guy, I just worshiped him as a kid." — *Brian Bonin, Gopher 1992-96*

"David Keon was my childhood hero, and I later got to play with him with the Fighting Saints and Hartford Whalers." — *Bill Butters, Gopher Player 1971-73; Assistant Coach 1985-95*

"Grant Bischoff. In fact, I wore No. 22 up until I was a pro because he was my favorite player." — *Ben Clymer, Gopher 1996-98*

"Tommy Pederson was my guy growing up. I never forgave Larry Olimb for beating Tommy out of the Mr. Hockey award, I was a total homer from Bloomington!" — *Mike Crowley, Gopher 1994-97*

"Donny Beaupre and Gilles Meloche, the old North Stars goalies were great, and so was Robby Stauber, who I looked up to a lot when he was a Gopher too." — *Steve DeBus, Gopher 1995-98*

"Mike Antonovich, he was Greenway's best ever." — *Ken Gernander, Gopher 1988-91*

"My dad was my hero. He played at UMD and was also my coach. I really admired him, he was just a huge influence on my life." — *Gino Guyer, Gopher 2003-Present*

"Peter Hankinson, my big bro." — *Ben Hankinson, Gopher 1987-91*

"Peter and Ben Hankinson, my two big-bros. That might sound corny but it is the truth. I just worshiped those guys back then, and believe it or not, I still do." — *Casey Hankinson, Gopher 1994-98*

"I was in awe of Corey Millen. He was so fast and was just electric whenever he got into open ice." — *Peter Hankinson, Gopher 1986-90*

"Mike Crowley, he was my guy." — *Chris Harrington, Gopher 2002-Present*

"As for Gophers, I would have to say Robb Stauber." — *Adam Hauser, Gopher 1998-2002*

"Neal Broten, it wasn't even close. I just worshiped the guy as a kid." — *Darby Hendrickson, Gopher from 1991-93*

"Mario Lemieux" — *Danny Irmen, Gopher 2003-Present*

"It would have to be Neal Broten, he was just the best." — *Craig Johnson, Gopher 1990-93*

"Growing up in Wisconsin I really enjoyed watching Mark Johnson, he was just a great all-around player." — *Phil Kessel, Gopher 2005-Present*

"Neal Broten, and he hates when I tell him that! He is so humble, but it's the truth. I mean that guy lived the dream: he played in the state tourney; for the Gophers; the Miracle on Ice; and then the North Stars. I got to play with him when I was with the Stars and it was almost surreal to play alongside your childhood hero." — *Trent Klatt, Gopher 1989-92*

"Wayne Gretzky was my guy." — *Ryan Kraft, Gopher 1994-98*

"Being from Elk River, it would have to be Joel Otto." — *Paul Martin, Gopher 2000-03*

"Neal Broten was my hero as a kid. In fact I had a big poster of him on my bedroom wall growing up. I had never met him or anything before and then back in 1995, when I was playing with the New Jersey Devils, he got traded to us from Dallas and we wound up being roommates. I was like a school girl I was so excited. I never had enough guts to tell him that his poster was probably still hanging in my old bedroom at my parents house though! We got to become good friends and I just think the world of him. I mean Neal Broten IS Minnesota hockey. What a classy guy." — *Chris McAlpine, Gopher 1990-94*

"As a kid it was Gretzky, and later it was Tommy Chorske." — *Jason Miller, Gopher 1987-91*

"Neal Broten, hands down. I just worshiped that guy." — *Nate Miller, Gopher 1996-00*

"Billy Baker was my guy as a kid. He was from Grand Rapids too and really made a name for himself with the Gophers and then with the 1980 U.S. Olympic hockey team. I will never forget, I was at home sick when he came in with his gold medal to speak to my fourth grade class. I was so bummed out! He definitely inspired me to become a Gopher though." — *Jeff Nielsen, Gopher 1990-94*

"I liked the local Warroad guys; Cal Marvin, Billy & Roger Christian, Blaine Comstock and Henry Boucha. I grew up around those guys and they certainly had a big influence on my life." — *Larry Olimb, Gopher 1988-92*

"I really liked Curt Giles. He was a smaller defenseman like myself and I tried to pattern a lot of aspects of my game after his." — *Tom Pederson, Gopher 1988-91*

"I loved Wayne Gretzky, he was just the ultimate ambassador to the game." — *Lance Pitlick, Gopher 1986-90*

"My hero changed every year and was basically whoever was the best player in the high school tournament that season, whether it was Darby Hendrickson, Mike Crowley, Jamie Langenbrunner or whoever, that is who I idolized. My dad was my coach and the pinnacle of our hockey season as kids was to always get to go up to the tourney and be a part of that. In fact, I had never been to a North Stars game and had actually only been to one Gopher game before I came to school there. So, for me it was all about the tourney, and that is still my favorite aspect of hockey in Minnesota today." — *Johnny Pohl, Gopher 1998-2002*

"Tony Hrkac, a UND legend. Grand Forks went nuts for that guy the year he won his Hobey with the 'Hrkac Circus.' " — *Grant Potulny, Gopher 2000-04*

"Eric Lindros" — *Ryan Potulny, Gopher 2003-Present*

"Neal Broten. I mean he played with the Gophers, the Olympic team and the North Stars, he just did it all." — *Travis Richards, Gopher 1989-93*

"It would have to be Neal Broten and Corey Millen." — *Troy Riddle, Gopher 2000-04*

"Growing up in Warroad you could take your pick. From Henry Boucha to the Christian Brothers to Larry Olimb, we had so many great players up there that we all looked up to." — *Wyatt Smith, Gopher 1995-99*

"Maurice Richard and Gordie Howe. They were the best." — *Glen Sonmor, Former Gopher, North Stars & Fighting Saints Coach; Current Gopher Radio Broadcaster*

"It would have to be Brett Hull, he was a Duluth hockey legend." — *Dave Spehar, Gopher 1996-2000*

"I would have to say Neal Broten. He was a Gopher and then went on to have success in the NHL, and he did it with such class — so he is certainly someone who I have tried to pattern myself after." — *Barry Tallackson, Gopher 2001-05*

"I was always a big Steve Yzerman fan." — *Dan Trebil, Gopher 1992-96*

"Growing up in Austria my idol was Mario Lemieux." — *Thomas Vanek, Gopher 2002-04*

"My dad, Tom. He has had a huge impact on my career both as a coach and as my parent, and I have always looked up to him." — *Mike Vannelli, Gopher 2003-Present*

"My dad, Pat, who was a Gopher Captain back in 1970. I grew up wanting to follow in his footsteps." — *Erik Westrum, Gopher 1997-2001*

"For sure it was Brian Bonin, he was so smooth." — *Blake Wheeler, Gopher 2005-Present*

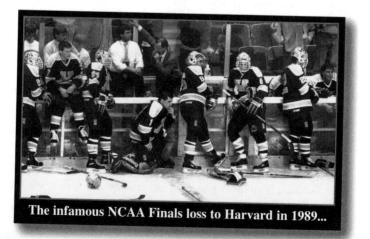

The infamous NCAA Finals loss to Harvard in 1989...

CHAPTER 7
WHAT WAS YOUR MOST MEMORABLE GOPHER GAME?

"Sadly, it would probably have to be the loss to Michigan my freshman year when Mike Legg scored on an unbelievable wrap-around goal. He went behind the net and was able to pick the puck up and just slam it into the top corner in one fluid motion, it was amazing. It was even the Play-of-the-Day on ESPN that night. It was just a devastating loss for us though, because it pretty much ended our hopes for moving on into the post-season." — *Mike Anderson, Gopher 1995-99*

"I would have to say my first game when I got to suit up in Duluth. That was it, I made it." — *Mark Bahr, Gopher 1991-94, Current Director of Hockey Operations*

"It would have to be beating Maine to win the 2002 NCAA title in St. Paul. What an amazing run that was. When Matty Koalska got the equalizer, I just knew that we were going to pull it off. Then, when Grant got the game-winner, it was like a dream come true. It was fitting that Johnny Pohl and Jordan Leopold got the assists on that goal too, because those were our three team leaders for sure. Those guys just carried us all year." — *Keith Ballard, Gopher 2001-04*

"I would say it was against Northern Michigan at the WCHA Final Five at the old Civic Center back in 1993. They were national champs and a pretty big rival back then. I will never forget, it was late in the third and they had their goalie pulled. The highlight for me came in the last shift when I caught one of their players with his head down and absolutely killed him. He went down like a ton of bricks. Johnny Brill then skated over and put the puck into the empty net to seal the win for us. I remember seeing the kid over on his bench with a bunch of coaches asking him how many fingers they were holding up. He was in rough shape. After the game my dad never even congratulated me on the big win, he just said 'Oh, what a great hit!', that was so cool. That was our first Final Five title and one I will always remember." — *Scott Bell, Gopher 1991-95*

"I would have to say my first game up at Michigan Tech, we won it 4-2. I got to start my career on a line next to Brian Bonin, who went on to win the Hobey that year, so that was pretty neat. The first time you get to put on that jersey, it is just really sinks in that you finally made it." — *Reggie Berg, Gopher 1995-99*

"I hate to say it, but it has to be the Harvard loss back in 1989 in the NCAA Finals at the Civic Center. I was just crushed. I remember after the game going to Grandma's Bar over in Seven Corners with Benny Hankinson. We were so bummed out at that point and just wanted to forget about what happened over some cocktails. Well, as soon as we got there, the DJ announced the score of the game and it was like the party came to a screeching halt. What a buzz-kill! It was almost surreal. People were so bummed out and we had to sit there and go through it all over again. That loss still eats at me even to this day." — *Grant Bischoff, Gopher 1987-91*

"I would probably have to say it was the team's third national championship back in 1979, under Herbie (Brooks), when they beat North Dakota to win it all. I was in Detroit for that game, and it was just incredible to be there. I had never seen anything like it before. You see, I grew up in Pipestone, a little town in southwestern Minnesota, where there was no hockey. Well, when I moved up to the Twin Cities in the mid-1970s, I wound up becoming friends with some girls who loved hockey. As a result, I started going to North Stars and Fighting Saints games with them. It was OK, but nothing special. Then, when they took me to a Gopher game,

I was hooked. I immediately bought season tickets and have been a die-hard ever since. The fans and the atmosphere were so great, I just loved it. Anyway, we went out to watch the team in Detroit that year and it was something that I will never forget." — *Patty Bjorklund, Longtime Gopher Hockey Administrative Assistant*

"I would have to say my very first game as a freshman. It was at old Mariucci against North Dakota. I was awe-struck just being there. I couldn't believe I had actually made it and was skating on that ice. I will never forget that night. I even scored a goal, which made it even more special." — *Brian Bonin, Gopher 1992-96*

"I would say beating North Dakota to win the WCHA Final Five my freshman year at the Xcel Center. It was so loud in there, it was just amazing." — *Kellen Briggs, Gopher 2003-Present*

"Most people would probably guess it would be the game against Colorado College, where I dove into their bench and took em' all on, but for me, I would have to say it was a game against Wisconsin back in 1971 where we were down 5-0 in the third period and came back to win, 6-5, in overtime. That was pretty amazing." — *Bill Butters, Gopher Player 1971-73; Assistant Coach 1985-95*

"I would have to say the overtime win over Maine last year where Barry Tallackson scored the game-winner. That was just insane." — *Kris Chucko, Gopher 2003-Present*

"You know, I basically only had one season at Minnesota, so all of my games there were special. If I had to pick another most memorable game, it would have to be the night we beat Calgary in Game Seven to win the Stanley Cup in 2004. Jordan Leopold was playing for the Flames, so it was sort of a Gopher game. Other than being a Gopher, having my name on Lord Stanley's Cup is about as good as it gets for me. I will never forget bringing the Cup back home to party with it. I got to have it here with me in Minnesota for two nights. The first night I took it out to dinner at Chino Latino, in Uptown, with about 10 people. We just showed up with it and the people there just went nuts. We took over the joint; people were drinking out of it and it got pretty out of control. Then, the next day I took it to my old stomping grounds, the Bloomington Ice Gardens, which was really cool. That night I had a party out at Olympic Hills Golf Club and invited like every player, coach, neighbor, friend, and family member I have ever known since I was five years old to come out and celebrate with Stanley. It was insane. From there we took it to Sally's on campus, followed by the bar, Drink, and then to bed. It was a whirlwind tour and something I will never forget." — *Ben Clymer, Gopher 1996-98*

"I would have to say beating Colorado College in Madison my freshman year to make it to the Frozen Four." — *Mike Crowley, Gopher 1994-97*

"Anytime we played Wisconsin, I just loved to beat those guys. They were a huge rival and really brought out the best in me." — *Steve DeBus, Gopher 1995-98*

"As bitter sweet as it was, I would have to say the overtime loss to Harvard in the Finals back in 1989. To play for a national championship right there in your back yard and come up short was tough. It is still tough even to this day." — *Ken Gernander, Gopher 1988-91*

"I would have to say being in the Frozen Four up in Grand Forks in 1983 was a big deal, but we didn't win, so that was tough." — *Mike Guentzel, Gopher Player 1981-85; Assistant Coach 1994-Present*

"No question, winning the NCAA title game over New Hampshire in 2003." — *Gino Guyer, Gopher 2003-Present*

"Unfortunately, I would have to say the Harvard loss back in 1989 at the Civic Center. That was one of the toughest things I have ever had to deal with, but certainly something I will never forget." — *Ben Hankinson, Gopher 1987-91*

"I would say playing in the Frozen Four my freshman year, 1995, out in Providence. We lost to BU, but it was a thrill just to be there." — *Casey Hankinson, Gopher 1994-98*

"My first ever game as a Gopher, against Colorado College back in 1986. I will never forget it, it was on homecoming weekend at the 'U.' I started out playing on the junior varsity. Well, it was a Friday night and we just got back from playing the Rochester Mustangs and we were all out at the bars celebrating that night. Meanwhile, it turned out that Brett Nelson had gotten injured in the Gopher varsity game that night, so they needed to bring in another player. Well, that was me. But, they didn't know how to get a hold of me. So, the team trainer called my parents in the middle of the night to track me down so that they could get me on a plane to Colorado Springs. Of course, this is the pre-cell phone era, so nobody knows how to find me. Finally, I get back to my dorm at about three in the morning and I see a note saying that I have an emergency message. Anyway, I call home and before I know it I am on a flight a few hours later heading out to join the team. I had no time to sleep or anything. But, I got into the line-up that night and played well enough to stay there indefinitely. It was pretty incredible how the whole thing happened, I will never forget it." — *Peter Hankinson, Gopher 1986-90*

"Without a doubt, beating New Hampshire to win the National Championship in 2003." — *Chris Harrington, Gopher 2002-Present*

"It would have to be the national championship in 2002. Winning that game with my team-mates was the ultimate way to end my college hockey career." — *Adam Hauser, Gopher 1998-2002*

"While nothing can compare to beating New Hampshire to win the National Championship in 2003, I would have to say beating North Dakota, 5-4, in the Final Five in 2004 was pretty sweet too." — *Tyler Hirsch, Gopher 2002-Present*

"I would have to say beating UND at the Xcel Center to win the Final Five last year. We just took it to them." — *Danny Irmen, Gopher 2003-Present*

"It would have to be the overtime game-winner I scored against North Dakota in the WCHA Playoffs back in 1993. What was so special about it was the fact that it was the last goal ever scored at Mariucci Arena. That was one I will never forget." — *Craig Johnson, Gopher 1990-93*

"How about all of them, they were all memorable to me. I loved them all. Just to be out there wearing the big 'M' on my chest was memorable for me." — *Trent Klatt, Gopher 1989-92*

"Nothing in my life will probably ever come close as to how amazing it was to score the equalizer against Maine in the 2002 National Championship game. I can't explain it but I was just in the zone that night. The puck came to me and I put it in the back of the net, what can I say? It was the most amazing feeling, I was really fortunate to have been in the right place at the right time. The most important thing about it though by far, was the fact that it just gave us a chance to win it in overtime. When Grant (Potulny) got the game-winner shortly thereafter, it was just indescribable." — *Matt Koalska, Gopher 2000-04*

"It would have to be the game where we beat Wisconsin at home in 1997, when we clinched a share of the WCHA title with North Dakota. We hung out together out on the ice after the game, listening to the Sioux game on the radio over the loudspeaker. When they lost we all went nuts, it was pretty sweet." — *Ryan Kraft, Gopher 1994-98*

"I will never forget the 1989 title game where they lost to Harvard in overtime over at the Civic Center. I just remember how the Gophers outplayed them that night but wound up losing a heartbreaker in the end. That was a tough one." — *Bob Kurtz, former Gopher Broadcaster*

"For sure it would have to be the national championship game against Maine in 2002. That was one of the greatest moments of my life and certainly something I will never, ever forget."
— *Jordan Leopold, Gopher 1999-02*

"Sadly, it's gotta be the national championship game that we lost to Harvard in overtime at the Civic Center. I have never, ever seen one highlight or replay from that game. It's just too painful. I never want to either. Sadly, it was the biggest highlight as well as the biggest low-light of my career." — *Cory Laylin, Gopher 1988-92*

"Not even close, beating Maine to win it all in 2002." — *Paul Martin, Gopher 2000-03*

"My first game, back in 1986. I was up in the booth with Wally Shaver for a WCHA Playoff game between the Gophers and Denver. I remember being in awe at the speed of the game, it was just so fast. It was funny, just prior to that, Tom Greenhoe, the Gopher Sports Information Director, asked me if he thought I could keep up with the pace. I said 'Tom, for crying out loud, I have been broadcasting minor league and NHL games for nearly 10 years now, of course I can keep up...' Well, it wasn't long after the game started that I was literally out of breath. The pace was just up and down, up and down. It was incredible. So, I will never forget my first Gopher game, it was special." — *Frank Mazzocco, Longtime Gopher TV Analyst*

"Even though we lost, it would have to be that damn Harvard game back in 1989, when we lost in the NCAA Finals at the Civic Center. We should have won that game. Sixteen years later it still bothers me." — *Jason Miller, Gopher 1987-91*

"It was against Boston College during my senior year when I wound up getting the overtime game-winner. That was just an amazing feeling and definitely something I will never forget it.
        "My other most memorable game would probably have to be the 1980 'Miracle on Ice' game where we beat the Soviets. Yes, my claim to fame, I played John Harrington in the Disney movie 'Miracle' a few years back and it was a blast. Being a Minnesota kid I grew up learning about the Miracle and about all of the local guys on the team under Herb Brooks. So, to be cast in it and to be a part of it was the thrill of a lifetime. I was in between teams while I was playing in the minors at the time and luckily got cast for the role. It was a wonderful diversion from the year world. I am just bummed that I didn't win an Oscar!" — *Nate Miller, Gopher 1996-00*

"Unfortunately, it would have to be the Harvard Finals loss back in 1989. There were other big games; fun games; and significant games, but none was more infamous than that one. It does-n't get any bigger than that." — *Larry Olimb, Gopher 1988-92*

"It would have to be the game against Harvard, where we lost in overtime in the NCAA Finals. That was big. It still haunts me. I hit the post with six minutes left and then Skarda hit it in overtime. Who knows what coulda been?" — *Tom Pederson, Gopher 1988-91*

"It's gotta be the 1989 loss to Harvard in the NCAA Finals at the Civic Center. I have yet to this day ever watched any of that game, it is too painful. I will never forget when (Randy) Skarda hit the pipe in overtime, I thought we won it right there. Then, to lose the way we did, on a funny bounce — it is still so painful even to think about it to this very day." — *Lance Pitlick, Gopher 1986-90*

"No question about it, the 2002 national championship. It was the most memorable game of my life!" — *Johnny Pohl, Gopher 1998-2002*

"Not even close, the 2002 national championship game over Maine." — *Grant Potulny, Gopher 2000-04*

"My first game as a Gopher. Coach Lucia put my brother Grant and I on the same line to start the game. It was the first time we had ever played together, at any level, and was something I will never forget. What made it even more special was the fact that my mom and dad drove down to watch it and it was my dad's birthday. I will never forget that night." — *Ryan Potulny, Gopher 2003-Present*

"I would have to say the night we beat Wisconsin to win a share of the WCHA title. After our game was over we all came back out onto the ice and sat around and listened to the North Dakota game on the radio over the loudspeaker. Like half of the fans stuck around and we wound up skating around on the ice and throwing a football back and forth. Then, when UND lost, we all went nuts and celebrated. That was just an amazing memory." — *Erik Rasmussen, Gopher 1995-97*

"It would have to be the game against Wisconsin back in 1997 where the players all stayed out on the ice after the game to listen to the Fighting Sioux game over the radio on the P.A. system. The fans all stuck around and the players were playing around out on the ice with a football as they were listening. Then, when UND lost, the Gophers all celebrated because they had clinched a tie for the WCHA title. That was really neat. — *Tommy Reid, Former Gopher TV & Radio Announcer*

"I think when we beat Northern Michigan my senior year to win our first ever WCHA Final Five. We had had a tough year and weren't really sure if we were even going to get an invitation to the NCAA's, so we just played like we had nothing to lose. That was pretty sweet." — *Travis Richards, Gopher 1989-93*

"While the two national championships were amazing, I would have to say my most memorable game was actually my last home game at Mariucci when we had senior night. To know that you were going to be skating there for the last time was really, really emotional. We had gone through so much and I just did not want it to end." — *Troy Riddle, Gopher 2000-04*

"It's not even close, the first national championship victory over Maine. It was by far the most thrilling moment I have ever experienced in hockey." — *Wally Shaver, Longtime Gopher Radio & TV Announcer*

"I would say it was my sophomore year in 1997 when we beat Wisconsin to win a share of the league championship. North Dakota was playing Denver that same night and after our game was over we all stayed out on the ice to listen to the game over the loudspeaker on the radio. We were throwing a football around out on the ice, tossing it up into the crowd, it was a blast. About half of the fans stayed with us and we all listened together, it was really neat. When the final score was announced, the fans just went nuts. I will never forget that." — *Wyatt Smith, Gopher 1995-99*

"The loss to North Dakota in the WCHA Final Five back in 1997. That was tough. But, I will always remember my first game up in Duluth my freshman year too. They had the 'Spehar Sucks' shirts out in force that night, it was definitely a memorable homecoming to say the least. We wound up losing and after the game UMD's Coach, Mike Sertich, went sliding head first into the net. That was one I will never forget." — *Dave Spehar, Gopher 1996-2000*

"While it was always fun playing North Dakota and Wisconsin, nothing will ever compare to winning the national championship in 2002 the way we did in St. Paul." — *Jeff Taffe, Gopher 1999-02*

"I think it would have to be the second national championship game against New Hampshire. I scored two goals and really felt a sense of accomplishment when we won that game and ended the season on such a high note." — *Barry Tallackson, Gopher 2001-05*

"I would say the game against Colorado College my senior year when Crowley scored the game-winner late in the third. Mariucci (Arena) just went nuts, I will never forget that." — *Dan Trebil, Gopher 1992-96*

"It's gotta be the 2003 national championship game where we beat New Hampshire. Even though I am playing in the National Hockey League now, that one will be tough to top for as long as I play this game." — *Thomas Vanek, Gopher 2002-04*

"I would have to say beating Cornell in 2005 to make it to the Frozen Four. That was a huge thrill and something I will never forget." — *Mike Vannelli, Gopher 2003-Present*

"I would say it was the playoff game against Colorado College in 2000, when we won in over-time, 3-2, out on their ice. That was huge. We kind of had the Lucia revenge factor going for us in that one too, with him having just left their program. So, that was memorable for sure." — *Erik Westrum, Gopher 1997-2001*

"That's easy, and for all the wrong reasons. It was the Harvard loss in the NCAA Finals back in 1989 at the Civic Center. That was so tough. It was one of those games that went down in infamy." — *Dean Williamson, Gopher 1987-90*

"I remember rallying back from like three goals down to beat North Dakota my freshman year. Peter Hankinson got the game-winner and it was just a very memorable game. It was at home and our fans went crazy. I can still see us all jumping over the boards after the game to pile on everybody out on the ice. That was special." — *Doug Zmolek, Gopher 1989-92*

CHAPTER 8
WHAT WAS YOUR MOST MEMORABLE GOPHER GOAL?

"I would have to say my first goal. It was against Alaska-Anchorage at home in Mariucci. It was surreal because I had been dreaming about what that would feel like since I was a little kid. And yes, that puck is sitting on my bar at my house here in Chicago — still in the case that Harry Broadfoot, our equipment manager, made for me." — *Mike Anderson, Gopher 1995-99*

"You know, I never scored any goals as a Gopher, but the most memorable goal that I was ever a part of was scored by Chad Roberg, against Team Latvia back in 2003. Just prior to the game he came into my office and told me that he wanted to quit. He said his grade point average was down to like 3.7 and he had had enough. I told him to hang on and just stick it out. It was real-ly emotional. Then, when he scored that goal, it was just amazing. The crowd absolutely went nuts. They were chanting 'Rudi-Rudi-Rudi!'. It was a very touching moment for me. He stuck it out and now he is a partner in a very successful banking business up in Duluth. We are still good friends and I couldn't be happier for the guy." — *Mark Bahr, Gopher 1991-94, Current Director of Hockey Operations*

"I can't even really remember one that stands out to tell you the truth." — *Keith Ballard, Gopher 2001-04*

"I would probably have to say the overtime goal I scored against Denver during the playoffs back in 1995. Bonin set me up and I put it in the net to win it. I wasn't a big goal scorer, in fact I could have used a shovel for most of them because they were usually right inside the crease, but that one is one I will never forget." — *Scott Bell, Gopher 1991-95*

"My first one, it was up at Michigan Tech. You never forget your first one, that one is special."
— *Reggie Berg, Gopher 1995-99*

"I would have to say it was in a playoff game against Michigan State in a total-goals series my freshman year. I came down on a two-on-one with Jay Cates and he passed it across the slot where I buried it. It turned out to be the series-winning goal, so that one was pretty special."
— *Grant Bischoff, Gopher 1987-91*

"I would probably have to say scoring an overtime game-winner against Duluth my freshman year, that was something I will never forget." — *Brian Bonin, Gopher 1992-96*

"I had so few goals, it shouldn't be that hard to remember! Well, it would have to be against Wisconsin where I scored a couple of goals in a 4-2 win. We were struggling that year, but that was a big win for us. Plus, that win knocked them out of the playoffs, which made it even sweeter." — *Bill Butters, Gopher Player 1971-73; Assistant Coach 1985-95*

"I would have to say scoring my first goal ever. It was an over-time game-winner against Mankato. I will never forget that one, it was really special." — *Kris Chucko, Gopher 2003-Present*

"I scored a natural hat-trick against Michigan Tech my freshman year. What was unique about it was that one was short-handed; one was even-strength; and one was on a power-play. So, that was pretty special." — *Ben Clymer, Gopher 1996-98*

"I would have to say the game-winner I got against Colorado College my sophomore year at Mariucci Arena. That was one I will always remember." — *Mike Crowley, Gopher 1994-97*

"Anytime our guys scored against Wisconsin was as good as it got for me, it really didn't matter who scored it, just as long as we beat those Badgers." — *Steve DeBus, Gopher 1995-98*

"I scored a goal in my first ever game as a Gopher, it was against Notre Dame. It all transpired back in that same dungeonous corner at the Old Barn where I used to watch the team as a kid, under that overhang. The puck took a weird bounce and landed on my stick. So, I just put it in the back of the net. It might have been the easiest goal I ever scored. The first one is so special because it just makes you feel like you are really a part of the program. I mean once you tally, it's official — you're in the books." — *Joe Dziedzic, Gopher 1990-94*

"I remember one in particular that I scored against Michigan Tech where I came in from my own blue line and then shot a slap shot outside of their blue line and somehow it went in. It was so stupid it was memorable. I later wound up playing with that goalie out here in the minors and he told me that he still remembered that goal. He said it was his first ever game and he was so nervous that he could hardly stand up. I felt bad for the guy, but hey, that's hockey."
— *Ken Gernander, Gopher 1988-91*

"My first goal, it came against the Badgers in Wisconsin." — *Mike Guentzel, Gopher Player 1981-85; Assistant Coach 1994-Present*

"Playing Michigan in the Frozen Four, we were down 2-1 in the third period, and Barry Tallackson threw the puck through traffic to me and I one-timed it home through the goalie's five hole to tie it up. That was amazing. Vanek then got the game-winner shortly thereafter to send us to the championship game." — *Gino Guyer, Gopher 2003-Present*

"My first one, against North Dakota. It was an ugly one too, right off my skate or shin or something. Yeah, I got to keep the puck, and I think my kids have long since deposited it into a snow bank out back somewhere!" — *Ben Hankinson, Gopher 1987-91*

"I had a couple of overtime game-winners as a freshman against Duluth and North Dakota.

There is just nothing more thrilling than jumping on your teammates after something like that." — *Casey Hankinson, Gopher 1994-98*

"It would have to be my first one. It came against UMD in my first home game. I won the face-off and got the puck back to Craig Mack, he then shot it and luckily I went right to the net and got the rebounder. It wasn't pretty but it was definitely memorable." — *Peter Hankinson, Gopher 1986-90*

"It would have to be my first one against Alabama Huntsville at Mariucci. And yes, that puck is on the fireplace mantle at my parent's house as we speak." — *Chris Harrington, Gopher 2002-Present*

"I have had so many at all of my levels of hockey, from the high school tourney to the Gophers to the Olympics to the NHL. If I had to pick one most memorable game I would have to say it was the Game Seven contest against Colorado on the road in the Stanley Cup Playoffs back when I was with the Wild. That was just something I will never forget." — *Darby Hendrickson, Gopher from 1991-93*

"I would have to say my first one, against Ohio State, in my first ever game. I got to keep the puck but to be honest, I have no idea whatsoever where it is." — *Tyler Hirsch, Gopher 2002-Present*

"Beating Wisconsin at home last year, I scored on a penalty shot late in the third period to win the game. We were short-handed with about eight minutes to go in the game. Briggs made a huge save and kicked the rebound out to me. The Badger player then dove at me and the ref blew the whistle. It was pretty controversial at the time. I wound up deking the goalie with a pretty good move and it wound up being the game-winner. It was just an amazing feeling." — *Danny Irmen, Gopher 2003-Present*

"I remember beating Denver I think it was to win the WCHA title back in 1992. After the game we were all skating around out on the ice with the MacNaughton Cup, just having fun and kicking back a little bit. It was a great memory, really special." — *Craig Johnson, Gopher 1990-93*

"My first one, it was against the Badgers in Wisconsin. That puck is sitting in my basement right now with the white tape and magic marker description of who it was against and the date still on it." — *Trent Klatt, Gopher 1989-92*

"My first goal, which came against UMD up in Duluth my freshman year. That puck is in my parent's basement as we speak." — *Ryan Kraft, Gopher 1994-98*

"I scored the over-time game-winner against Denver in my first ever series at Mariucci Arena. I will never forget that, it was such an amazing feeling." — *Cory Laylin, Gopher 1988-92*

"If I had to pick one, I would have to say the Mike Crowley game-winner against Colorado College at Mariucci back in 1996. It was really dramatic. He just held onto the puck for what seemed like forever and then came in and scored to break a 2-2 tie. If I had to pick one more I would pick the Keith Ballard overtime goal against North Dakota in the playoffs back in 2002 that started in our own end when Keith turtled a guy, or pulled his jersey up over his head, and then raced down the ice and slammed home a rebound that turned out to be the game-winner. That was something else." — *Frank Mazzocco, Longtime Gopher TV Analyst*

"It would have to be my first goal. It came my freshman year up at North Dakota against Eddie Belfour. I will never forget that one." — *Jason Miller, Gopher 1987-91*

"Scoring the game-winner against Colorado College in my first ever game as a Gopher. I whacked in a Nick Checco rebound out front and that was that. I was in the books, it was official." — *Nate Miller, Gopher 1996-00*

"I got the overtime game-winner to beat Lowell in the NCAA quarterfinals back in 1994. That was a really emotional win for us and a game I will always remember." — *Jeff Nielsen, Gopher 1990-94*

"I would have to say my last goal. It came against North Dakota in a best-of-three playoff series at Mariucci Arena. I got the game-winner in the third game to put us ahead for good. It was pretty special." — *Larry Olimb, Gopher 1988-92*

"My first one sticks out, against Colorado College." — *Tom Pederson, Gopher 1988-91*

"I scored the second goal in the 2002 national championship game, which put us up 2-1. That was pretty memorable. It was such a lucky shot too. I grabbed the puck and came down the left wing. I was tired, so I didn't even try to make a move or anything, I just shot it at the net. I had my head down and never even looked at the goalie. It was just a prayer and it got answered." — *Johnny Pohl, Gopher 1998-2002*

"Hmmmm. Let me see. OK. Got it. Scoring the overtime game-winner to beat Maine in the 2002 national championship game..." — *Grant Potulny, Gopher 2000-04*

"My first goal, I scored it against St. Cloud. It was special to me because I had five assists through my first eight games as a freshmen, and then I blew my knee out. So, I was on the shelf for a long time before I was able to come back. I thought I was going to be out that entire year, but luckily was able to return sooner than expected. I was really happy for all the other freshmen when they got their first goals, but I was jealous, I wanted my own. So, when I finally got healthy and was able to find the back of the net in my first game back, it was a big deal to me. Vanek shot the puck and the rebound came right to me and I buried it. It was even the game-winner which gave us the home-ice advantage for the playoffs, so it was a big one on a lot of levels for me." — *Ryan Potulny, Gopher 2003-Present*

"I would have to say my first one, because it took me a while. It was against St. Cloud and it wasn't pretty." — *Erik Rasmussen, Gopher 1995-97*

"My first one. I crashed into the net like a zamboni against Northern Michigan. John Anderson passed the puck across the slot and I just tried to tip it and wound up plowing into the goalie." — *Travis Richards, Gopher 1989-93*

"Probably my first one, against Notre Dame." — *Troy Riddle, Gopher 2000-04*

"I would have to say my first ever goal, against Alaska Anchorage in 1995. That puck is in my parents living room as we speak." — *Wyatt Smith, Gopher 1995-99*

"I remember one time playing against Colorado College. I came in on a break-away and totally pooched a shot over the net and it bounced off the glass in front of the net, where I batted it out of midair and into the net. That one was awesome." — *Dave Spehar, Gopher 1996-2000*

"I would have to say scoring in the Michigan game during the 2002 Frozen Four. I got my picture in the paper the next day and was pretty excited about contributing to the effort which ultimately got us into the Finals." — *Jeff Taffe, Gopher 1999-02*

"It would have to be scoring the overtime game-winner against Cornell in 2005 to put us back into the Frozen Four. That was just amazing, I will never forget it." — *Barry Tallackson, Gopher 2001-05*

"The most memorable goal I ever saw was when Nate Miller scored an overtime game-winner to upset then No. 1 ranked Boston College back in 1998. It was just one of the prettiest hockey goals I have ever seen in my life. He worked his butt off; threw a check; skated hard; and just wound up scrapping for a loose puck out front. I even refer to hard-working goals now with my son as 'Nate Miller Goals.' Nate is probably my favorite all-time Gopher too, he is just a great kid. He was the nicest guy off the ice, but when he was playing — watch out. He was a real competitor. I thought it was so neat that he got a role in the movie Miracle too, that was a lot of fun." — *Dan Terhaar, Former Gopher Radio Announcer*

"Probably my first one, it was a little wrister from the blue line against Michigan Tech." — *Dan Trebil, Gopher 1992-96*

"Scoring the game-winner in the 2003 national championship game, it doesn't get any bigger than that. It was a three-on-two and Matty Koalska passed it over to me. I just went around the defensemen and wound up beating the New Hampshire goalie, it was amazing." — *Thomas Vanek, Gopher 2002-04*

"I scored one against Michigan in 2004 that was pretty sweet. We were ranked No. 1 and they were No. 2 at the time, so it was a big win for us." — *Mike Vannelli, Gopher 2003-Present*

"It would probably have to be my first one, it came against North Dakota when I was a freshman. Anytime you can score against the Sioux it is great, but that one was special for sure." — *Erik Westrum, Gopher 1997-2001*

"My first one. It was by far the most memorable and important one I ever scored as well. It was up at Duluth and I got the overtime game-winner. I was just filling in that game because a bunch of guys were sick and a few others had to sit out for fighting. I mean it was like I was the last guy on the bench, so I got in there by default. It was my only shot of the game too, so I was batting 1.000. As a result, I got put into the line-up for that next weekend against Colorado College, where I got my second goal — which also happened to be an overtime game-winner. So, my first two goals were overtime game-winners. It was amazing. I should have retired right then and there, because it was all down hill after that!" — *Dean Williamson, Gopher 1987-90*

"I got the overtime game-winner one time to beat UMD, which was pretty rare because I didn't light the lamp very often." — *Doug Zmolek, Gopher 1989-92*

CHAPTER 9
SHOULD THEY STILL BE THE ALL-MINNESOTA GOPHERS?

"No. The tradition was great at the time, but I would much rather see our program stay at the top and keep on winning national championships. If that means bringing in other top players from outside of the state, so be it. I am all for it. I mean how do you turn down a kid like Phil Kessel, who is from Wisconsin? You don't. I would hope, however, that if all things were equal, and it came down to a kid from Minnesota versus a kid from Canada, that they would give the scholarship to the Minnesota kid. That is just me. Overall though, I think Lucia is doing a great job and I am all for the way he is going about establishing his own identity." — *Mike Anderson, Gopher 1995-99*

"Wooger tried it for years and came close so many times, but just couldn't get it done. Sure, it was a cool tradition, but it isn't realistic anymore. There are so many kids leaving high school now to play juniors and they all want full-ride scholarships, so it is tough to get all of the top local kids. The way Coach Lucia has integrated other kids into the program has been great and I think the resulting two national championships pretty much speak for themselves." — *Mark Bahr, Gopher 1991-94, Current Director of Hockey Operations*

"No. If you can get the best players from Minnesota, then that is where you should start. It is most kids' dream around here to grow up and play for the Gophers, so I don't think we will ever see the core nucleus ever be anything but that. I also think that if you don't recruit the top kids, regardless of where they come from, then you are eventually setting yourself up for failure. I mean the game has grown so much over the past several years. It used to be that the only place top kids came out of was Canada, Minnesota, Michigan and Massachusetts. Now, look around, we are seeing top-flight talent coming from all over the place, including the west coast and Europe. So, Coach Lucia is a great recruiter and will never steer this program in the wrong direction." — *Keith Ballard, Gopher 2001-04*

"Sure, it would be great if they were still all Minnesota kids, but that is simply not realistic anymore. Recruiting is way too tough these days and there is way too much competition. There aren't a lot of kids like myself, who took a quarter scholarship over a full-ride elsewhere, just to fulfill the dream of playing for the Gophers. Nowadays things are much different and the program has had to change and adapt in order to be successful. Hey, it's hard to argue with their results. Thomas Vanek, for instance, was from Austria. He was also an extremely special player. That is what I like. If they are going to get kids from far, far away, then hopefully those kids are going to be special, memorable players who really make a difference. Grant Potulny was from North Dakota, he was an amazing leader. Phil Kessel is from Wisconsin and by all accounts has the potential to be one of the great ones. So, I am all for giving Minnesota kids opportunities and scholarships, first and foremost, but I also understand the business of hockey. I was just lucky to have played there when it was all Minnesota kids and I will leave it at that." — *Scott Bell, Gopher 1991-95*

"Well, it's kind of hard to argue with the results that they have gotten! Coach Lucia obviously knows what he is doing. Sure, it was a special time for us, being a part of the Woog era that did that, but times change and I am OK with it. College hockey is so competitive and you have to get the best players available nowadays, regardless of where they are from. Hopefully that competition just raises the bar for Minnesota kids to make them want to come there even more." — *Reggie Berg, Gopher 1995-99*

"How do you argue with what Donny Lucia is doing down there. Of course, I am a little biased, being that we are both from Grand Rapids and all! Really though, it was a neat tradition under Woog when I was around, but college hockey is so competitive now — they need to get the best kids in order to stay on top." — *Grant Bischoff, Gopher 1987-91*

"I never had a problem with it being all-Minnesota kids. That was how Doug (Woog) recruited and he believed in it, so I supported him for that. He was my boss and that was he wanted. Don (Lucia) was a different coach and he believed that you needed to have some diversity to be successful. I totally support his decision too. Hey, you certainly can't argue with the results." — *Patty Bjorklund, Longtime Gopher Hockey Administrative Assistant*

"I don't think so. We need to be competitive and we need to open it up to more players. Yes, it was a neat tradition, having all Minnesota kids, and I was lucky to be a part of it. But times have changed and we needed to move on. You know, part of it I think was the fact that the coaches needed to do that in order to convince all of the Minnesota kids that they needed to go spend a couple of years playing juniors before they could suit up. Most kids several years ago didn't want to do that, but when they saw the level of competition coming in they didn't have a choice. This league is so tough now, I don't know how an 18 year-old can play right out of the gates. They need some seasoning and that is why they are all playing juniors. Like it or not, I think that is just the reality of college hockey nowadays. Beyond that, there are five division I schools here now and quite frankly, it was getting tougher and tougher to get the top kids from Minnesota every year. Kids have more options and they want to go where they will have the best chance of getting ice time and winning. So, it is an entirely different ballgame." — *Brian Bonin, Gopher 1992-96*

"Ummmm… Being that I am from Canada, that would have to be no." — *Kris Chucko, Gopher 2003-Present*

"I feel very strongly that they should still be all-Minnesota kids. I may be in the minority saying that, but that is just how I feel. To be able to play with the guys that you grew up with is so special and so unique. That was the greatest tradition in all of college sports in my opinion. It's like the Montreal Canadiens in the NHL when they sign up all the French Canadian guys — it is just an amazing source of pride for those people. I mean Minnesota for sure has enough great players to win it all. No question. They came so close on so many occasions under Wooger. Who knows? If they would have won it any one of those times, maybe Woog is still coaching and we aren't even having this conversation." — *Ben Clymer, Gopher 1996-98*

"All I can say is that I loved playing with all Minnesota guys when I was there. It was so special and so unique, I wouldn't have traded that experience for anything. Now it is a totally different deal. Not only are they recruiting kids from other states, they are looking in Canada and Europe as well. The bottom line is that they are winning and they have won two national championships, so how can you argue with that?" — *Mike Crowley, Gopher 1994-97*

"I have feelings both ways. On one hand I think that there are enough good Minnesota kids who can get the job done. On the other hand, how can you turn down other good players out there who want to come to the 'U' and be a Gopher? You gotta take them and get the best guys who can help you win national championships, that is the bottom line. Selfishly though, I would still love to see the all-Minnesota Gophers, that was a really fun era." — *Steve DeBus, Gopher 1995-98*

"No, I don't think it is necessary. I think Lucia has handled it perfectly to tell you the truth. He is getting the elite talent from Minnesota and then filling in the gaps elsewhere. How do you say no to Thomas Vanek, from Austria, or Phil Kessel, from Wisconsin? You don't. Or how about Grant and Ryan Potulny, from North Dakota? It is still mostly Minnesota kids and the diversity can only help the program down the road as far as I am concerned." — *Jeff Dubay, KFAN Radio Host & Longtime Gopher Fanatic*

"I personally liked it when it was all Minnesota guys, but how can you knock Coach Lucia for what he has accomplished? More power to him for believing in that and then backing it up the way he did." — *Joe Dziedzic, Gopher 1990-94*

"I think so. That was a great source of pride for the state. I mean that is where all your support comes from, right? So, why not. You have plenty of kids to draw from and you have the best facilities around. I say heck yeah, that was a great tradition. I am not against other kids from outside the state, I am just for Minnesotans." — *Ken Gernander, Gopher 1988-91*

"I am a Minnesota boy, so I really liked that tradition. Times change though and now it's kind of like saying we should still have a governor on a lawn mower. So, truthfully, I would have loved for them to say all-Minnesota, but I don't know if they could have kept up with the Jones'. So, in the final analysis, if we are seeing the best college hockey players here and are still winning titles, then I am OK with it." — *Eric Gislason, Former Gopher Radio & Television Commentator*

"I believe very strongly in what Don (Lucia) is doing. Times change. When I was an assistant under Doug (Woog) I supported that policy, but it is a much different situation now in college hockey. We will always be predominantly Minnesota kids because there is such an abundance of talent here. But, it is our job to field the best team possible, and if that means bringing in a certain special kid, then that is what we will do. We can't be close-minded enough to shut kids out of coming here just because they aren't from here. And hey, with two national champi-onships it is sure hard to argue with the results." — *Mike Guentzel, Gopher Player 1981-85; Assistant Coach 1994-Present*

"In theory, it would be great if we could still go with only the Minnesota guys, but times change and we need to stay competitive with everybody else. The players coming in are older and more experienced nowadays, so every team has had to raise the bar talent-wise. I think that Don (Lucia) has done a great job of picking the right players and has been very respectful of the entire situation. It is still primarily Minnesota kids, which is great, and the other guys just enhance the diversity of the program. That is a good thing. I mean let's face it, Grant Potulny, from North Dakota, and Thomas Vanek, from Austria, were arguably the two biggest factors in each of the national championships. So, how do you argue with that?" — *Ben Hankinson, Gopher 1987-91*

"I don't think so. I think that was a great time and a fun era, but those days are long gone. Lucia has been very respectful about who he has recruited and he is just an awesome coach. You can't argue with the success the team has had and the bottom line is that everybody still enjoys the product out on the ice. Nobody looks at the team any differently now than they did under Woog's tenure. In fact, one of the negative things about having all-Minnesota kids was the fact that there was always a pecking order in the locker room. Guys felt that just because they might have been better than other guys in high school, then that should translate into the college game too. So, as close as we all were, you would always have a little bit of that stuff. Now, I don't think you have that because guys are coming from different states, different countries and of course, from junior hockey as well. So, it's all good." — *Casey Hankinson, Gopher 1994-98*

"When I started back in 1986 we had Steve MacSwain and Johnny Blue, who were from Alaska and California, respectively. Those were just great guys, really good people. From there, Wooger started his system of taking only Minnesota kids. So, it was neat to have all Minnesota guys, but certainly having players from different backgrounds is healthy for your team's chem-istry too. I think the way Lucia is doing it now is great, with the core group of guys being from Minnesota, while still taking other out-state kids too." — *Peter Hankinson, Gopher 1986-90*

"There are a lot of different debates about this. I grew up in a time when that was the tradition and it was really unique and special. That all changed when Coach Lucia came in though and it is hard to argue with the results that have followed. So, I am OK with it, programs have to evolve and change and this is a prime example of that. They have brought in some great kids who have really contributed and that is the most important thing. We have five division one schools here now and times have changed. Not every kid wants to play on the third line with the Gophers when he could be a first liner at Bemidji or Mankato. So, with the competition for the top kids today and with so many kids playing junior hockey after high school, I think we need to get the top kids who will give us the best chance of winning national championships." — *Darby Hendrickson, Gopher from 1991-93*

"Ahh, being that I am from North Dakota, that would have to be a big fat NO!" — *Danny Irmen, Gopher 2003-Present*

"It's debatable but I don't think so. The talent level outside of the state has really improved for one thing, and the other is the fact that high school kids in Minnesota don't play enough games. That is why they are all having to go play juniors now before coming to college. I think the recruiting outside of Minnesota is fine, as long as those guys are excited to be Gophers and wear that 'M' proudly." — *Craig Johnson, Gopher 1990-93*

"Personally, yes. I loved that tradition, it was so special to suit up and play alongside so many great guys from your home-state. But, in order for the team to win and be successful, I think that they needed to look elsewhere. If they went with all Minnesota kids they would be at a serious disadvantage. All of the other programs are taking kids who played two years of jun-ior hockey and have 80, 90 even 100 games of experience as incoming freshmen. Meanwhile, our high school seniors in Minnesota play just 22 games. I know that a lot of Minnesota kids are playing juniors too, but in order for the program to keep a lot of the top talent, they have to promise those kids roster sports as freshmen and then let them develop. If they don't, they will go elsewhere where they can play right away and still get their full ride. So, it is a tough situation. Overall though, I am glad the way Coach Lucia has made the transition, and he obviously knows what he is doing given the fact that he just won two national championships." — *Trent Klatt, Gopher 1989-92*

"I don't think so. Times have changed. What Doug Woog did was a special thing, and I was lucky to be a part of that. But, in order to win a national championship in today's competitive environment, I think they had to make a change. So, Lucia did the right thing by bringing in some other key guys. I mean for the most part it still is and probably always will be a predominantly all-Minnesota team, so that is OK. Hey, if they need to go outside of the state to get a certain player, then I am all for it if it will help the team's chances of winning more NCAA titles." — *Ryan Kraft, Gopher 1994-98*

"While Woog's philosophy of using all Minnesota players was great, I think college hockey has become much more global. I guess I never thought straining from the state borders was ever a bad idea. So, when Lucia came in and brought in some kids from out-state, it turned out to be just what the program needed. I mean it is hard to argue with the results, that is for sure." — *Bob Kurtz, former Gopher Broadcaster*

"For as long as Minnesota had hockey, it was only that brief 12 year period or so that we didn't recruit non-Minnesota kids. What I always say is that they are all Minnesota hockey players, where they were born doesn't make much difference. Once you put that 'M' sweater on, you're representing the state of Minnesota and you are a Gopher. Period. To me 'Pride on Ice' does not mean an all-Minnesota team, it is taking in pride in the hockey program at the University of Minnesota and supporting whoever is wearing a maroon and gold jersey." — *Don Lucia, Current Gopher Head Coach*

"No. Doug (Woog) had Herbie's (Brooks) vision, of taking Minnesota kids, but he also had the great timing when there was a bounty of players coming out of Minnesota high schools. I don't think we have that depth any more. You can argue against that, but if we do, then there are definitely more schools plucking away at them. So, to win a national championship, you have to have national players. You have to draw from the best available pool to win, and that is OK. Doug stuck to his guns for as long as he could though and you have to respect that, because it was great while it lasted." — *Frank Mazzocco, Longtime Gopher TV Analyst*

"No. They had a great run doing that and it was certainly a neat tradition that I was proud to be a part of, but times have changed. To be competitive they need to bring in the top kids nowadays. With kids going on to juniors now, the high school talent isn't what it used to be in years past, so you have to adapt. You know, even back when I was playing we used to sometimes question why we never went out and got that one big goal scorer or a seasoned goaltender. You were always going up against the tougher Canadian kids, who were older and had more experience, and maybe that would have gotten us over the hump earlier. Who knows? We did OK, and Coach Lucia is obviously doing great, so he doesn't need any advice from me." — *Chris McAlpine, Gopher 1990-94*

"As a coach, you have to stay competitive. So, from that perspective I would have to say no. But, as a player, personally, I loved that tradition and feel really lucky that I was a part of it when I played." — *Jason Miller, Gopher 1987-91*

"Hey, the ultimate goal should always be winning national championships. So, if bringing in outside guys to help you do that is what it takes, then so be it. Let's face it, Minnesota is always going to draw the top local kids, but if you can get key guys elsewhere who can help, then that is fine." — *Jeff Nielsen, Gopher 1990-94*

"No. It is not necessary to force the coach to have to do that. It was a great thing Doug Woog did, but that was another era of Gopher Hockey. I admire him for doing it as long as he did, but times change and you have to move on. The tradition is the same and that is what matters most." — *Larry Olimb, Gopher 1988-92*

"No. I think it was stupid. Everybody knew that we were a Minnesota team, but it wasn't necessary to exclude other kids just because they weren't from here. Correct me if I am wrong, but was Grant Potulny from Minnesota? There is your answer right there." — *Tom Pederson, Gopher 1988-91*

"I don't think so. You have to go after the best kids first and foremost. I mean what are the odds that the best kids are going to be from Minnesota each and every year? Not very good. So, you have to mix it up nowadays and bring in kids from different areas to compliment your core group of Minnesotans. The kids today all come out of junior hockey too, which has changed the landscape of college hockey recruiting immensely. Plus, there is so much competition for our state's blue-chip kids, that it is impossible to get all of them. Even the ones you do get are going to insist on coming in as 18 year old freshmen, which means they are already behind the curve of the other freshman who are 20. Those extra two years that they get down in the juniors are huge. They play three times as many games as do the high school kids and they pack on an extra 20 pounds of muscle too. So, it is a whole new ballgame today." — *Lance Pitlick, Gopher 1986-90*

"Come on. Do you mean to tell me that Grant Potulny shouldn't be a Gopher just because he is from Grand Forks? No way." — *Johnny Pohl, Gopher 1998-2002*

"Seeing that I am from North Dakota, I would have to say a big NO!" — *Grant Potulny, Gopher 2000-04*

"I would hope not, otherwise I wouldn't be here..." — Ryan Potulny, Gopher 2003-Present

"No. I think if you have a chance to get a kid who is going to fit in well with the program, then you take him — regardless of where he is from. It was great having it be all Minnesota kids when I was there, but it certainly didn't have to be. In my opinion it is not about taking the most talented kids, it is about taking the right kids who are going to be the best fit with the program. Lucia has done a great job with that and has really turned the program around. It is so great to see us back up on top again." — *Erik Rasmussen, Gopher 1995-97*

"I thought it was a really cool tradition and we were for sure good enough to win it all, we just didn't catch a lucky bounce here or there. So, it could have been done, no question. As for now, sure, if they want to bring in other kids then that is fine. It is sure hard to argue with the success that they have been having as of late." — *Travis Richards, Gopher 1989-93*

"No way. I mean come on. Grant Potulny is one of my best friends. Under the old system I never would have even met the guy, let alone been able to play hockey with him. Just because a guy is from North Dakota doesn't mean he should be denied the opportunity to be a part of this great tradition. Hey, where would we be without Grant right now? We certainly wouldn't be back-to-back national champions, that is for sure. So, I think the way Coach Lucia has done it has been great. I am sure that the team will always be mostly Minnesotan, and deservedly so, but we should always have room for great players who want to help us win and be successful. That's what this is all about." — *Troy Riddle, Gopher 2000-04*

"No. Times have changed and I am glad they went that way. Sure, it was great while it lasted, but they needed to go in a different direction to get to the next level. I can tell you too, from being in the National Hockey League, that they got a lot of respect on a national level, outside of Minnesota, for doing that. I know that a lot more top recruits want to go there now and that can only be good for the program's success in the long run. Plus, having a good mix of guys from diverse backgrounds is good for the team's chemistry. Not that it was bad when I was there or anything, but overall I think it is good for guys to be around different people. They learn a lot both on and off the ice." — *Wyatt Smith, Gopher 1995-99*

"I'm all for change, because change is good. Having said that, I will say that when we were all-Minnesota kids it was awesome. But, times change and you certainly can't argue with the results of what has happened over the past few years. Overall, having kids from other states and other countries is just a credit to the University of Minnesota. So, it's all good." — *Dave Spehar, Gopher 1996-2000*

"No. It's not fair to prevent guys from coming here to be a part of this. Obviously, we all want the best Minnesota kids to come here, but guess what, every other school is probably going after those guys as well. So, it is really competitive nowadays and we need to get the top kids from all over to stay on top." — *Jeff Taffe, Gopher 1999-02*

"There are a lot of die-hards who wish that they never would have changed their policy on that, but it is pretty hard to argue with what Coach Lucia has done. I enjoyed it while I was there, but things change. So, it is OK." — *Dan Trebil, Gopher 1992-96*

"It all happened during my senior year, when we had the coaching transition from Woog to Lucia and we started taking guys from outside of Minnesota. Lucia figured that if we were going to be able to compete at the elite level, which I would consider to be the top four teams in the nation, then you have to go outside your comfort zone. For so long that comfort zone was to get the top Minnesota kids. Well, now with so much competition and all the kids going the junior hockey route, things had to change. To open that door and extend opportunities to other guys, such as Grant Potulny from North Dakota or Thomas Vanek from Austria, that just makes everyone better. So, I am OK with it." — *Erik Westrum, Gopher 1997-2001*

"No. I mean my dad was from Canada and he was a Gopher All-American back in his day. So was Lou Nanne. Those guys were a huge part of Gopher Hockey. So, the program has always had a lot of diversity in it, other than the small window of when Woog was coaching. Now, I was a part of that era and thought it was amazing. But, I certainly don't think we should discriminate from allowing other players from out-of-state to come here and contribute and enjoy our rich tradition. Of course, the majority of our talent is going to come from this pool, but in order to compete and thrive, we need to get the best kids, regardless of where they come from. Plus, with college hockey being so ultra competitive now, all of the other schools raid Minnesota for the top talent. A lot of kids can get full rides elsewhere, whereas here they may only get a partial scholarship. So, we aren't going to get every blue-chipper ever year, there is just no way. So, we need to expand our talent pool. Plus, it is healthy for a program to have kids from elsewhere. I mean my first year I was great friends with Steve MacSwain, who was from Alaska. He added a ton to the team's chemistry and was just a great guy. And hey, I think a big part of the team's success the past few years has been because of their chemistry." — *Dean Williamson, Gopher 1987-90*

"For me, it all went back to John Mariucci's dream of giving the American kids a chance to play college hockey. I guess I took that one step further at the University by going after only Minnesota kids. My vision was a tribute and a thank you to Maroosh for all that he did for us. And really, to see that evolution and to give our kids the opportunity, that may be more important to me than coaching for 45 years. A lot of people don't know the history of all this, but it goes way back to American kids just not having the chances to play at the next level. Back in our day there were so few opportunities. Thank God for John Mariucci, who just gave me the chance, because at the time there were very few of them out there for us. Because most of the coaches were Canadian, the vast, vast majority of the scholarships then went to the Canadian kids. Then, even after those kids graduated and went on to play professionally, they took most of those jobs too. It was a double whammy.

"So, it was tough for our era of players, and I just wanted to make sure that our kids had more opportunities than we did. Was it controversial? No question. But we stuck to it and were proud of our decision. It was nothing against anybody else. It wasn't anti-Canadian by any means, it was just pro-Minnesotan. That's all. John (Mariucci) wasn't anti-Canadian either, he was just anti-older Canadian players, the 22 year old freshmen who competed against our 18-year-old kids. But hey, you know, with a couple of breaks here or there, there is no question in my mind that we would have won some titles along the way. So, do I have any regrets? None.

"You know, it is tough to get all the top local kids nowadays. With so many kids playing junior hockey and all five D-I programs here, as well as North Dakota and Wisconsin, players are going to go where they A) get the best deal, and B) get the most ice time. I remember guys like Scotty Bell who had a full-ride offer at CC, but came here on a quarter scholarship. Heck, our first seven captains, guys like Benny Hankinson and Lance Pitlick, were all half-scholarship guys. You don't see much of that anymore today. The top players want the full-rides and they have a lot more options to get what they want.

"Now, as far as what Donny (Lucia) has done? I think he is an outstanding coach and has done such a great job of recruiting. I am glad he is doing it his own way and on his own terms. He knows what he is doing and he has two national championships to prove it." — *Doug Woog, Former Gopher Player & Coach; current Gopher Hockey TV Analyst*

"No. It was special to be a part of 'Minnesota's Pride on Ice,' with all the local kids, but the game has changed so much in the past 10 years or so that it is just unrealistic. I am great friends with a lot of Canadian hockey players from my time in the NHL and I couldn't imagine now not letting them come here just because they aren't from here. So, it was a good decision to change it." — *Doug Zmolek, Gopher 1989-92*

CHAPTER 10
ARE ENOUGH GOPHERS GOING ON TO THE NEXT LEVEL?

"In my opinion, if a kid really wants to go to the National Hockey League, he shouldn't even bother going to college. They should go straight to Canada to play major juniors and learn that system right out of the gates. So, for the kids from the collegiate ranks who actually do make it, that is even more impressive when you really think about it. Having said that, I think Minnesota kids have done really well and have been getting into the pro ranks. Would I like to see more? Absolutely. But, those guys also leave here with a college degree and the memories of playing at the best college hockey program in the country. So, you have to look at it that way too I think." — *Mike Anderson, Gopher 1995-99*

"I definitely think so. In fact, now that the NHL has its new agreement in place for rookies, I think we could be seeing a lot more players making the jump to the pros in the ensuing years to come too." — *Mark Bahr, Gopher 1991-94, Current Director of Hockey Operations*

"I think so. We have had a lot of great players come through here over the years and many of them are playing pro hockey right now. Success is contagious I think. I mean because of our success the past couple of years, that is only going to attract more top kids and the cycle will just keep repeating itself. So, you watch, over the next five years we are going to see a ton of Minnesota kids up in the NHL. I am thrilled to be with Phoenix right now, and I hope to be playing against a bunch of my old Gopher teammates up in the big leagues in the very near future — that would just be awesome." — *Keith Ballard, Gopher 2001-04*

"I think so. It is great to see guys like Jordan Leopold and Paul Martin doing so well. Would it be nice to see more guys playing in the NHL? Sure, but I look at it as not just the number of Gophers that are making the jump, but the number of Minnesota kids. When you look at those numbers, I think we are doing really well. We have a lot of kids who are playing at the top level right now and that is just fantastic for Minnesota hockey as a whole." — *Scott Bell, Gopher 1991-95*

"I think that every kid who plays for the Gophers has aspirations of playing in the NHL, I know that I certainly did. But as many of us find out, it is a tough transition. I think we are getting a lot of guys into the pros, but even from the minors to the NHL is a big step. As long as guys continue to work hard and keep plugging away though, then eventually good things will happen for them. By the time you get to that level so many things have to happen in order for it to work out and you really need to catch a break." — *Reggie Berg, Gopher 1995-99*

"I think that there is a reason as to why we have seen several All-American defenseman come out of here over the past few years in Leopold, Martin and Tallackson. That big ice sheet at Mariucci Arena forces guys to be really quick, especially the defensemen. They have to be extremely mobile in order to cover that extra room out there. As a result, when those guys play on the smaller sheets of ice in the pros, they are just on top of their opponents even that much quicker. It is no coincidence that all three of those guys went directly to the NHL and have had immediate success in my opinion." — *Grant Bischoff, Gopher 1987-91*

"You know, I don't think it is the coach's job to get kids onto the next level. Their job is to win games and to foster good student-athletes. Hopefully, they can teach them and encourage them to get onto the next level, but in the end that is up to the individuals. College hockey shouldn't be the NHL's minor league. No way. It should be about kids developing, learning, winning and having fun. Having said that, coaches have to realize that the top kids coming into their programs all want to use that school as a stepping-stone on their way up to the NHL. So, it is a delicate situation to say the least. Trust me though, the college game is entirely different from the pro game. It is not even close. The players are so amazingly good in the NHL it is not even funny. Guys like Peter Forsberg and Joe Sakic are light years beyond what I could ever imagine doing. In college you have skill players, whereas in the pros you have skill players playing alongside goons who are out their to crush people. To make the leap to the pros, you have to play a certain role and you have be damn good at that role in order to make it. The NHL is about mistake-free hockey, whereas college hockey is about smaller guys developing and learning from their mistakes. It is night and day, and really, that is why not a lot of college hockey players make it at the next level." — *Brian Bonin, Gopher 1992-96*

"Yes, the Gophers are putting players in pro hockey. Now, are enough players going on to the NHL? Perhaps. There are a lot of other Minnesota guys making it too, guys from here but didn't necessarily play for the Gophers. We have had some success stories, certainly with guys like Martin and Leopold as of late, and there are others too. I know that I recruited and coached a lot of guys from my era who made it, guys like Doug Zmolek, Lance Pitlick, Darby Hendrickson, Randy Skarda, Craig Johnson, Trent Klatt, Tom Chorske, Tommy Pederson and Joe Dziedzic, to name a few. So, there were a ton of guys who had decent NHL careers and there will certainly be more as we move forward." — *Bill Butters, Gopher Player 1971-73; Assistant Coach 1985-95*

"I think so. I think the total number of Americans playing in the NHL is only about 15%, so we are not talking about a ton of people here. I think that number is going to go way up in the future though, particularly because they are recruiting blue chip kids from other states as well as in Canada and Europe. Plus, those kids are getting more exposure there now than ever. Just wait, there will be more Gophers coming down the pipeline." — *Mike Crowley, Gopher 1994-97*

"It seems like it. We have had a whole bunch of guys sign NHL contracts as of late and that is just fantastic to see. Several of them are already playing with the big clubs and a lot more are waiting in the wings in the minors just waiting for their opportunities. So, it is going well and

I think more kids will be joining them in the future from Minnesota too." — *Steve DeBus, Gopher 1995-98*

"I think we are getting back on track as of late, with guys like Paul Martin, Thomas Vanek and Jordan Leopold, but we were definitely in a little dip for a while there. So, that is great to see. The fact that more and more kids are coming out of junior hockey now, and are much more seasoned coming into the program, will result in a lot more Gophers making it at the next level in the ensuing years I think. You know, when I was playing in the NHL I saw how hard it was for guys to make it. I was lucky, I was a bigger guy and found a role as a third liner and embraced it. Frankly, a lot of the college guys don't want to have to pay their dues and do the dirty work down in the minors. They have a safety net in their college degrees, whereas a lot of the Canadian kids don't have that. So, they may be more inclined to tough it out for longer than the college guys because they have more to lose. I don't know, just a theory." — *Joe Dziedzic, Gopher 1990-94*

"That is not the essence of college hockey I don't think. I mean they are not recruiting guys who they think will be good pros. If you are fortunate enough to have players who are good enough to go on to the next level, that is great, but that shouldn't be the focus in my opinion. I think they should worry about making sure kids have a great four year experience, play hard, and leave with a degree. That is what it is all about." — *Ken Gernander, Gopher 1988-91*

"You always want to see more, that is for sure. That is what we as fans live for, seeing one of our own making it at the highest level. That makes us all feel proud. But hey, it is tough, otherwise more of our guys would be up there. There are a lot more Europeans in the league now too, which has made a big difference. You know, it is cyclical. I can remember just starting out as a reporter up in Duluth back in the early '80s and covering guys like Brett Hull, Billy Watson, Tom Kurvers, Jimmy Johnson and Norm Maciver — all of whom went on to play in the pros. So, the Gophers have had their share make it and they will certainly have more in the future — especially with the new rules in the NHL which benefit the skill players. We'll be OK." — *Eric Gislason, Former Gopher Radio & Television Commentator*

"Yes. I think we have a very fair representation of players that leave our program to go play professional hockey. You know, pro hockey is not for everybody, myself included, but I think we do a great job of preparing guys for that next step in life — whether that is their life in hockey or their life out of hockey. Either way, these student-athletes are going to get an opportunity to earn their degrees from the University of Minnesota. What they do with it at that point is on them. Hopefully they will use that along with the exposure that they got here and any contacts that they have made to parlay that into their business careers. It is the same way in hockey too. Once our kids leave here to make the jump to pro hockey, it is up to them to take their games to the next level and then hope to catch a break. Overall though, I think we have had a lot of kids make it in the NHL and a whole bunch more are waiting on the doorstep playing in the minor leagues." — *Mike Guentzel, Gopher Player 1981-85; Assistant Coach 1994-Present*

"As of late, definitely. Over the past five years or so we have certainly been amongst the leaders of most college programs with regards to getting kids onto the next levels. Is there room for more? Absolutely." — *Gino Guyer, Gopher 2003-Present*

"Yes, absolutely. I mean some programs might have a little bit more success in terms of getting their kids onto the NHL, but those teams are recruiting a lot more kids out of the major junior ranks in Canada too. So, we are doing OK and hopefully that will continue to grow in the future." — *Ben Hankinson, Gopher 1987-91*

"Absolutely. However, it amazes just how may more players from Boston wind up becoming NHLers than we do. My theory on that is we only play 22 games a year in high school, which just isn't enough. Of course, that is a catch-22 because we are all complaining about our kids playing too much hockey these days. Well, that may be so at the youth levels, but not so at the high school level, where kids are in their peak developmental years. The guys I played pro hockey with couldn't comprehend that. They were playing 70-game seasons at that point, so it is an entirely different deal all together. So, I am not saying that what Massachusetts is doing is better, I am just saying that is probably why they have more kids in the NHL than we do." — *Casey Hankinson, Gopher 1994-98*

"I don't know why we aren't getting more of our guys onto the NHL. We have a ton of players playing pro hockey, but not nearly enough are in the NHL. Sure, we have had a lot of guys make it up over the years, but not since Neal Broten have we had a real star. Hopefully that will change in the future. One explanation I can think of is that for a lot of Canadian kids, there is no fall back option. I mean college kids have a degree to fall back on if things don't work out, whereas the Canadian kids just go for broke because for many of them it is all or nothing. So, they have more incentive to work their tails off and make it at all costs. I played three years of minor league hockey, including one year up in Canada, and I definitely saw that hungry attitude from a lot of those guys. Even the guys who weren't that skilled were willing to make it as fighters, just to make it. A lot of college kids wouldn't do that." — *Peter Hankinson, Gopher 1986-90*

"Are enough Gophers? Yes. Are enough Gopher goalies? No. The bottom line is that the state of Minnesota is not producing goalies like it should be. Heck, the United States is not producing enough goalies. The top goalies in the NHL are from either Canada or Europe. So, we have to ask ourselves what those guys are doing in order to get better. I would also say that in no way should we be up on our high horse thinking that we rule the country in terms of youth hockey and high school hockey. That is just my personal perspective from spending a lot of Summers working at camps and being around kids, especially goalies. On a positive note though, I wound up playing against Kenny Gernander last year out in Hartford. We are both Greenway High School alums, but had never played with or against each other at any point in our lives except for then. So, that was pretty cool." — *Adam Hauser, Gopher 1998-2002*

"I think that right now we are in a great cycle of kids getting called up, which is just a great statement for our team's success. We have really gotten a lot of guys onto the NHL the past few years and that just speaks volumes about our program and about the quality of our players. Hey, the Wild drafted me in the third round a few years back, and what a thrill it would be to go from playing in Mariucci Arena to the Xcel Center. I mean every college player's dream is to play in the NHL, so I hope it will come true for me the same way getting to play for the Gophers did. Wow, it just makes me want to work that much harder to help my team win so that I can go out on top. What a thrill and honor it would be to be able to wear that green and red sweater one day." — *Danny Irmen, Gopher 2003-Present*

"It's tough to make it to the NHL. You have to have the right people recognize you and then you have to be a little bit lucky. I certainly was. Beyond that it is just a lot of hard work. I have been very grateful for the opportunity to play here as long as I have, it has been a tremendous experience for sure. As far as enough Minnesota kids getting here, I don't know. We are getting a lot of guys onto the next level, but certainly it would be nice if more could make the leap. I think the most important thing for the vast majority of college players is to get their educations, have fun and become a better person. That is what it is all about." — *Craig Johnson, Gopher 1990-93*

"I'd obviously love to see more, we all would. It's tough. I was very fortunate to have stayed up there for as long as I did. That pyramid just keeps getting smaller and smaller when you advance up to the next level. Fewer and fewer players move on to each level, and you are left with the cream of the crop. I would also say that the NHL game is so drastically different from the college game too. It is like night and day. College hockey is a wide open skating game played amongst a lot of skill players. The NHL is just a totally different style of hockey. So, when college guys make the jump, they have to go through a pretty significant transition and really learn a whole new system. The latest thing with the new rule changes is that the NHL game is going to open up more and that that will inherently help the college guys, who play that way. Well, I can tell you that after 15 years in the NHL, they have been saying that forever. So,

I will believe it when I see it." — *Trent Klatt, Gopher 1989-92*

"No, not even close. And I won't go into it because I could talk all day and all night about it." — *Ryan Kraft, Gopher 1994-98*

"To me, the most important thing is that when kids come into our program that they play here and have success both on and off the ice and then leave with a degree. That has always been far more important to me than playing at the next level. To me, the next level is the NHL. I am not a big believer in going to spend a bunch of time in the minor leagues because I think by then it is time to get on with life. I do think, however, that it is all cyclical. You have your run of kids who are blessed with size and speed, and it goes in spurts. You have to remember that some of the greatest college players are never going to play in the NHL. It is an entirely different game when you get to that level." — *Don Lucia, Current Gopher Head Coach*

"I think so. I think that a whole bunch of guys from my era are going to make it and that is just awesome to see. The program has had just a ton of kids get drafted really high over the past few years, so it is going to be exciting to see which of those kids make it." — *Paul Martin, Gopher 2000-03*

"Oh yeah, I think so. We have so many kids who have gone on to play professionally, whether that is in the NHL, the minors, or over in Europe. You know, there are so many more opportunities for kids nowadays. The NHL has 30 teams, the AHL has a ton of teams since it merged with the IHL, and there are a lot of teams in Europe which are top notch. So, I think we are getting a fair shake. As for the guys playing in the NHL, that is a very elite group. There are so many more Europeans coming over now too, which hurts us I think. We've got some guys who are doing all right though, the Leopolds, the Martins, the Rasmussens — so, we're doing OK." — *Frank Mazzocco, Longtime Gopher TV Analyst*

"I think so. I am coaching in an elite high school league right now, so I am pretty up to date with what is going on at that level. I think that we have some of the most skilled players in North America. In my opinion we may have the best skaters in the entire world. But the one knock that we have against us is that by the time our kids get to the NHL level, they are not used to the smash-mouth style of hockey that is played there. Up there a skill player can dingle and dangle his way through three or four players, but the fifth guy, who may have half the skill that he does, will lay him out and put him on his butt. So, our kids get a little shy playing that way. It is much, much different up there. Now, I am not saying that we should play that way at all and hinder kids' creativity, I am just saying that if we want more kids to play at that level then we need to teach them and prepare them to play that style of hockey. Again, that isn't my preference, it is just my opinion after having played in the NHL for the past 10 years. College hockey is fun and the kids are great, but to take that jump to the big time takes a special kid who can perform a real niche. It is a business by the time you get that high in the ladder and it is treated as such. So, I don't think our kids are prepared for that part of the game, which, again, is just my opinion." — *Chris McAlpine, Gopher 1990-94*

"No. And I am not sure what the reason for that is. Hopefully we can get it turned around in the future though." — *Jason Miller, Gopher 1987-91*

"No. I think it is changing though. I think a lot of guys have suffered from the Canadian bias a little bit over the years. They wanted the kids who played in the major juniors and didn't always give a fair shake to the college kids. They felt that college players were too soft; they weren't physical enough; and they couldn't adapt to the pro style. I think that has changed somewhat though over the past several years and we are getting more guys up to the big leagues. We have had a lot of guys get drafted pretty high these past few years and those teams are going to put more of an investment into those players because they are going to need to see a return on them. So, we will have more opportunities down the road I think." — *Nate Miller, Gopher 1996-00*

"I think that the guys who are good enough are certainly getting the opportunities. There are so many scouts out there looking at kids of all ages, that if you are good enough you are going to get discovered and you will get an opportunity. What kids do with that opportunity is up to them. You know, when you get to that level the pyramid shrinks pretty quickly. The talent up there is just amazing and it takes a lot of hard work and you need to catch a break somewhere along the line too. So, are we getting enough kids to the NHL? I guess I would always say that there is plenty of room for more." — *Jeff Nielsen, Gopher 1990-94*

"I don't know. It is not something I spend a lot of time thinking about. I still follow the Gophers but don't have a lot of interest in the pro game to tell you the truth." — *Larry Olimb, Gopher 1988-92*

"We have quite a few guys who are playing in the NHL right now, but there is certainly room for more. A lot of guys are right there on the doorstep, guys like Johnny Pohl, who really deserve a shot I think. You know, I just think that college kids are much better suited to make the transition versus kids who came out of major junior hockey. College guys understand the work ethic; the structure and routine; about practicing hard; and about the discipline of what it takes to go to school and be a student-athlete. I just think that they are better equipped to weather the ensuing adversity. I mean so much of junior hockey is about riding a bus, playing cards, drinking beer, and then playing hockey. I just think college prepares you more for life and about how to deal with the pressure of playing at the next level." — *Tom Pederson, Gopher 1988-91*

"I am not sure. You know, if you can play past college, that is just gravy as far as I am concerned. The odds are against you, that is for sure. Who knows? Maybe the new NHL rule changes will benefit the college kids with the new open style of play that they are trying to achieve. Plus, a lot of the Europeans may stay put now too, knowing that they can make just as much money playing over there. That may open up more opportunities for our boys as well. We have some guys who are doing great, but there is always room for more. So, we will have to stay tuned and hope good things happen in the future." — *Lance Pitlick, Gopher 1986-90*

"Trust me, you are going to be seeing a lot more Gophers playing in the NHL in the near future. A big part of that is because of the new rules in the NHL, which benefit kids who played the wide open style of hockey they play in college. Take a guy like Brian Bonin for example, he had a ton of skill, speed and play-making ability. He was a phenomenal college player but struggled at the pro level because of all the clutching and grabbing. The NHL game used to be all defense and no offense. The big, physical guys ruled and little guys like Brian got stymied. Well, now, a guy like Brian would be a superstar. So, in the future we are going to see more Gophers getting on to the next level because of the style we play on that big sheet of ice at Mariucci Arena. That is also a big reason why we are seeing guys like Paul Martin and Jordan Leopold having success up there too, because they learn to play defense on that bigger Olympic sheet of ice, and then take that speed to the NHL-sized rink which is much smaller. So, they can cover so much more ground than the bigger defensemen, and still be a factor on offense too. In the new NHL, the better skating team will win 95% of the time. And now, defensemen have to be able to actually skate. That is why a guy like Keith Ballard, who is only five-foot-ten, can make it in the NHL. He can skate and defend without having to cross-check, hook and grab guys, like so many other players do. I think these new rules are good for Gophers, but also for all college players, which is great." — *Johnny Pohl, Gopher 1998-2002*

"Let's just look at the 2002 team: Pohl, Riddle, myself, Taffe, Welch, Koalska, Leopold, Ballard, Martin, Demarchi and Hauser. All of those guys signed pro contracts and several are in the NHL right now. Ah... I would say we are doing OK. Throw in Vanek from 2003, who is starting for Buffalo right now, and it is a resounding yes in my book." — *Grant Potulny, Gopher 2000-04*

"I think so. I mean look at the Stanley Cup Finals in 2004, we had Leopold playing against Ben Clymer when Calgary played Tampa Bay. That's' two Gophers right there. Then you've got guys like Tallackson, Martin, Vanek and Rasmussen too. Is there room for more? Sure, but we are doing all right I think." — *Ryan Potulny, Gopher 2003-Present*

"I think we are going to see more and more Minnesota kids playing in the NHL as the years go by. It is cyclical and I think we are on the front end of a cycle which is going to have a good number of kids get their shots. Pro hockey is a different mentality than college hockey, it really is. I am not saying college kids don't have the mentality to make it, a lot of it just comes down to being in the right place at the right time and catching a break. There are a lot of politics and luck involved at this stage of the game, without a doubt. As for Gophers, Ben Clymer has done great. Paul Martin and Jordan Leopold are going to be here for a long, long time. There are other Minnesota kids who weren't Gophers that have made it too, with guys like Mark Parrish and Matt Cullen. The new NHL rule changes are certainly going to help college kids. They are trying to make it a skill game now, which is going to help a ton. Teams aren't going to be able to afford having huge guys who can hit but can't skate very well. So, it seems like there has been a jinx on the Gophers for whatever reason, but hopefully that is going to change in the not so distant future." — *Erik Rasmussen, Gopher 1995-97*

"You know, one of the problems that we have with the development of college players is that the ice surfaces at the collegiate levels vary by size so much. A lot of rinks are standard size, which are 200' x 85', and others, such as Mariucci Arena, are Olympic size, which is 200' x 100'. Some players really prosper on that bigger, Olympic ice sheet. When you have that extra seven and a half feet on each side of the ice, or 3,000 square feet of extra space, you have more time to do things. It is also much less physical on the Olympic sheet because there is more room for faster guys to get around people. But, when those players try to make the jump to pro hockey, which is all on standard size ice sheets, they struggle. Because they are so much smaller, those players can't react quite as quickly and it hurts them a great deal. They can't adapt and as a result don't advance onto the next levels. So, for me, I would like to see a uniform size rink at all levels of hockey, preferably Olympic. I don't think it will ever happen though, because the pro arenas would have to take out several rows of the most expensive seats in order to make their rinks bigger. Now, a lot of Gophers have made the adjustment just fine, don't get me wrong, but this is just one reason as to perhaps why more kids don't." — *Tommy Reid, Former Gopher TV & Radio Announcer*

"There are a bunch of guys making it in pro hockey today. Sure, I would love to see more guys get to the NHL, but that is so tough. As a career minor leaguer, I can certainly attest to that. You know, I have been playing pro hockey for over 13 years now and have had just three NHL games on two call-ups with the Dallas Stars. I am kind of like 'Moonlight Graham,' from the movie 'Field of Dreams' that way. So, that has been bittersweet. It was always my goal to make it up in the big leagues, but sometimes that is just not in the cards, so you make the best of it. As for Gophers, I think that we are pretty well represented up there though. You know, I have played against a lot of former Gophers over the years in the AHL and IHL and it is always fun to see those guys and to reminisce a little bit." — *Travis Richards, Gopher 1989-93*

"As of lately, absolutely. At one point we had like 16 guys on the team who had been drafted. So, that is amazing. As far as making it to the big leagues, the jury is still out. That takes time. A lot of us have to pay our dues and hope to catch a break. Certainly, to see Leopold, Martin and Vanek making it is pretty sweet. That just drives the rest of us to follow them too, because we all want to get there." — *Troy Riddle, Gopher 2000-04*

"I think so and I think there are going to be a lot more coming too. It is a big jump, no question, but a lot of our guys are there and some more are on the way. You know, the biggest difference between college and the NHL is the ability of those athletes to play different systems as well as they do. I mean if they want to go into a lock-down defense, they do it. They are that good and they are that quick. They know where to be positionally and can adapt to virtually any opponent on any given night. That is what makes the NHL even sort of boring, because the players are just that good and can react so quickly to shut down the other team. College kids are still learning the game and that is why it tends to be more entertaining at times, because you get some good mismatches along the way. Our guys have been making the adjustments

though and making us proud — guys like Jordan Leopold, Paul Martin, Wyatt Smith, Erik Rasmussen, and now with Keith Ballard. Hopefully there will be a lot more in the future too."
— *Wally Shaver, Longtime Gopher Radio & TV Announcer*

"I think so. There are a lot of Gophers who are doing well and have a good shot at making it in the NHL. It is tough to make it up here though, you have to dedicate your whole life to it and make a lot of sacrifices along the way. There are plenty of Minnesota kids who have the talent to play up here, no question, it just comes down to opportunities and hard work. Beyond that, guys need to catch a break here or there and then take advantage of it." — *Wyatt Smith, Gopher 1995-99*

"I don't think it has happened yet, but I think it is going to in the not so distant future. With the new rule changes in the NHL I think that more and more college kids are going to get their chances. You look at Leopold, Martin and Vanek, and that is a pretty good start. As long as our kids are given a chance, they will prove to the hockey world that they can play with anybody." — *Glen Sonmor, Former Gopher, North Stars & Fighting Saints Coach; Current Gopher Radio Broadcaster*

"I think a lot of Gophers do go on to play at the next level and I think even more could go on if they wanted to. Playing at the University of Minnesota affords you a lot of opportunities after college outside of the game of hockey and for a lot of guys they are ready to hang it up at that point. I know I was. I knew that I was never going to get that far and wasn't interested in spending a bunch of time in the minors when I could be out starting my career in the real world. So, that was my choice." — *Dave Spehar, Gopher 1996-2000*

"Lately, for sure. From our era alone there are at least a dozen guys who are either in the NHL or right there in the AHL. So, hopefully we will be able to keep that all going and get more guys on up to the next levels." — *Jeff Taffe, Gopher 1999-02*

"I believe so. If you look back to the early '90s there were only a select few who went on to play at the next level. Now, we have had a bunch of guys getting drafted in the higher rounds and a lot more guys are getting their chances to compete. That is what it is all about." — *Barry Tallackson, Gopher 2001-05*

"While I am thrilled to see so many Minnesota kids going on to play pro hockey, I am surprised by the fact that there haven't been as many who have found success in the NHL. I think we have had a little resurgence lately, with Martin and Leopold and Vanek, but not nearly as many have made the jump as there should be." — *Dan Terhaar, Former Gopher Radio Announcer*

"I think so. Sure, there could always be more, but I think we are getting there. I would say though that there is somewhat of an inherent disadvantage in that Minnesota kids are playing on the bigger, Olympic-sized rink at Mariucci Arena. When they make the transition to the smaller rink in pro hockey they have to make a lot of timing adjustments. Aside from that I think college hockey is a different mentality than that of a lot of the Canadian kids, who have more of a do-or-die mentality with regards to making it at the next level to a certain extent. Overall, we are doing fine and when guys leave here I think they are well prepared." — *Dan Trebil, Gopher 1992-96*

"For sure, especially lately we have seen a lot of guys making the jump. Look at Paul Martin, Grant Potulny and Thomas Vanek, those guys are kicking butt. A lot of guys are putting in their time in the AHL too, and that is OK. They are making good money and paying their dues. Hopefully they will get up to the NHL before long, we will just have to see how it all plays out. So, overall I think we are going in the right direction." — *Mike Vannelli, Gopher 2003-Present*

"It's cyclical I think. Early on, particularly after the Herbie Brooks era, there were a ton of guys who went on to play. Then it slowed down a little bit, with some peaks and valleys in between. Now, with the recent success the program has had with the two titles, we are going to see a bunch of guys from that era making it too. So, we are doing all right." — *Erik Westrum, Gopher 1997-2001*

"I think so. Kids are developing here and are able to bring their games to the next level. I think as times goes on we will see more and more Gophers playing in the National Hockey League." — *Dean Williamson, Gopher 1987-90*

"I don't know what the answer to that is. We have a lot of talented kids who come out of here, that is for sure. It is a whole different world once you get out of college hockey though. Some players are effected a little bit by the intimidation of not being able to wear a mask, and the intimidation of fighting. That added a lot of stress, believe me. Because now you had to not only raise your game to a new level as far as skating, shooting and passing, but you also had to keep your head on a swivel. I know that when I was on my way up, those things were definitely concerns of mine. The other thing is that maybe the elite junior leagues up in Canada push their top-end kids a little bit harder than we push our top-end kids. I don't know. We had four first round draft picks this year, so maybe it goes in cycles." — *Doug Zmolek, Gopher 1989-92*

CHAPTER 11
HOW IS THE STATE OF THE STATE OF HOCKEY IN MINNESOTA TODAY?

"There are several thousand people on both the Gopher and Wild season ticket waiting lists. That says a lot about the State of Hockey." — *Mike Anderson, Gopher 1995-99*

"I think it is getting a lot better. A lot of guys from Minnesota who are back in town after retiring from pro hockey are getting involved with youth organizations and that is just awesome to see." — *Mark Bahr, Gopher 1991-94, Current Director of Hockey Operations*

"It's great. I think having the Wild back is huge. That gets a lot of the kids excited about playing and that is where it all starts. The biggest problem in my eyes is the lack of ice time in the area. There are so many youth levels now and so many girls teams playing that it is almost impossible for some of these teams to find enough of it. Kids are playing super early in the morning and super late at night, so hopefully we can get that figured out." — *Keith Ballard, Gopher 2001-04*

"Overall, I think it is really good from top to bottom. The biggest thing nowadays though is the fact that so many kids are either skipping high school to play junior hockey, or they are playing in juniors for a few years prior to playing Division One. We are also seeing a lot of kids who maybe don't like their coaches at the high school level or are having problems in their community and are transferring schools. That is too bad I think. There were 17 seniors on my high school team and we were all good buddies. No one left early or transferred out, we wanted to play together and have fun. You don't see that anymore, which is sad. The state of hockey is in great shape though and as a coach that is nice to see." — *Scott Bell, Gopher 1991-95*

"There are so many more opportunities to play hockey now than when I was a kid. They can play all year round nowadays if they want to. Now, I don't think that is necessarily the smartest thing for young kids to do, but it is there for them if they so choose. I still think that kids need to be well-rounded and play several different sports in each season. We are losing some of that now with the specialization, and that is probably the biggest concern that I have. One bright spot for sure is the growth of the girls' programs. That has been unreal to watch that take off. So, we are OK I think." — *Grant Bischoff, Gopher 1987-91*

"I think it is pretty good. The way guys are training and working, I think we are producing a lot of really talented kids with very high skill levels. I think we have a whole bunch of kids who will have opportunities to excel at the collegiate level and beyond. The problem is the fact that not enough kids are learning the game outdoors, on the lakes and ponds, or by playing street hockey. That to me is sad. Kids today are on high tech skating tread mills and that type of thing, and are on serious weightlifting programs. So, they are bigger, faster and stronger, but oftentimes they lack that sixth sense or instinct that you get from playing out in the elements with no coaches around yelling and screaming. I don't think that bigger kids who are faster and can fly around the ice creating problems are necessarily better hockey players. Where did they learn the game? Can they think out on the ice? I don't know and only time will tell on stuff like that." — *Brian Bonin, Gopher 1992-96*

"I think our youth players put too much of an emphasis on playing league games. I mean when peewees and bantams are playing 55 games, plus the playoffs, that is too much. The European kids don't do that stuff, they work on skill development instead. It is no coincidence that 13 of the top 20 goal scorers in the NHL are from Europe. I think our society is so intent on winning at a young age that we don't take human growth and development into the equation. We cut some kids because they don't go through the pylons in 6.4 seconds or whatever, and we don't give them a chance to develop. Size is another huge thing. The NHL doesn't want guys who are five-foot-nine, so those guys don't stand a chance unless they are like Jason Blake and can scooter around the ice a million miles per hour. Then, you look at high school football and basketball and you've got tons of six-foot-two, six-foot-three kids just standing around on the sidelines who don't have a prayer to ever even make a Division III program. Well, if a lot of those guys didn't get cut from hockey early on, because maybe they were uncoordinated as a peewee, they might have had the opportunity to really develop out on the ice. Who knows? The smaller communities as well as the European communities develop more kids because they spend more time with them. They don't cut them early on, they stick with them and let them develop. That is so important. Our coaches need to look at those things. It is a win-at-all-costs society and sometimes that isn't right." — *Bill Butters, Gopher Player 1971-73; Assistant Coach 1985-95*

"I am very impressed with it. Coming from Canada, obviously, we take great pride in our youth hockey. But this is just as good if not better than what I grew up with, so that says a lot I think. The fans here are extremely educated too, more so than I expected. They are just so supportive of their teams. I was the most amazed by the high school hockey tournament. That was just amazing to go watch over at the Xcel Center. I mean you would never see anything like that up in Canada. None of us ever played high school hockey up there, it wasn't even an option. So, that was pretty cool to experience, for sure." — *Kris Chucko, Gopher 2003-Present*

"At the risk of sounding like a proud Minnesotan, I think it is better than it has ever been. We have five Division One college hockey programs for both the men and the women for starters, which is great. We are also producing a ton of talent for other college hockey programs outside of Minnesota as well. The high school tournament is probably the only element of Minnesota hockey which isn't quite as good as it once was, and that is because so many of the top kids are leaving school early to go play juniors. Beyond that, the Wild are kicking butt and are more popular than the North Stars were in their last years for sure. So, we are doing great." — *Jeff Dubay, KFAN Radio Host & Longtime Gopher Fanatic*

"I am coaching youth hockey now, so I am pretty in tune with what is going on out there. The biggest thing that I see now is a movement to have less games and more practice — especially at the youth levels. That is the European model. They have been doing that for a long time and have been developing more talented kids as a result. For them, it is a necessity because they have so few rinks and are forced to do a lot of dry-land training. Here, we have parents and politics and egos, and it is out of control. Everybody wants to play games and win games, and we are losing a lot of skill development I think. Then they want to be on Triple-A this and Triple-A that, I mean do we really need that? Or do we think it is good for mites and squirts to be playing 40, 50 and even 60 games throughout the entire year, including in the Summer? No way. Let these kids be kids and let them put their skates away in the off-season to do other things, otherwise we are going to lose them to other sports when they burn out.

"I also hate it when I see parents carrying their kids' bags into the rinks for them; of when they are tightening up their skates. I think kids should figure that stuff out on their own and toughen up a little bit. That is just me. I think that sissy mentality carries over sometimes too in that kids nowadays don't really want to play outside anymore either. That is where they could have unlimited ice-time, but hey, it is too cold I guess. That just kills me.

"I would also add in regards to the older kids, that when you look at the number or rinks that we have here in Minnesota, compared to the number of players we are getting on to the NHL, it isn't even close to what it is in Russia or in parts of Europe. So, we have our work cut out for us moving forward, but I think we are on the right track." — *Joe Dziedzic, Gopher 1990-94*

"We just had an entire year lay-off in the NHL due to a labor dispute and the first Wild game after all that time was a sell-out. In fact, there are still thousands and thousands of fans on a waiting list to get season tickets which will probably become available years down the road. That says a lot about the 'State of Hockey.' I have a son who is a bantam and I follow youth hockey pretty closely. I think it is really healthy. The bantams today look and play like high school players back in my day. They have just developed so much skill-wise over the years. So, for me, the state of hockey in this state has never been better." — *Eric Gislason, Former Gopher Radio & Television Commentator*

"I can answer that emphatically as very good. Our kids are doing great, especially with things such as the USA Hockey Select Festivals as well as the U.S. Select 17 team. I was just over in Europe watching the Select 17 team and five of their top players are from the state of Minnesota, including their leading scorer. I just saw a recruiting service newsletter today about the pro hockey rankings for the draft next year and they were raving about the 1988 and 1989 birthdates in Minnesota. Those classes are loaded with talent, which is so great to see. It even said that it might be possible that next year you could have a world junior team playing with as many as 14 of the 20 kids being from Minnesota. That is unheard of. We are producing some really elite top-end players and I think in 5-10 years from now we will see many of those kids playing in the NHL. So, we are in great shape right now, collectively, as a state." — *Mike Guentzel, Gopher Player 1981-85; Assistant Coach 1994-Present*

"I think it is great across the board. I think the fact that more and more high school kids are going to juniors before they play in college is a testament to the fact that the competition and skill levels have gone up over the years. The state tournament is still a really big deal and girls hockey is booming, so I think we are doing all right. Hockey is and always has been very important to the people of Minnesota, and that is great to see. I guess you could say that the state-of-hockey is great in the state of hockey." — *Gino Guyer, Gopher 2003-Present*

"One of the best things that I have seen lately is this high school elite league, which allows seniors to play for their high school teams without having to play junior hockey on the side. Too many kids are missing their proms and everything else by having to pack up and move away their senior years, which I always felt was unfortunate. That entire phenomenon is here to stay though, and that is just the reality of the business of hockey. For the most part, kids have to get some more games under their belts in order to play at the Division One level. This has been second nature in Canada for a long time, where kids leave home at 14, 15 and 16 years old to go play junior hockey. It is a tough call for kids today, that is for sure. You can't fault them for trying to better themselves and certainly going on to play after high school requires a lot of hard work and sacrifice.

"The fact of the matter is that high school hockey in Minnesota, as good as it is, is not on the same level with the Canadian junior leagues or even the Triple A leagues or prep schools out East. Don't get me wrong, the tourney is still an awesome thing and is practically sacred here in Minnesota. But more and more kids are having to play junior hockey instead of playing on their high school teams in order to get into good college programs, and that is just the way it is.

"In terms of our youth levels and the girls, however, they are doing really well I think. In fact, I think that over the past five years the United States has taken bigger steps than anybody else, including Canada as well as the Eastern Block countries in Europe. Hockey is a year round sport now and the skill levels are way up across the board. We aren't seeing the Larry Olimb's and Neal Broten's nowadays, guys who were two to three strides ahead of everybody else, because everybody has gotten that much better as a whole.

"You know, when you look at the top American talent, the Roenicks, the Modannos, the Tkachuks, the Amontes, the Guerins — you can go on and on, and none of them are Minnesota kids. It is crazy if you think about it. But a lot of that I think has to do with the fact that here our kids grow up playing four lines pretty evenly and no one really rises above the pack that much. Some people call this the 'robot effect,' where kids are kind of programmed to play a certain way. Beyond that, it is just a function of ice time, our kids only get so much of it compared to other places. So, kids have to seek it out elsewhere, such as elite leagues and junior hockey. It is a personal choice for kids and for families. But, times are changing and kids are progressing faster, so the future looks very bright in my opinion. Will the next generation of American superstar players come from Minnesota? That remains to be seen." — *Ben Hankinson, Gopher 1987-91*

"I don't know how it could get any better. The Wild have been doing great; girls hockey is just phenomenal the way it has taken off; the high school tourney is still a huge draw; and our kids seem to be doing well too at the youth levels. The one negative I would have would be how all-year round youth hockey has become. I think it is still really important for kids to play other sports and to be well-rounded, otherwise they will get burned out and quit. Overall though, I think it is really solid." — *Casey Hankinson, Gopher 1994-98*

"You know, I coached my daughter in the Edina lower girls mites program for first, second and third graders, this past year. What amazed me was that they had 98 kids sign up for the team. And, it went for like five full months, which is a really long season for kids that young to be in such a structured environment. Some of the parents had those kids skating all year round too. That was shocking to me. So, I think youth hockey has become really one dimensional nowadays and sadly, a lot of these kids are only going to get to play one sport. That specialization is wrong and a big problem in my eyes. Our kids need to play a lot of different sports all year round and not even think about specializing until they are way older. That's just my opinion." — *Peter Hankinson, Gopher 1986-90*

"I think youth hockey is great here. The one thing I don't like about it, however, is the amount of specialization we see now. Kids are playing almost all year round at younger and younger ages and that is not good. Kids need to play other sports and have a life or they will get burned out by the time they are 15. Overall though, it looks good from top to bottom, with the girls taking off and the state tournament still going strong. So, we are in good shape I think. It's just good to see a lot more people playing hockey here, at all levels, and I think the Wild has helped out in that regard too." — *Chris Harrington, Gopher 2002-Present*

"I think it is really good. It has grown tremendously with the girls and all of that, which is great. I think the triple-A programs have gotten a little watered down though, due to the fact that too many players' fathers have started programs of their own after their kids didn't make the cut. That has gotten out of hand over the past couple of years if you want my opinion. But, overall it is good. People are staying involved and they are enjoying it, so that is all you can really ask for." — *Tyler Hirsch, Gopher 2002-Present*

"I think it's awesome. To see the women's program grow the way it has; to see the five Division One programs giving opportunities to all those Minnesota kids; to see the state tournament still drawing so many fans; and to see the Wild selling out night in and night out — that all speaks volumes about what is going on here. We have great hockey fans here and they absolutely love the game. That is great to see." — *Trent Klatt, Gopher 1989-92*

"I think that at the high school level in particular, it is down. Back when I was a kid watching the tourney I couldn't believe the skill level of the kids. Now, most of the top kids skip the tourney to play juniors, which is OK, but it has diluted the tourney talent-wise. Beyond that, a lot of kids in general just seem to have other things going on in their lives. Kids are busy nowadays and they have a lot of options as to what to do with their free time, whether that is playing video games or being on the internet or just working so that they can afford to buy stuff. So, I don't see the same commitment level in today's kids that I did a while back. That is just my opinion. You know, kids don't want to skate outside that much anymore either, which is really too bad. When I was a kid we used to go over to Sylvan Park on the corner of Rice and Maryland everyday in the Winter to skate. There were actually too many kids out there, that is how popular it was. That is where I learned how to skate and where to stickhandle, right out there with they boys. Now, they don't even put up the boards or flood the rink anymore. That is really sad. Another thing that bugs me is the fact that we have Triple-A hockey for mites. For Mites! I mean how do you differentiate between a Triple-A mite and a regular mite? It is insane. The parents have gone overboard on some of this stuff and I think a lot of kids aren't having fun with hockey. Burn-out is huge and that has to change. Hockey needs to be fun or why bother?" — *Matt Koalska, Gopher 2000-04*

"I think we are doing great. I come back and work with kids in the Summers and from what I can see, the skill levels are very high. I don't think we have lost a step to tell you the truth. I mean we have a lot of Minnesota kids going off to play in the U.S. Developmental camp in Michigan every year. So, I think that is a great testimonial to the state of hockey. It is also a great compliment to all of the coaches who work with those kids and help them to develop. The bottom line is that we are producing a lot of good talent, both boys and girls, and that is what it is all about." — *Ryan Kraft, Gopher 1994-98*

"I can only really comment on the top of the hockey pyramid, and from there I can say that it is very strong. The Wild are doing extremely well, and continue to sell out their building night in and night out. We have five division one programs now too, which is great to see as well. That just gives more Minnesota kids scholarship opportunities, both men and women, and that is great. Beyond that, it appears that more and more kids are making the leap to play at the next level. So, from that standpoint things look pretty good I think." — *Bob Kurtz, former Gopher Broadcaster*

"I think we are in the midst of a pretty good run right now as far as producing some elite players. This group of kids, the '88's (kids born in 1988), are as good as its ever been here with the Gophers and that speaks volumes about our high school kids which are moving up the ladder. So, I do think that we are on the right path. I do worry though about kids dropping out because of the expense of the sport. That really troubles me, the fact that our sport has become so elitist. I also have a problem with all of the traveling teams at younger and younger ages. Kids are getting burned out and moving on to other sports before we find out maybe if they will become a good player at 14, 15 or 16 years of age. That is too bad." — *Don Lucia, Current Gopher Head Coach*

"I think we had a little dip talent-wise a while ago at the high school level, but now I think it is getting better again. The tournament is certainly different nowadays with so many kids going to play junior hockey. But the addition of the girls tourney has just enhanced it all the more. In fact, I think there's times when the enthusiasm of the girls is rubbing off on the guys. So, top-to-bottom we are in good shape, but there is always room for improvement at all levels. There was an interesting article in the paper about a year ago which basically said that participation in almost every high school sport had dropped off, largely because kids were going to work…because they want money to buy cool things or to go to school. Hockey, however, had not dropped off anywhere near what the other sports have. So, I think that says a lot about hockey and the dedication you see from the youth levels on up." — *Frank Mazzocco, Longtime Gopher TV Analyst*

"I think it is great when you look at the overall picture. Having said that, I think the one area where it is a little bit out of hand is at the youth levels, where we've got kids playing way too many games. Let's face it, hockey is a year round gig nowadays which is kind of sad. Kids don't get to play other sports now, they are totally specialized in one sport. That is why we see so much burn-out. I know a 13 year old kid who has his own personal trainer. Wow! What were you doing when you were 13? I think we are lacking athletes. We have a lot of hockey players, but we are lacking athletes. When kids specialize so young and don't get to play other sports, they don't develop those sixth sense skills that great athletes possess. Look at Paul Martin. He was a stud football player in high school, and, he was a straight-A student, just the complete package. He is going to be a star in the NHL, just watch. And you couldn't meet a nicer kid either. So, we are doing well in a lot of areas, but need to work on some others. We'll be OK." — *Chris McAlpine, Gopher 1990-94*

"I think it is great. I coach youth hockey up here in Waconia, so I am on the front lines of some of this stuff. The numbers are up across the board and the players keep getting better. Kids have more opportunities these days, at every level of the game, and the girls game has just doubled the popularity as a whole. So, things are good in my opinion." — *Jason Miller, Gopher 1987-91*

"I think it is really good. I coach at a lot of hockey schools and stay in touch with a lot of this stuff. Obviously, the trend is for high school seniors to leave a year early to play juniors, and the verdict is still out on whether or not that is the best way to go. You can't fault kids for wanting to get more ice time so that they can get scholarships, but you wonder if they are giving up too much in the process. I am a big fan of the high school tournament and am sad that it isn't what it used to be. It is still strong, and the numbers are still there, but the majority of the top kids aren't. Maybe if they added more games, that would be enough to entice kids to stay put. Who knows? Overall though, I think we are getting kids into Summer programs and they are doing well. Plus, we are adding ice sheets, which is a big deal too. I think that the Wild have had a real positive impact too, because kids are more into hockey now than ever. We had a lull there for a while when the North Stars were gone, but now kids can grow up watching that and dreaming about playing with them the same way I did. And, when the Gophers are winning, then that is a real keystone to the overall success of Minnesota hockey as well." — *Nate Miller, Gopher 1996-00*

"I think that Minnesota hockey is definitely on the right track. From peewees to bantams to high school to college, we have a lot of great volunteers who are working with our kids and don't always get a lot of credit. Those are the people who have made our hockey tradition here in Minnesota what it is. Without them we would be nowhere." — *Jeff Nielsen, Gopher 1990-94*

"It's great that kids have a million opportunities today at all levels. We have great volunteer coaches at the youth levels; we have tons of support across the board; and we have lots of indoor ice — so we are in good shape in that regard. However, sometimes I worry that we are putting too much emphasis on hockey, collectively. I think as parents, sometimes we tend to get too involved, rather than just let the kids play. Maybe those days are gone, I don't know." — *Larry Olimb, Gopher 1988-92*

"You know, hockey at the youth levels all over the place is out of control. It is getting diluted. I coach kids out here in California and everybody wants to be Triple-A, everything is about Triple-A. So, I joke around that I am going to start a new league, Quadruple-A, and really raise the bar. You can put as many damn A's in front of your name as you want to, it doesn't mean much unless you are willing to be a team player and work hard. I grew up as a Double-A player and it seemed to work out OK for me." — *Tom Pederson, Gopher 1988-91*

"I have been coaching youth hockey in the Wayzata system for about four years now, so I have a pretty good idea of what is going on out there. I think that the associations are doing an awesome job, I really do. They have a real proactive approach to teaching and on skill development and that is refreshing to see. I also am seeing more of the 'rink-rat' kids too, who are playing outside more and more. That is hopefully a trend that will continue because we definitely got away from that for a while. The biggest problem that I see is the specialization today. When I was a kid we weren't training year round in hockey. Well, today the top kids are almost all one-sport athletes and that is really sad to see. It is almost like the days of the three-sport athlete are gone. I think that the parents are really pushing kids and want to see a return on their investment. I don't know. There is so much money being spent on training, on camps, on equipment and on travel expenses. In some ways it is almost out of control. Kids now want to make it in high school and beyond, and sadly, they feel that the only way that they are going to achieve that is by sacrificing so much so early on. We are going to see a lot of burn-out with these kids too, just watch. So, that is the biggest thing in my mind." — *Lance Pitlick, Gopher 1986-90*

"My brother Tom is playing for the Gophers now, so I follow it pretty closely. Hockey has always been strong in Minnesota and it always will be in my mind. I think that we are producing a lot of players onto the next levels and I think our youth hockey programs are moving kids along too. The big change now is how high school kids are playing junior hockey and missing out on their high school experiences. You know, I was able to play juniors with the Vulcans, but did so after my season was over. There was no way I was going to miss playing with my buddies in the state tourney. No way. So, I wish maybe that more kids would do that kind of stuff, rather than skipping it altogether. They tourney has definitely suffered from all of that, with the top kids not being there with their old teams. Look, I don't have a problem with kids wanting to play juniors, because that is a great way to improve your game in order to get a college scholarship. If a kid really sees hockey as his future and it is his dream though, then I don't have a problem with him leaving home at 16 or 17, because if you are going to play in college — hockey is basically your job anyways. So, you might as well get used to that.

"One thing I am not a big fan of, however, is all the Triple-A Summer hockey for little kids. I mean kids playing 100 games a year, that is ridiculous. I worked at a camp one Summer and after the camp was over I was talking to the kids. They were all talking about what they were going to do that weekend, and one of them said he was going to his cabin and another said he was going to a baseball game. Then, this other kid said that he was going up to Ottawa to play in a tournament. I was floored. I mean this 10 year-old kid just spent a week in a camp and was now on his way up to Canada for more. You know that it is the dads pushing that stuff, and that is scary. In my eyes kids that age don't get any better doing that stuff either. They are much better off taking the Summer off, or maybe going to one camp, and then having fun by playing baseball and soccer or whatever. Kids need to be well-rounded and do other things or otherwise they will burn-out and get sick of it." — *Johnny Pohl, Gopher 1998-2002*

"You hear about Texas football and Indiana basketball, well we have Minnesota hockey. The state tournament draws over 100,000 fans; the best women's players in the world are from Minnesota; as many as six Minnesotans will be on the men's Olympic team in Turin, Italy, next year; four kids went in the first round of the NHL draft this past year; and the youth programs here are among the very best in the nation. So, I think it is outstanding. In fact I would say that Minnesota is hands down way above everybody else across the board." — *Grant Potulny, Gopher 2000-04*

"I think it's awesome. There is no state out there that loves hockey more than they do here. Other states may say that they do, but they don't follow hockey as closely as they do other sports. Here, they say it and they back it up. And it doesn't matter what level it is either. People love their hockey here and they totally get behind it and support it from the grass roots levels on up. To see the kids out on the outdoor rinks just skating for the love of the game — that to me is where it starts and what it is all about." — *Ryan Potulny, Gopher 2003-Present*

"I think we are doing pretty well. However, I think that a lot of people are losing sight of why we play this game. When I was a kid I skated because I liked it, not because I had a dream of playing college hockey. I never dreamed of concentrating on just one sport, and that is what is so alarming today — the specialization of young kids who are focusing on just hockey. There is no reason kids should be playing hockey 12 months a year. That is a major problem I think. So, we need to follow the dream of Herbie Brooks and give this game back to the kids. They need to play outside way more I think too. I mean when I was a kid that is all I did. We would go from hockey practice in the afternoon to skating outside on the pond. We loved it. Times have changed though and hopefully we can address some of these issues before they get too out of hand." — *Erik Rasmussen, Gopher 1995-97*

"There are a lot of peaks and valleys I think. Some years it looks really good and some years it looks not so good. I think it goes back to the development systems. One thing I don't like, especially at the youth levels, is the fact that a lot of kids have to practice every day. Then, if they don't show up for practice then they can't play in a game as punishment. They are driven by their parents to succeed at that level and in some instances it is just out of hand. I think there has to be some restrictions on this stuff, particularly for the younger kids. There is no doubt in my mind that 40, 50 even 60 games for kids as young as 9, 10, 11 and 12 years old, is far too much. There are a lot of other areas where kids should be allowed to develop, whether that is in other sports or theater or music or academics or whatever. The burn-out factor for our kids is way too high and we need to look at why that is happening. So, overall hockey is doing fine in Minnesota, but we need to look at some of these things as we move forward I think." — *Tommy Reid, Former Gopher TV & Radio Announcer*

"It is fantastic. I have a seven year old son who is growing up here in Michigan, where I live, and it is night and day comparing here to Minnesota. It's football and basketball here, and hockey comes in somewhere down the line. So, we hope to get back there at some point so he can grow up in that environment. Who knows? Minnesotans just really love their hockey. You can't appreciate that until you live away from there for a while. All in all though, I think we are pretty strong from the youth levels on up." — *Travis Richards, Gopher 1989-93*

"I think it is really healthy and in very good shape, I really do. We have a lot of great coaches out there teaching our kids to play the game the right way and that is what it is all about. You know, Minnesota had over 100 kids playing professional hockey at some level in 2004, and that was with no NHL. I think another telling statistic is the number of Minnesota kids who are on the U.S. National Teams as well as the elite select camps. At one recent national U-17 tournament, fully 25% of the kids were from Minnesota, which is pretty impressive.

"As for some things that we need to work on, I think a lot of our problems stem from ice time. As a result of not enough ice time, kids are playing more games and are being forced to practice at all hours of the night. So, I agree with Herbie Brooks, in that what some of these hockey associations should be doing is instead of raising money to build these Taj Mahal arenas, they should be building inexpensive artificial sheets of ice either outdoors or in scaled down open buildings with just a roof. They could still have games in their main arenas, but they could totally utilize the extra ice sheets to accommodate the demand for ice time with the boys, the girls, the youth teams, the senior teams — all of them, much more effectively. Hey, look at the John Rose Oval up in Roseville, that thing costs less to run than the indoor arena next door, which is four times smaller. So, this can be done and it should be done." — *Wally Shaver, Longtime Gopher Radio & TV Announcer*

"I think it is better than it has ever been. High school hockey has taken a little bit of a hit though in that so many kids are leaving school early and going on to play juniors. Sadly, that is a trend that is probably here to stay. Beyond that I think it looks great at the youth levels and with the girls too. Overall though, I think it is good. Hey, as long as Warroad beats Roseau every year, then the state of the state of Minnesota hockey will always be great as far as I am concerned!" — *Wyatt Smith, Gopher 1995-99*

"I think it is as good as its ever been and it keeps getting better. At the prep level I think that the elite high school league, which has been going on for the past several years, has really opened the door for a lot of our top kids in particular. It has doubled the number of games these kids get to play and that is a really big deal. Minnesota kids can't make it with just 25 games a year. So, they need to get additional ice time in order to compete with the older, more experienced kids. This essentially is what the Canadians and Russians have been doing for so many years. They get the best players playing against the best players. They have outstanding coaches and it is really making a difference. I mean we had four high school kids selected in the first round of the NHL draft this past year, that is unheard of. All of the top kids are in this league and that is just going to enhance Minnesota's stock well into the future.

"The college game is thriving here too. In 2005 all four of the teams in the Frozen Four were from the WCHA, and there were a ton of Minnesota kids on those teams. We have five D-I schools here now and that is so great to see.

"Beyond that, the girls programs are doing well and progressing nicely; the Wild is in great shape after the lock-out; and our youth programs seem to be doing OK too. So, we are doing well in what they appropriately call 'The State of Hockey.' " — *Glen Sonmor, Former Gopher, North Stars & Fighting Saints Coach; Current Gopher Radio Broadcaster*

"I think it is phenomenal. Obviously, women's hockey is booming. The state tournament is still strong and the youth levels look strong too. Sure, we are losing kids to the developmental programs, but people have to do what they have to do in order to get where they want to go. You can never fault kids for trying to better themselves. But the big picture looks good. I know it's a cliché, but I truly do believe that we are the 'state of hockey.' " — *Dave Spehar, Gopher 1996-2000*

"I think overall it is good, particularly at the youth levels and with the girls. The high school level is going the wrong way though, and unfortunately a lot of that has to do with the fact that so many kids are being pressured into playing junior hockey instead of sticking around. The trickle down effect from this recent trend is starting to take a toll. Eventually, there won't be any good kids playing in the tourney and that will really be sad in my opinion. I mean I guess you can't fault kids for wanting to improve themselves so that they have a better chance of getting a scholarship, but at what cost? I think you only get one shot to be a high school senior and to play with your buddies in the state tournament. For me, I played juniors in Rochester before my senior season and then afterwards. I wouldn't have ever wanted to miss out of playing with my high school buddies though, so I was there during hockey season. Hey, I got to play about 25 additional games, but didn't have to miss out. I wish more kids did that kind of stuff I suppose." — *Jeff Taffe, Gopher 1999-02*

"I think it is going really well. I mean the only place that could come close to what we have from top to bottom is maybe Boston. Minnesota is just synonymous with hockey and that is something we should all be very proud of. We have five Division One schools here now, so there are just a ton of opportunities for the men and the women to go on and play after high school. The youth levels are doing well too, and a big part of that is due to all of the great volunteers who donate their time." — *Barry Tallackson, Gopher 2001-05*

"I am the president of the Andover Youth Hockey Association and also have three kids who play, so I am in real touch with that level of hockey right now. I think things are going really well at the youth levels. The numbers are growing, which is real positive. College hockey has never been stronger with both the men and the women, having five D-I programs flourishing now. I am also involved with the state high school tournament and I think that is on its way back too. And, the Wild are doing fantastic and should only benefit from the aftermath of the recent NHL lockout. So, things look good at all levels and appear to be alive and well." — *Dan Terhaar, Former Gopher Radio Announcer*

"I think we are at a cross-roads when it comes to high school hockey now. Who knows, maybe in the future we will go away from high school hockey altogether and just have midget Triple-

A leagues? Kids are in such a rush nowadays, with junior hockey and what-not, and that is too bad I think. I remember back to my playing days at Bloomington Jefferson and how much fun that was. I wouldn't trade a year of that to get ahead by a year in my hockey career, no way. But, that is just me. For me, the NHL was a goal, it wasn't the be-all-end-all. Kids are becoming so specialized now too, which is not good either. I see peewees quitting other sports to focus on hockey, and they are missing out. They also have to guarantee that they will be at every game and every practice all Summer, or else they can't play on the team. I am sorry, but that is just wrong — and it is not good for the long-term growth of our sport." — *Dan Trebil, Gopher 1992-96*

"I honestly think that if you were to take a poll of NHLers and ask them which is the top state for hockey, not only in terms of where guys grow up and develop, but also where guys want to play during their careers — Minnesota would probably be No. 1, followed by Massachusetts and Michigan. The Canadian guys I play with can't even fathom our state high school tournament, that is the coolest thing for them to see whenever they are in town here in March. So, we are doing all right I think, but we never want to become complacent either." — *Erik Westrum, Gopher 1997-2001*

"I think it is as good as it has ever been. The numbers are up in about every association around the state, which is awesome. With the Wild here now I think that helped a lot. Kids are interested in playing the game and that is what it is all about. From there, we have the best high school tournament in the country; five Division One college teams; and a pro franchise in the Wild that is just a great organization. So, we are doing great I think." — *Blake Wheeler, Gopher 2005-Present*

"I think we are doing great. There are a lot of opinions on this, but my take on it is that when you look at the core nucleus of our youth feeder programs, we are solid. The girls programs have basically doubled the fan base too, which is great. I also think that Gopher Hockey is so important to all of this because it is such a pillar here that will never falter. I mean high school hockey will have its ups and downs, its cyclical, and so will the Wild. But the Gophers are a constant. The names and faces change, but the tradition and pride always stay the same." — *Dean Williamson, Gopher 1987-90*

"At the youth levels all I can say is that there is too much money being spent on stuff that is not so important. There is way too much traveling; there are too many all-star, Triple-A, elite teams; and too much specialization with the younger kids. I also think that we have too many parents getting involved for the wrong reasons and too many 'boards.' It has gotten so political and so legal, even at the youth levels. It's like 'we'll sue you...' or what have you. Coaches are getting scared away from all of this.

"You know, as parents for some reason we want our kids to play; to learn the sport; learn sportsmanship; learn teamwork; and to simply keep them off the streets and out of trouble. So, why do we do so many dumb things to discourage or embarrass our kids from doing the thing we really want them to do in the first place. Things like our behavior in the car on the way home; criticizing the coach; and ranting and raving at the rink. A lot of parents are just too invested and they want to see a return on that investment. There are just too many juries, too much entitlement and too much scrutinizing going on. What ever happened to playing for fun? That is how we grew up, and it's sad to see how some of this has evolved.

"On the positive side, we are still developing players; we have a lot of rinks; and we have a lot of tremendous youth coaches who are giving their time to these kids to help them get better. That, in my opinion, is what it should all be about." — *Doug Woog, Former Gopher Player & Coach; current Gopher Hockey TV Analyst*

"I think it is pretty good overall. Kids today really are better skaters with much better technique than I ever had at a young age, that is for sure. The big problem that I see in our association is that a lot of kids seem to be in way over their heads. So, I don't know if they are having as much fun as they should be. I think our society is too worried about playing at this level or that level, rather than playing at a level where they will excel and just enjoy the game. Kids develop at such different rates. A kid at 10 years old might not be the same kid at 16. We need to stick with our kids so that they don't get too frustrated or burn out. We need to help them develop and work with them. We also need to let them be kids and play other sports. There is no reason little kids should be playing hockey all year round. The important thing is that kids are having fun and that they want to come back year in and year out, and that they want to get better." — *Doug Zmolek, Gopher 1989-92*

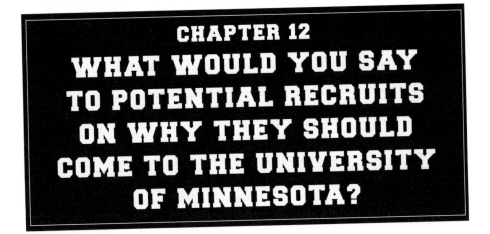

CHAPTER 12
WHAT WOULD YOU SAY TO POTENTIAL RECRUITS ON WHY THEY SHOULD COME TO THE UNIVERSITY OF MINNESOTA?

"Whenever I talk to recruits or their families, I don't talk so much about Gopher Hockey nowadays, instead it is about the opportunities that they will have when they are done playing. That is the key. I talk about the TV exposure that they get and how that translates into business connections after hockey." — *Mark Bahr, Gopher 1991-94, Current Director of Hockey Operations*

"Every recruit is different. If he is a blue-chip recruit then he will for sure get to visit the top programs: the Michigans, the Boston Colleges the North Dakotas and of course, the Minnesotas. Each of those schools is great for their own reasons but for me Minnesota was the perfect fit. It comes down to being comfortable with the guys and being comfortable with the city you will be playing in. Plus, you want to get the most out of your education while you are here, and that was big for me too, being able to come to a great academic institution. Plus, we have great coaches here. Coach Lucia is definitely a players-coach and understands that in college hockey you need to just let your players play the game — and that is what he does. He makes you feel very comfortable and gets the best out of his players. He has a fun system to play under and as a player that is all you can ask for. He also stresses the importance of academics and never let us forget that we were student-athletes. He just keeps his players very focused and really has a plan. I respect him so much, we all did." — *Keith Ballard, Gopher 2001-04*

"I think it is the best place to play in all of college hockey. I don't think you will find a better atmosphere, night in and night out, anywhere else. The program is solid from the top down and it has consistently always been that way. As a player, knowing that if you come here you will always have a chance to compete for a national championship each and every year, that is a huge selling point. Being on TV every week is pretty sweet too. All of that factors into the big picture. Beyond that, you will get a great education here and then be able to tap into the old-boy network which is alive and well here in the Twin Cities. Lastly, I would say too that it is pretty amazing to know that almost all of your teammates are going to wind up living here. I mean if you go to North Dakota and your teammates are from all over Canada, from the East Coast, and Colorado, odds are you will lose touch with most of those guys over the years as you get older. For me, it is so awesome knowing that all of my teammates are still here and that our families can hang out together for the next 50 years. Those friendships are what it is all about when it is all said and done." — *Scott Bell, Gopher 1991-95*

"I would tell them that there is only one University of Minnesota, and it's the best college hockey program in the country. It is the best of the best; the best arena; the best fans; the best players; and the best tradition. What more could you ask for?" — *Reggie Berg, Gopher 1995-99*

"To get a chance to put on that 'M' sweater is something only a select few get to do, so if it happens — congratulations. To be a part of that tradition and history is pretty special. I can honestly say that it was the greatest four years of my life, no question. And the friendships will last a lifetime." — *Grant Bischoff, Gopher 1987-91*

"First, I am not allowed to talk to potential recruits. However, if I were to say something to a kid off the street, who wasn't coming here (laughing), I would tell him that we run a pretty straightened arrow program here. They follow the rules here and they do things by the book. That is a big part of why they have been so successful." — *Patty Bjorklund, Longtime Gopher Hockey Administrative Assistant*

"Once your career is over, you start to realize pretty quickly that there is more to life than hockey. You realize how important your education is and you realize how invaluable the friendships and relationships that you made here are. Going to the U of M was one of the best decisions I ever made in my life. The connections I have now are invaluable. So, unless you are guaranteed to make it to the NHL and be set for the rest of your life, there are other things that you need to think about. Beyond that, the tradition here is second to none; the arena is amazing; and the fans are amongst the best in the world. Do you enjoy playing in front of 10,000 fans and being on TV every week? Come on, what else do you want? The U of M is the entire package, it really is." — *Brian Bonin, Gopher 1992-96*

"The coaching staff here is the best in the business, just a really great group of guys. Aside from that, the tradition here is just incredible. Playing hockey at the University of Minnesota is truly a life-changing experience." — *Kellen Briggs, Gopher 2003-Present*

"First of all, if you are going to live here after hockey, there is no better place to play. People know you and they will help you out. Secondly, the fans here are just great. Third, the hockey program is second to none and it has a wonderful tradition and history. Lastly, it is a great school, which means most importantly, that you will get a good education here." — *Bill Butters, Gopher Player 1971-73; Assistant Coach 1985-95*

"I would tell them to walk out onto the ice and take a look up at all of those banners. Then, I would tell them to walk through the finest college hockey arena in the country and look at all the old photos of all the great players who have passed through here. Beyond that, I would tell them that if they are looking for a program that is rich in tradition, then this is the place they should be." — *Harry Broadfoot, Gopher Equipment Manager 1986-Present*

"The first thing is that you will be playing for a national championship each and every year here. Secondly, for me, it was about coming to a Division One school where hockey was the main sport. I mean I went to check out the University of Michigan, which is a great school with great sports, but the fact of the matter is that the fans there would much rather watch the Wolverines play the Gophers in football rather than in hockey. So, that was a big factor for me. Thirdly, the atmosphere here with the fans and the facilities is just amazing. I mean you can't beat it. It is such a great campus atmosphere here. You don't get that in Canada at all. The people really rally around their teams here and that is so cool to see. I just love living here, there is so much stuff to do, like watching the Vikings and the Timberwolves. So, it is really the complete package when you factor all of those things into the equation." — *Kris Chucko, Gopher 2003-Present*

"Not only is it the best college hockey program in the country, it also has an amazing academic program. There are so many opportunities for kids there educationally, and that is a big part of it. Beyond that, the college atmosphere is so much fun there, being in the city. Plus, if you are talented enough to make it in the NHL, going to Minnesota will only enhance that. You will be playing under the top coaches; playing and training in the finest facilities; and will get so much television exposure that it is not even funny. So, if they want you, you should feel very fortunate. Congratulations." — *Ben Clymer, Gopher 1996-98*

"The media exposure that you will get there when you are playing is second to none in college hockey. That exposure helps not only with your chances of turning pro, but also when you go out and look for a job after hockey. On top of that, you will get to play in arguably the premier arena in the country and in front of 10,000 fans each and every night. Throw in the pride and tradition factor, and it is the complete package. Trust me, the memories and friendships will last a lifetime." — *Mike Crowley, Gopher 1994-97*

"I would tell that recruit to think of all the tradition and of all the great players who have skated for this program in years past. Then, I would take him to a game and let him see what it is like to skate in front of 10,000 screaming fans who care so passionately about that team. Gopher hockey means so much to people all over the state of Minnesota and it is a privilege to wear that 'M.' Hopefully, they will realize that if they come here, that they will be a part of something really meaningful. Plus, they will be playing in a state-of-the-art facility and getting a ton of media exposure, which will not only help their hockey career down the road, but also their business career after hockey. It is a once in a lifetime opportunity to play here and hopefully that is something they will want to be a part of. And hey, if hockey doesn't work out, then at worst they will leave here with a world class education from one of the best universities in the Midwest." — *Steve DeBus, Gopher 1995-98*

"From all of the Gophers who I have known over the years, I have always heard a common thread about why they like it here: the guys are good friends; there are no big egos; and they don't have any problems with cliques on the team. From their vantage point, it's like having 20 best friends. There is a real brotherhood amongst Gopher hockey players which is really special that you don't always see with other programs where the players are from all over the place. The team chemistry is just phenomenal here and that is a big part of why they have had so much success
     "The biggest testimonial as to why a recruit should come here in my eyes is Grant Potulny. Grant grew up in Grand Forks, the heart of Sioux country, dreaming of being a Gopher. That guy just lives Gopher hockey, it means so much to him even to this day. I remember last year being out in Columbus for the Frozen Four. We are losing to UND, 4-0, late in the game and my cell phone rings. I answer it and it's Grant calling from Binghamton, New York, where he was playing in Ottawa's minor league system. He is watching the game on ESPN and he is just beside himself. He was so passionate and upset about how the team was playing. So, we are talking and all of a sudden the Gophers score two quick goals late in the game to make it interesting, and Grant is going nuts. He is actually screaming the rouser 'M-I-N-N-E-S-O-T-A!' over the phone and can hardly contain himself. Well, the Gophers lost that game, but it just goes to show you how much some of these guys really do care. It is the passion that guys like Grant Potulny have for this program that make it what it is today. He epitomizes the cliché 'Once a Gopher, always a Gopher,' and you have to totally respect that." — *Jeff Dubay, KFAN Radio Host & Longtime Gopher Fanatic*

"I would definitely recommend it. I think it is truly the best of both worlds in that they have a great hockey program with great facilities, coaches, fans and tradition. Then, you've got an opportunity to leave there with a great education which will take you a long ways, especially if you want to live in Minnesota after hockey." — *Joe Dziedzic, Gopher 1990-94*

"I think you come to Minnesota because that is where you want to be. It is a great experience and something you will never regret. There are more opportunities both on and off the ice at the U of M than anywhere in the country. It has it all. If you are a Minnesota kid there is no greater honor than to wear the 'M' in my opinion." — *Ken Gernander, Gopher 1988-91*

"I am a big tradition guy and as far as tradition goes, this is as good as it gets. I mean Gopher Hockey in itself is like no other University sport based on folklore alone. I think that there is some magic in that and that is why kids grow up dreaming of wearing that big 'M.' It is just a very special program with so much pride and respect behind it. So, any young man or woman who gets the opportunity to come here to play hockey and get a great education should look at it as a privilege." — *Eric Gislason, Former Gopher Radio & Television Commentator*

"I think if you look at location, facilities, resources, academics, coaching, commitment by the university to the program, media exposure, and tradition — I think the Gophers rank No. 1 or 2 in every one of those aspects. So, if any of those criteria are important to you in selecting a school, then the University of Minnesota is for you." — *Mike Guentzel, Gopher Player 1981-85; Assistant Coach 1994-Present*

"The tradition that is at Minnesota is just second to none. To put on that maroon and gold sweater is the ultimate and I would say that if you get the chance to play here, take it, because it will probably be one of the best decisions you will ever make in your life. The program is just first class from top to bottom and arguably the very best in the nation." — *Gino Guyer, Gopher 2003-Present*

"First, the hockey program here is second to none. If you come here you will have a decent shot at playing for a national championship year in and year out. Second, you have to look at life after hockey. When you are out looking for a job, people know you and that goes a long, long way. You really become a part of the community when you are a Gopher and as much as that is a big responsibility, it is also a huge blessing down the road." — *Ben Hankinson, Gopher 1987-91*

"It is really the complete package. If you want to settle in Minnesota after hockey, then there is no better place. Period. To play in front of your home-state fans in a world class facility, then this is the place for you. And, if you want to come here as a part of your bigger plan to get to the next level, then that is great too, because the hockey program here is just fantastic. We have had so many players go on to play in the NHL from Minnesota and that pipeline has been built up over years and years of great players and great teams. Plus, the media exposure that kids get here really helps that too. So, it is a great overall place to go to school and if you are lucky enough to get the chance to play here, you would be a fool not to." — *Casey Hankinson, Gopher 1994-98*

"There are so many things to do in the Twin Cities, that was a huge motivating factor for me. I mean it is a Big 10 school; there are pro sports here; a great nightlife in downtown; you have the arts and theater, if you are into that; you just have so much to do. That, of course, is all on top of playing hockey at arguably the best college program in the country. Beyond that, your business career will be greatly enhanced by going to school here. That in itself is huge, believe me." — *Peter Hankinson, Gopher 1986-90*

"The hockey program here is one of the elite in the nation, but what really separates the University of Minnesota from the other schools is the entire package. The school itself is amazing and that is so important for life after hockey. Beyond that, the tradition and pride that the program has is just unbelievable. Most of us players all grew up watching the team and dreaming of wearing the 'M' and we all share that in common. As a result, we all get along; we all hang out with each other; and we all have a lot of fun together. We don't have any cliques on our team, we are all just great friends, which is great. So, it is just the overall experience, which is just second to none. It is truly a once in a lifetime opportunity to play here and something you will never regret." — *Chris Harrington, Gopher 2002-Present*

"For me, I just grew up dreaming of being a Gopher so it wasn't even a choice. I was so proud and happy when they took me that I couldn't believe it. That was me. For other guys, it is all about the best fit for them and about where they think they will have success. I will say this though, you won't find a better all-around program anywhere else that is even close to the University of Minnesota. It is the best. Period." — *Darby Hendrickson, Gopher from 1991-93*

"As a recruit I think you have to consider what is the best option for you. I think that most kids from around here would say that the University of Minnesota would be their top choice, but things don't always work out for everybody. Plus, a lot of guys would rather go to a different program if they know that they will have a better chance of getting more ice time. For me, I think this is one of the top hockey programs in the country. The tradition and history speaks for itself." — *Tyler Hirsch, Gopher 2002-Present*

"Just to be a part of this winning tradition is enough for most kids. I mean to go to one of the best programs in the nation is such an honor. It is a great school; you get tons of media coverage here with TV and the radio; and the facilities are the best in the country. The best part about it though, without a doubt, is the fact that everybody on the team genuinely gets along and likes each other. The coaches do a great job of creating good chemistry amongst the players and because of that we just have fun. I saw that right away on my recruiting visit, there were no cliques and the guys all seemed to be genuinely good friends. That is my favorite part for sure." — *Danny Irmen, Gopher 2003-Present*

"I think the tradition speaks for itself. The campus, the city, the education — it is the entire package. To have the opportunity to represent your state and to be able to play big-time college hockey in an environment like that is pretty amazing." — *Craig Johnson, Gopher 1990-93*

"In my opinion, Minnesota is the best hockey school in the country. The fans are great and the atmosphere is just second to none. Aside from that, they have a great coaching staff which really cares about its players. So, it is just a great program." — *Phil Kessel, Gopher 2005-Present*

"Because it's the best. Do you need any more of a reason?" — *Trent Klatt, Gopher 1989-92*

"The tradition and the fans here are second to none. I think a great testimonial to our program's success is the fact that whenever we play other teams, they always really want to 'Beat Minnesota!'. It's like the Yankees a little bit in that teams always come gunning for us maybe even more so than when they play other opponents. You never have a night off when you are a Gopher because every team you line up against is full of guys who wanted to play here but never got the opportunity to do so. So, they bring it and they bring it hard to make a statement. I think that says a lot. Beyond that, this is such a great school with so much to do here in the Twin Cities. We just had a ball together and the friendships I made here are going to be with me for the rest of my life. What else could a guy ask for?" — *Matt Koalska, Gopher 2000-04*

"Not only is it a great program where you are going to get noticed, it is also a great lifestyle. And when I say lifestyle I mean both while you are at school, living in the Twin Cities, as well as after hockey when you want to settle down and establish your career. I have already made connections that will set me up for the rest of my life. You will meet people here who will give you direction and reassurance that there is life after hockey. You will also have a strong feeling and sense of belonging with the community as well. That is really gratifying. Beyond that, the friendships and relationships that you foster here are priceless. So, it is the complete package, it really is." — *Ryan Kraft, Gopher 1994-98*

"Number one it is a good school, academically. Number two it has solid program with a fabulous arena. Number three it is a great media market, so you will get a lot of exposure on TV while you are here. Factor all of those things together and you realize pretty quickly that this is a tremendous place to play." — *Bob Kurtz, former Gopher Broadcaster*

"It's a Minnesota pride thing. It's the pinnacle of college hockey and probably the best hockey institution in America." — *Cory Laylin, Gopher 1988-92*

"To me it's easy. There is no better college hockey program in the country. Not when you factor in the academics, the facilities, the location and all of the media attention. I mean between the TV, radio and newspapers here all covering us, we are like a mini NHL franchise. That exposure is great not only in a hockey sense, but also for when you are done playing the game and want to begin your business career here in the Twin Cities. It is just an incredible experience to play here in the state of hockey and is really just the complete package." — *Don Lucia, Current Gopher Head Coach*

"Come take a tour; check out the arena; the locker room; the weight room; the pictures up on the walls of all the great players and great teams; and then ask yourself if you want to be a part of that." — *Paul Martin, Gopher 2000-03*

"You will not find a better school in terms of the exposure you will get here; you won't find a better rink; you won't find a better big city campus that has such good academics; and you won't find a better all around program. It is just second to none. You have so many different things at your fingertips here, and the entire experience is just unbelievable. I still miss it." — *Chris McAlpine, Gopher 1990-94*

"The tradition is so amazing there. They have always had a successful hockey program as well as a solid academic program. Going to class; getting good grades and getting our degrees was always emphasized big-time. So, if you are serious about being a student-athlete at one of the best hockey schools in the country, then this is the place for you." — *Jason Miller, Gopher 1987-91*

"All in all it is such a great school. There are a ton of opportunities for kids there both on and off the ice. You are in a great city and you are going to play in a first class arena with amazing fans. The tradition is second to none and for sure one of the top overall programs in the country. It is a great place to grow up and learn about life. The friendships you will make there will last a lifetime and the experiences and memories are just priceless." — *Nate Miller, Gopher 1996-00*

"It is such a great program with such a rich history. Coach Lucia is doing a great job over there and he really develops his kids to play hockey the right way. Beyond that, getting your degree from the U of M is a big deal, especially if you want to live and work in the Twin Cities after college. That combination of athletics and academics is what makes the program the best in the country in my opinion." — *Jeff Nielsen, Gopher 1990-94*

"The atmosphere in Mariucci Arena should almost be reason enough. The fans; the tradition; the history; the facilities; the coaching staff; the fact that they are in the hunt for the national championship year in and year out; and the great education that kids get there. It is all of those things and really so much more." — *Larry Olimb, Gopher 1988-92*

"When you come to Minnesota you get the whole package. You get to live in the big city; go to a great school; and play hockey in the best program in the country. If I had the chance to do it all over again I would do it in a second, it was just an awesome experience." — *Tom Pederson, Gopher 1988-91*

"There is a history of excellence here. It is just a great place to come get a solid education while also playing college hockey for the best program in the country. Beyond that, it is just a fabulous place to come and to lay down your roots. If you want to stick around the Twin Cities after your playing days are over, then this is definitely the place for you. The media exposure and the contacts you will make here are invaluable. This program is big-time, it's the real deal from top to bottom." — *Lance Pitlick, Gopher 1986-90*

"You know, I honestly think that Coach Lucia could walk up to any recruit out there and say to him 'What do you want?' Any answer that the recruit could give, the University can realistically satisfy that. If the recruit says he wants to play for the national championship every year; done deal. If the recruit says he wants to play in a fantastic rink; done. If he wants to be on

TV and get a lot of exposure; done. And, if he says he wants to get a great education and go to a great, well-rounded school; so done. Or, if he doesn't care about school that much and just wants to make it in the NHL; he can do that too, that is up to him. So, the 'U' has everything and that is why it is the best college hockey program in the country." — *Johnny Pohl, Gopher 1998-2002*

"For starters, you have to look at who is steering the ship. Right now I don't think there is a better coach in college hockey than Lucia. He is not a 'my way or the highway' type of coach. He is a great recruiter and he is extremely well respected by his players. He just demands excellence and his players want to play hard for him. Beyond the coach, the program has one of the best arenas in the country; one of the best weight rooms in the country; and the media coverage is second to none. The academics are amazing here too, with a ton of career options for kids to choose from. On top of all that, you get to live and go to school in a huge city with so much fun stuff to do. The job opportunities for alumni are huge too, because people here love their Gophers. If you want to go on to play at the next level, there is just no better place. So, if you are very serious about being a student-athlete and are serious about winning, then this is the place for you." — *Grant Potulny, Gopher 2000-04*

"I would say that they were crazy if they didn't come. The tradition and history pretty much speak for itself. Just walk around the arena and look at all the pictures of the All-Americans and Hobey Bakers winners. It is amazing. It is also pretty humbling to be a part of all that. When we bring in recruits they like seeing the arena and the facilities, but what makes them stay is the guys. We all genuinely like each other and that type of sincere chemistry is extremely unique in sports. Aside from all of that, it is about the friendships that you make. It is like a big family. On and off the ice we are all buddies. Even when guys move on we still stay in touch. In fact, all of the guys come home in the Summers and we still skate together. That is so awesome. Being a Gopher is the bond that holds us all together and that is so special." — *Ryan Potulny, Gopher 2003-Present*

"If you get the opportunity to go to the University of Minnesota, and you turn it down, I think that would be a huge mistake. As a life decision, there is no better place to go. I mean you have to feel comfortable with your surroundings, a la being in a big city, and you obviously have to be in a financial situation that you are OK with, a la a scholarship. If that is all good, then it is a no-brainer. I mean at the U of M, it is like a pro atmosphere. You are on TV every week; you are on the radio; and you are followed by two big papers. You are really treated like a professional there, so you need to act like a professional. You are given every benefit that you could ever want there, and you get a top-notch education on top of that. Then, above and beyond all of that, you will make so many great contacts for life after hockey. I certainly plan on retiring there and starting my business career there. It was all set up on a silver platter." — *Erik Rasmussen, Gopher 1995-97*

"When you look at the University of Minnesota's program over the years, it has certainly been one of the top in the country, if not the top, in terms of the entire package. From academics to the facility to the tradition to producing star players — it has it all. Plus, those kids get a ton of exposure that players at smaller schools couldn't dream of." — *Tommy Reid, Former Gopher TV & Radio Announcer*

"You know, most of the top teams have fancy new arenas nowadays, but Minnesota's program is just head and shoulders above everybody else. Hockey rules in Minnesota and it doesn't play second fiddle to any other sports like you see elsewhere. So, if you get the chance to wear the 'M,' consider yourself extremely lucky to have been asked to join one of the most exclusive clubs in sports." — *Travis Richards, Gopher 1989-93*

"The tradition here is so amazing. Plus, it is the most fun you will ever have in your life. It is the No. 1 program in the country and if you get the chance to be a part of it, take it, you will never regret it." — *Troy Riddle, Gopher 2000-04*

"It's a top-notch program with a winning tradition as well as a world class university. So, it is really the best of both worlds. Furthermore, look at the alumni contacts you can make by coming here and then living and working here after hockey." — *Wally Shaver, Longtime Gopher Radio & TV Announcer*

"It is the best program in the country, hands down. From the education you will get there; to being in a big city; to the amount of exposure you are going to get on TV; to the coaching staff; to the facility; to the success and tradition that the program has — it is the complete package." — *Wyatt Smith, Gopher 1995-99*

"Minnesota has got such a great program. If you are a great player, you will thrive here in this environment and will undoubtedly be well on your way to having a successful pro career. No question. I would also say that if you want to live here after hockey, then you would be crazy not to go here. I mean with the exposure you get nowadays, you can parlay that a long ways into your business career well after your playing days are over. Beyond that, it is an excellent university and you will get a very good degree there. It is the complete package, athletics and academics, it really is." — *Glen Sonmor, Former Gopher, North Stars & Fighting Saints Coach; Current Gopher Radio Broadcaster*

"The University of Minnesota is just so rich in tradition. To play in the state of hockey at a program like that is just amazing. Then, to have so many opportunities waiting for you after you graduate, that is hard to say no to. Plus, you grow up a lot living in the big city, away from your family, which is good too. It is just a great stepping stone, whether you want to play in the NHL or whether you want to be a doctor or lawyer. It's just a great place and trust me, you will have a lot of options when you are ready to hang up your skates." — *Dave Spehar, Gopher 1996-2000*

"If you are lucky enough to come here, you will have the privilege of playing in front of the greatest college hockey fans in the world. This program is big-time. From the history, to the packed arena, to the TV coverage, to the big city life, to the coaches, to the mystique — it's got it all." — *Robb Stauber, Gopher 1986-89; Current Gopher Goalie Coach*

"I just can't say enough about how great it is to live and go to school and play hockey in the Twin Cities. I used to love going to pro sports games and going out downtown Minneapolis with the guys, it is just an awesome place to be when you are in college. That for me was the biggest thing. Obviously, the hockey, the fans and the tradition of the program, that all speaks for itself." — *Jeff Taffe, Gopher 1999-02*

"There is such an incredible tradition here. The facilities are all top notch too, from the arena to the locker room to the weight room, it is all first class. Plus, you get treated so well, like a real professional. Add to that the fact that you get to go to one of the best academic schools in the Midwest and it makes it the complete package. It has to be one of the top one or two programs in the nation, without a doubt." — *Barry Tallackson, Gopher 2001-05*

"Most Minnesota kids grow up watching and listening to the Gophers, and then dream of playing there. I think those kids will always be loyal to Minnesota. The draw for the kids outside the state is the fact that this is the only WCHA school that is in a major city with a big-time facility packed full of fans. And with that comes a lot of media exposure, which is a big selling point to kids who want to take their hockey careers as far as they can. It is also a big selling point for life after hockey too, which makes the U of M a very attractive program both on and off the ice. Add to that the fact that you have one of the best coaches in all of college hockey and the future looks pretty bright for the Gophers. I don't think they are done winning titles yet, not by a long shot." — *Dan Terhaar, Former Gopher Radio Announcer*

"Looking back, I wouldn't trade my college experience for anything. I could have gone out East to some schools which maybe had better academics than the University of Minnesota, but when you look at the entire package of school and hockey, and life-after-hockey, it was a no-brainer. This is one of the best all-around college hockey programs in the country, without a doubt. It is just a great place with so much tradition and history. To be a part of that was priceless." — *Dan Trebil, Gopher 1992-96*

"I would tell them to look at the program's winning tradition, that is what I looked at. When you come here you are expected to win, so if you want to be a part of that then this is for you. Aside from that, they have great facilities; great fans who understand hockey; and it is just a great place to live and go to school." — *Thomas Vanek, Gopher 2002-04*

"When a new recruit comes in for a visit it is really important to Coach Lucia that we spend time with him and that he sees us hanging out together. I think he takes pride in the fact that all of us genuinely like each other and we all choose to hang out with each other. There is no dissension among us, we enjoy each other's time. So, as a result, the recruits see that and immediately feel comfortable. Chemistry is an important thing and that goes a long way in keeping our roster full of top talent. Beyond that, I would just tell recruits how I honestly feel: this is the best college hockey program in the country. Plus, it is a lot of fun, which is what it is all about." — *Mike Vannelli, Gopher 2003-Present*

"In my opinion there is not a better program in the country when you look at both hockey and school. It has it all. Aside from the tradition and the pride, when you graduate from the University you will have an outstanding education that will take you places, especially here in Minnesota. There are a lot of job opportunities here and the exposure that you get while you are with the team only enhances your career after hockey. So, it is the complete package as far as I am concerned." — *Erik Westrum, Gopher 1997-2001*

"Why go anywhere else? Everything you would ever need is right here. You will be pressed to find a better rink in all of college hockey and you will be pressed to find a better coach in all of college hockey. The tradition; the pride; the history — it is all just second to none. If you are lucky enough to be recruited here I don't know how you could possibly pass it up. It is just the best of the best." — *Blake Wheeler, Gopher 2005-Present*

"In my mind this is without question the premier college hockey program in the country. The history, tradition and pride are huge. Beyond that, you have to look at life after hockey and all of the opportunities you will have here when your playing days are over. Those connections are invaluable. You know, I have several friends who played college hockey up at North Dakota. They were great players and had a great time up in Grand Forks, but when they moved on, that chapter of their lives stayed behind up there. For me, even 20 years later, I am still living here in the Twin Cities and am still a part of the program. I am in the community, my business has thrived here because of my affiliation with Gopher Hockey, and on top of that, I still get to hang out with my old teammates. In fact, I live about a sand wedge away from former Gophers Wally Chapman and Benny Hankinson. Now, our kids all play hockey together, which is so great to see. So, it is the total package both now as well as in the future." — *Dean Williamson, Gopher 1987-90*

"This is a professional media market and kids who play here will get a lot of exposure on television and on the radio. No place in America covers college hockey like the Twin Cities. That is so invaluable for life after hockey. To be known in a hockey community like this, where people understand and appreciate hockey, is such an advantage career-wise. Beyond that, kids who come here will be very well coached and they will always be in the hunt for a national championship. You will get to play at a world class university in a world class facility. The opportunities are endless here. Come on, what more do you want?" — *Doug Woog, Former Gopher Player & Coach; current Gopher Hockey TV Analyst*

"I liked the University because it prepared you for the real world. The classrooms were huge and you were on your own there to either do good, or to do bad. There was no in-between. Nobody held your hand there, you had to grow up or you would get thrown out. You don't have that at smaller schools, and that is not for everybody. The hockey program, meanwhile, simply speaks for itself. All the past glory, the tradition, the players — it should be a no-brainer." — *Doug Zmolek, Gopher 1989-92*

CHAPTER 13
WHAT WOULD YOU LIKE TO SAY TO THE FANS WHO HAVE SUPPORTED YOU OVER THE YEARS IN GOLD COUNTRY?

"Thank you for making a young kid's dreams come true." — *Mike Anderson, Gopher 1995-99*

"Our fans are so great. They give us so much support, whether we are playing at Mariucci or on the road in Boston. They are so loyal and so passionate about the team and that is what makes it so special." — *Mark Bahr, Gopher 1991-94, Current Director of Hockey Operations*

"Just thanks. We have the best fans in the world here and I couldn't even begin to tell them how much I appreciated their support." — *Keith Ballard, Gopher 2001-04*

"The fans are what makes Minnesota hockey. Period. They are so loyal, so positive and so passionate about their Gophers, and I was just so lucky to have been a part of that. They are so smart about the game and really appreciate hard work and dedication. It was a joy to play for them and believe me when I say that the pleasure was all mine." — *Scott Bell, Gopher 1991-95*

"Thanks wouldn't even come close. They are the best hockey fans a player could ever ask for. They are there night in and night out, cheering for you whether you win or whether you lose, which was amazing. They are just second to none. I was very lucky to have gotten the opportunity to play at Mariucci Arena in front of 10,000 screaming fans every Friday and Saturday night during the season. I will never forget those memories, they are priceless." — *Reggie Berg, Gopher 1995-99*

"I want to particularly thank the guys in the 'NE' section! Our fans are the best, but the student section was always the loudest and craziest by far. They were awesome to me and just made my entire experience there so memorable. They were the ones who created that home-ice winning atmosphere. So, thanks." — *Grant Bischoff, Gopher 1987-91*

"I would like to say thanks to the fans for supporting this program so loyally through the years. I would also like to thank our coaching staff for being such good people too. I am now at the age where some of the parents are younger than me, so that is how long I have been here. When anybody asks me how many years I have been with the program I tell them that Coach Guentzel was a junior on the team my first year here. That long! So the moral of the story is: be good to your players because you never know when they are going to come back and be your boss." — *Patty Bjorklund, Longtime Gopher Hockey Administrative Assistant*

"I have often dreamt about finding a way to say thanks to the fans who supported me all those years. I just always tried to play my hardest and the fans really appreciated that. They were so good to me. All of them, from the fans at Mariucci to the people I met in the street. I appreciated it so much and just want them to know that. The college fans are so much better than the pro fans. In college it is intimate, you can really get to know the fans. We have functions where we get to know them and we embraced them. In the pros everybody is so private and stand-offish. It is totally different. Gopher fans are amazing. They feel like they are a part of the program and that they make a difference. And they're right, because they do. They got to know us and genuinely cared about us. The die-hard fans here are like family, they really are. I am sure that the same fans who cheered for me are still there, cheering for the next crop of kids. So, for me, the way to give back is to be around; to go to the games; to be accountable; and to teach the next generation of kids who shared the same dream that I had of one day being a Gopher." — *Brian Bonin, Gopher 1992-96*

"The fans here really know their hockey, so they don't just cheer for things that don't matter. Then, when they do cheer, it really reinforces that you did a good job. As a goalie that is really important. They are there every night too, which is the best feeling ever. They give us a big home-ice advantage too, which is huge for us. So, thanks, it means a lot." — *Kellen Briggs, Gopher 2003-Present*

"I would like to say thank you to the loyal fans who have always been there for Gopher hockey. Gopher hockey to me was never about any one person or player. Gopher hockey is a tradition that was built up by players who bought into the program and were proud to wear the 'M.' So, it wasn't about me, it was about the entire program. So, thanks to everybody who has been loyal and supported this program. The fans are a part of this program, make no mistake about it. They matter." — *Bill Butters, Gopher Player 1971-73; Assistant Coach 1985-95*

"Thank you. They have been great to me. Minnesota fans don't accept anything less than the best, and that is how it should be. They are so supportive of us and I just really appreciate it. Mariucci Arena is always full and that means the world to us." — *Kris Chucko, Gopher 2003-Present*

"My only regret is that I didn't stay longer. I am so envious of the players who did. It wasn't in the cards for me, but the fans always treated me great and for that I humbly say thank you. I am so grateful that I was able to spend a season there and to be a part of that amazing tradition. I will never forget it." — *Ben Clymer, Gopher 1996-98*

"Those were the greatest times in my life. The support we got from our fans was amazing. I am just sorry that we weren't able to win a national championship for them. That is my only regret. So, thanks for making my experience so special, it was truly the thrill of a lifetime." — *Mike Crowley, Gopher 1994-97*

"Thank you for being so supportive of me. The fans here cheer for a good game, they are extremely intelligent. It was a pleasure to play for you and I appreciated your support." — *Steve DeBus, Gopher 1995-98*

"Just thanks. It was so much fun. There were times when you were down and struggling, but they always brought you back up. It was amazing what a lift you got as a player when the band played the Rouser and the fans started cheering. We really do have the best college hockey fans in the country here, they are just awesome." — *Joe Dziedzic, Gopher 1990-94*

"I am so grateful and fortunate for having the opportunity to have played there. I couldn't even begin to try and express my gratitude as to how much I appreciated everything that they did for me." — *Ken Gernander, Gopher 1988-91*

"Our fans are the best. They live and die with us. They are so loyal, so enthusiastic, so knowledgeable and so passionate. They have stuck with us through the thick and thin and I couldn't thank them enough for their support. We owe them a lot for what they do for our program. We wouldn't be here without them. Because of their interest level we have a state-of-the-art arena and as a result we are able to make a commitment level to our program that is just second to none." — *Mike Guentzel, Gopher Player 1981-85; Assistant Coach 1994-Present*

"I have played in so many rinks around the country and I can honestly say that we have the best fans in the world. They are by far the most knowledgeable hockey fans around too. They make you want to play hard for them and to reward them for all of their support. When Mariucci Arena gets rockin', watch out, the players totally feed on that and they get pumped. I love our home ice advantage, it is amazing. So, thanks to all the fans who have supported me and rooted me on, I really appreciate it." — *Gino Guyer, Gopher 2003-Present*

"Gopher hockey just meant the world to me and the fans were so darn good to me over the years. I couldn't thank them enough for all of their support. I had so much fun going to school at the University of Minnesota and playing hockey there, it was just the thrill of a lifetime. Hey, every now and then I even see guys walking around with Gopher jerseys that say 'Kill Ben, Kill!'. I want to go up and hug those guys! Those were great, I just loved that kind of stuff. Our fans were so great, they really were." — *Ben Hankinson, Gopher 1987-91*

"They are the reason Gopher Hockey is so special. Mariucci Arena is the best college hockey arena in the country for one reason, the fans. They create an atmosphere in there that is so contagious and that is why the teams do so well in there, they don't want to disappoint those fans. I mean a great testimonial to that is the fact that when the Wild came to town and sold out 18,000 season tickets, or however many that number was, the Gopher season ticket base didn't budge. Gopher fans are so loyal and so passionate about their teams. That is why they are the best hockey fans in the country. So, thanks for your support over the years, it meant the world to me." — *Casey Hankinson, Gopher 1994-98*

"Thanks, it was the best. To play in your hometown in front of your hometown fans, it doesn't get any better than that. Our fans were so great too. They really understand the game and are so knowledgeable about it. Plus, they really respect the tradition here and have so much enthusiasm for the team." — *Peter Hankinson, Gopher 1986-90*

"They have been unbelievable to me. They are just great fans and extremely smart about hockey. They support us through the good times as well as the bad and we really appreciate that a lot. I love to go up into the crowd after games and to visit with them, that is so much fun. I have appreciated their support so much and couldn't begin to thank them enough for everything that they do." — *Chris Harrington, Gopher 2002-Present*

"Well, there were two different groups here for me. For the fans who liked me and supported me, thank you. I really appreciated your support. Now, for the other group of fans, the ones who weren't real comfortable with me in the net, I guess I don't have much to say. It was no big secret that a lot of people didn't like me and were not too supportive of me when I was playing. Apparently KFAN Radio had a bit where they said that the University of Minnesota would never win a national championship as long as Adam Hauser was in net, or something like that. That was difficult to handle. The one thing I will say to those guys, however, is that I understand now. Three years removed from college hockey, I have just now taken a look at old video tapes of me playing. It is humorous for me to watch. Now that I have been out on my own and have been studying pro hockey goaltenders, I have completely changed the way I play. So, looking back to the way I played back then I can see how I made them nervous. Hey, I made myself nervous watching the tapes. I am not mad now and I don't blame anybody for feeling the way they did. I am over it. I will say though, that one of the greatest moments in my life came after we won the national championship in St. Paul and I was walking off the ice at the Xcel Center. The first people that I saw were Jeff Dubay and Paul Allen, from KFAN, and as I was walking by I said to them 'How do you like me now?' Those two then came over to me in the locker-room and apologized to me for saying what they did. They said that I had proved them wrong, and that made me feel pretty darn good. I understood where they were coming from though. Jeff Dubay is a huge Gopher fan at heart and wanted so badly to win. So, I am Ok with all of that now." — *Adam Hauser, Gopher 1998-2002*

"I am really fortunate to play for a program that has so much fan loyalty. It is a really family friendly atmosphere at the arena and it is just an honor to be a part of that great tradition." — *Tyler Hirsch, Gopher 2002-Present*

"I would just want to say thanks to the greatest fans in college hockey. The way they support us is incredible, both on and off the ice. Gopher fans have always been there for their teams, through the good times and the bad, and that is what separates them from the other band-wagon jumpers that follow some of the other sports in town. You know, the biggest thing for me was when I saw grown men weeping after the team won its first national championship. Those are die-hard fans. That is what Minnesota hockey is all about." — *Danny Irmen, Gopher 2003-Present*

"Thank you. It meant a lot to me then and it still means a lot to me now. Minnesota hockey fans are everywhere, from Los Angeles to Germany, I see them all over, wearing their jerseys proudly. So, they are great and have been just wonderful to me over the years." — *Craig Johnson, Gopher 1990-93*

"The fans were tremendous to me while I was here and I will forever be grateful for that. The one thing I learned early on in my college hockey career was to put forth an effort on every shift that I was out on the ice. Otherwise you are cheating yourself; your teammates; and especially the fans. So, thanks for your awesome support." — *Trent Klatt, Gopher 1989-92*

"Just thanks for being there and for taking the time to be so supportive — it meant the world to me." — *Matt Koalska, Gopher 2000-04*

"Thank you for being the best fans in college hockey, bar none. They were always supportive, always positive, always uplifting, and they were always appreciative towards us. They are just the best." — *Ryan Kraft, Gopher 1994-98*

"All I can say is thank you. Hopefully they enjoy my style and that I have made some of their evenings entertaining." — *Bob Kurtz, former Gopher Broadcaster*

"Our fans were the best. They gave us so much energy and such an emotional lift. They were amazing. I couldn't begin to thank them enough, they really did make a difference." — *Cory Laylin, Gopher 1988-92*

"The people here have been so great to me and my family, and we really appreciate that. This is my fourth coaching job and while they have all been great, it is particularly special to be back in Minnesota and having success. The fans here are so smart and so enthusiastic and that makes our jobs so much easier as coaches. It is so sweet to see that the whole state embraces our hockey program, even though there are four other division one schools within the state. That just does not happen anywhere else and I am very lucky to have that kind of support. It is special. So, I am just on this train ride for a short time and when I get off, somebody else will get on and do a great job as well.

"The fans are what makes our program so special. I mean we have 10,000 seats sold for every game and another 2,000 people on the waiting list hoping to get tickets. That is amazing. Gopher hockey is very special to the people in our state and all I can say is thanks for your support, our entire program really appreciates it." — *Don Lucia, Current Gopher Head Coach*

"I wouldn't even know where to begin. They are the reason why we play, so it is truly all about them. They are like the sixth-man out there too, rooting us on and supporting us. That was a huge help to us to be able to count on that home-ice advantage." — *Paul Martin, Gopher 2000-03*

"Thank you, deeply. If the fans didn't care as much as they do, I wouldn't enjoy this job nearly the way I do, and may not even be doing it. I really appreciate their caring and their support, it means a lot to me. I am just glad to be there for them." — *Frank Mazzocco, Longtime Gopher TV Analyst*

"I would just say, hey, thank you for making the experience so memorable. It was the best time of my life playing here. To play in front of a packed house night in and night out, regardless of how we were playing, was just amazing. They're what make it so great, they are just the best fans in the world." — *Chris McAlpine, Gopher 1990-94*

"I would just say thanks for taking time out of your busy schedule to support us. The barn was always packed and it was always loud. It was just the best home-ice advantage we had there and as players, we really appreciated that." — *Jason Miller, Gopher 1987-91*

"Thank you. It was an amazing experience to be a part of that tradition. It was so fun to play in Mariucci Arena and to have all of those people rooting for us. Everywhere we went, both on and off campus, fans are always great to us and we really appreciate it. They are so educated here too. I have played all over and trust me, our fans know and understand the game. They aren't just loud, drunk idiots like at some other arenas, they get it. I mean they might be on their feet during a key penalty kill, stuff like that, which really got us as players going. The fans here just really, sincerely care about their team and about the players. Their enthusiasm was contagious. They set extremely high expectations for us and we tried to repay them by winning and being respectful." — *Nate Miller, Gopher 1996-00*

"The fans were so good to me here, both with the Gophers as well as when I was with the Wild. Our fans really understand hockey here and they follow their teams very passionately. So, thanks for your support, it meant a great deal to me and really enhanced my experience as a player." — *Jeff Nielsen, Gopher 1990-94*

"I see people even to this day who tell me that they enjoyed watching me play when I was a Gopher. Well, all I can say is that it was as much fun for me playing the game as it was for you to watch. So, thank you for your support. Minnesota fans are smart hockey people. They understand good hockey and they know what it going on out there. I have been to enough arenas in my day and have seen so many bad fans; people who are there to see fights or show poor sportsmanship. We had the best fans, we really did. It was a privilege to play there for them and I just appreciated everything that they did for me." — *Larry Olimb, Gopher 1988-92*

"It was the time of my life, so thank you for all your support. Gopher fans are some of the smartest hockey fans in the country, bar none. I have played in a lot of hockey rinks from coast to coast, and I can honestly say that they are the best of the best. I hope to return home sometime in the near future and give back by working with the kids there. That would be the best way I could think of to thank them, is by giving back and carrying the tradition on the next generation of kids." — *Tom Pederson, Gopher 1988-91*

"Minnesota is just a great place to live and play hockey. The people here are amazing. The fans get it and they are so supportive. You know, I used to love playing professional hockey up in Canada, because it reminded me of being in Minnesota. Everyone was friendly and you just wanted to play hard for them. So, thanks for your support, it was very appreciated." — *Lance Pitlick, Gopher 1987-90*

"Thanks for sticking with us when we weren't that good and thanks for being there when we were really good. You guys are awesome. Hopefully you enjoyed it half as much as we did." — *Johnny Pohl, Gopher 1998-2002*

"If I was ever lucky enough to someday win a Stanley Cup, I don't think it would be as special as winning the 2002 national championship. I say that because of what it meant to our fans. They are the best fans in college hockey, without a doubt. The people of Minnesota just live and breathe Gopher Hockey, and I was so thrilled to be a part of giving that to them. So, thanks for making my dreams come true, it was all for you guys." — *Grant Potulny, Gopher 2000-04*

"I could not even begin to thank them enough. I could sit here and thank them forever and it still wouldn't be enough. We have the best fans in the world, we really do. They are always there; they are always behind us; they always trust us; and they always support us — through the good times as well as the bad. And they are such genuinely nice and caring people too, which is what I love the most about them. As a result, we all want to play so hard for them every time we step onto the ice. That is why we have such a successful program, the fans." — *Ryan Potulny, Gopher 2003-Present*

"The fans are so special to play for there. They get it. They appreciate the history and they appreciate the tradition. As a player, it was so great to play in that environment. You could sense their emotions and feelings out on the ice, you really could. It was awesome. So, thanks for everything, your support meant a ton." — *Erik Rasmussen, Gopher 1995-97*

"They have been just great to me. Do you know what? As much enjoyment as they may get from me in doing the broadcast, I get that much more enjoyment back from them. They have always been very supportive of me and I really appreciate that. They always bring so much enthusiasm and just make it so much more enjoyable for me to do my job. So, thank you very much for your continued support." — *Tommy Reid, Former Gopher TV & Radio Announcer*

"Just a big thanks. I look back now it means so much to me. I mean I played in the Olympics and made it to the NHL, but nothing will ever compare to my four years in Gold Country. It was just fantastic. Our fans are so great there and just made the whole experience even more memorable." — *Travis Richards, Gopher 1989-93*

"We have such incredible fans here, they are so amazing. You can't really appreciate how smart, respectful and loyal they are until you play in some other arenas around the country. It isn't even close. So, thanks for supporting me and for rooting for me, it meant the world to me." — *Troy Riddle, Gopher 2000-04*

"I know how much everybody in the state of Minnesota loved my dad, Al, who did North Star's games for so long, and I always dreamed of being able to do the same thing. So, thanks to everybody out there who have allowed me to live my dream. If I can entertain hockey fans just a fraction of what my dad did, then I would consider that to be a real honor. The fans here are great and I just really appreciate the support that they have given me over the years. You know, hockey has been my whole life, that is all I have ever done and all I do now. So, it means the world to me to be able to do what I love." — *Wally Shaver, Longtime Gopher Radio & TV Announcer*

"Just a big, huge thank you. Playing for Minnesota was the greatest. The fans there are so classy too. They totally embrace the players and cheer for us, win or lose, and that meant so much. We went through some tough times during my last couple of years there but the fans still supported us and I will never forget that." — *Wyatt Smith, Gopher 1995-99*

"The two words that come to mind for starters are 'thank you.' The fans here were absolutely wonderful. They supported me through thick and thin and I really appreciated that so much. From the Gophers to the Fighting Saints to the North Stars, it was just amazing. Fans still stop me on the street to talk to me and are so complimentary, and that just means the world to me. It is so wonderful to have people come up to me and tell me that they enjoy listening to me. I really appreciate that. I am lucky to have an on-air partner as good as I do in Wally Shaver, he is just outstanding. I have been fortunate to work with some of the best in the business over the years, from Al Shaver to Dan Terhaar to now, Wally. The greatest compliment we get is when people say to us that we sound like we are having fun. That is what it is all about, it is truly so much fun to do what we do. It is a real labor of love and my enthusiasm for this program and for these kids is genuine. I love it." — *Glen Sonmor, Former Gopher, North Stars & Fighting Saints Coach; Current Gopher Radio Broadcaster*

"Thank you very, very much. The fans were always supportive, yet they were always honest.

If you weren't playing well they let you know about it in a respectful way. They were great to me, however, and I owe them more than I could ever repay them. It was just so special to have played there and I will forever be grateful for that. All of us players owe the University and the coaches a great deal, and hopefully we gave them something in return." — *Dave Spehar, Gopher 1996-2000*

"They are the best. They are just awesome. They are the best hockey fans in the world, they truly are. I have played in a lot of arenas over the past 15 years and I can honestly say that Gopher fans are the best. They are so knowledgeable; so passionate; so appreciative; so understanding; so supportive; and so loyal. I watch them now from up in the press box when I am coaching and I am always so impressed with them. They are just very respectful not only of the players, but of this program's tradition and history. They are always there for the players, win or lose, and they give the players such a home ice advantage. They just love Gopher Hockey and I feel so proud to have played for them. They are why we play this game and I am so humbled by the way they treated me. So, thanks, believe me it was my privilege." — *Robb Stauber, Gopher 1986-89; Current Gopher Goalie Coach*

"The fans there were always so good to me. They know the game and they respect it, and that is why they are the best fans in college hockey. So, I guess I would just say thanks, it was a lot of fun playing for you." — *Jeff Taffe, Gopher 1999-02*

"If it wasn't for them none of us would be here, so thanks for your support." — *Barry Tallackson, Gopher 2001-05*

"The fans here are fabulous. They are so passionate about Gopher Hockey and just really appreciate hard work and dedication. They were great to me when I was here, that was for sure. I think they appreciated my passion for the program and that meant a lot to me." — *Dan Terhaar, Former Gopher Radio Announcer*

"I guess thank you, for starters. There was nothing like being out on the ice when the crowd was just into it. They made a huge difference and I hope that they realize that. They have created just a very special atmosphere there that makes the program what it is today." — *Dan Trebil, Gopher 1992-96*

"I would just want to thank them for all their support. They made me feel so at home here and I really appreciated that. They were there for us every weekend at Mariucci Arena, through the good times and the bad times. It was always so much fun to play in front of 10,000 fans though, that just made our home-ice advantage that much better. It was very enjoyable to play for them and to be able to make their evenings enjoyable too." — *Thomas Vanek, Gopher 2002-04*

"We have the best hockey fans in the world, we really do. They are why we are out there and we appreciate everything that they do for us. So, thanks!" — *Mike Vannelli, Gopher 2003-Present*

"We appreciated all their support so much. I think that our fans were just amazing. They gave us such a home-ice advantage and really made it undesirable for other teams to come in here and face us. That was huge. So, thanks for taking care of us, and for your unwavering loyalty. You're the best." — *Erik Westrum, Gopher 1997-2001*

"I know that I haven't been here very long, but thanks for your support. It is amazing to skate at Mariucci Arena and to see the fans all there cheering for you. They are just fantastic fans. I don't know if they always realize how much they matter and how much they get us into a game. When they are loud and rowdy it really has an impact and gets us going. So, thanks for your encouragement, I totally appreciate it and promise to work hard for you." — *Blake Wheeler, Gopher 2005-Present*

"God bless you. You know, I had a funny story happen to me the other night that best exemplifies what type of fans we have here. I was walking into Braemar Arena in Edina to register my kids for hockey. I was there with Lance Pitlick and Benny Hankinson, whose kids were also signing up. Anyway, I am walking in and this guy comes up to me and says 'Hey, are you Dean Williamson?' I said 'Yes, who are you?' He then proceeded to tell me that he has been a lifelong Gopher season ticket holder since 1977 and he recognized me and just wanted to say hi. I mean I haven't been in school for almost 20 years and here I am with a hat on and two kids hanging all over me. So, I started talking to him and he really knew his history, a real die-hard. I wanted to really test his memory, so I grabbed Benny Hankinson's kids and I said to the guy 'All right, these kids' dad was a Gopher too, who was he?' Sure enough, he says 'Are they Hankinson's?' I couldn't believe it. We just have the best fans ever, and they are so respectful and loyal. I just couldn't even begin to thank them enough for what they have meant to me and my entire family." — *Dean Williamson, Gopher 1987-90*

"You know, I really miss the 'WOOOOOOOOOOOOOOOG!' cheers, that was just the best. So, thanks to those fans for cheering for me and sorry to the fans who were 'BOOOOOO-ing' me. It all sounded the same! Really though, the fans were great to me and I appreciated their support over the years so much." — *Doug Woog, Former Gopher Player & Coach; current Gopher Hockey TV Analyst*

"I would just like to say thank you. Our fans were great. When they cheered for you it was just the best. They were also very smart about hockey and weren't afraid to get on you when you weren't pulling your weight. So, we were just lucky to have such loyal fans who supported us the way that they did. I think its great that the Gopher fans support all of the sports at the University of Minnesota. That is what being a true fan is all about. I totally respect that." — *Doug Zmolek, Gopher 1989-92*

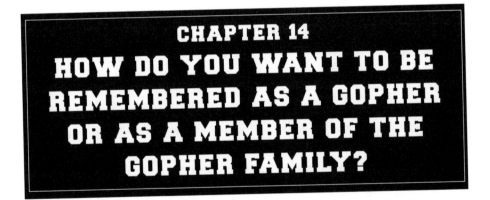

CHAPTER 14

HOW DO YOU WANT TO BE REMEMBERED AS A GOPHER OR AS A MEMBER OF THE GOPHER FAMILY?

"I would hope to remembered as a guy who respected the opportunity he was given and made the most of it by giving 100% every time he stepped onto the ice." — *Mike Anderson, Gopher 1995-99*

"Hey, I would be thrilled just to be remembered at all!" — *Mark Bahr, Gopher 1991-94, Current Director of Hockey Operations*

"I would like to be remembered as a quality player who played hard for his team and didn't leave anything behind. I also want to be remembered as someone who really respected the tradition at the University of Minnesota and tried his best to keep it going and to make it better." — *Keith Ballard, Gopher 2001-04*

"I would like to be remembered as a really hard working player; someone who had a passion for the game; and a real team player. You know, I never scored a lot of goals, but I did a lot of the little things to help my team win. I joke around with Woog and Lucia by asking them when they are going to add a new wall, next to the All-American wall, which will feature guys who just worked hard, grinded it out and showed up every day. I mean somebody had to dig the puck out of the corner to feed the 'glory guys,' right! How about a wall for us grunts, come on!" — *Scott Bell, Gopher 1991-95*

"I would hope to be remembered as a guy who gave it his all every night. Just to be thought of as one small piece of this incredible tradition is so humbling." — *Reggie Berg, Gopher 1995-99*

"I would hope that people would remember me as a team player who was a steady contributor. I just had so much fun there, I really miss it." — *Grant Bischoff, Gopher 1987-91*

"I would want to be remembered as a hard worker and as a dreamer. You know, I was just lucky to have gotten the opportunity to be a part of this program and that is something I will never take for granted." — *Brian Bonin, Gopher 1992-96*

"My biggest concern is winning a national championship and hopefully I will be remembered for that." — *Kellen Briggs, Gopher 2003-Present*

"I would want to be known as a guy who worked hard; was consistent and reliable; and who listened. When it is all said and done it is more than just hockey with these kids, it is about being a real person. I get to talk to these kids not as their coach, but as their friend, and those relationships that I have fostered over the years are priceless to me. So, I hope too that I would be remembered as a good friend." — *Harry Broadfoot, Gopher Equipment Manager 1986-Present*

"Everyday I showed up and did my best. I wasn't the most talented guy, but I worked hard with the ability that the Lord has given me. I competed hard both as a player and as a coach and I am proud of that." — *Bill Butters, Gopher Player 1971-73; Assistant Coach 1985-95*

"Hopefully as a national champion, that is my main goal." — *Kris Chucko, Gopher 2003-Present*

"I don't know if I was even there long enough to be remembered! If I am remembered though, I hope it would be as a solid player who worked hard and was proud to be a Gopher." — *Ben Clymer, Gopher 1996-98*

"I want to be remembered as an unselfish player who worked hard every night; was a team player; and had fun." — *Mike Crowley, Gopher 1994-97*

"I would hope to be remembered as a player who went out tried his best and tried to be a good teammate. Hopefully I was what a Gopher Hockey player was supposed to be." — *Steve DeBus, Gopher 1995-98*

"I would like to be remembered as a hard worker who played physical and was a good teammate. You know, I never really got going in my full stride while I was at the 'U' because of so many injuries that I suffered. I mean I had two busted arms, a separated shoulder, back problems and a host of other things, so it was tough for me to keep my momentum going. But, I was lucky to be there and to be a part of that amazing tradition." — *Joe Dziedzic, Gopher 1990-94*

"I just tried to do the best I could while I was there." — *Ken Gernander, Gopher 1988-91*

"That he worked hard; that he cared about his teammates or his players, both from the coaching and playing standpoint; he gave everything he could; and that he was respected." — *Mike*

"I want to be remembered as someone who came out and worked hard every night; was consistent in all three zones; played tough defense; contributed on offense; and was a great team player." — *Gino Guyer, Gopher 2003-Present*

"It is such a compliment to be remembered at all. I would just hope to be thought of as a guy who maybe didn't have that much talent, but figured out a way to help his team win hockey games. I would also hope to be thought of as a good team player who played hard and most importantly, had fun." — *Ben Hankinson, Gopher 1987-91*

"Just even to be remembered at all is good enough for me. That in itself would be a tremendous honor. If I was going to be remembered, however, I would hope it would be a package deal, as one of the three Hankinson brothers." — *Casey Hankinson, Gopher 1994-98*

"Just to be remembered at all is enough for me." — *Peter Hankinson, Gopher 1986-90*

"As a winner. I would hope to be remembered not as an individual, but as a part of my team." — *Chris Harrington, Gopher 2002-Present*

"You know, I guess they can put all my stats on my tombstone, I am proud of that. I still own the all-time career records for 'Games Played,' 'Minutes Played' and 'Wins,' not just for the Gophers, but for the entire WCHA. Beyond that I was proud to be on a great team my senior year and we took it all the way." — *Adam Hauser, Gopher 1998-2002*

"I hope to be remembered as a player with two national championships. I have one under my belt and another year to get another." — *Tyler Hirsch, Gopher 2002-Present*

"I want to be remembered as a guy whose teammates knew that they could always count on. I also want to be thought of as someone who gave it his all both in practice as well as in games. When the game was on the line I just always wanted to be out on the ice." — *Danny Irmen, Gopher 2003-Present*

"I would hope to be remembered as a good hockey player, but maybe more importantly I would want to be remembered as a good guy." — *Craig Johnson, Gopher 1990-93*

"I would hope to be remembered as a guy who went out and played hard every single night. You know, I learned very early on that for me to be successful I had to elevate my game to a certain level and then bring it every single night. If I ever took a shift off or a night off, there was going to be someone right there ready to replace me. I learned so much as a Gopher and those lessons carried me through 15 years in the National Hockey League. Now that I am retired, I have been able to look back and reflect on just how significant it was to be a Gopher. It meant so much to me. For now, I am just happy to be able to spend some time with my family, away from the game for a while. I was lucky. I have a broken nose; I'm missing a couple teeth; I had a mess of concussions; and I've got a bad knee; other than that though, I was thrilled to be able to leave a pretty big contract on the table and walk away from this game on my own terms. For me, it was all about life after hockey with my kids and I didn't to A) miss any of it and, B) not be able to play around with them because my body was a wreck. So, I am excited about the next chapter of my life and I know that now that I am home I will be able to follow my Gophers even that much closer." — *Trent Klatt, Gopher 1989-92*

"For me, to be a winner is what it was all about. I always want to be known as a winner, both on and off the ice. I think I was a vocal, upbeat guy and I tried to lead by example, whether that was by playing hard of by just cracking jokes and being funny to keep it light — that was all a part of it for me. Beyond that, I would like to be remembered as somebody who was able to bring his teammates together. You know, we did a lot of bonding together, which really helped to build our team chemistry. I used to take the whole team up to my cabin and we would hang out with each other a lot during the season as well as the off-season. We all became sincere friends and I was really proud of that because I think it went a long way in our success." — *Matt Koalska, Gopher 2000-04*

"I would like to be remembered not only as a great player, but as a great team player." — *Ryan Kraft, Gopher 1994-98*

"As an announcer I would hope to be remembered as somebody who was fair, and not a somebody who was homer. Beyond that, hopefully people have enjoyed listening to my style and that I have made some of their evenings entertaining along the way." — *Bob Kurtz, former Gopher Broadcaster*

"I want to be remembered as a hard working guy who put his heart on the line every shift. I wasn't the most talented player, but I had a drive to help my team win games at all costs." — *Cory Laylin, Gopher 1988-92*

"I want to be remembered as a champion, period. That was my goal when I first got there and I finally got to experience it four years later. It was an honor to help rebuild that program and I hope that they will be able to win many, many more titles in the years to come. My teammates and I went through a lot, but we came together under a new coaching staff and got it done." — *Jordan Leopold, Gopher 1999-02*

"I hope that when it is all said and done we have turned a lot of boys into men. I also hope that we not only had success, but we had success the right way in that we graduated our players and we tried to have them all reach their potential. So, as a coach I would hope to be remembered for things like that." — *Don Lucia, Current Gopher Head Coach*

"I would hope to be remembered as a guy who put on his sweater and showed up everyday to help his teammates win. I just tried to be positive and have as much fun as I could. Fortunately, we won a pair of championships while I was here and I am honored to be a part of that wonderful bit of history. You know, I had a really tough time leaving the University and leaving my teammates a year early. It was a business decision though and something that I have no regrets about. I didn't really have anything left that I felt like I needed to accomplish at that point and figured it would be better to give my ice time to the next guy who wants to fulfill his hopes and dreams. That's what it's all about. I am a semester or so shy of graduating, but I will definitely get my degree in the near future and when my professional hockey career is over I hope to come home and become a teacher and coach, so that I can give back the way others helped and encouraged me." — *Paul Martin, Gopher 2000-03*

"I am not sure that I want one. It's about the guys on the ice, not me. Whether I leave today or 15 years from now, the program is going to go on, as it went on way before me. How would I like to be remembered? As a professional. You know I always wanted to set a course for the long term so that I could be palatable to the fans for a long number of years. So, if I could accomplish that, then that is legacy enough. I don't need to have it written anywhere." — *Frank Mazzocco, Longtime Gopher TV Analyst*

"I would like to be remembered as a guy who, aside from getting a lot of penalty minutes, could actually play the game. I just played hard and loved wearing the 'M.'" — *Chris McAlpine, Gopher 1990-94*

"I would hope to be remembered as not only a good student-athlete, but as just an all-around good guy both on and off the ice." — *Jason Miller, Gopher 1987-91*

"I would like to be remembered as a hard worker who gave it his all. I hope that I will be thought of as a good leader who could always be counted on by his teammates to do the little things to help his team win. You know, every time I put on my jersey I always thought to myself what I was representing and what a special opportunity I had been given. Just being there was something I had dreamed of and I never wanted to take that for granted. When I took off my jersey for the last time it was really, really tough. I cried. I put so much into it and it was a very sad day knowing that I was done there and was going to move on. I just wanted to honor the 'M' on my chest as respectfully as I could each and every time I wore it. I was so lucky to play there and I still miss it." — *Nate Miller, Gopher 1996-00*

"I would like to be remembered as a gritty player who scored a few goals; killed some penalties; and just did the little things to help his team win." — *Jeff Nielsen, Gopher 1990-94*

"I would like to be known as a Gopher Hockey player who had fun and who did whatever was needed to help his team win. You know, old-time hockey!" — *Larry Olimb, Gopher 1988-92*

"I want to be remembered as a tough-ass, hard-hitting, hard-shooting, mean S.O.B. whenever I was out on the ice. As a defenseman I enjoyed putting the hurt on people, and I was proud of that. There were a lot of guys who were bigger and better than me, but I worked hard and did whatever I could to help my team win. I just tried to always be the first guy on the ice and the last guy off. I had desire, and you can't teach that." — *Tom Pederson, Gopher 1988-91*

"I felt very fortunate to be able to have played for the Gophers and to have been given that opportunity. I just want to be remembered as a guy who made the most of every minute that he was there." — *Lance Pitlick, Gopher 1986-90*

"Hopefully my tombstone will say something simple, like: A player that Gopher fans were happy to see come to the 'U.' " — *Johnny Pohl, Gopher 1998-2002*

"If I could have one word on there it would be: winner. I am the luckiest kid in the world to have been able to be a part of this and I wouldn't trade it for the world." — *Grant Potulny, Gopher 2000-04*

"I hope to be remembered as a true Gopher; a hard working player who wore the 'M' with pride and did whatever he could to help his team win." — *Ryan Potulny, Gopher 2003-Present*

"I would hope to remembered not so much as a hockey player, but as just a good guy." — *Erik Rasmussen, Gopher 1995-97*

"I think as someone who was fair. As an announcer you will always be slanted towards your own team, but you never want to take away from what the other team has accomplished. I have always remembered that." — *Tommy Reid, Former Gopher TV & Radio Announcer*

"I would love to just be remembered as a hard worker." — *Travis Richards, Gopher 1989-93*

"I hope people remember me as a team guy who energized his team and even snuck a puck in every now and then too." — *Troy Riddle, Gopher 2000-04*

"How about, 'Wally the Weasel and his love affair with the Gophers…' (That's my nickname and the name of my senior hockey team.) Really though, I hope to be remembered as somebody who made a difference doing what he loved. I truly believe that I've got the best job in town." — *Wally Shaver, Longtime Gopher Radio & TV Announcer*

"I would want to remembered as a player who was accountable; who never took a shift off; who worked hard; and who showed up to play every night. I am so proud to say that I was a Gopher, it meant everything to me." — *Wyatt Smith, Gopher 1995-99*

"To be a part of such a wonderful program means so much to me. So, I would hope to be remembered as somebody who cared a great deal about his players; as somebody who cared very much about winning; as somebody who did the best job he could to help his team win; as somebody who just enjoyed every minute of what he was doing; and as somebody who was very appreciative that he had the chance to do what he loved to do for a living for as long as he did. I have such a great appreciation of what a privilege it is to make my living doing something I love to do." — *Glen Sonmor, Former Gopher, North Stars & Fighting Saints Coach; Current Gopher Radio Broadcaster*

"I just want to be remembered as a guy who worked hard to be a part of the Minnesota hockey family and tradition." — *Dave Spehar, Gopher 1996-2000*

"Occasionally I meet people and they tell me that they will never forget the way I played, because it was so different than all the other goaltenders. I just think that is the ultimate compliment and definitely how I would like to be remembered. I was different and I did it my own way and on my own terms. That might not have always been the best way, but it was always the way I felt would give my teammates the best chance of winning. I just loved to lay it all on the line and challenge guys, whether that was out at the blue line or in front of the crease. That was what it was all about for me, the competition and the amazing feeling you got when you got swarmed by your teammates after a great win." — *Robb Stauber, Gopher 1986-89; Current Gopher Goalie Coach*

"I would want to be remembered as a national champion. That means more to me than anything else." — *Jeff Taffe, Gopher 1999-02*

"I would want to be remembered as a clutch player; and as a guy who was always there for his teammates, no matter what." — *Barry Tallackson, Gopher 2001-05*

"I think the word that comes to my mind the most is passion. I hope people will remember that when I called a game I was very passionate, whether the Gophers were ahead or behind. You know, it wasn't just a job to me, I really cared about the team and about the players." — *Dan Terhaar, Former Gopher Radio Announcer*

"I would hope to be remembered as someone who showed up every day and was unselfish. My dad was my coach growing up and those were the two things that he always tried to instill in me. He always instilled in us to play the same way against the last place team as you would against the first place team. So, if I was thought of that way, that would be something I would be very proud of." — *Dan Trebil, Gopher 1992-96*

"I just want to be remembered as a winner." — *Thomas Vanek, Gopher 2002-04*

"I hope to be remembered as a guy who came in and helped his team to win a championship. That hasn't happened yet, but I certainly am going to work hard to see that it does." — *Mike Vannelli, Gopher 2003-Present*

"I would hope to be remembered as a hard-nosed competitor. I was proud to wear the captain's 'C' as my dad once did when he was a Gopher, and hopefully I too was a good leader." — *Erik Westrum, Gopher 1997-2001*

"I would hope to be remembered as somebody who left it all out on the ice after every game. I hope people will think of me as a team player who played with a lot of heart and helped his team win. That's what it is all about." — *Blake Wheeler, Gopher 2005-Present*

"For me, to be a Gopher was the thrill of a lifetime. I would just hope to be remembered as a player who gave it his all; who respected the game; and who appreciated every moment of being a Gopher. To follow in my father's footsteps there, just means more to me than words can even describe. I get really emotional even thinking about it. It did so much for me and I want to do so much for it. It will never leave my heart and soul. I truly do bleed Maroon and Gold." — *Dean Williamson, Gopher 1987-90*

"I want to be respected by the guys I respect the most. When you have the respect of the guys who I would call 'champions of their game,' then that is something special. I also want to be thought of as someone who won with dignity and performed with dignity." — *Doug Wooog, Former Coach & Current TV Analyst*

"I would like to be thought of as a good teammate; a guy who worked hard both on and off the ice; a guy who wanted to get better every season; and as a guy who had fun. What I would most have liked though is a championship ring, and I am sorry that we weren't able to get that. We had some great teams, but just came up short. It was a great experience though, something I will never take for granted." — *Doug Zmolek, Gopher 1989-92*

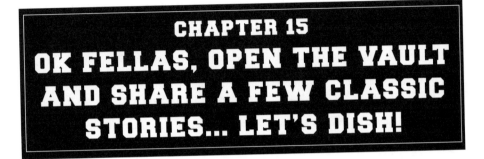

CHAPTER 15
OK FELLAS, OPEN THE VAULT AND SHARE A FEW CLASSIC STORIES... LET'S DISH!

"One of my favorite stories in college had to do with the 'Bud Truck,' which was Casey Hankinson's Honda Accord. I will never forget one night when Willy Marvin and I borrowed it and 'allegedly' had a little too much fun. All I can say is that the next morning when Casey got up to go to class he had no mirrors, no muffler, and a phone call from a cop wondering if his car had been involved in an incident where a bike got run-over. Casey, sorry bro, but Willy and I have no idea what happened, we were at church that night..." — *Mike Anderson, Gopher 1995-99*

"When I was playing I used to live with Dave Norqual and we had an apartment down on Cole Avenue, off of Como. We used to have some of the greatest after-bar parties down there. Eventually the cops would always come break it up, but they knew that we were hockey players, so they took it easy on us. Usually they would say 'Save us a cold one for when we get off work...'. And sure enough, they would come back at two or three in the morning and hang out with us. It was awesome." — *Mark Bahr, Gopher 1991-94, Current Director of Hockey Operations*

"OK, here is one of the all-time classics. One time we were up in St. Cloud for a series and we wound up staying at a hotel. Well, the next day I get a call from the hotel manager who proceeds to tell me that a maid found some poop in an ice bucket in one of our rooms. So, Don (Lucia) was like no way, it was definitely not one of our guys. Anyway, the next day we are at practice and Don tells the players what happened and asks if anybody wants to come forward to claim responsibility. By now you could hear a pin drop it was so quiet. Finally, after a while, Erik Westrum raises his hand and calmly says 'I did it.' Don was flabbergasted and literally speechless. Westy then says with a perfectly straight face, 'Haven't you ever sh-- in an ice bucket?' Don's like NO! Well, Don skated him like I have never seen anybody skate before. He could hardly walk after that. I give the guy credit for fessing up though, a lot of guys wouldn't have done that. Apparently, Westy was playing a practical joke on his roommate, Aaron Miskovich, while he was in the shower. I don't know where it went from there, but let's just say the item in the bucket never got properly disposed of. Needless to say, he learned his lesson after that one. The whole thing was just hilarious. Westy is a great guy, super funny, and we all love him." — *Mark Bahr, Gopher 1991-94, Current Director of Hockey Operations*

"I was always a big fan of the alarm clock re-setting or the bogus hotel wake-up-call prank. I had been the victim of a few of those over the years and was on the other end as well, serving them up to unsuspecting freshman. It is just hilarious to see guys waking up and getting ready in the middle of the night because they have no clue what time it really is." — *Keith Ballard, Gopher 2001-04*

"Whenever I scored a goal I just tried to be all cool about it and skate right back to the face-off dot like I had scored a thousand goals before. Well, I think I only celebrated one goal in my entire career with the Gophers and it came against St. Cloud. Woog and Butters had been on our case all week that we were playing flat and without any emotion. So, it is the third period of this game and I am out there with Brandon Steege and Steve Magnuson. I guaranteed them that I was going to score a goal that shift and then I made them promise me that if I did, that they would ride their sticks with me right down the center of the ice in a blaze of glory. Well, sure enough, I back-hand shelfed a goal with a guy on my back after a hellaciously long shift. From there, I just took off straight down the ice riding my stick like a broom. I looked back and sure enough, Steege and Magnuson, who were already on the bench because they were so tired, hopped over the boards and rode their sticks right behind me as well. It was so sweet. Well, by the time I got down to Tom Newman, our goalie, I could hear Woog screaming at me at the top of his lungs. We were toast. Here I thought I was doing exactly what he wanted, pumping up the team and showing some emotion, but he was livid. Afterwards I had to go apologize to the St. Cloud coaches, it was awful. Woog told me that my goal was one of the top 10 he had ever seen at Mariucci, but my celebration was in the top five for worst ever. I said, 'Hey, at least I scored one of the top 10 goals ever, right...?' Needless to say, I caught hell over that one, let me tell ya." — *Scott Bell, Gopher 1991-95*

"One time in practice I was playing around with Bill Butters and we started play fighting. Well, we got into it a little bit and eventually I pulled his jersey over his head. Well, then he started swinging at me for real. I was like whoa, he was a tough guy who fought a lot of battles in the NHL. So, I backed off and said 'Hey, what's up?' He said 'I was OK with it until you pulled my shirt up and showed everybody my fat roll... that's where I draw the line!' We made up after that, but he is definitely not a guy you want to piss off out there, no way." — *Scott Bell, Gopher 1991-95*

"One of my favorites was when Casey Hankinson and Mikey 'Sugar' Anderson filled up our team trainer, Bob Broxterman's, briefcase with snow up in Michigan one time. Broxie had filled up their skates with water before practice, so that is how they retaliated back at him. Broxie was so pissed. That was a classic." — *Reggie Berg, Gopher 1995-99*

"I only missed two series during my entire career as a Gopher. One of them was because I was really sick and had a super high fever. The other one was from an injury that was really an embarrassing story-behind-the-story. The 'official' story of how I separated my shoulder was that I tripped and fell on the ice off my front porch. But, what really happened was that I was out one night with Sean Fabian and Lance Werness at the Pub Down Under, in Dinkytown. Anyway, we were walking home and we went through the Burger King parking lot right next door. Well, they had these permanent cement picnic tables out there, and I was acting like a rock star in my current state so I proceeded to jump up on one of them, only it broke in half. I fell super hard right on my shoulder and that next morning I couldn't even get out of bed. Meanwhile, we had a game out in Colorado College that night and I was completely out of commission. So, I had to go in and talk to Woog that morning and fabricate a story to save face. It was awful. 'It was really icy coach and I fell...'. Woog was like, 'Sorry, I hope your OK...'. Bill Butters, our assistant coach, was on to me though. He looked at me all disgusted and said, 'Grant, you're a hockey player, we don't fall on the ice...'. Needless to say, I didn't eat any Whoppers after that for a long, long time. So, Wooger, I am sorry. That's the real story, I am coming clean!" — *Grant Bischoff, Gopher 1987-91*

"When I was a sophomore I lived in a house with a bunch of guys. We didn't have any artwork anywhere so one day I got bored and made a big yellow WCHA sign that I hung up on the wall.

Then, I cut holes in it to put all of the team pucks in there. Well, it became a challenge at that point, to physically collect each of the team pucks from around the league. One by one, when we would travel to each rival city, I would get a game puck with a logo to display on our wall. Finally, North Dakota was the last one I needed and time was running out. As luck would have it, I got a penalty late in the game and found myself in the penalty box. Wouldn't you know it, but that is where they kept the bucket of game pucks. So, I very quietly took one and shoved it in my nut cup. Well, as I was skating from the box back over to our bench, it fell out onto the ice. Of course, I pretended not to notice, but I was pissed because that was the final piece to the puzzle." — *Brian Bonin, Gopher 1992-96*

"I remember when I was a freshman, John Brill, Eric Means and some of the other seniors, had a hockey house where they used to have huge parties after games. Eventually, when too many people showed up, they would just call the cops. The cops would show up and the players would tell them to clear everybody out because they were tired and just wanted to have a few guys over for a beer. So, they would clear everybody out and then we would all come back and hang out to finish off the beer. Meanwhile, those guys made enough money to pay for rent, so it always worked out." — *Brian Bonin, Gopher 1992-96*

"One guy who I was always enamored with was Travis Richards. He was a great guy. Travis was one interesting dude. I will never forget, he used to always wear his hockey underwear underneath his clothes all the time. You know, those baby blue Bauer long johns that players wear under their equipment. Well, Travis just loved those things and I think he had like two pairs. He would wear one and then switch over to the other one at the rink, where he would have it washed after practice for the next day. It was hilarious. Then, I remember too he used to always show up to practice like 10 minutes before we had to be out on the ice with a bag of Taco Bell. He would chow a bunch of tacos as he was getting dressed and then hit the ice right before we had to work out. I don't know how the heck he did that without puking, but that was his deal. It's funny the things you remember sometime, especially the little things about what happened in the locker-room. Everyday there was some silly story or some drama, and that was half the fun." — *Brian Bonin, Gopher 1992-96*

"I love pranks. One of my favorite pranks is to mess with guys' composite sticks. Some of my favorite things to do are to take out the butt-end and then fill it up with either water or pennies, and then put seal the plug back in. Then, we replace it while we are in practice, maybe during a break, so that they can't switch it. That is always a classic moment to see that guy grab his stick for the first time after that and just freak out.

"Other fun pranks are to cut guys' skate laces in half so that when they tighten them up they snap. That is a particularly good gag for guys who are always late for practice and are rushing to get dressed. Nothing is worse than snapping a lace when you are in a hurry." — *Kellen Briggs, Gopher 2003-Present*

"I used to always talk about fishing with Nick Checco and he used to always ask me a million questions about river fishing for carp. He was just really curious about how big they were; about what they looked like; just everything about them. Well, one day I went home after practice and decided to go fishing. Sure enough, I caught this huge carp. Just as I was about to let it go, I decided to take it back for Nick. So, I wrapped it up and brought it in to work with me the next day and put it in Nick's laundry bag. Then, we got all the guys around and watched him as he grabbed his bag and realized that there was this giant smelly carp in there. His eyes just got huge. I don't think I can repeat what he said next. It was hilarious. From there, Bob Broxterman, the team trainer, took the fish and hung it in Doug Woog's locker stall. Now, Doug was running late for practice that day so he came rushing in and sat down in his stall to get changed into his skates. Meanwhile, the carp's tail is hanging on a hook and actually rubbing on his bald spot. He was so focused on not being late that he didn't even notice the stinky carp rubbing on his head. Everybody died laughing over that one, that was a classic." — *Harry Broadfoot, Gopher Equipment Manager 1986-Present*

"My greatest memory as a Gopher was just being on the same ice with Mike Antonovich. He was right up there with John Mayasich as far as being the best ever to wear the Maroon and Gold, he was literally that good. He had so much fun out on the ice, the guy was just unbelievable. The things he could do with the puck were amazing. He was just a joy to watch. It was a privilege to play with him. Well, my favorite story about Mike came on a road trip one time. I was sitting with him and Dean Blais and they were talking. Now, Mike and Dean were roommates and the best of friends, just super close. They used to hate each other though, because Mike was from Greenway and Dean was from the Falls, and they were bitter enemies. Glen (Sonmor) put them together as roommates though, just to be funny. Well, they wound up becoming the best of friends. Anyway, we are on the bus and Mike says to Dean 'Hey, did you remember the tooth brush?' Dean says 'No, I thought you packed it...' I laughed so hard I almost fell out of my seat. Those two guys are still great pals, and that is what Gopher hockey is all about, memories and great friendships." — *Bill Butters, Gopher Player 1971-73; Assistant Coach 1985-95*

"The funniest thing I remember was when Casey Hankinson showed up one day in a neck brace while Nick Checco came in on crutches. They made up this ridiculous story before practice about how Tommy Nevers was driving their car and they all crashed, but were able to walk away. Well, this reporter was there and he just got sucked in to what they were saying, totally believing them. Well, the funny thing about it was that the reporter stuck around for practice and actually saw all three guys out there skating with everybody else, but never put two and two together. He bought it and wrote a story that next day, not realizing that they had duped him. It was pretty funny.

"Another funny media story that I remember happened one time when Casey Hankinson and I were on the Ryan Lefebvre Show and we wanted to have some fun, so we made up stories about what we were going to be doing in the off-season. Well, I don't know where it came from, but I blurted out that I was going to be the long-snapper on the Gopher Football team that Fall. What was so funny about it was the fact that it was in Sid Hartman's column that next Sunday. I remember seeing Sid a few weeks later and he let me have it pretty good. Sid spent all of his time with the football team and rarely covered Gopher Hockey, so we used to love to play pranks on him whenever he came around." — *Steve DeBus, Gopher 1995-98*

"I remember one time being up in Grand Forks for a Gopher-Sioux game back in about 1990 and watching Benny Hankinson and his Dad each get into a brawl. Benny got into it with out on the ice with David Hakstol, a goon defenseman who is now UND's head coach, and while that was going on his Dad, John, a former quarterback on the Gopher Football team, is going at it was some idiot rube in the stands. It was insane. I had never seen a dueling father-son brawl before, so that one ranks right up there in my personal highlight reel." — *Jeff Dubay, KFAN Radio Host & Longtime Gopher Fanatic*

"One of my favorite stories about Gopher Hockey came from Nate Miller, who was cast in the movie 'Miracle' a few years back. Well, they were filming the movie at the same time the Gophers were in the Frozen Four out in Buffalo. According to Nate, I guess Kurt Russell, who played Herb Brooks in the movie, was just a huge hockey fan. He even had a satellite in his trailer so that he could watch the Gophers beat New Hampshire in the Finals. Apparently, Nate was filming a scene that Kurt wasn't required to be in at the time, so he would run out on to the set between periods to grab Nate and give him updates on the games. He said that he was even reenacting Vanek's spectacular goal for him frame-by-frame. What a rube!" — *Jeff Dubay, KFAN Radio Host & Longtime Gopher Fanatic*

"I will never forget when Doug Zmolek and Eric Means decided to turn their dorm room into a barber shop one time. They were offering guys free hockey mullets, so I said 'Sure, why not?' I remember sitting there in the middle of their room with a pile of hair about two inches thick across the entire floor, it was so disgusting. Well, I left and about two weeks later I stopped by to say hello and sure enough, they had yet to vacuum it all up. Those guys were such pigs, it was hilarious. To make matters worse, I caught hell from my dad who drove down and just about passed out when I took my helmet off for the National Anthem and he saw my new doo.

Man, we had some bad hair back then!" — *Ken Gernander, Gopher 1988-91*

"Most of my favorite stories about Gopher Hockey usually had something to do with Glen Sonmor, who I used to do the play-by-play with on the radio. Glen used to get so excited about coming in to work that he actually forgot to turn his car off in the parking lot at Mariucci Arena and left it running for so long that it ran out of gas. He did that twice! He was in such a hurry to get up here that pulling the key out just slipped his mind. You gotta love Glen, he is just the best." — *Eric Gislason, Former Gopher Radio & Television Commentator*

"I think the most meaningful story that I can share has to do with Jordan Leopold. What a guy. Jordan came over to my house last year and hung out with my kids; signed their hockey lockers in our garage; gave them some sticks; and took them took them for rides in his Corvette convertible Stingray. Does it get any better than that? My kids thought that was just unbelievable. What a classy guy. He epitomizes Gopher Hockey in my opinion. You know, there have been some great guys come through that program over the years; guys like Casey Hankinson, Mike Crowley and Ryan Kraft — who have all taken time out to spend time with my kids, and that is why people are so passionate and loyal about this team, it's the kids." — *Eric Gislason, Former Gopher Radio & Television Commentator*

"There have been so many stories and so many memories over the years. I remember playing under Brad Buetow, he was a big, intimidating tough coach. He was such an emotional guy. I remember one of my first freshman practices, he would dump the puck in your corner and then follow it at full speed to test your mettle and see what you were made of. He wanted to see how you handled the pressure with a big guy coming down on you, knowing you were going to pay the price for going into the corner soft. Then, if you didn't do it well, he would blow the whistle and throw another puck right back into your corner and come breathing down your neck even harder the next time. He wanted to see if you would crack under the pressure. He wanted to make you tougher. Sometimes with Brad we wouldn't touch pucks all week long, and then the first time we would see one would be on Friday night during the pre-game warm-up. He was tough, but we came together and played hard for him." — *Mike Guentzel, Gopher Player 1981-85; Assistant Coach 1994-Present*

"You know, when you are in college you are always broke and never have enough cash it seemed like. Well, one day I had an epiphany as I was leaving practice and heading back to campus. I was walking out with John Hamre, our equipment manager, and we were walking through the parking lots next to Mariucci Arena. Well, there was a high school basketball tournament going on next door at Williams Arena and the fans were filing into the parking lots. It wasn't a University event, so the parking was free. So, me and John, who is like the most honest guy on planet Earth, are walking by and I got a great idea to start stopping cars and charging them for parking. It was brilliant. I must have stopped 40 or 50 cars and when I finally ran out of correct change, we headed over to Rocky Roccocco's over in Dinkytown for pizza and beers. That was hilarious. And believe me, if the Hammer hadn't been so nervous and such an honest guy, I would probably still be over there right now collecting money!" — *Ben Hankinson, Gopher 1987-91*

"Lance Pitlick is one of my favorite people of all-time, and I tell you what. I have never known another guy who was tougher than Pit. I will never forget watching him go toe-to-toe with this cornerback who played on the Gopher Football team one time at a bar in Dinkytown. These two got into it and it got heated. Lance just went after this guy and absolutely cleaned him up. I guess this guy was a big-time boxer, but Pit just would not back down. This guy must have hit Pit right dead, straight on between the eyes at least a 100 times. I bet Pit went down a dozen times, but he got up every time and went back for more. He eventually took care of him, it was just incredible. I was standing there with Randy Skarda and a whole bunch of other tough S.O.B.'s too, but we couldn't help out because the entire damn football team was there. So, we sat back and watched Pit go at it with this guy. I have never seen a fight like that before, just bare-knuckle brawling at its best. The next day Pit's face was so swollen that he looked like Howdy Doody. Woog just looked at him and said, 'Pit, I don't even want to know...'. I had so much respect for him after that. I played in the NHL for several years and got into my share of scraps, but I can honestly say that I have never known another human tougher than Pit. Guys feared him out on the ice when he played pro hockey, no doubt about it. He wasn't that big, but man, that guy could pack a punch. He was just an animal." — *Ben Hankinson, Gopher 1987-91*

"I will never forget my freshman initiation shaving. I got ambushed and tied down with duct tape. Marty Nanne and Randy Skarda blindfolded me and they got me pretty good. They were squirting me with warm water from a water bottle, and I of course thought the worst. It was just brutal, let me tell ya. I was bleeding like hell from that razor, it was awful. You know, you could always tell how much of a smart-ass guys were by how badly they got trimmed up for their initiation. Let's just say that Tommy Peterson looked REALLY bad!" — *Ben Hankinson, Gopher 1987-91*

"I will never forget one time during my freshman year when I found Wooger sleeping in my bed back in my dorm room. Apparently, he had taken a recruit around campus and was showing him the dorms. Well, he had a couple hours of down time before practice, so he just helped himself to my bed. I remember coming back to the room and before I went in I saw my roommate, Jake Enebak, who says 'Don't go in there, Wooger is taking a nap...'. I am like, 'Yeah right, whatever!' So, I go in and flip on the lights. To my horror, I see Wooger laying in my bed with the tightest Fruit of the Loom undies that I have ever seen. It was the funniest and most horrifying thing I have ever seen in my life. That was Wooger though, just one of the guys." — *Ben Hankinson, Gopher 1987-91*

"As crazy as this sounds, I actually used to wear these 'Switch-It' hockey skates that were popular for a while back in the late 1980s. You could switch them from hockey skates to in-line skates by just popping them out. They were like, recreational skates, at best. Well, even though we got all of the top-of-the-line equipment that we wanted, I just liked these things so I wore them all the time. Sure enough though, we are playing against Duluth and the damn blade popped out. I had to gimp all the way back to the bench from the far corner of Mariucci's big ice sheet, back to the bench, where steam was literally coming out of Woog's ears. (Bill) Butters was just laughing at this point because he knew that I was going to catch hell, which I did. Then, to make matters worse, I had to gimp all the way across the ice at the next whistle so that I could go down to the locker room and get it fixed. So, I get it fixed and I am back out on the ice, and sure enough, not more than a few shifts later the other damn blade popped out and I had to gimp around all over again. Needless to say, I got my ass chewed hard for that one. Guys used to give me so much crap for wearing those things, but I loved them. I even wore them in the NHL. I should have gotten a huge endorsement deal or something from the company, but they thought that I was giving them bad press by having them fall off all the time. Well, they went broke not too long after that, so maybe I had a part in that — who knows? How funny is that?" — *Ben Hankinson, Gopher 1987-91*

"One of my favorite Benny stories happened off the ice and on the golf course. I will never forget playing golf in Chicago several years back out at Cog Hill with my two brother and my dad. They had several courses there, and the main one was hosting the Western Open that weekend. Anyway, our tee-time was at about 4:30 and we are all there ready to go except Ben. We can't find him anywhere. Finally, we look over and there's Benny, who had gone back to the car to put on a pair of nice pants, on the putting green with all of the tour pros. He is standing there, putting next to Greg Norman and Vijay Singh, and all of these famous golfers, just having a ball. Nobody questioned him, he just walked over there and started putting. It was hilarious. The guy is like Ferris Bueller, he could just get away with stuff nobody else could dream of." — *Casey Hankinson, Gopher 1994-98*

"My favorite prank of all time happened during my senior year. It was a bye-week for us, so it was a little bit laid back. Anyway, one of my roommates was Willy Marvin, who was our goalie. Well, I had a crazy idea to switch gear with him so that he would wear my stuff and I would suit up in his goalie pads. So, we both got dressed in the bathroom, where nobody else could see us, and then headed out onto the ice. It was hilarious. We must have been out there for at least 20 minutes, doing shooting drills and running through our regular routine. All of the guys knew what was up, but Wooger was clueless. Finally, he blows his whistle and says 'OK, break-aways on Willy...', which signaled the start of a new drill. Well, he took the first break-away shot and skated down on me from the opposite end in front of the entire team. The best part of it was that I stuffed him, and hey, he was a former Gopher All-American! He still doesn't know it's me in there at that point because I am wearing the big goalie mask, and he probably never would have if it wouldn't have been for a three-on-three drill we wound up doing after that where Willy just couldn't keep up. Wooger was just screaming at him, saying 'Casey, come on, pick it up, start skating, what the hell's the matter with you?!' I am just dying of laughter at this point. Finally, he is so pissed off at me, or who he thinks is me, and he comes over to Willy to bitch him out for loafing. Just then he realizes what has been going on and he just about died. Luckily, he thought it was pretty funny and he took pity on us. We went and got undressed after that and came back out. Afterwards I was razzing him about denying his break-away, and telling him not to feel bad because the extent of my goaltending experience came from playing in my back yard with the little neighbor kids. He just laughed. I love the Wooger, he is just the best. That one was a classic." — *Casey Hankinson, Gopher 1994-98*

"My favorite story came back during my freshman year. Woog had Grant Bischoff and Kenny Gernander in on a recruiting visit. We go to the pre-game meal at Stub & Herbs Restaurant, and Woog had not decided who the last guy was going to be in the starting line-up that night. He had penciled in 19 of the 20 spots, but was undecided between Marty Nanne and Scott Bloom. So, after the pre-game meal Woog asks me if he can bring these two recruits over to see my dorm room over at Frontier Hall, to shown them around a little bit. I said 'sure.' So, about a half an hour later he shows up and Randy Skarda, my roommate, and I let them in. We show them our room and start talking to the guys about hockey and what not, and then, out of the blue, Woog says 'Oh, Geez! I almost forgot, I have to make a decision on who to start tonight, Nanne or Bloom.' Then he says, 'Do either of you guys have a quarter?' Honest to God, he says 'Heads its Nanne; tails its Bloom.' He then flips it and it comes up heads. 'Woog looks right at me and says, 'Two out of three.' I couldn't believe it. Sure enough, Nanne wound up not playing that night for whatever reason. We were just shocked that Wooger would do that in front of us, let alone in front of some recruits. But, he was a great coach and I am sure there was some lesson or method to his madness. I will always remember that though, it was hilarious. Grant and Kenny just looked at each other and were like 'Whoaaa!'. We all laughed about it later." — *Peter Hankinson, Gopher 1986-90*

"One time my brother Ben and I were playing a game against each other in the minor leagues, and a fight broke out. We both stood by each other, and were talking on the ice. Then a goon named Bundy, skated by us and said threateningly, 'Cut this pussy Minnesota B.S. right now, and get the hell out of here!' I felt like keeping my teeth, so I told Ben we'd just talk after the game." — *Peter Hankinson, Gopher 1986-90*

"I remember one time we were in the locker room between periods of a game and we had been playing pretty bad. So, Coach Lucia comes in and he is just pissed. Now, he is normally a pretty calm guy, so when he gets upset you know that he means business. Well, he is yelling at us and to make his point, he goes over to the corner of the locker room and kicks this garbage can super hard. Well, it was in the corner, so it didn't move. So, he grabbed it and threw it across the floor. But instead of it falling over, it kind of makes a big loop and stays standing up. By now he is just steaming because this stupid garbage can will not cooperate. Finally, on the third try, he came over and just shoved the thing down to the ground. By then one of the players just busted out laughing and we all totally cracked up. Poor guy, he just left completely dejected after that. It was pretty hilarious." — *Danny Irmen, Gopher 2003-Present*

"Back when I lived in the dorm I had a bird named Igor and I just loved that thing. Anyway, Darby Hendrickson and Jeff Nielsen came over one time and hid Igor in a box and then left the window open to make it look like he had escaped. So, I get home from class and realize what has happened and am about to freak out. I'm just beside myself and just as I am about to go out combing the campus for him, those two clowns come running in with Igor laughing hysterically. I was too relieved to even be mad at them, it was pretty funny." — *Craig Johnson, Gopher 1990-93*

"All I can say is that two of my teammates had a notorious "Booger Wall" in their dorm room. I won't name names, but you two know who you are. And they wondered why they didn't ever have any dates..." — *Trent Klatt, Gopher 1989-92*

"You know, it was the little pranks that kept us on our toes. I used to love calling the front desk at the hotel to request 3:00 AM wake-up-calls for Troy Riddle when we were on the road. Call me crazy, but that never got old.

"I got him with a few 'leaners' over the years as well. Leaners were when you would fill up a garbage can full of water and lean it up against a guy's door. The key was to be able to knock and then have a good place to hide, because you knew he was coming after you.

"Another funny thing we did was 'shoe-checking,' like a hockey check, only this was totally different. A shoe check was when you would sneak under a table at dinner and smear ketchup all over a guy's shoes when he wasn't looking. Riddle got Travis Weber at Mancini's Restaurant one time and Travis got so pissed. He had these brand new white tennies on that he just got and they were totally red. It was hilarious.

"Paying out fines was another good source of comedy. We had a big 'M' on the carpet in the middle of the locker room and if anybody ever walked on it they had to pay a fine to what we called the 'sin-bin.' So, we would shove guys into it and then pound on them for walking on the 'M.' Dumb stuff like that was hilarious. One of my biggest fines came between periods when I was being interviewed on TV by Clay Matvick. Well, I dropped an 'F-Bomb' by accident and that one cost me dearly. I am a potty-mouth, so that stuff killed me. The guys were thanking me though because all of the fine money went towards the end of the year party for the team.

"Telling stories and debriefing on Sunday mornings was the best. Us seniors lived in a house our last year, it was me Rids, Waibel, Joey, Pauly and Grant. We would wake up on Sundays after the season was over and stumble down to the living room around noon, where we would try and piece together what happened the night before. Half the stuff that happened we couldn't even remember because we were so tanked the night before. It was hilarious to hear about who hooked up with who at the bars, or who got punched where, and what other stupid stuff guys might have done that night. Our favorite bar was the 'Library,' because we could tell our mom's that we were honestly going to the library that night. Good stuff. Those were the days, I will never forget those great memories." — *Matt Koalska, Gopher 2000-04*

"My first fight was a doozy. It was with Davis Payne, who was a six-foot-three, 210 pound thug who played for Michigan Tech. After the fight everyone on the bench started calling me 'Homer Hanky' because of the way he was waving and tossing me around out there so much." — *Cory Laylin, Gopher 1988-92*

"I will never forget being at Danny Welch's freshmen get-together. By the end of the night he was crashed on the couch where he proceeded to poop his pants. To this day he claims he didn't, but we all know better. We have had many laughs about it, that is for sure. I know he will get me back for divulging this, but all I can say is... GAME-ON-DANNY!" — *Jordan Leopold, Gopher 1999-02*

"I lived in a hockey house with Matt Koalska, Troy Riddle, Jon Waibel and Joey Martin. Grant Potulny technically lived with us too, but had a girlfriend, so we never saw him. Anyway, one time Joey Martin passed out after a party at our house. So, just for fun we permanent markered his face all up. Now, we knew that he had a test that next morning, so we all got up early to see him off to school. Well, he rolled out of bed and threw a hat on, not even noticing the trainwreck that his face had become. We sat with him and had breakfast, talking about that last night, and he just kept eating his toast completely oblivious to what was going on. We were beside ourselves trying not to laugh. Finally, he left and went out to his car. We then all ran to the window and saw him just absolutely freak out as he backed out of the driveway and saw himself in the rear-view mirror. It was hilarious. He had to come back in and scrub his face until the skin practically fell off, it was awful. He was late for his test and everything, we felt pretty bad after that one. I guess the lesson there is don't pass out if you live in a hockey house with a bunch of idiot roommates!" — *Paul Martin, Gopher 2000-03*

"Working with Tommy Reid was always an adventure. I remember one time in Denver he brought me to tears, literally. The game was going on and the puck bounced up and landed in Erik Wendell's hand. Then, for whatever reason, he took the puck out by the blue line and came in at the top of the circle and just threw it into the net. We couldn't believe it. I mean it was a great shot, but totally illegal. Tommy started laughing so hard that he began crying. In fact, he laughed so hard that his contact lens got flushed out of his eye. When I saw that I just lost it. His laughter just destroyed me. I was done for. My eyes filled with tears as I began watching him and I couldn't even speak I was laughing so hard. Luckily, we got a commercial break, because neither of us could stop laughing. It was insane. I will never forget that moment." — *Frank Mazzocco, Longtime Gopher TV Analyst*

"I remember one time I was doing a series in Denver back in the late '80s and Wooger forgot to pack enough dress shirts for the trip. So, he sent one of his student-managers to go out and buy him one. Well, the kid comes back with the most God-awful, ugliest shirt anybody had ever seen. It had more colors and more patterns than anything I had ever seen before. Doug was stuck, it was game time and he had to either wear a terribly smelly shirt from the night before, or wear this thing. Let's just say he should have gone with the smelly one. That was a beauty, let me tell ya'. It was his birthday that night too, so to this day we refer to it as 'Wooger's obscene birthday shirt.' And of course, as soon as I saw that thing we immediately started doing close-ups of him on the air and then just laughing about it. It was a classic. Doug never forgot his shirt again after that one." — *Frank Mazzocco, Longtime Gopher TV Analyst*

"One of my all-time classic memories of being at old Mariucci Arena, was when I finally figured out that you, as Goldy, had been getting the crowd to chant 'Frank & Wally.' I don't know how long you had been doing the shtick, where you would get the one side of the crowd to yell out 'Frank!' and the other 'Wally!' I had no idea. Wally and I were up in the press box with our head-sets on and we were oblivious to everything that was going on outside of the game. Well, one time during a commercial break I took off my head-set and listened to this loud cheer. I thought to myself, 'What in the world are all of these people saying?' Then it dawned on me, there are 6,000 people in here screaming my name! So, I nudged Wally to take his head-set off and to listen to what was going on. He was shocked. It was so much fun. I had no idea that anybody knew who we were, and that was really nice to be recognized like that. From there on out, Wally and I loved it whenever you would get that chant going. It was great." — *Frank Mazzocco, Longtime Gopher TV Analyst*

"When I was a freshman, Bennie Hankinson was our captain. Well, he had been growing this fu-manchu goatee that he was really proud of. Anyway, we were all at a New Year's Eve house party one year and Benny wound up having a few too many cocktails and passing out cold. So, Jake Enebak and Sean Fabian somehow talked me into shaving off half of his goatee. Well, I did, for whatever reason, and it was pretty hilarious. Benny, meanwhile, eventually woke up and when he looked in the mirror he was not very happy. Needless to say, he started throwing large objects into the wall. At that point I proceeded to run as fast as I could back to my dorm room, where I hid in utter fear. OK, a few days and then weeks go by and I just assumed that he had forgotten about it and just chalked it up to a good prank. I was still super cautious and never took long showers or anything after practice because I knew Benny was probably up to something. So, we are up in Houghton one weekend for a series with Michigan Tech. We wound up winning and I went out afterwards with my roommate, Doug Zmolek, to grab a few beers. From there, we headed back to the hotel and when we got there I opened the door, only to see the entire team in there waiting for me. I was like oh, sh--! Benny is there and says 'Remember this?' and he pointed at his goatee. I was dead. So, they threw me down and held me while Benny thoroughly shaved my head. Then, to make matters worse, he pulled out a scissors and proceeded to trim me up real good down south of the border, if you know what I mean. It was awful. The worst part was the wait, because Benny had it all planned out. Just when I thought I was home free and wound up letting my guard down, sure enough, there was Benny and his damn scissors. I learned my lesson after that one." — *Chris McAlpine, Gopher 1990-94*

The most bizarre fight I ever got into during my 10 years in the NHL came when I was playing with St. Louis and we were playing Edmonton one night. A big mêlée breaks out and I wind up tying up with Edmonton's tough guy, Kelly Buchberger. We are locked up and I am just praying he is not going to connect with me. Meanwhile, our fighter, Kelly Chase, comes over and says 'Hey, Cow Pie, I got him, let him go...' Let me preface that by saying that he and Brett Hull had given me this ridiculous nickname which somehow derived from saying McAlpine real fast, which sounded like 'McCow Pie.' Well, they eventually dropped the Mc, and just went with 'cow pie.' Hey, who was I to argue with those guys, right? Anyway, Kelly comes skating over to me while I am locked up with this guy and wants to take him, because he was a fighter and he had my back. Well, as he says this, Kelly Buchberger just starts laughing hysterically and can't stop. He is just dying out there. He looks right at me and says 'cow pie?' He thought that was the funniest thing he had ever heard. So, here I am in the middle of this bench-clearing brawl, tied up with this notorious goon who I think is going to kill me, and he is laughing so hard I probably could have pushed him over. The worst part about it was afterwards, whenever I would skate past the Edmonton bench they would all yell out 'HEY, COW SH--! COME BACK OVER HERE COW SH--!' So, for people who wonder what really goes on in those things, there is one story they won't soon forget. That was pretty funny though, and hey, it got me out of an ass-whooping." — *Chris McAlpine, Gopher 1990-94*

"Did you know that I am the only Gopher in team history to get scratched from the line-up because of a Pop-Tart? It's true. I was home one day and was hungry, so I threw in a Pop-Tart. Well, I cooked the thing too long and the toaster started smoking. The smoke alarm is blaring, so, I ran over and yanked it out of the toaster really fast. But because it was so hot, I just tossed it straight up into the air. Then, I didn't want it to hit the floor, so I caught it like an idiot. Unfortunately for me, the melted frosting totally burned my hand. It blistered up and everything and I wound up having to go to the hospital. It was crazy. I caught so much crap from the fellas over that one, it wasn't even funny!" — *Jason Miller, Gopher 1987-91*

"My best memories from those days usually came from my junior year when I lived in a hockey house. I lived with Chris McAlpine, Eric Means, Tom Newman, John Brill and Jed Fiebelkorn. We were such slobs, I can't believe the filth we lived in. Man, what a dump! We had so many keg parties and never cleaned up afterwards. The carpet just wreaked of beer, it was so nasty. Looking back, it probably should have been condemned, seriously. So, sadly, most of my stories are probably not appropriate for your readers, sorry!" — *Jeff Nielsen, Gopher 1990-94*

"It was the little things: like being escorted out of the bar and back to our hotel by the local authorities up in Houghton, Michigan, where we were greeted by our coach fully two hours past curfew; or getting tattoos after a series sweep out in Colorado. So many of my best memories happened off the ice, when it was just the guys, hanging out and having fun." — *Larry Olimb, Gopher 1988-92*

"I will never forget when I showed up for my first practice, I had a mohawk. Wooger just came up to me and said 'I like your hair-cut, can I practice hitting my wedge off of it?' " — *Lance Pitlick, Gopher 1986-90*

"The credit card game is an old game that pro hockey players play when they are at a restaurant out on the road. If you have a big group of guys, everybody throws their Visa card in to a hat, and then the waitress pulls them out one by one at the end of dinner. The last card in the hat has to pick up the entire tab. Well, for whatever reason, a group of us did this at a Macaroni Grill in Ann Arbor my senior year during a series with Michigan. It was myself, Leopold, Taffe, Wendell, O'Leary, Riddle, Potulny and Koalska — who is notoriously cheap. So, we all eat and then, after dinner, we all toss our cards into a hat. The waitress comes over and starts taking them out one at a time. We are all praying that our name gets called, so we don't have to pay. Well, finally, there are three cards left and she pulls out a card and says 'Lawrence...'. Just then, Erik Wendell jumps in and says 'Yup, that's me!' That bastard put in his dad, Larry's, credit card! We are all like 'Dude, that is so weak!' Anyway, that left Koalska and Taffe as the last two. Koalska is just dying at this point and is now begging Taffe to split it with him. Taffe would not do it though, he just wanted to see Matty squirm. Well, as luck would have it, she pulled out Matt's card, which left Tayfer with the bill. It was hilarious. I will never forget that night, because those little things are the memories that stay with you forever. I miss it." — *Johnny Pohl, Gopher 1998-2002*

"I will never forget the aftermath of a horrible series we played in out in Denver. We got swept out there and then for some reason, we all got busted by the coaches afterwards for partying too much. In fact, they busted us several times because we kept moving the party to different hotel rooms. So, when we got back to the Cities that Monday and showed up for practice, we realized that there were no nets and no pucks out on the ice for a reason. We were toast. We skated or asses off, it was sick. We did nothing but up-downs, mountain-makers and lines for three straight hours. Nick Anthony puked. Riddle and I, who had been out all night at a Dave Mathews Band concert, were completely spent. Finally, we are all doing push-ups and sit-ups and Pat O'Leary's body literally ballooned up from a condition called over-training syndrome. It was insane. We still talk about that practice to this day. I wouldn't wish it on my worst enemy. Needless to say, we kept our noses clean after that." — *Grant Potulny, Gopher 2000-04*

"How about my favorite ritual, going to Sally's Bar in Stadium Village after every win. The next morning we would all show up with freshly shaved mustaches. They were our own version of NHL playoff beards, only a lot less hairy — just a 'Dirty Sanchez' look. We used to wear our 'I love New York' tee-shirts and hang out telling war stories all morning, it was the best. I miss those days." — *Grant Potulny, Gopher 2000-04*

"Billy Kohn was a huge pro wrestling fanatic and used to love doing this shtick where he would act like Hulk Hogan and tear his shirt off in the locker room. Well, one time somebody recorded him doing it and then got a copy over to the school newspaper, the Daily. They then ran story about it and poor Billy just took crap for it forever. It was absolutely hilarious." — *Erik Rasmussen, Gopher 1995-97*

"I remember being on a road trip one time up in Marquette, Mich., doing an MSC (TV) game with Frank Mazzocco. Well, we went out on the town after the Saturday night game and then headed back to the hotel to get some rest because we had an early flight that next morning. Anyway, 'somebody' called down to the front desk and said 'My name is Frank Mazzocco and I need a 4:30 AM wake-up-call. Now, I know that I am going to sound grumpy, but you need to call me at least four times every 15 minutes, no matter what. Even if I tell you not to call back, don't listen to me, you have to keep calling so that I can wake up...' Let's just say that old Frank was a little bit tired and upset that next day. That was a classic." — *Tommy Reid, Former Gopher TV & Radio Announcer*

"One time we were coming home from a series out in Michigan and the TV station had chartered a small plane for our crew to fly back on after the game. Well, we had to fly right through a blizzard and it was pretty scary. Anyway, I wound up sitting up in the front seat next to the pilot and I remember asking him about these blue lines of static electricity that were dancing across the windshield of the plane. He reassured me that it was normal because of the storm outside and it would only be a problem if it cracked the windshield. Not more than a few minutes later I heard a loud noise and saw the window crack right down the middle. I looked at the pilot and he said 'OK, now we need to put her down...'. Meanwhile, I was as white as a ghost thinking we were going to crash and burn. So, we starting descending and luckily wound up landing at the airport in Eau Claire, Wisconsin. I remember looking for a runway and it was just pitch black because of the storm. Nobody was home! Then the pilot told me that he could turn on the runway lights via remote control, so we were OK. When we landed we wound up driving right into an open hanger, where we made some coffee and waited for another plane to come pick us up. That was one night I will never forget!" — *Tommy Reid, Former Gopher TV & Radio Announcer*

"Some of my best memories of being a Gopher happened off the ice. I remember rooming with Larry Olimb and Jeff Stolp, and we lived next door to Jake Enebak and Sean Fabian. We used to have some of the most heated basketball games behind our house. It was total prison rules out there. I mean guys would get into fights and we would just beat the crap out of each other. Neither Jake or Faybs could dribble a basketball to save their lives, but they won all the time because they would just elbow you in the chops whenever you came inside on them. It was brutal. So, those are some of the dumb things I will always remember." — *Travis Richards, Gopher 1989-93*

"We had a pretty good house war going on for while one time with another hockey house. They started it by coming over to our house and taking all of our light bulbs. We got home and thought our electricity was off. So, we called the electric company and an electrician came over to basically tell us all that we were retarded. So, we retaliated by taking all of their remote controls and then took every shoe lace in their house and tied them into a giant knot. We finally called a truce after that, but that one was pretty good." — *Troy Riddle, Gopher 2000-04*

"Working with Glen Sonmor is the biggest perk of my job, by far. To listen to Glen tell stories is one of my favorite things to do in the world. One of my favorite stories about my time with Glen happened one time up at Michigan Tech. We were there doing a series and just before we were about to head over to the rink for the game, I get a call in my hotel room. Well, it was Glen and he says 'Wally, I lost my eye...' Now, for those who don't know this, Glen lost an eye many years ago while playing in a hockey game, so he wears a glass eye. I asked him where he put it but he couldn't remember. He said he looked all over the room and couldn't find it anywhere. So, I went down to his room and we spent at least a half an hour on our hands and knees just scouring this hotel room for his eye. By now we had to get going or we were going to be late for the game. Glen says, 'No problem, we'll just head over to the drug store on the way over and I will pick up a pirate patch.' Again, for those who may not remember, the last time Glen lost his eye and had to wear the patch, all hell broke loose up in Boston in one of the greatest brawl-fests of all-time when he was coaching the North Stars. Great, now I am thinking it could get real ugly if somebody makes fun of his patch and he goes after them! Well, luckily, just then he found it — it was hiding on the bed spread. Apparently it had popped out and he lost track of it. Anyway, all was well and we headed off to the game. That eye has been around, let me tell ya! He even lost it on the bench one time during the National Anthem when he was coaching the North Stars. The lights were off at the time and all the players were feeling around for it, it was a classic. Glen is the best. He makes my job so much fun, I just love the guy." — *Wally Shaver, Longtime Gopher Radio & TV Announcer*

"In Duluth there was this one fan who always sat in the same spot, and gave the opposing players hell all game. Well one time this loudmouth reached over and grabbed Mike Antonovich's stick when he was checked over by the boards near him. I was looking for an excuse to nail this idiot, and figured this would be as close as I would get. So, I jumped up from the bench, and beat the snot out of him but good. I knew he wasn't a fighter because he just kept grabbing my shirt, while I bloodied his face. It was a big production, and Herbie (Brooks) even came down to my defense from the press-box. I guess I showed that drunk son of a bitch a thing or two about messing with a Gopher!" — *Glen Sonmor, Former Gopher, North Stars & Fighting Saints Coach; Current Gopher Radio Broadcaster*

"You know, when I was playing with New York I got to know the Bentley brothers, who played for years with John Mariucci in Chicago, when they were with the Blackhawks. Now John, as you know, was the ultimate warrior out on the ice. He knew his role as a fighter and he loved it. He knew that he wasn't there to score 50 goals, he was there to play solid hockey and to protect his teammates. So, one time I asked those Bentley brothers about what it was like to play hockey with that big Dago. They said that playing with John made hockey fun for them again. Before John got there other players used to intimidate them and make runs at them because they were the stars of the Blackhawks. Well, when John got there it took just one trip around the league for every team to learn not to even look funny at the Bentley brothers. They left them alone after that because anybody from that point on knew that if they tried anything with those guys, that John was coming to get them. And back then you didn't have any of the penalties or rules about coming off the bench to mix it up like they do now. I remember Max (Bentley) saying, 'Anybody who tried to intimidate us had to have some pretty big balls because as soon as they went after us they would have to turn around and get ready for big John, who would come flying off the bench in a hurry. And there wasn't any doubt as to why he was coming either, because he left his stick and gloves back on the bench!' John used to love beating the crap out of guys and he was pretty darn good at it. Those Bentleys told me that after that no one would mess with them with the exception of one guy, Black Jack Stewart, who played for Detroit. They said that Black Jack would get bored out there sometimes and decide to make it interesting so he would take a shot at one of the Bentley's just so John would come after him. Those two used to love brawling with each other, and then they would go out and have beers together after the game. It was crazy, but that was the kind of guy John was, he would knock you down and then pick you back up. I miss that old son-of-a-gun, he was really a character." — *Glen Sonmor, Former Gopher, North Stars & Fighting Saints Coach; Current Gopher Radio Broadcaster*

"Once during a game I turned around and asked a woman who was heckling me, "Excuse me ma'am, how much do you charge to haunt a three-bedroom house?" Another time after a bad call during a game, I popped out my glass eye and offered it to the ref and told him, "Here, you take it, you need it more than I do!" — *Glen Sonmor, Former Gopher, North Stars & Fighting Saints Coach; Current Gopher Radio Broadcaster*

"One time we were going up to Billy Kohn's cabin for a team bonding trip before the season started. Well, we are driving along and we see this go-kart track along the side of the road, so we pull in to check it out. Nobody was around, so we helped ourselves to a little test-drive just for fun. Before long we are all out there racing around the track and smashing into each other, really having a ball. Just then, we hear police sirens. Sure enough, the owner of the place showed up and we were totally busted. So, this guy goes nuts and we wound up apologizing and paying for gas and all that. It was absolutely hilarious. Needless to say, I think the guy was a Sioux fan." — *Dave Spehar, Gopher 1996-2000*

"I will never forget my recruiting visit to come see the 'U' campus. I took a Greyhound bus from Duluth down to the Cities and Jack Blatherwick, the team's strength and conditioning coach, picked me up in his old truck. I am all excited to go see campus and check out the arena, but Jack says he has a better idea. He says 'You and I are going to go play golf...' I said 'Sure, I love golf, this is going to be fun.' So, he is telling me about the course, Oak Ridge Country Club, out in Hopkins, and he is telling me how nice it is. Well, we drive up to the course, but instead of going to the club house to check in and get me a set of rental clubs to use, he drives down this dead-end road and parks. He gets out of the truck, throws his clubs over the fence, and hops over. 'Come on,' he says, 'let's golf!' I couldn't believe it. I mean here I am, a 17-year old high school kid dressed in jeans and a t-shirt, with no clubs — sneaking into one of the poshest country clubs in town with one of my new coaches. I just thought 'Welcome to the big city, kid.' I just went with it and do you know what, we had a ball. We shared clubs and wound up having a blast. Luckily nobody caught us either, because that one would made for an interesting story. So, that was how I spent my recruiting trip to the Gophers. Unbelievable! I will never forget that." — *Robb Stauber, Gopher 1986-89; Current Gopher Goalie Coach*

"The worst freshman initiation I ever saw was up at Tim Berglund's cabin in Thief River Falls. The seniors got Scott Bloom really good. Bloomer was a pretty confident guy, which is why he was such a good hockey player. Some of the older guys thought he was a little bit cocky though, so they let him have it pretty good. They shaved him from top to bottom and even got both of his eyebrows. That poor bastard. Luckily they grew back a few weeks later, or he would have been bumming big-time! That was pretty funny." — *Robb Stauber, Gopher 1986-89; Current Gopher Goalie Coach*

"I always get a kick out of our annual Christmas party where we all exchanged gag gifts. I had a serious girlfriend my freshman year and the gift I got was a dog leash. I took a lot of crap over that, but it was pretty funny." — *Barry Tallackson, Gopher 2001-05*

"Traveling with Glen Sonmor made for terrific stories every week. We were out in Colorado Springs one time doing a Gopher-CC series. Well, after a game one night Glen told me to swing by his room that next morning and pick him up for breakfast. So, that next morning I knocked on Glen's door to go to breakfast. I hear some shuffling around in the room and finally after several knocks on the door he lets me in. He is standing there in his tightie-whities and his room looked like a tornado had just gone through it. Stuff was everywhere. I asked him if he was all right. He said, 'My eye fell out in the middle of the night and I couln't find the damn thing! Well, I finally found it over there behind the curtain.' I just about died laughing. He said it so matter of factly, and that was that. He said he would throw on some clothes and be with me in a minute. Sure enough, he popped his eye back in and we went and had breakfast. You know, I learned so much from working with Glen, the guy is just a brilliant hockey mind. I mean he is much older than I am and only has one eye, but he could see things out on the ice that I would never pick up on. I was just amazed at the things he could see and how much he understood the nuances of the game. I love Glen, he is just the best." — *Dan Terhaar, Former Gopher Radio Announcer*

"We used to have an annual team Christmas party where we would exchange gag gifts with everybody. Now, the rule was that whatever you got as a gift, you had to hold it up and you had to read the card out loud. Well, my roommate was Greg Zwakman, and he had written this totally sappy love letter to his girlfriend one time. Anyway, she wound up leaving the letter at our apartment, so I took it and wrapped it up and then gave it to him as his present. He just about died when he opened that thing up. But, he was a trooper, and he read it to the entire team. He got heckled pretty good for a while after that one. That was classic." — *Dan Trebil, Gopher 1992-96*

"I love doing pranks, everything from scotch-taping guys' skates just before they walk out onto the ice, which is always funny to watch. I have gotten both Smaagaard and Stevens with that and you would think it would get old, but nope. It's still funny watching those guys fall flat on their faces every time!" — *Mike Vannelli, Gopher 2003-Present*

"Some of my best memories were just hanging out at our hockey house with all the fellas. I remember playing ping pong out in the yard and drinking beer, it was awesome. Then, Leo (Jordan Leopold) would come over, and being the electronics guru that he was, would hook up all the wiring so that we could have the TV and stereo outside so that we could watch the Stanley Cup Playoffs. That guy was like 'MacGyver,' he just loved hooking up stuff and fixing stuff with duct tape. He was hilarious. Anyway, we would sit out there in our boxer shorts all day getting tanked, it was awesome." — *Erik Westrum, Gopher 1997-2001*

"I will never forget losing to St. Cloud in 2000 at the WCHA Final Five and just being totally bummed that our season was over. So, a few days later I was out at the bars with Matt Leimbek and Nick Anthony, and I told them that I needed to get away for a road trip. It was spring break and dammit, we deserved a good break. So, it's like two in the morning and I said pick a spot, let's go. We found a map and pointed south. South Padre Island, Texas, was the closest spot to my finger, so that is where we went. I told them that they had a half an hour to pack their bags and then we were leaving. So, we are all jacked, listening to tunes and getting psyched to see the ladies on the beach. Well, we are about an hour outside of the Cities and just outside Albert Lea, we hit a deer. It was a total buzz-kill. We had to sit there for five hours while our car got fixed. We finally hit the road again, and the only problem was that the cruise control didn't work. OK, so Nick is driving now and we are somewhere in Iowa. He is tired, so he hits the cruise control. Sure enough, I am awoken from a dead sleep in the back seat by the sound of the engine getting munched by the cruise control. Now, we are stuck in Iowa to get the damn thing fixed yet again, it was crazy. I was beside myself I was so pissed. Leimbek is now totally spent and just wants to go home. I am like 'Dude, we are not going home, we are going to Texas. Period!'. He didn't care, he wanted his mommy, so I said 'Fine, go home!', and I dropped him off on the side of I-35 in the middle of nowhere, Iowa. That was it, I was like 'You are not going to take down the team morale of this vehicle anymore, get the hell out!' So, he hiked like 10 miles in his sandals and wound up at a Greyhound Bus depot. The bus was full though, so he wound up sleeping in the stairwell that night. Nick and I didn't care, we just pressed on. We were on a mission, by God, and we were not stopping for anything. Finally, we got to South Padre and we shacked up in this rat nest hotel for like eight days. It was the best. Then, we had to get home, so we are driving back north through Texas and a massive tornado comes up on us along the road. It is like pitch black and hailing so hard we can't even see out the window. Well, we were broke and tired and just wanted to get home, so we turned off our car lights, put on our sunglasses, and just plowed straight through it like maniacs. It was completely insane. We drove all day and all night until we finally got home. Needless to say, Leimbek was not too pleased to see us when we got back."— *Erik Westrum, Gopher 1997-2001*

"OK, one night I went out with Lance Pitlick, Marty Nanne and Randy Skarda, three of the biggest tough guys on our team. Well, we wound up over at a house party at St. Thomas. As soon as they found out we were Gopher Hockey players though, we got shuffled out of there pretty quickly. Anyway, we are leaving and a bunch of guys who were at the party jump in their car and try to chase us to see if they can pick a fight. Of course I wanted no part of this. I am five-foot-nothing and a hundred and nothing. So, we pull up to a stoplight and Pit jumps out and just runs straight over to their car and drop kicks it super hard. These guys are so freaked out that they just take off. Meanwhile, Pit comes back to the car with his adrenaline is pumping and says 'I don't feel so good.' Well, we look down and his foot was about the size of his head, just totally swollen. It turned out he broke his foot. So, the next day in the paper there was a story about how he broke his foot after getting hit with a slap-shot in practice — which was total damage control propaganda on our parts. Thank goodness nobody ever found out the real story. That was an evening I will never forget." — *Dean Williamson, Gopher 1987-90*

"One of my favorite memories was when we won the MacNaughton Cup back in the late '80s one time and the players picked me up and put me right inside of the cup. That was great! — *Doug Woog, Former Gopher Player & Coach; current Gopher Hockey TV Analyst*

"One of my favorite memories in Gold Country was when we took Johnny Brill out to Solid Gold for his 21st birthday. He wound up getting into a mud-wrestling match with some of the ladies and we all sat outside the ring cheering him on. It was like the scene from the movie 'Stripes,' it was pretty hilarious." — *Doug Zmolek, Gopher 1989-92*

CHAPTER 16
WHERE ARE THEY NOW?

Mike Anderson presently works as a futures trader in Chicago.

Mark Bahr, now in his 12th year with the program, serves as the Director of Hockey Operations for the Gophers. He and his wife Tammy, a former Gopher Hockey cheerleader, have two children and presently reside in Crystal.

Keith Ballard presently plays for the NHL's Phoenix Coyotes.

Scott Bell retired from pro hockey in 2000 and has been coaching at various levels around the country ever since. Today he serves as the head coach at Hamline University. He and his wife Jaci, a former Gopher Hockey cheerleader, and their two boys presently reside in Minneapolis.

Reggie Berg continues to play professional hockey with the Florida Everblades of the East Coast Hockey League. He and his wife have one child and presently reside in Estero, Fla.

Grant Bischoff works as a real estate appraiser in his hometown of Grand Rapids, where he also coaches youth hockey. He and his wife have four kids and presently reside in Grand Rapids.

Patty Bjorklund is in her 23rd year as Hockey Administrative Assistant and her 25th year as a member of the Golden Gopher staff. She and her husband, Denny, presently reside in Victoria.

Brian Bonin retired from pro hockey in 2005. Presently he works with Edina Realty and resides in White Bear Lake with his wife and two children.

Harry Broadfoot is in his 20th season as a member of the Gopher's staff. Twenty of those seasons, however, have been as the Head Equipment Trainer for Gopher Hockey. Harry presently resides in Minneapolis.

Bill Butters works as a missionary with Hockey Ministries International, which sponsors 36 Summer camps in six countries. Bill and his wife have three children and presently reside in White Bear Lake.

Ben Clymer currently plays for the NHL's Washington Capitals.

Mike Crowley retired from pro hockey in 2002 after tearing his achilles tendon during training camp with the Minnesota Wild. Today, Mike works as a futures trader in Chicago, where he and his wife have one child.

Steve DeBus works as an instructor at Robb Stauber's Goalcrease Academy in Edina. He and his wife have one child and presently live in South Minneapolis.

Jeff Dubay serves as one half of the ever-popular "P.A. & Dubay" show on KFAN Sports Radio and presently resides in the Twin Cities.

Joe Dziedzic retired from pro hockey in 1999 after suffering a career-ending eye injury during a game. He presently coaches a team in the Minnesota high school elite league; operates several youth skill development camps, including a high school prep camp with former teammate Chris McAlpine; and also runs Mounds View's Youth Hockey Program. He is single and presently resides in Minneapolis.

Ken Gernander retired from pro hockey in 2005 and serves as the assistant coach of the AHL's Hartford Wolfpack. He and his wife have three children and presently reside in Hartford.

Eric Gislason is the co-host and executive producer of the "Kent Hrbek Outdoors" television show. He and his wife have three kids and presently reside in Burnsville.

Ben Hankinson retired from pro hockey in 1998. Since then he has become an NHL Certified Agent and has his own agency called SPS Hockey. Benny represents about 40 players, including several current Gophers: Paul Martin, Keith Ballard, Wyatt Smith and Barry Tallackson. Among his former clientele who have since retired are: Chris McAlpine, Doug Zmolek, Lance Pitlick, and his own brother, Casey. Ben and his wife have three kids and presently reside in Edina.

Casey Hankinson retired from pro hockey in 2005 and presently works in the commercial real estate business. In addition, for the past five years he has operated his own hockey school, "Hankinson-Hockey," at Edina's Braemar Arena. He and his wife have one daughter and presently reside in Edina.

Peter Hankinson works in the insurance business in Minneapolis. He and his wife have two girls and presently reside in Edina.

Adam Hauser is currently in the Los Angeles Kings minor league system, playing for the AHL's Manchester Monarchs.

Darby Hendrickson headed overseas to play Salzburg, Austria, in the Fall of 2005. Darby and his wife have three children and presently reside in Inver Grove Heights.

Craig Johnson is playing professional hockey in Düsseldorf, Germany. He and his wife, along with their three children, presently reside outside of Los Angles in nearby Irvine, Calif.

Trent Klatt recently retired from pro hockey in 2005, after 15 seasons in the NHL. He and his wife have three kids and presently live just east of Grand Rapids.

Matt Koalska currently plays for the AHL's Bridgeport Sound Tigers, the farm-team of the NHL's New York Islanders.

Ryan Kraft is playing pro hockey in Germany. He and his wife have one child and presently reside in Apple Valley.

Cory Laylin is playing hockey in Denmark. He and his wife Stayce, a former Gopher Hockey cheerleader, have two boys and presently live in St. Michael.

Jordan Leopold currently plays with the NHL's Calgary Flames. Leo married his college sweetheart after his senior year at Minnesota and together they have one daughter.

Paul Martin currently plays professional hockey with the NHL's New Jersey Devils.

Frank Mazzocco continues to serve as a television analyst for Gopher Hockey. He and his wife have two grown children and presently reside in the Twin Cities.

Chris McAlpine retired from pro hockey in 2005 and is coaching youth hockey in the Twin Cities as well as finishing his degree back at the U of M. He and his wife have three kids and presently reside in Shoreview.

Jason Miller works in the land development business in the Twin Cities. He and his wife have three kids and presently live in St. Bonifacius.

Nate Miller works in sales for an orthopedic medical device company in the Twin Cities and presently resides in Brooklyn Park.

Jeff Nielsen works for a wealth management firm in the Twin Cities and presently resides in South Minneapolis.

Larry Olimb works in the commercial real estate business in the Twin Cities, specializing in property management. He and his wife have three kids and presently reside in Plymouth.

Tom Pederson is a coach in the San Jose Sharks system, working as the head coach of several Junior Sharks youth and developmental teams. Tom and his wife have three kids and presently live in San Jose, Calif.

Lance Pitlick retired from pro hockey in 2002. He is currently a youth coach in the Wayzata

Hockey Association and also works as a skill development coach for several other programs. In addition, he also owns his own company called 'Sweet Hockey' and is the inventor of the 'Sweet Hands Hockey Trainer,' an innovative stick handling product. He and his wife have two kids and presently reside in Plymouth.

Johnny Pohl was traded by the St. Louis Blues to the Toronto Maple Leafs in the Fall of 2005. He currently plays for their AHL minor league affiliate, the Toronto Marlies. *(And yes, for those of you who really want to know, he and Krissy Wendell are still an item...)*

Grant Potulny currently plays for the AHL's Binghamton Senators in the Ottawa Senators farm system. He and his wife have one child and presently reside in the Twin Cities.

Erik Rasmussen is in his 10th year of pro hockey and is currently playing with the New Jersey Devils. He and his wife have one child and presently reside in New Jersey.

Tommy Reid serves as the radio analyst alongside Bob Kurtz for the Minnesota Wild. He also owns a restaurant in on West Seventh Street in St. Paul called, appropriately enough, "Tommy Reid's Hockey City Pub." Tommy and his wife presently reside in Eagan.

Travis Richards serves as a player/assistant coach for the American Hockey League's Grand Rapids Griffins. Travis and his wife have three kids and presently reside in Grand Rapids, Mich. *(Incidentally, Travis' older brother Todd, also a former Gopher, is an assistant coach with the AHL's Milwaukee Admirals.)*

Troy Riddle presently plays in the St. Louis Blues system for the Peoria Rivermen of the American Hockey League.

Wally Shaver presently serves as the Gopher's play-by-play radio announcer. In addition, Wally also works with Let's Play Hockey Magazine and the Hobey Baker Award. He and his wife presently reside in Apple Valley.

Wyatt Smith currently plays for the NHL's New York Islanders. During the off-season he resides in Eden Prairie and has a 10 year old daughter.

Glen Sonmor presently serves as a Gopher Hockey radio analyst and also scouts for the Minnesota Wild. At 76 years young, Glen remains one of the best in the business and is still having a ball. He currently resides in Bloomington.

Dave Spehar works for an investment bank in Chicago and presently lives with his wife just outside the Windy City.

Robb Stauber currently owns and operates his own goaltending academy in Edina called "Stauber's Goalcrease." He has two children and presently resides in Eden Prairie.

Jeff Taffe currently plays professional hockey and was recently traded by the NHL's Phoenix Coyotes to the New York Rangers in the Fall of 2005.

Barry Tallackson currently plays for the NHL's New Jersey Devils.

Dan Terhaar presently works for WCCO Radio and serves as the TV play-by-play announcer for the Minnesota Wild. He and his wife have three children and presently reside in Andover.

Dan Trebil retired from pro hockey in 2001 and works in real-estate investment banking for a firm in Bloomington. He and his wife have two kids and presently reside in Eden Prairie.

Thomas Vanek currently plays for the NHL's Buffalo Sabres.

Erik Westrum currently plays in the NHL as a member of the Minnesota Wild's minor league affiliate, Houston Aeros. Erik and his wife presently reside in Eagan.

Dean Williamson serves as a vice president with a major commercial real estate firm in the Twin Cities. He and his wife have two kids and presently reside in Edina.

Doug Woog serves as a color analyst for Gopher Hockey TV broadcasts. Woog also works for Learfield Sports Properties, doing sales and marketing for Gopher Sports. In addition, Woog continues to own and operate a hockey camp up in the Brainerd Lakes area. Doug and his wife have three grown kids and several grandkids, and presently reside in South St. Paul.

Doug Zmolek retired from pro hockey in 2001 and works for the Rochester Youth Hockey Association. He and his wife have three boys and presently reside in Rochester.

CHAPTER 17
A FEW WORDS OF COACHING WISDOM FROM DON LUCIA & DOUG WOOG...

CATCHING UP WITH COACH LUCIA...

Don Lucia grew up in Grand Rapids and went on to graduate from Grand Rapids High School in 1977. There, he led the Thunderhawks to a pair of State High School Hockey titles in 1975 and 1976, as well as a pair of third-place finishes in 1974 and 1977. The sturdy defenseman not only earned all-state honors in hockey his senior year, but also on the gridiron as well as a linebacker on the football team. He was later was drafted by the Philadelphia Flyers of the National Hockey League. From there Don went on to play hockey at the University of Notre Dame, where the team captain graduated in 1981. Lucia's first coaching job came at the University of Alaska-Fairbanks, where he served as an assistant from 1981-85. In 1985 he moved over to the University of Alaska Anchorage, where he served as an assistant until 1987 before taking over as the head coach. Lucia served as the head coach at Alaska-Fairbanks for six years, posting four winning seasons and an overall record of 113-87-10, before leaving the Nanooks in 1993 to take over as the head coach at Colorado College.

At CC Lucia took over the reins of the program and had not experienced a winning season in the previous 13 campaigns. How would he do? He guided the Tigers to a record of 23-11-5 and the WCHA regular-season title in his first season. The league title was the program's first

Don Lucia

in 37 years. Lucia was honored at the conclusion of that season with the Spencer Penrose Award as National Coach of the Year. Lucia he didn't stop there though, guiding the Tigers to an unprecedented three straight outright regular-season league titles in his first three years behind the bench. Colorado College won a school-record 33 games in 1996, and made it all the way to the NCAA championship game. For his effort Lucia was named WCHA Coach of the Year that same season, and added a second league coach of the year trophy at the conclusion of the 1997 season as well when he led his Tigers back to the NCAA Frozen Four semifinals. In all Lucia would spend six seasons in Colorado Springs, racking up a 166-68-18 record along the way.

On April 9, 1999, the University of Minnesota announced that Don Lucia would become the 13th head coach in Golden Gopher Hockey history. Nearly three years to the day later, Lucia raised the NCAA Championship Trophy above his head at the Xcel Energy Center in St. Paul. Led by Hobey Baker Award winner Jordan Leopold, and All American Johnny Pohl, the Gophers hung on to beat Maine in one of the greatest Finals in history. Amazingly, he would do it again that next year too, making it back-to-back national championships as the Gophers this time beat New Hampshire in the Frozen Four in Buffalo, NY.

Entering the 2005-06 season, Lucia currently has an overall record of 441-232-50 (.645). He has established himself as one of the premier collegiate coaches in the nation and has put the Gophers back on top of the hockey world once again. In all he has coached 13 All-Americans, 41 All-WCHA players, 77 WCHA All-Academic team members, six Hobey Baker Award finalists and five WCHA Defensive Players of the Year. And, he is one of just six coaches in NCAA history to lead two different teams to the Frozen Four. Lucia has also been active with USA Hockey for the last decade, having served as head coach of the national-16 team that competed in Finland in 1996, as well as for Team West at the U.S. Olympic Festival in Denver in 1995. Lucia also served as the president of the American Hockey Coaches Association in 1999. Don and his wife Joyce live in Plymouth and have four children: Alison, Jessica, Anthony and Mario.

HOW WOULD YOU DESCRIBE YOUR COACHING STYLE?
"Number one I give my assistants a lot of responsibility in what we do and they have a lot of say. I think it is a team effort, it is not just about me, so I want a lot of input from my staff and players. Ultimately I have the final say in things, but communication is very important to our success. I have always tried to have my teams play on an even keel night in and night out. I don't think you can get all fired up for Friday night and then have a let down on Saturday, so consistency is important to me."

HOW DO YOU MOTIVATE YOUR PLAYERS?
"Number one, you have to coach to your own personality. I don't think you can copy what a certain coach does and then try to be the same thing, that is impossible. So, I try to treat my kids fairly. I want them to respect me, but there also has to be a line where they know who is in charge. Then, I try to give the leaders of our team a lot of say in what we are doing. I also think that as I have gotten older as a coach I have begun to realize more and more that you just have to try to make each individual team the best that that particular team can be. And that changes from year to year. My philosophy has always been that I want our team to reach its potential, and I don't ever want my players to play with the fear in that if they make a mistake they think will get benched. Hockey is a game of read and react and you have to play with confidence. When you play with confidence, that is when you play your best."

WHO WERE YOUR COACHING MENTORS?
"My father was my high school football coach and he had a big impact on me. Then, Mike Sertich and Jim Nelson were my high school hockey coaches, and I had a lot of respect for those guys too. So, you take pieces of those people that you have been around your whole life and that kind of formed your style. I remember as a kid admiring Bud Grant's calm and cool on the sidelines, and I have always felt that that was a very important quality to have."

WHAT ARE THE CHARACTERISTICS OF WINNERS?
"Commitment, character, and teamwork."

LOOKING BACK WHAT ARE YOU MOST PROUD OF IN YOUR CAREER?

"I would hope that most of the players who have played for me can look back and feel that they were treated fairly, reached their potential and had a great time."

HOW DID YOU BUILD TEAM UNITY & CHEMISTRY?

"I don't believe in hazing or rookie initiations. I am big believer that once a player is on the team then everybody should be treated the same."

WHAT'S THE BEST PIECE OF ADVICE YOU EVER GOT FROM ANOTHER COACH?

"Mike Sertich, former UM-Duluth head coach, once told me to 'take care of the game.' And by that he meant that the game is bigger than any one person, any one player or any one coach. So, try to make decisions that benefit our sport."

ON WINNING BACK TO BACK NCAA CHAMPIONSHIPS:

"You know, it is like when I go out recruiting players to come here and I always ask them the question, 'if you could win a national title, who's jersey would you want to be wearing?'. And I certainly feel that way as a coach that there is no better place to win a title than at the University of Minnesota because of how much pride there is in this state with Gopher Hockey. I am so happy to be back in Minnesota. This is just an incredible program and it is really a once in a lifetime opportunity to serve as the coach of the Gophers."

WHAT ADVICE WOULD YOU HAVE FOR YOUNG COACHES STARTING OUT TODAY"

"Coach to your personality, be patient and treat your players like you would want your son to be treated."

WHAT ROLE HAS YOUR FAMILY PLAYED IN YOUR SUCCESS?

"I couldn't have had the success I have had without the support of my wife. She has had to hold down the fort at home while I have been out coaching and recruiting all across the country. Whether it is recruiting dinners or team meals at our house, she has been there and that has made my job so much easier. And, the team has become more of an extended family to our own, and that helps build team unity too."

WHAT MOTIVATES YOU?

"I am also really into my family and I try to spend as much time as possible with them as I can.

WHAT'S THE BIGGEST THING YOU'VE LEARNED FROM COACHING THAT YOU'VE BEEN ABLE TO APPLY TO YOUR EVERYDAY LIFE?

"To be disciplined in everything I do."

John Mariucci & John Mayasich

You don't write a Gopher Hockey book without these two. Period.

CATCHING UP WITH COACH WOOG...

Doug Woog grew up playing hockey in St. Paul and went on to graduate from South St. Paul High School in 1962. There, he earned all-state hockey honors for an amazing three consecutive years and also starred on the football team as well. Next, Doug fulfilled a life-long dream by accepting a scholarship to play for the University of Minnesota and learn the game from one of the all-time great coaches, John Mariucci. Woog went on to a fabulous career in Gold Country, earning All-American honors his junior season after leading the team in scoring. He was named as captain for his senior season en route to leading the team to a 16-12-0 record, and a second place finish in the WCHA. For his efforts he was named the team's MVP. From 1964-1966 the speedy center scored 48 goals and 53 assists for 101 career points. Woog went on to graduate with honors from the U of M in 1967.

From there Woog went on to play for the 1967 U.S. National Team and was a candidate for the 1968 U.S. Olympic team. After that, however, it was off to the real world as he went on to teach Geography and coach football and hockey at Hopkins West Junior High School. Then in the fall of 1968, he took a job at his high school alma mater, where he became the head soccer coach as well as an assistant on both the hockey and baseball teams. While coaching at South St. Paul, Woog's soccer program won six conference titles and twice finished as runner-up's for the state championship.

From 1971 through 1977 Woog branched out to coach the St. Paul Vulcans and the Minnesota Junior Stars, who he led to two U.S. Junior National titles. During that time, in 1973, Doug fulfilled another dream when he earned his Master's Degree in guidance and counseling from St. Thomas University. In 1978, Woog was chosen to lead the West Team in the U.S. Olympic Festival, where his squad won the gold medal. It would be the beginning of a long relationship with USA Hockey. (At the 1989 Olympic Festival Woog duplicated that feat by winning the gold medal with his South squad. Woog was also the assistant coach of the 1982 U.S. National Junior Team and then served as an assistant coach for the 1984 Olympic team that competed in Sarajevo, Yugoslavia as well. In 1985 Woog coached the U.S. National Junior Team; in 1987 he served as the assistant coach for Team USA in the 1987 Canada Cup; and in 1989 he was the head coach of the of U.S. Select 17 team. In addition, he served as a national committee member for the AHAUS and was chairman of the National Skating Committee for USA Hockey.)

In 1985 the "Wooger" returned to his college alma-mater. There, he guided the Golden Gophers to seven league championships (four regular season and three post-season) over his illustrious 14-year career. During his tenure in Gold Country the Gophers were among the nation's very best, garnering WCHA Final Four/Five and NCAA appearances in 12 of 14 seasons, posting seven 30-win seasons, and appearing in six NCAA Final Fours. In 1999 Woog resigned as the University of Minnesota's head hockey coach to take an assistant athletic director position at the school. He would leave as the program's all-time winningest coach with a gaudy 389-187-40 record (.664).

Doug Woog

Today, in addition to his work as a television analyst for Gopher Hockey games, he runs his own summer hockey camp up in Brainerd. Woog has been instrumental in initiating and maintaining youth athletic organizations in his community and is an overall good friend to hockey. In 2002 Woog was honored by being inducted into the U.S. Hockey Hall of Fame in Eveleth.

HOW WOULD YOU DESCRIBE YOUR COACHING STYLE?

"It's experiential. It all starts from the coaches that you played for because as a coach, that is what you know. I learned a lot from several different coaches and that all went into creating my own style. It was a real mixed bag and in retrospect, that was great because I had several different styles to choose from when we played different kinds of teams. I mean the European style to was so different than the North American style, it that was all part of it. From there I just believed in hard work and good teamwork. I believed that you should treat kids the same way you would want your own kid treated. You want them to be taught well, you want them to have a chance to win, and you want them to have opportunities to succeed."

HOW DID YOU MOTIVATE YOUR PLAYERS?

"You know, that has really evolved. From the time I was coaching in high school until the end of my college coaching days, my style of motivation really changed with the times. I realized that there were a lot of different ways to motivate kids and that helped me become a better teacher. I just loved teaching, that was what it was all about for me."

WHO WERE YOUR COACHING MENTORS?

"I learned a great deal from my high school coach, Lefty Smith, and of course from John Mariucci at the University of Minnesota. I also learned a lot about the international style from Lou Vairo."

WHAT ROLE DID YOUR FAMILY PLAY IN YOUR SUCCESS?

"They were great. You know, to coach my sons was very special to me. They were good players and it was a great to see them get the opportunity to play college hockey. From there it was great too that my family was not only very supportive, but that they stayed out of the spotlight. I mean my kids didn't get into any trouble, they didn't do drugs, they were just great kids, and that was big because those are the kinds of distractions that can be detrimental to your career. Really though, I couldn't have asked for more in terms of what they gave me in terms of the freedom of doing what I loved to do. I think back to when I first started out. I was coaching junior hockey, coaching the South St. Paul soccer team, serving as a high school counselor and going to graduate school all at the same time. Then, I had a couple of kids in diapers at that same time, so my wife was a saint. Her support was incredible and I am very lucky to have a great family."

LOOKING BACK WHAT ARE YOU MOST PROUD OF IN YOUR CAREER?

"I am just proud of all the good kids that we have had in our program over the years. None of our kids got into trouble and they have since gone on to do some great things in their lives. That is very rewarding as a coach. Then, to have made so many friendships along the way, and to be genuinely appreciate by the fans and supporters — that means the world to me."

HOW DID YOU BUILD TEAM UNITY & CHEMISTRY?

"We had a lot of traditions that we did that built chemistry. For instance, we used to take some of the seniors hunting every year down in Iowa. We used to have golf tournaments, social outings, dinners, and even maybe taking the guys to a North Stars game. We wanted to get guys into social situations where they could become friends outside of hockey and that led to better team unity. I think even the dorms helped out too, where the kids lived with one another. The other thing that was because all of the kids were from Minnesota, they had that in common. They all knew of each other, or had played with or against one another at one time over the years as well, and that helped too."

WHAT'S THE BIGGEST THING YOU'VE LEARNED FROM COACHING THAT YOU'VE BEEN ABLE TO APPLY TO YOUR EVERYDAY LIFE?

"Happiness. I have been so lucky to have had all of the opportunities that I have had. To be able to spend my entire career here in Minnesota was extremely gratifying. I count my blessings for all of the great people that I have been lucky enough to meet and have an impact on in this business, and I really appreciate it. I also haven't had to sell my values or cheapen myself along the way and that makes me happy too."

The Genesis of Gopher Women's Hockey

Krissy Wendell grew up in Brooklyn Park, as, well, just one of the guys. That's right, Krissy was never afraid to compete against the top athletes, even if that meant playing alongside the boys. In fact, she attributes much of her success in athletics to the fact that the guys accepted her and let her play with them. Not only did she succeed on her youth boys' hockey teams, she also starred with the fella's out on diamond as well. Back in 1994 she even played catcher on the boy's baseball team that made it all the way to the Little League World Series — becoming just the fifth girl in America ever to do so.

Krissy went on to star at Park Center High School, where, as a junior, she became the first high school player (boy or girl) in the nation to score 100 goals in a season, when she tallied 109. She posted 110 her senior year just for good measure. Oh, and by the way, she accomplished all of that as a defenseman! Incredible. In all, she tallied an insane 335 points in just 62 games, en route to leading her Park Center Pirates to the 2000 Girls High School State Championship. For her efforts, she was named as the recipient of the coveted Ms. Hockey award that same year. Hockey wasn't her only gig either. Krissy was also a two-time all-state catcher for the Pirates who hit over .500 batting clean-up. Not bad.

Krissy then went on to play for Team USA as a member of the 2002 U.S. Women's Olympic team, where she won a silver medal in Salt Lake City, Utah. From there, the most highly recruited freshmen, maybe in women's college hockey history, opted to stay put and attend the University of Minnesota. As a Gopher, Krissy simply dominated the college hockey landscape. Alongside her partner in crime, Natalie Darwitz, she lit up goaltenders from Bemidji to Boston, en route to leading her squad to a pair of back-to-back national championships in 2004 and 2005. For her efforts, she was named as the winner of the 2005 Patty Kazmaier Memorial Award presented annually to the top player in NCAA Division I women's hockey.

When it was all said and done, the two-time first-team All-American had rewritten the record books during her illustrious career in Gold Country. Despite playing only three seasons, she finished second in career scoring with 237 points; second in career goals with 106; second in career assists with 131; third in career plus/minus with +156; and just to show that she was no sissy… she finished third in career penalty minutes with 153. Equally as impressive, Krissy graduated in just three years with a degree in Communications. As for the future? The five-time U.S. Women's National Team member is likely to represent the United States for her second Olympic hockey tour at the 2006 Winter Games in Turin, Italy.

Arguably the greatest women's hockey player in the history of the sport, Krissy Wendell is as humble as she is talented. A budding superstar in sports-entertainment, Krissy also recently signed a contract with Octagon, a leading sports and marketing company, which works with such well-known female athletes as Mia Hamm. They see Wendell as the next big thing, as evidenced

Krissy Wendell

by the fact that she will soon have her own hockey equipment deal. As for now, her goals are simple: to win the gold in Turin, and then do it all over again in Vancouver, where she has every intention of leading that Olympic team in 2010 as well. Stay tuned!

As for the state of the state of women's hockey in Minnesota, Krissy is optimistic and realistic about her sport's future.

"I think overall it is awesome, I really do," said Krissy. "We are way ahead of the curve. The numbers are growing every year and that is what it is all about. We are far more advanced than any other state with regards to development and that is a testament to all of the youth coaches and volunteers out there who really do make a difference. The game has grown so much over the past ten years, it is just amazing. This is the state of hockey and there are opportunities for everybody out there, regardless of what age or what level you play at. From kids playing youth hockey to senior women playing in adult leagues, the game continues to grow for women and that is so great to see."

"I think the biggest growth has been at the youth levels, where more and more kids are coming out for the sport and giving it a try. I have a little sister who is a U-10 right now and she has so many opportunities for ice time, which is fabulous. She can play in summer leagues, girls' hockey camps, and even skate with the boys. Girls that age have just as many opportunities as the boys, and I never thought I would see that so soon. I remember when I was her age, I was playing with the boys pretty much exclusively. We just didn't have the numbers to support a lot of teams and leagues back then, so we did what we had to do in order to get ice time.

"While I am happy for the girls in that they have so many more outlets to play on, I don't ever regret all of the years that I got to play with the boys. Plus, it was so much fun. And, that is why we will probably never see the scoring records that were established during the era in which I played high school hockey be broken. The competition has leveled out and there aren't any more seventh grade phenoms like Natalie Darwitz dominating at such a young age. There are so many girls playing now and the talent level has risen across the board. Playing with the boys is such an advantage though, it really is. The intensity and atmosphere that the boys play with is hard to match with the girls.

"As for some of the problems in the game today? Well, I think little kids are out on the ice way too much in structured practices. Young kids do not need to be practicing every-day. When I was a kid we used to practice for an hour inside and then head out to the pond,

Just call her "Wendell"

where we would skate for hours and hours amongst ourselves just having fun. I don't see that as much nowadays and that is too bad. Kids need to be kids and have fun with hockey. They also need to be well rounded and play other sports as well, that is so important. We just need to make sure that they are enjoying themselves while they are growing and learning, otherwise they are going to get burnt out and quit the sport — which is counter-productive.

"When I was a kid my parents literally took my skates away from me and hid them in the Summer. I wasn't allowed to skate in the Summers until after my freshmen year. My parents wanted to make sure that I played other sports in the off-season and didn't get burnt out. By the time Fall started I was so excited and was practically begging them to let me play. I had that fire and drive again and that probably wouldn't have been that way if I had skated all Summer long. Being a well-rounded athlete is so important. You learn so much from playing other sports and from being in different situations. I remember when I played on the boys little league team, I learned so much from that experience and that totally helped me to become not only a better athlete, but a better person."

As for her time in Gold Country, it was all good...

"Being a Gopher meant everything to me," said Krissy. "It was a real dream come true for me and something I had looked forward to ever since I was a little kid. Just to have that opportunity is something that I will always be very grateful for. My big brother, Erik, was a Gopher from 1999-2002 and I saw what a great experience he had there. I will never forget seeing him with his jersey on with the name 'WENDELL' on the back. It looked so cool and I knew that someday I wanted one of my own. So, for me to follow in his footsteps and keep it all going was just awesome. We all grew up watching the team and then to finally put on that maroon and gold jersey was truly an amazing feeling."

"Everything about my experience with the Gophers was tremendous, especially winning the two national championships. They were so awesome. What else can I say? To be able to share those memories with 20 of your closest friends, your sisters, is something you will never forget. The entire experience of being at the University of Minnesota was wonderful, but to win the national championships — that was just icing on the cake. We worked so hard to achieve them and when they became a reality it was just indescribable. The first title was really exciting because we had gone through so much that year. We had a bunch of highs and a bunch of lows, but came together in the end when it all mattered. When we won it and got to throw our gloves in the air and pile on top of each other out on the ice, that was just the most amazing feeling in the world.

"Plus, by then we had really established a great rivalry with Duluth and that made everything so much more interesting for our fans. We had so much fun playing against those guys, who had won three straight titles of their own just prior to that, and for us to get past them and win it all was so huge. Then, the second one was just as incredible, but different. We set some really high goals for ourselves at the beginning of the season to repeat as national champs, and when it happened it was so sweet. There was a lot of pressure on us that year and we were able to come through when it counted. That was really special too. To go out on a winning note is amazing, I was very fortunate.

"A huge part of our success definitely came from the fact that we had our very own arena. That was such a huge advantage. We were so spoiled it wasn't even funny. To be the only college program in the country to have our own building, just for women's hockey, was so special and so unique. There are so many advantages to having your own rink, from getting your own ice time whenever you want it, to creating your own winning atmosphere that you don't have to share with anybody else. It was a huge deal for us and something none of us took for granted. Plus, it was great to have my family at every one of my games, having that support is something looking back I probably took for granted."

"Being a part of that atmosphere was truly incredible. It is the best of the best. Minneapolis has everything you could possibly ever want and that makes the entire experience so much more fun. The school itself has it all too, from academics to athletics to fan support, you name it — it's got it. Plus, your network here for when you want to get a job is second to none. There are so many alumni who live here and work here and they totally support their own. I don't think any other university can compete with the entire package that we have here. We have our own arena, no other program in the country can say that. It's just the best and I am so proud to say that I went there.

"With regards to our fans, I couldn't even begin to thank them enough for all of their support. The support we got here, from the administration on down to the fans was just amazing. I am so blessed to be able to say that I played for the Gophers and I was so happy that we were able to share our two national championships with everybody in the state of hockey.

"When it's all said and done, I would hope to be remembered as a winner; as a competitor; and somebody who worked hard both on and off the ice. That is what it is all about."

FOREWORD BY
NATALIE DARWITZ

In a word, Natalie Darwitz is a phenom. Growing up, she would spend hours playing street hockey in front of her house with her big brother, Ryan. Her grandfather even had to custom build her a net, because the store-bought kind usually didn't stand up to the relentless pounding of her slap-shots. She used to stay out at the neighborhood rink all night, and oftentimes when the rink shut off the lights at 10 p.m., her dad would pull the family car up and turn on the high beams for her to continue skating.

As a 6th grader Natalie was voted as the captain of the boys peewee A team, where she led the squad in scoring. The next year she was asked to try out for the new varsity girls team. How would she handle the transition from playing with 12 year-olds to high school seniors? By most accounts she did pretty well, scoring a mere 90 goals and 32 assists for 122 points, en route to leading her Eagan Wildcats to the state title game. From there, Natalie, who also starred on the softball diamond, simply dominated girls hockey in Minnesota, seemingly scoring at will. When it was all said and done she had netted 312 goals and 175 assists for an incredible 487 points in just 102 career games. Amazing. Then, in 1999, at the age of just 15, Natalie was invited to try out for, and made, the U.S. Women's National Team.

Natalie spent her junior and senior seasons of high school playing for Team USA. Then, after playing on the U.S. National team, she made the 2002 U.S. Women's Olympic team, where she won a silver medal in Salt Lake City. Natalie next got to fulfill a childhood dream when she accepted a scholarship to play at the University of Minnesota. As a Gopher, she simply dominated. Alongside her partner in crime, Krissy Wendell, she lit up goaltenders from Duluth to Dartmouth, en route to leading her squad to a pair of back-to-back national championships in 2004 and 2005.

By the time the smoke had cleared, the two-time first-team All-American had rewritten the record books during her illustrious tenure in Gold Country. Despite playing only 99 games in three seasons, she finished first in career scoring with 246 points; first in career assists with 144; and third in career goals with 102. As for the future? The five-time U.S. Women's National Team member will be representing the United States for her second Olympic hockey tour at the 2006 Winter Games in Turin, Italy. But, the All-WCHA Academic selection still has one year of college eligibility left. Could she return to the Gophers following the Olympics or will she capitalize on future endorsement deals which may come her way? Either way, she remains one of women's hockey's greatest ambassadors. Stay tuned!

As for the state of the state of women's hockey in Minnesota, Natalie is optimistic about her sport's future, but knows that there is much work to be done moving forward.

"I think that our sport grew a lot after the 1998 Olympics in Nagano, Japan," said Natalie. "Winning the gold medal did a ton to promote our sport and kids began playing hockey in record numbers right after that. Since then, the progress has been steady but nothing like it was back then. We need another shot in the arm."

"I have definitely been seeing a lot more girls

Natalie...

at the rink lately though, which is very positive. Ten years ago you might have seen a couple of girls at the rink with 20 guys. Now, you see a whole team. That is serious progress and that is awesome to see. As far as talent, I have seen a few girls who can fly around the ice, but the talent levels have plateaued over the years. Hopefully that will improve get better over time.

"You know, I am also a big fan of the girls playing with the boys up until they can't anymore. What I found by playing with the boys is a certain level of competitiveness; you learn a no-fear attitude; you gain more confidence; and you become a better all-around player. Playing with boys gives you things you just can't get by playing with the girls and that is just a fact. I think that they should integrate the boys and girls together at the really young levels such as mites. It helps the boys learn to work together more and it helps the girls get so much better by being a part of that.

"The talent level is growing, especially at the high school level. You don't see girls dominating the game like we did five years ago and that is good, because it means the talent levels have evened out and gotten deeper. Now, teams have three solid lines that can skate and it is a much improved game. I also think that the success of the state tournament has really helped to grow the sport as well. The younger girls can see the action and see the top levels of competition and that just gets them excited to play. While the numbers are up across the board at the youth levels, our sport still has a ton of room to grow. It is a process and hopefully that can start over in Turin, where a gold medal would do wonders for jump-starting our game again. Anytime you can get your sport national coverage on TV, good things are going to happen.

As for her time in Gold Country, Natalie wouldn't change a thing...

"Being a Gopher meant so much to me," she said. "It was a huge honor. Like a lot of kids in Minnesota, I grew up watching the Gophers every Friday and Saturday night on TV. Watching guys like Mike Crowley and Casey Hankinson just made me want to play there so badly. I mean at that point in my life I had been playing on boys teams and figured that since there was no Gopher women's team, that I could become the first girl ever to play with the boys. It was a dream of mine that seemed so real at the time. Then, when they got the women's program, it was so amazing to be a part of that. I had dreamed of wearing that big 'M' on my chest and when it finally happened it was almost indescribable. I am so lucky and proud to have been given the opportunity to play there and for that I will forever be grateful. The fans have treated me so warmly over the years and I couldn't even begin to thank them for what they have done for me.

"Having our own arena was huge too. Playing over in Mariucci was great, but to have our own building, something no other team in the country can say, is such a big deal. Having a place to call our own was just a giant advantage for us. A lot of teams that we played against talk about our 'home ice advantage,' and that makes me feel very proud. Our fans love it and we love it. When you go to games out East it just feels weird playing a team in this big arena with only a couple hundred people there. And, with 10,000 seats, it looks like there are only about 10 people there. At Ridder the fans are right there on top of you and it is really intimate. Then, to have your own locker room, to have your own private lounge where you can relax — those things go a long way in building a successful program. So, our arena is a big advantage for us and we certainly don't take it for granted. When you play in an arena that you love, trust me, you play a lot harder and a lot better.

"Winning the two national championships were among the greatest experiences of my life. To be a part of that, twice, is something I will never forget. Winning that first one was my first championship at any level of hockey for me, so to throw off my gloves and pile on the goalie after that final buzzer meant so much.

...Darwitz

That was such a big highlight for me in my career. We had such great teams those two years. I was just fortunate to play alongside some great players from very diverse backgrounds, and we all came together under a solid coaching staff. All of the players genuinely liked each other too. No, we weren't all best friends, but we all got along and we all respected each other. We played for each other though and that is why we had so much success the past few years.

"I will tell you another reason as to why I was so motivated to win a second national championship. You see, after we won our first one, I had already made plans to go on my first Spring break to Mexico with a couple of teammates. Well, when you get invited to go to the White House to meet the President, they give you a week's notice. We had already booked our flights and were out of luck, so we missed it. We were totally bummed out! Luckily we got to meet him the second time though, which was definitely one of the highlights of my career.

"Going to the University of Minnesota was just an amazing experience. Being able to play for the best team in the country just 20 minutes away from where I grew up was a big part of that too. To know that my parents could be at all of my games was huge for me. It gave me so much comfort and so much happiness to know that they were there, along with so many of my friends and family. That support is invaluable and is a really big selling point as far as why I think other top players come to the University of Minnesota. Beyond that, the connections you make while you are there are just incredible. At some point in the future I am going to begin my career and I know that I will have so many business opportunities from our network of alumni here in the area. That is so important and a very beneficial resource.

"As far as being a 'pioneer of the sport,' as some have labeled me? All I can say is thanks. None of that will ever really sink in though until I am an old Grandma and can look back at what I helped to start. Really though, I was just one of many people who did so much to grow the sport and take it to the next level. Certainly somebody like Krissy Wendell is right there with me, she has been great for the sport too and we have had a lot of fun together over the years playing hockey. We both know that there is still a long ways to go.

"Women's hockey is so new that I feel obligated to go the extra mile and promote the sport. We have to do the little stuff, the extra stuff to get fans into our arena. It all starts when the girls are young because that is when they can choose to play hockey as one of about a dozen different youth sports. So, I go to a lot of camps for little kids and I put in the time to give back, that is so important. It is even more than that, like getting asked to go read books to kids at elementary schools. That stuff is so rewarding and so humbling. You know, the guys don't have to do a lot of the extra stuff to grow their sport because it is already established. We, on the other hand, are just in our infancy and are trying to grow into the mainstream the way women's soccer and basketball have. Will that ever happen? I don't know, but I can tell you this — I am going to do whatever I can to help get it there.

"I also think that it is my responsibility and my duty to be a positive role model. That wasn't something I asked for, it was just something that happened. I am proud of that though and really take a lot of pride in it. If I can be an ambassador for my sport and really make a difference, then great. I want to make the most of my opportunity and help the next generation of little girls who have dreams of playing college hockey or Olympic hockey or even professional hockey. Krissy Wendell and I have certainly put the spotlight on our sport and that makes us both very proud. We need all the recognition and support that we can get in order to grow the game well into the future.

As for my future? Well, my goal is to continue playing hockey for as long as my body will let me. Right now I am bound and determined to bring home the gold in Turin. Would I play in the 2010 Winter Games in Vancouver? Hey, if I can make the team and they will have me, why not!? That would be awesome. The Olympics are a huge deal. I have just been so fortunate to have been able to put on the USA jersey and to represent my country. A lot of people have worn the 'M,' but very few have been able to wear the Red, White and Blue, which makes me very proud. There is just nothing like the Olympics. To be selected to play with the best of the best is the ultimate honor.

You know, hopefully my accomplishments such as playing in the Olympics and helping my teams win a pair of national championships will go a long way in growing the women's tradition at the U of M into what the men's tradition has become over the past 100 years. If I had a small part in that success, then that would truly be an amazing legacy.

CHAPTER 18
IN THE BEGINNING...

The history of women's hockey goes back for more than a century in North America, with the first recorded women's hockey games taking place in 1891, in Barrie, Ontario, and also in Ottawa. The ladies' game soon spread to the State's after the turn of the century to both the East Coast and also into Minnesota and Upper Michigan's Copper Country. In 1916, according to U of M yearbooks, some 30 women tried out for the first-ever Gopher Women's team. This article appeared in the "Gopher" that same year describing the team:

" 'But girls can't play hockey,' protested everyone when they heard that the girls at Minnesota intended to indulge in this strenuous sport. Just to prove that they could, and could do it well, the girls organized four strong class teams, with subs for each one. They didn't need to learn how to skate, for they were already experts, so they devoted arduous hours of practice under skilled coaches to developing teamwork. This resulted in a tournament of fast games which called forth an unusual amount of interest, and convinced people that girls really could play hockey. The first game was between the Freshmen and the Juniors, and the newly entered girls succeeded in winning from the upper classmen 5-0. The Sophomores lived up to their reputation as a fast team by defeating the Seniors 2-0. On February 27, the Sophomores and Freshmen fought for the class championship. Both teams displayed remarkable teamwork and the Sophomores only succeeded in carrying off the title by the narrow margin of 1-0."

The Gopher women's program sported at least two squads per year, with 15 ladies on each roster. Although most of their competition came against other U of M teams, there was an annual cup awarded for the school's championship team. In addition, each woman that tried out had to have at least a C average in their studies to be considered. The teams often practiced their stick handling skills in the gymnasium, until after the Christmas break when they would venture outdoors to practice on the skating rink at Northrop Field. While Gopher men's hockey coach Emil Iverson helped to coach them on occasion, the majority of the women's teams' coaches were fraternity boys who were also playing intramurals. The women played through the 1920s, often times drawing big crowds to come see their games.

The women wore long dresses and overcoats, always remaining "lady-like" on the ice. But, while they wanted to play like the boys, they surely didn't want to take a beating like the boys. In fact, in 1927, to protect her face from flying pucks, Queen's (Canada) goaltender Elizabeth Graham became the first recorded hockey player ever to wear a face mask - more than three decades before Montreal Canadiens' keeper Jacques Plante, then considered the originator of sporting a cage over the old melon.

This came at an empowering time for women, who were now in the midst of the women's suffrage movement which challenged society for equality in education, work and play. In addition to fighting for equal rights (Incredibly, women were finally allowed the right to vote in only 1926!), women were having to prove to the world that they could do anything men could do. Male doctors were even claiming that the women's unique anatomy, coupled with their moral obligation to bear children, was not suitable for vigorous physical activity, especially with something as rough as hockey.

The 1925 Lady Gophers

But large numbers of women pressed on and continued to compete for the love of the game.

In 1929 the University of Minnesota women finally got a home of their own, when a hockey rink was constructed behind the old library on campus. These were the heydays for women's hockey, as the Gophers now were playing teams from Duluth and the Iron Range, as well as from nearby Carleton College. In addition, the Gopher women played against other women's club teams, co-ed fraternity and sorority teams, and even some men's teams. While other women's sports were emerging on campus, it was thought that many of the school's most talented female athletes were hockey players.

But, when the Great Depression hit in the early 1930s, the women's program at the U of M came to a halt. Women's hockey blossomed during the war years, however. With most of the men overseas, women began working, supporting their families, and enjoying a new independence they had not known before. While women's baseball flourished during this time other women's team sports, including hockey, were oftentimes the only game in town. But, after the war ended, men's hockey began to boom, which ultimately meant less ice-time for the ladies, and as a result, the growth of the women's game slowed down.

By the late 1960s women's-only programs began forming throughout the U.S. and Canada, and by the early '70s, teams had popped up in Scandinavia, Europe and the Far East. By now, several U.S. college varsity and club teams had formed throughout the East Coast, and also in the Midwest. The Lady Gophers re-established a club team during the early '70s as well. The girl's game was developing quickly, but still had a long way to go at this point. Soon special protective chest and pelvic gear was designed especially for women, as their game began to evolve into its own style.

In the mid 1970s, in addition to community-based grass-roots programs, girls ice hockey was starting to be included in the athletic programs of several Minnesota school districts. Inspired by Billie Jean King, who defeated professional male tennis champion Bobbie Riggs in a "Battle of the Sexes" tennis match broadcast around the country, little girls everywhere saw that they were capable of achieving anything. Peewee, bantam and even midget tournaments popped up around the state, and before long the demands for more opportunities for women's hockey were being heard.

In the late 1970s a woman by the name of Lynn Olson, the venerable "Godmother" of women's hockey in Minnesota, started the Minnesota Women's Hockey League. With no age limit per se, high school aged girls as well as middle aged women in their 40s all came together in the new league to have a little fun and play some competitive hockey. Several teams, including the Blue Jays, Rink Rats, Shooting Stars and Gold Diggers, emerged as the team's to beat in the league. Into the early 80s, as the sport continued to grow, a new elite midget team from Wayzata, called the Checkers, burst onto the Minnesota hockey scene. (One of the people that helped a lot in the development of the girls game was Dr. Bob May, who, in addition to helping start the Checkers, also coached at North Dakota.) In 1980 the Checkers came home with the national Open B Division women's title. Then, led by Laura Halldorson

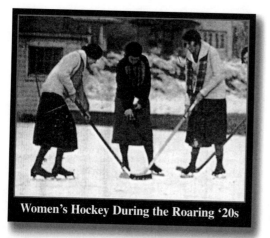

Women's Hockey During the Roaring '20s

(today the Gopher women's hockey coach), and Jill Pohtilla (the Augsburg women's hockey coach), the Checkers went on to win a couple of USA Hockey National Midget Championships in the early-1980's in both the 15-and-under, and later in the 19-and-under categories. In 1987 a new powerhouse team called the Thoroughbreds took the women's game to a new level. The elite team from Minneapolis dominated league play and oftentimes played against the best amateur club teams from around the nation.

By 1982 there were 116 teams registered in the women's division of USA Hockey, covering the spectrum from squirts through seniors. In 1984 Providence College won the inaugural Eastern College Athletic Conference Women's Championship, which would later come to serve as the equivalent of the women's college hockey national title. In the Minnesota Women's' Hockey Association was formed, which then became a part of the Minnesota Amateur Hockey Association (MAHA) and USA Hockey. This really opened the door for women everywhere to get involved in hockey. International women's hockey was growing too, as the U.S. defeated Sweden, 5-0, to win the bronze medal in the first-ever Women's World Invitational Tournament held in North York and Mississauga, Ontario, in 1987.

In 1989 the girl's and women's section of USA Hockey was established for the purpose of overseeing the development of girls' hockey throughout the country. In addition to legislating rules and regulations, the division would also help run national tournaments and developmental training camps as well. The director of the new program was Lynn Olson, a position she would hold for six years. One of the first big hurdles Olson faced was the issue of recognition.

"When I first started, the girls' program was not really recognized," said Olson. "That's the way I felt and so did a lot of the rest of the country and we were very happy to see that USA Hockey was appointing a director to help establish a better program. We grew from 150 teams to over 700 teams; just the visibility that was created and the credibility of being a part of USA Hockey helped establish that."

There would be other issues as well, including the fact that at that time, there were a lot of men who simply were not comfortable with the idea of girls playing hockey:

"I believe USA Hockey is firmly behind the program but not everybody at the amateur level is necessarily interested in promoting it because it takes time away from their sons," Olson would say. "It has been a problem over the years, but it's getting better."

Although the sport went through somewhat of a lull in popularity during the late '80s, it really picked up speed in the early '90s. In 1990 Minnesota had 29 amateur youth teams in the state. That same year, Minnesota led the nation in the total number of registered women's hockey players, with just less than 6,000. By this time the age classification for girl's hockey was broken down into 10-and-under, 12-and-under, 15-and-under and 19-and-under, or midget.

A big boost to the development of the game came that same year when, as part of a gender equity requirement set forth by state and federal laws, schools were required to give equal athletics opportunities to both boys and girls. That next year, according to a Minnesota Department of Education survey, only 35 percent of Minnesota's high schools were in compliance with these new gender equity regulations. In an attempt to become compliant, many state schools introduced the game of ringette (a game similar to hockey that uses a straight, bladeless stick to slide a rubber ring across the floor and into a goal). While the game was pretty well received, most girls wanted to play the game of ice hockey.

By 1992 there were 39 girls and women's teams registered with MAHA and USA Hockey in Minnesota, and a record 25 teams took part in the five divisions of the MAHA State Hockey Tournament that year as well. After that season, the Minnesota State High School League took a survey called "Girls Really Expect A Team!" or (GREAT!) to gain a more accurate assessment of which sports high school girls were most interested in playing. Nearly 8,000 girls signed a petition saying that they would love to play high school hockey if it were only offered. With that, the wheels of progress starting turning...fast.

On November 19, 1994, South St. Paul and Holy Angels played the first high school girl's hockey game in state history. Later that year, in response to the overwhelming outcry for more organization in the sport, eight teams representing 11 state schools hit the ice for the inaugural girls state tournament, which, incidentally was not yet sanctioned by the MSHSL. Blaine/Coon Rapids beat Anoka/Champlin Park, 3-0, for the "unofficial" 1994 state title. That same year, there were 78 amateur youth teams registered in the state, up from 29 only four years earlier.

In 1995, after seeing how the experiment would fare, the Minnesota State High School League's Representative Assembly took a giant leap of faith by voting to become the first such organization in the country to sanction girls' ice hockey as a varsity sport. The news was viewed as a major advancement for women's sports everywhere.

"Now the younger girls will have role model's and know that they can get better," said Olson. "It will give them more encouragement to start playing."

Twenty-four varsity teams took to the ice that season, while an additional 12 schools featured junior varsity squads, giving more than 1,000 girls in Minnesota the chance to play hockey at various high school levels. Then, on February 24, 1995, with the eyes of the nation upon them, the MSHSL sponsored the first-ever girls' state high school hockey tournament. Held at the 3,500-seat Aldrich Arena in Maplewood, the inaugural tournament field included teams from Stillwater Area, Apple Valley, South St. Paul and Henry Sibley. There, the undefeated Apple Valley Eagles, in front of a standing-room-only crowd in the title game, beat the South St. Paul Packers, 2-0, to claim the first ever girl's high school hockey championship.

As high school hockey grew, so too did the college game. In 1995 Augsburg College made history by becoming the first fully funded women's varsity hockey program not only in the state, but in the nation. At the same time, the Minnesota Legislature was making strides to help the girl's game grow as well. Believe it or not, a lot of the women at the state capital liked to skate themselves, and many even play in a league of their own on Sunday nights. They wanted to do their best to see to it that girls everywhere had the same opportunities that the boys did. So, in 1995 the legislature passed a bill requiring that 15 percent of all ice time in both public and private rinks, be reserved for girls, increasing to 30 percent in 1996 and 50 percent in 1997. Arena owners throughout the state could no longer get away with giving the girls undesirable time slots either at the crack of dawn or in the middle of the night, and report that they had filled their quota. In addition, the Minnesota Amateur Sports Commission, the body runs all amateur sports in the state, received funds through the legislature called the Mighty Ducks Bill, which was earmarked for either the construction of dozens of new arenas or for the renovation of existing ones. In 1995, 23 grants totaling nearly $3 million were awarded to 23 communities throughout the state, and to date more than $20 million has been awarded for the sole purpose of giving more kids the chance to play hockey in Minnesota.

The University of Minnesota women's team turned varsity in 1996, due in part to rising gender equity issues at the collegiate level. Both the Big 10 Conference, as well as the NCAA were enforcing strict rules about equity and making sure that member school's were providing an equal number of sports for both male and female athletes. This was one way the school saw fit to satisfy them both. Former Colby College coach Laura Halldorson took over as the team's first head coach that year, as the team hit the ice at the new Mariucci Arena. One of their biggest problems out of the gates was a lack of competition. Other than Augsburg, there weren't any other varsity programs in the area, so many of the team's games that year were played on the East Coast, against the more established programs. Aside from those teams, they played local club teams which were playing in the Midwestern Collegiate Women's Hockey Alliance, including: Carleton, Gustavus Adolphus, Mankato State, UM-Duluth, St. Catherine's and St. Thomas, St. Cloud State, St. Mary's and St. Olaf.

The 1997-98 hockey season was a huge one for women's hockey everywhere. For starters, the U.S. women's Olympic hockey team defeated Team Canada, 3-1, at the Winter Games in Nagano, Japan, to win the first-ever Olympic gold medal in women's hockey history. The upset victory was huge for the growth of American hockey. Following the game, which was televised throughout the world, USA Hockey was inundated with thousands of phone calls from curious girls around the country who wanted to start playing hockey, as well as women of all ages who wanted to start their own leagues. While the game certainly did not have the same global implications of the 1980 Lake Placid *"Miracle on Ice"* men's game, it did represent just how far women's sports has come. Fully each of the women on that team had been told at least once in her life that she couldn't play ice hockey, and most had to scrape by for years on unappreciative boy's teams because there was simply no other alternative.

That same year, the upstart University of Minnesota Women's Gopher hockey team shocked the college hockey world by finishing fourth at the American Women's College Hockey Alliance National Championships. More than 80 years after it all began on frozen pond near Dinkytown, the Lady Gophers were back in business. Here is their story...

The 1997-98 Inaugural Season...

The dream of many came to fruition on October 31st, 1995, when it was announced that women's hockey was officially going to be the 11th varsity sport in Minnesota Women's Athletics history. Assigned to assemble a team and build a new program from the ground up was Plymouth native, Laura Halldorson. Halldorson, a four-sport prep athlete at Wayzata High School, went on to star at Princeton University, where she emerged as an all-conference winger en route to leading the Tigers to three Ivy League titles during the mid-1980s. After serving as an assistant at Princeton for two years, Halldorson took over as the head coach at Colby College, where, after seven seasons, was named as the ECAC Co-Coach of the Year in 1996. From there, Halldorson got the opportunity of a lifetime when she was asked by women's athletics director Chris Voelz to come home and serve as the program's first-ever head coach. It was an offer she simply couldn't refuse. A tenacious worker, Halldorson wasted little time in assembling her first team — a roster of student-athletes who would eventually go on to finish fourth in the inaugural 1998 American Women's College Hockey Alliance National Championships.

The 23-member squad would consist of 17 freshmen and five sophomores. Julie Otto, who spent three seasons at Northeastern University, the team's lone senior, was named as the inaugural team captain and was going to be counted on to serve as the team leader. Among the other ladies who would be counted upon that season included Center Kris Scholz, who had previously played for the Minnesota Thoroughbreds senior team prior to that, and Winger Angela Borek, one of two University of Minnesota club team members to make the Gopher squad. In addition, there were a pair of players who had participated in their countries' Olympic selection process: Forward Ambria Thomas, who attended the USA Hockey Olympic tryout camp, and Center Nadine Muzerall, who attended Canada's Olympic team evaluation camp. Leading the defensive corps was Brittny Ralph, who also played for the Thoroughbreds and also attended the USA Hockey Olympic tryout camp that Summer. Joining her on the blue line was Ms. Hockey finalist Kelly Olson, an all-stater who had just led her Roseville Raiders to an unbeaten season and a state title in 1996. Finally, the lady between the pipes was none other than Erica Killewald, who had previously played club hockey out of Detroit, Mich.

The Lady Gophers burst onto the collegiate hockey scene in style by setting a national single-season attendance mark in their inaugural game on Nov. 2, 1997, when nearly 7,000 fans filed into Mariucci Arena to witness them crush Augsburg College, 8-0. Fittingly, it was senior captain Julie Otto who scored the first ever goal in Gopher women's hockey history, just 1:55 into the opening period. Ambria Thomas led the charge with the first hat trick in program history, while goalie Erica Killewald turned away all 11 shots she faced to secure the historic shut-out. After falling to Harvard and New Hampshire, Minnesota posted its first victory over a Division I opponent when they defeated fifth-ranked Princeton in the opening game of the Princeton Thanksgiving Tournament — a tourney they went on to win, thus giving them their first national ranking.

Coach Laura Haldorson

The team continued to play well into the new year, sweeping St. Lawrence, 6-1 and 5-0, in early January. From there, the team went on to secure wins over Boston College and Yale, before battling Northeastern to pair of tough ties, 2-2 and 1-1. On February 7th the Gophers crushed Wisconsin, 10-0, behind Goalie Sarah Harms' first career shut-out. Minnesota concluded its first regular-season with a 21-5-3 record and was invited to compete in the American Women's College Hockey Alliance national tournament in Boston. The Gophers drew top-ranked New Hampshire in the semifinal game, however, and wound up losing to the eventual national champion Wildcats, 4-1. In the third-place game, the Lady Gophers got blanked by Northeastern, 4-0, to finish a very successful inaugural campaign with a 21-7-3 record and a fourth-place national trophy to boot.

As for individual honors and accolades, Forward Nadine Muzerall wound up leading the nation in scoring with 32 goals and 32 assists for 64 points, and was rewarded with one of the 11 nominations for the prestigious Patty Kazmaier Award — women's college hockey's Hobey Baker equivalent. In addition, Nadine Muzerall and Brittny Ralph were named to the Women's Hockey News All-America Second Team, while head coach Laura Halldorson was honored as the American Hockey Coaches Association National Coach of the Year.

The 1998-99 Season...

Heading into the 1998-99 campaign, the Gopher women were very optimistic about their chances. They had gotten a taste of post-season success and clearly wanted more. The team returned 15 letter winners that season and a recruiting class that featured an Olympic gold medalist in Jenny Schmidgall of Edina; a transfer from Colby College who earned first-team All-America honors the season before in Courtney Kennedy; and Winny Brodt, a former Ms. Hockey Award winner from Roseville, who returned home to Minnesota after two years at New Hampshire, where she was just named as the MVP of the national championships.

Among the other newcomers were Shannon Kennedy, the older sister of Courtney, who also transferred from Colby. The Gophers added another Ms. Hockey Award winner as well in Laura Slominski, who rewrote the record books at Burnsville High School. Tracy Engstrom also joined the team from the Minnesota Thoroughbreds, a club team she captained to the semifinals of the midget national championships in 1998, tallying 48 points along the way. Another great addition was Winger Amber Hegland, who, in 1994, became the first female in Minnesota history to play and register a point in the boys state high school tournament.

The squad opened its season with an 11-1 pummeling of MSU, Mankato, followed by a tough 3-1 loss to Harvard at home. They rallied to get a 1-1 tie a few nights later against New Hampshire, thanks to Jenny Schmidgall's third period equalizer. From there, the team rolled over most of its undermatched opponents, posting no less than five 10-0 scores over the next 15 games en route to establishing a school-record 17-game winning streak along the way. In early February the team swept Cornell, 6-1 and 5-0, and then swept Providence, 1-0 and 5-1, a few weeks later. They could only manage one point, a 1-1 tie, against Brown though, as they lost Game One of that series 2-1. After outscoring their next three opponents 26-1, the team headed into the post-season that March with high hopes.

Minnesota earned its second berth into the AWCHA national tournament, which was hosted by USA Hockey at Mariucci Arena. Indeed, they had made it back to the Final Four in '99 for their second time in as many years. There, the Lady Gophers took on a top ranked University of New Hampshire team in the semis in front of the Mariucci Arena faithful. The Gophers jumped out to an early 2-0 lead on a pair of goals by Nadine Muzerall. But, UNH rallied to tie it and then send it into overtime. After a back-and-forth exchange by both teams, Melisa Heitzman finally beat Gopher Goalie Erica Killewald at the 12:37 mark of the extra session to end the heart-breaking game. It was a crushing defeat for the Gophers, who, in just two

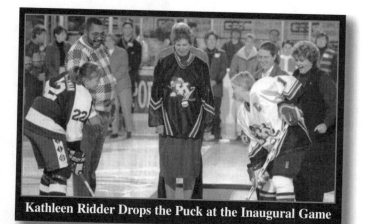

Kathleen Ridder Drops the Puck at the Inaugural Game

seasons had already emerged as one of the college hockey's elite teams. They came back strong that next night though to beat Eastern power Brown University, 3-2, on third period goals from both Tracy Engstrom and Nadine Muzerall, and win AWCHA third place honors.

"This was a huge win for us," said Gopher Coach Laura Halldorson. "Last year, we were just happy to be in this tournament and to come in fourth. This year, we knew we had to finish better. This continues our growth and gives us momentum going into next year. This is a team that is learning as we go, and the experience we're gaining means a lot to us."

The team ultimately finished with an impressive 29-4-3 record that year. The Gophers' defense finished first in the nation giving up 1.09 goals per game, while the offense was third nationally, scoring 5.94 goals per game. Forward Jenny Schmidgall, the first player to sign a women's hockey scholarship at Minnesota, earned second team AWCHA All-America honors in her first collegiate season. In addition, Nadine Muzerall and Courtney Kennedy were honored by being named to other All-America second teams as well.

Nadine Muzerall

The 1999-2000 Season...

The 1999-2000 season ushered in a new era of Gopher Women's Hockey with the advent of the newly created Western Collegiate Hockey Association Women's League. The upstart circuit hit the ice with seven charter members: Bemidji State University: University of Minnesota; University of Minnesota-Duluth; Minnesota State University, Mankato; Ohio State University; St. Cloud State University; and the University of Wisconsin. The teams would play a 24-game league schedule followed by a three-day conference tournament, which was to be held at the Bloomington Ice Gardens that March. The new league, a division of the American Women's College Hockey Alliance (AWCHA) gave the sport a lot more credibility throughout the Midwest and would do wonders in growing the game beyond the East Coast.

Minnesota returned 18 players from the previous year's squad and figured to be there at the end yet again. Much of those hopes lied with junior Goalie and team MVP Erica Killewald, who established herself as one of the nation's elite goalies by leading the nation with a 1.24 goals against average and a .947 save percentage. Also joining the mix this year for the Maroon and Gold were a pair of freshmen forwards from Roseville, Ronda Curtin, the 1999 Ms. Hockey Award winner who tallied 465 career points in 105 games, and Allyson Sundberg —both of whom had just led their undefeated Raiders to a state championship.

The 1999-2000 Gopher women's hockey team opened their season on October

Ronda Curtin

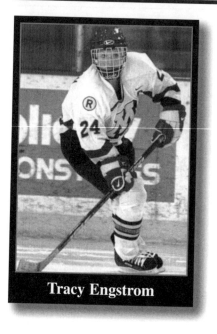

Tracy Engstrom

15th against St. Cloud State at home, where Nadine Muzerall's five points paced the team to an impressive 10-1 victory. Ronda Curtin and Tracy Engstrom then both recorded their first hat tricks up in St. Cloud that next night to complete the sweep by the identical 10-1 margin. From there, the team got third period goals from Curtin, Muzerall and Brodt to upend Providence, 3-1, on the road. Game Two of that series, however, saw the Gophers get blanked, 1-0, despite 26 saves from Goalie Erica Killewald. They managed just a split that next weekend too, at Northeastern, and then, after beating Brown, 4-0, got spanked by Harvard, 8-3.

The team stayed on the road for the next two weeks, earning sweeps over Ohio State and Wisconsin. Then, after beating MSU, Mankato, the Gophers faced off with arch-rival Duluth back at Mariucci Arena. Game One was a reunion of sorts and had a lot of drama as Jenny Schmidgall and Brittney Ralph, who both transferred to UMD that off-season, were about to face their old mates. They didn't disappoint either as both ladies scored a pair of goals each in this one en route to leading Duluth past the Gophers, 5-4. The next night was just as tough as Killewald came up with 28 saves, only to wind up on the wrong end of a 1-0 series sweeping loss. After taking a pair of games from Dartmouth that next week, the Gophers went on a tear, going unbeaten in 19 straight games. The only blemish on the record was a 2-2 tie at Duluth, in a series which saw the Gophers get revenge by taking three out of four points.

Minnesota rolled through the WCHA Playoffs, beating Mankato and Wisconsin, 10-0 and 5-0, to set up a rematch with the UMD Bulldogs in the WCHA tournament championship game. There, Duluth came out smoking and cruised to a tough 2-0 victory. Both teams were selected to participate in the AWCHA National Tournament in Boston, however, and as luck would have it they would go on to face each other one more time, with a national championship game berth hanging in the balance. It would be historic. With the Gophers down 2-0 early in the second period, Muzerall scored two consecutive goals to tie the score and set up Tracy Engstrom's thrilling power-play game-winner at 6:45 of the third period.

From there, the Gophers went on to face Brown in the Finals. Down 1-0 early, Minnesota roared back with four unanswered goals from Courtney Kennedy, Laura Slominski,

The 1999-00 AWCHA National Champs

Nadine Muzerall and Winny Brodt to capture their first AWCHA National Championship, 4-2. Kennedy got on the board first when she dramatically chipped in her own rebound while falling down in front of the net at 4:47 of the second period. Slominski scored with just over a minute left in the period to make it 2-1 and things were looking up. Then, early in the third, Muzzy got what would prove to be the game-winner, and Winny tallied less than a minute after that to put it out of reach. Brown added another goal late in the third, but it was too little too late as "Killer," who stopped 34 of 36 shots that night in goal, hung on down the stretch to give her team the amazing victory. The Gophers had officially arrived! Following the final buzzer the team went ballistic at center ice as they celebrated their incredible achievement.

Winny Brodt

The team finished with an impressive 32-6-1 record that year and fought hard for everything they got. Leading the team in scoring was Nadine Muzerall, who tallied 49 goals and 28 assists for 77 points. Following her were Ambria Thomas and Laura Slominski, who each scored 62 and 59 points, respectively. As for post-season honors and accolades, Winny Brodt was selected as the WCHA Defensive Player of the Year and joined Muzerall on the WCHA all-conference first team. In addition, Goalie Erica Killewald was named as the MVP of the AWCHA national tournament.

The 2000-01 Season...

Not that they needed any, but the Gophers got a lot of extra incentive in 2000 when it was announced that the NCAA would be hosting its first Women's Ice Hockey Championship... and that Mariucci Arena had been chosen as the site of the inaugural Frozen Four. The pressure was officially on. The team's fourth season in Gold Country looked promising though and they had 15 returning letter-winners along with a group of nine rookies ready to defend the title.

"Obviously, it would be tremendous to repeat what we did at the national championship last year," said Coach Halldorson. "It would he extra special to do so in our own rink. We also have some unfinished business in regards to winning the WCHA regular season and playoff championships. It's exciting to have this much talent. Our goal is to blend everyone together and try to put together a lineup that will be difficult to defend. It won't be easy, though. It's going to take hard work, discipline and a commitment to excellence. No longer are we the underdogs."

While Minnesota and Duluth were still the cream of the college hockey crop, it was becoming readily more apparent that the landscape of women's hockey was changing. More and more youth programs were popping up

Ambria Thomas

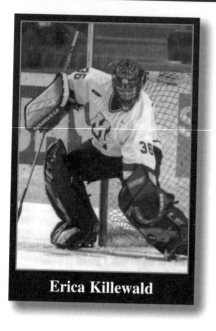

Erica Killewald

around the country and as a result, there was much more parity among the teams. This was particularly true for the Gophers as evidenced by the fact that the team got beat by the likes of Ohio State, St. Cloud State and Wisconsin that year — team's which they had dominated in years past.

Minnesota, led by hat tricks from Ambria Thomas and Laura Slominski, opened the season with a series sweep over St. Cloud State. The team then wound up splitting with Ohio State that next weekend, but came back to sweep Mankato on the road, 2-1 and 6-1. From there, the team headed east and wound up losing to Brown, 3-2, and then beating Harvard by that same score. They blew a third period lead for the first time in nearly 20 months against Brown, and then beat the Crimson on Ronda Curtin's third period game-winner. The team returned home that next week and played huge against rival UMD, blanking the Dogs, 4-0 and 8-0, to sweep the series. Muzzy scored a pair in Game One, while Ambria Thomas notched five points and La Toya Clarke chipped in a pair of power-play goals in Game Two. Erica Killewald played incredibly in both games, stopping all 44 shots she faced that weekend.

After taking three out of four points at Wisconsin, the Gophers swept Bemidji State to open the month of December. Muzzy and Clarke each netted hat tricks in the 9-1 opener against the Beavers, while Kris Scholz added a pair of her own in the 8-4 rematch. Tracy Engstrom notched seven points over the weekend as well, good for WCHA Player of the Week honors. Things got ugly from there though as the team got swept at Dartmouth the following week. They went on to beat Mercyhurst, Niagara and Mankato, however, before losing a pair to the U.S. Women's Select Team in an exhibition match. They rebounded from there, sweeping New Hampshire and Bemidji State on the road, and then split with St. Cloud State in a home-and-home match in mid-February. Clarke, Engstrom and Thomas each notched a pair of goals apiece in Game Two against Bemidji, while Muzzy tallied a hat trick in the win over St. Cloud.

Following a series split with Ohio State, the Gophers came back to sweep Wisconsin 6-2 and 3-1 to end the month of February on a positive note. March rolled in with the team heading to Duluth for the last series of the regular season. There, the Gophers managed to earn a tie in Game One, 2-2, but then lost Game Two, 3-1. Regardless, Minnesota had earned the WCHA Tournament's top seed heading into the tourney, but wound up getting spanked by Ohio State, 4-0, in the semifinal, followed by a disastrous 4-3 loss to Wisconsin in the third-place game. The result was the fact that the defending national champs now had to sit back and watch the Frozen Four being played on their home ice. Ouch!

The team did wind up with a solid 23-9-2 overall record though, good for a No. 5 national ranking and their first WCHA Women's League title. La Toya Clarke led the team with 53 points, while Ambria Thomas and Nadine Muzerall added 49 and 46, respectively. Muzzy would finish her illustrious career in Gold Country with a record 235 career points in 139 career games. Individually, several Gophers were recognized with post-season honors, including senior defender Courtney Kennedy, who was selected as the initial first team All-America selection in Gopher women's hockey history. Kennedy, the WCHA Player of the Year, was also named as one of just three finalists for the prestigious Patty Kazmaier Award — which honors the nation's top player. Senior goalie Erica Killewald joined Kennedy on the All-WCHA First Team, while Laura Halldorson shared her first WCHA Coach of the Year honor with St. Cloud State's Kerry Wethington.

The 2001-02 Season...

With the loss of nine players to graduation the Gopher women's hockey program was finally going to have to do a little rebuilding. The Gophers added 10 rookies to the roster to go along with the 12 returning players who had helped lead the team to their first conference crown. Tracy Engstrom and Laura Slominski were named as the team captains and would be counted on as team leaders.

The Gophers opened their season against Minnesota State, Mankato at Mariucci Arena, where they swept the Mavericks, 2-0 and 4-1. Goalie Stephanie Johnson stopped all 21 shots she faced en route to earning her second career shut-out in Game One. Meanwhile, Slominski, Stephens, Curtin and Engstrom each tallied in Game Two. From there, the Gophers headed north to take on the defending national champion Minnesota-Duluth Bulldogs. There, they got blanked, 7-0, in Game One but managed to earn a 1-1 tie in the rematch thanks to Gwen Anderson's first collegiate goal. Rookie Goalie Brenda Reinen started her first game for the Maroon and Gold and came up with 37 saves along the way.

From there, Minnesota went on a 24-game unbeaten streak that lasted from November 2nd to February 16th. During that span, the Gophers notched series sweeps over Ohio State, Wisconsin, St. Cloud State, Minnesota-Duluth and Minnesota State, Mankato. The Gophers also got huge wins against non-conference foes Brown, Harvard, Dartmouth, St. Lawrence and Findlay as well. Incredibly, the team endured 12 overtime games and 15 one-goal contests over that stretch. By the end of the streak, however, the Lady Gophers found themselves ranked No. 1 not only in the conference, but in all the national polls. They would retain that No. 1 ranking for eight consecutive weeks and rode that wave right into the WCHA Playoffs, where they won the WCHA regular season title for the second year in a row. In addition to that, on March 9th the Gophers also established another first in Minnesota women's hockey history when they defeated Wisconsin, 3-2, for the WCHA Final Five Championship. Kelly Stephens, La Toya Clarke and Brenda Reinen were all named to the all-tournament team, while Ronda Curtin was selected as the Tournament MVP.

From there, Minnesota headed to New Hampshire, where they faced off against Brown as the top seed in the NCAA Frozen Four. After a scoreless first period, Kelly Stephens scored midway through the second period to make it 1-1. Brown tallied again on a power-play goal that period though and the Gophers could not find the back of the net for the rest of the evening. Minnesota's Cinderella season then came to an end that next night when they with skated to a 2-2 tie with Niagara in the third-place game. Kristy Oonincx tipped in a Ronda Curtin slapper in the second period to put the Gophers out front, 1-0. La Toya Clarke then notched her 15th goal of the season late in the third, only to see the Purple Eagles get the equalizer past Brenda Reinen with just over two minutes to go. Kelly Stephens, who assisted on Clarke's goal, was named to the Frozen Four All-Tournament Team.

The team finished the season with a 28-4-6 record, as well as the WCHA Season and Tournament Champions. As for individual honors, Ronda Curtin was recognized as one of three Patty Kazmaier finalists. Curtin, who actually moved from forward to defense that season, led the team and the WCHA in points (45), assists (35), points by a defenseman and power-play points (22). Curtin was also named as a First Team All-American, only the second Gopher in women's hockey history to do so. (Incidentally, Ronda's sister, Renee, was a freshmen on the team that year but suffered a serious head injury early on which ultimately cut her collegiate hockey career short. Renee, who won the Ms. Hockey award earlier that year, tallied an incred-

La Toya Clarke

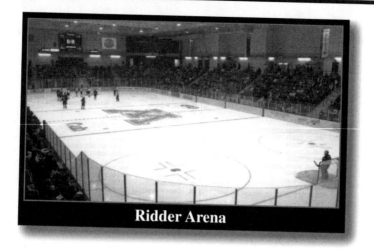
Ridder Arena

ible 544 career points at Roseville Area High School and set the high school points record for a boy or girl. The five-time all-stater led Roseville to a pair of state titles in both 1996 and 1999.)

While Ronda Curtin led the team in scoring, Kelly Stephens finished second with 43 points, followed by La Toya Clarke and Kristy Oonincx, who tallied 42 and 38, respectively. Incredibly, those four players also had 51 multiple point scoring games among them.

The 2002-03 Season...

The 2002-03 season was one of the most significant in the program's short history for several reasons. First, the Golden Gophers said goodbye to Mariucci Arena and moved into their new home, Ridder Arena, right next door. The state-of-the-art facility is known to be the first women's only college hockey arena in the country. Named after longtime contributors Bob and Kathleen Ridder, the bowl-shaped arena seats 3,000 people and includes a clubroom as well as nine suites. It is intimate, luxurious and the ladies absolutely loved it.

"Ridder Arena will be the premier women's hockey facility in the nation," Coach Halldorson said. "When you combine this tremendous facility with the talent we'll be putting on the ice this season, I expect us to generate an electric atmosphere and a great experience for Gopher women's hockey fans. It will also be a unique and exciting place for our student-athletes to play their collegiate hockey and create lasting memories of their hockey careers here at the University of Minnesota."

The Ridder Lockerroom

Second, while the Gophers returned 13 letter-winners from the year before, this season was special in that it had without question the single-greatest recruiting class in women's college hockey history. Leading the way were a pair of Minnesota high school hockey legends, Krissy Wendell and Natalie Darwitz, who starred at Park Center and Eagan High Schools, respectively. Both of the ladies played on the silver medal-winning U.S. Olympic team in Salt Lake City that past year as well. Having reloaded both barrels, the Golden Gophers were ready to compete for yet another Western Collegiate Hockey Association championship and a NCAA Frozen Four appearance.

Minnesota opened the season against Findlay on the road in Ohio. There, the Gophers crushed the Oilers, 8-1 and 7-2, as the two freshmen phenoms, Wendell and Darwitz, wasted little time in making names for themselves by tallying seven points among them in Game One. Darwitz then added a hat trick in Game Two for good measure, while Wendell added a goal of her own. These ladies were the real deal.

Kris Scholz

That next week the Gophers held their inaugural game at Ridder Arena on October 19th, when they hosted St. Cloud State. Minnesota drew 3,239 fans at the opener, the largest crowd for a regular-season game in the nation that year. As for the game itself, the Gophers, who rolled, 10-1, the night before up in St. Cloud behind Kristy Oonincx's first collegiate hat trick and Krissy Wendell's four points, crushed the Huskies, 8-0. Jerilyn Glenn made history by scoring the first goal in the "Rid" and that was all Goalie Jody Horak would need as she posted her fifth career shut-out. Eight different Gophers scored in the big game, which was complete with plenty of media coverage and local celebrity sightings.

The Gophers cruised from there, going unbeaten in their next 10 games against Ohio State, Wisconsin, Bemidji State, Brown, Harvard and St. Lawrence. The undefeated Gophers then got a taste of reality when the two-time defending national champs from Duluth came to town and swept them in a pair of one-goal thrillers, 4-3 and 6-5. Darwitz and Brodt each scored a pair of goals in the losing effort. The team got back on track after that though and rattled off sweeps over both Mankato and St. Cloud before losing, 6-3, at Dartmouth. After beating New Hampshire that next night, the team opened up the month of February on a positive note by sweeping Bemidji and Ohio State to set up a rematch with rival Duluth.

The Gophers got slammed in Game One up in the Zenith City, 7-1, but rallied back to take the revenge game, 4-2. Minnesota came from behind in this one and got goals from both Brodt sisters, Winny and Chelsey, to secure the big win. After sweeping Mankato that next weekend, the team split with Wisconsin at Madison, 2-1 and 2-0. With that, the team wound up playing the cheese heads yet again in the opening round of the WCHA Final Five

Laura Slominski

Andrea Nichols

Championships. There, they beat the Badgers, 3-1, up in Grand Forks, on goals from Darwitz, Brodt and Clarke.

The next night the Gophers faced off against Duluth for the title, but came up short, 5-3. Despite the loss, the team was still invited to participate in the Frozen Four that year, which were being held up in Duluth. There, the Gophers stunk up the joint and wound up getting pulverized by Harvard, 6-1. To make matters worse, they then fell to Dartmouth, 4-2, in the third place game to wind up in fourth. Darwitz and Wendell each scored third period goals in this one, but it was too little too late as the Big Green hung on to take the bronze. It was all over.

The Maroon and Gold ended the 2002-03 campaign with a 27-8-1 overall record and a 19-4-1 mark in the WCHA. As for individual honors and accolades, it was all about Darwitz and Wendell, who were named as two of the top 10 candidates for the Patty Kazmaier Memorial Award. Darwitz led the team in scoring with 33 goals and 35 assists for 68 points. She had four hat tricks, 10 power-play goals and five game-winning goals. Wendell, who missed eight games due to a fractured clavicle, played in 25 games but still managed to score 55 points — good for second on the team. Both ladies, as well as Ronda Curtin, were named as All-Americans. (Wendell was a second-team All-American.) In addition, Curtin, Darwitz and Jody Horak were named as all first-team All-WCHA selections, while Wendell was a second-teamer. Furthermore, Darwitz also garnered WCHA Rookie of the Year honors, while Curtin was named the WCHA Defensive Player of the Year.

Lastly, the Golden Gophers drew 27,208 fans during the season at Ridder Arena and averaged 1,943 per game — tops in the nation.

"Our first season in Ridder was amazing," said Coach Halldorson. "I think the atmosphere in that facility on game days was even better than I had imagined it would be. When we put 3,000 Gopher fans and the band in there, it gets awfully loud each time a goal is scored. I know that our players love playing in Ridder because the arena and our fans definitely give us a home ice advantage. It's a great environment for college hockey."

The 2003-04 Season...

With so much firepower, the Gophers were poised to make their third straight trip to the NCAA Frozen Four and land their first NCAA national championship. While the team had a great nucleus of young talent, it wasn't going to be easy. Gone were defensemen Winny Brodt, who holds the career record for the most points (134) goals (41) and assists (93) by a Gopher blue liner, and two-time All-American Ronda Curtin, who tallied 167 career points as a Gopher, ranking her third in school history.

With the theme of *"Get It Done,"* the Lady Gophers opened their 2003-04 season in style

Ashley Albrecht

against the Ohio State Buckeyes. Krissy Wendell had four goals that night en route to a 6-3 Gopher win. The Gophers followed with a sweep over the Buckeyes, 7-0, that next night behind Jody Horak's 23 saves. Wendell, who added two more points in Game Two, was named as the WCHA Offensive Player of the Week. Horak posted her second straight shut-out that following weekend against Wisconsin, winning the opener, 3-0, behind two goals and an assist from Natalie Darwitz. Brodt, Wendell and Clarke each then tallied that next night as the Maroon and Gold completed the sweep, 3-1. The downside to that weekend, however, was the fact that the team lost its senior co-captain, Kelsey Bills, to an ankle fracture.

While most of the team was enjoying a week off from competition in early November, four Gophers: Darwitz, Wendell, Kelly Stephens and Lyndsay Wall, flew to Sweden where they helped lead Team USA to a gold medal in the Four Nations Cup. Upon their return the Gophers proceeded to sweep St. Cloud State thanks to Darwitz's hat trick in Game One, fol-

Courtney Kennedy

lowed by La Toya Clarke's two goal effort in Game Two. From there, the team headed east to take on Brown, defeating the Bears in the first game, 5-2, and earning a sweep with an impressive 8-1 win in the rematch. While seven Gophers figured into the scoring for Game One, Darwitz added yet another hat trick in Game Two.

Minnesota then got all it could handle from much improved Minnesota State, tying the Mavs, 1-1, on Lyndsay Wall's first period goal. They rebounded, however, to take the nightcap, 4-0, on Brenda Reinen's 16-save shut-out. Returning home, the Gophers swept both North Dakota and Bemidji State to close out the first half of the season undefeated at 13-0-1. Kelly Stephens and Natalie Darwitz each had six points in the 10-1 Game Two win over the Fighting Sioux, while Goalie Jody Horak stopped all 23 shots she faced in the 7-0 shut-out over Bemidji in Game One of that series. In addition, La Toya Clarke notched seven points in the Bemidji series, earning her WCHA Player of the Week honors.

Things were about to get much tougher for the Maroon and Gold though as they started into the second half of the season. Over the next two months the team would face no less than five ranked opponents, starting with WCHA rival Minnesota-Duluth on the road. Despite having Bills back in the lineup after a five-week injury hiatus, the Gophers suffered their first loss of the year, dropping the opener, 4-1. They rebounded big-time in the rematch though, rallying from being down 3-1 to beat the Dogs, 4-3, in overtime. Darwitz scored late in the third to send it to the extra session, and then Kelly Stephens got the game-winner just 15 seconds into sudden-death on a sweet pass from Krissy Wendell. The celebration didn't last long though when it was learned that Darwitz would be sidelined with what appeared to be a season-ending elbow

Shannon Kennedy

Kelly Stephens

injury.

Even without Natalie, the Gophers went on to sweep No. 7 Mercyhurst, 5-1 and 3-1, as Wendell scored her second hat trick of the season, earning WCHA Offensive Player of the Week honors. Lyndsay Wall also went down with an injury during that series too, knocking out two of their top five scorers in just one week. Minnesota then suffered its second loss of the season, this time at the hands of Minnesota State, Mankato. After winning the opener, 3-2, the Gophers fell to the Mavericks, 3-2, in overtime, marking the first time in 26 tries that the Mavs had beaten them. The Gophers got right back on track though, sweeping Bemidji State, 4-1 and 4-0, while Krissy Wendell earned her third WCHA Offensive Player of the Week honor for her two-goal and five-assist weekend.

Back at Ridder Arena it was No. 1 vs. No. 2 when top-ranked Dartmouth came to town. The Big Green rallied in Game One to beat the Gophers on their own turf, 3-2. Minnesota came back strong in the rematch though, winning 7-3 behind the efforts of a dozen Minnesota skaters who earned a point that series. Leading the way was Melissa Coulombe, who had three points, followed by freshmen Andrea Nichols and Becky Wacker, who tallied two goals each. No. 5 Wisconsin then came to town and beat Minnesota in overtime, 2-1, to take Game One. What was significant about this was the fact that it would be the last time the Gophers would lose for the rest of the 2003-4 campaign. Then, in the rematch, Jerilyn Glenn set up Noelle Sutton for what proved to be the game-winning goal at 6:43 of the third. The team got some great news shortly after that, Natalie Darwitz, who was feared lost for the season, was set to return to the line-up that next week against Ohio State. But, how would she do after so much time off? She scored a hat trick to lead the Gophers to a 6-0 victory over the Buckeyes in Game Two. Not bad. Game One, incidentally, resulted in a 1-1 tie.

The Gophers then proceeded to win a two-game series at home against UMD, solidifying their spot as the top team in the WCHA. Minnesota won the opener, 4-2, and then rallied to score two short-handed goals in the same penalty kill late in the third to win the thriller, 7-5. From there, the team swept St. Cloud State to clinch the WCHA regular season championship for the third time in five years with a 19-3-2 conference mark. In the process, they also earned the top seed in the WCHA Final Five. After beating Ohio State in the first game of the playoffs, 5-1, Minnesota now had the challenge of beating UMD for the Final Five championship. Down early, the Gophers rallied back to score three goals in the second period and win it. It was one of the most emotional come-backs in program history. While Darwitz, Horak and Stephens all earned spots on the WCHA All-Tournament Team, Wendell was named as the tourney's MVP.

Minnesota then squared off against Dartmouth in the 2004 Frozen Four semifinal

Jody Horak

game at Providence, R.I. The Big Green tallied first but the Gophers came back behind three goals from Krissy Wendell and two more from Kelly Stephens to win the game, 5-1. Horak played huge in net, totalling 21 saves in the win and setting up a meeting with Harvard for all the marbles. The Crimson took an early 1-0 lead in the first period of this one, only to see the Gophers rally back to tie it on Darwitz's top-shelf goal at 4:51 of the second. Harvard went ahead on a power-play, 2-1, midway through the second period, but from there on out the best line in college hockey: Darwitz, Wendell and Stephens, dominated the action on both ends of the ice. Minnesota tied the game when Nichols scored on a perfect slot pass from Clarke to make it 2-2 heading into the third. The final frame was all Maroon and Gold in this one as the Gophers poured in four goals in the third period for the 6-2 win. Just how fast did the Gophers come out the gates that period? Well, Darwitz scored just nine seconds into the period to set an NCAA record for the fastest goal coming out of an inter-mission.

Lyndsay Wall

From there, Stephens added her third goal of the Frozen Four just 32 seconds later at :41 of the third. Amazing. Fittingly, Darwitz and Wendell each added one apiece for good measure to seal the deal and give the Gophers their first ever NCAA championship for any women's team sport at the University of Minnesota. The squad, which finished at 30-2-2, certainly made Minnesota proud.

Wendell led the Gophers with eight points in the Frozen Four and for her efforts was named as the tournament's Most Outstanding Player. Darwitz, Horak, Stephens and Allie Sanchez all landed All-Tournament Team honors as well. In addition, Wendell, who was named as a first-team All-American, was named as the WCHA Player of the Year. Furthermore, Wendell, Darwitz and Lyndsay Wall earned first-team All-WCHA honors, while Kelly Stephens and Jody Horak made the second team. Bobbi Ross was named as the WCHA Rookie of the Year as well. Let's not forget Coach Halldorson either, who was named as the WCHA Coach of the Year too.

From there, the party was on. The new media darlings of Minnesota were every-where, from throwing out first pitches at Twins baseball games to meeting with the governor. But the biggest thrill by far came on May 19, 2004, when the team got to go to the White House and meet President Bush, where they presented him with his very own Gopher jersey.

NCAA National Champions, WCHA Final Five Champions and WCHA Regular Season Champions —all three terms described the Gopher women's hockey team in 2003-04. The phrase *"Get it Done,"* had officially changed to *"Got it Done."*

The 2004-05 Season…

With 15 returning letter winners and most of the team's leading scorers back in action, the No. 1 ranked Gophers had to feel pretty good about their chances heading into the 2004-05 season. Krissy Wendell was back, Natalie Darwitz was back, Kelly Stephens was back, and one of the nation's top goalies, Jody Horak, was back. Indeed the bar had been raised, but yes, the Gophers were back.

Minnesota opened the season by destroying the Fighting Sioux up in Grand Forks, 8-0 and 7-1. Ten different Gophers scored points in the opener and Jody Horak stopped all 20 shots that came her way. Game Two featured a hat trick by Kelly Stephens as well as a pair of goals from Krissy Wendell. The score-fest continued that next weekend as the Gophers pound-ed on St. Cloud State, 7-0 and 7-1. Horak posted her second shut-out in just three games in Game One, while Lyndsay Wall and Andrea Nichols each added a pair in Game Two.

The 2002-03 Team with President Bush

Minnesota cruised from there, sweeping Bemidji State, Minnesota State and Ohio State, before meeting up with rival UMD midway through November. Incidentally, Kelly Stephens and Natalie Darwitz each had four-goal games against Minnesota State and Ohio State, respectively, during a stretch which saw the team outscore its opponents 37-4.

Against Duluth the Gophers took Game One, 4-2, as they rallied from a two goal deficit on tallies from Darwitz and Bobbi Ross to beat the Dogs. Wendell and Stephens each scored goals in the third period to seal the deal. The Gophers finally had their unbeaten streak broken that next night but left the port city still undefeated. The Gophers got on the board first in this one when Chelsea Brodt found the back of the net at 11:57 of the first period. UMD tied it up in the second only to see Gopher forward Liz Palkie get the go-ahead goal on a put-back out front just over five minutes later. Then, with under two minutes to go, UMD evened it up for good as the game ended in a 2-2 tie.

Minnesota kept rolling from there, beating up on Northeastern, 8-1, at the Harvard Tournament on Krissy Wendell's hat trick. The team won the tourney that next night when they then beat the hosts, 5-3, on yet another Wendell hat trick. The girl was simply unstoppable. Darwitz and Stephens each tallied while Horak stopped all 22 shots that came her way that next week against Wisconsin in Madison. Following the 2-0 win the Gophers got a third period goal by Stephens to save a 3-3 tie in Game Two. The streak came to an end that next though as Dartmouth upended the Gophers, 7-5, in the opening game of their series. Minnesota came back to win that next evening, as Kelly Stephens broke a 3-3 tie on a short-handed goal at 4:25 of overtime. It was a huge win and a real lift for the team.

From there, the Gophers went on an unbelievable run, winning 14 straight games over the likes of Bemidji, Brown, Ohio State, Wisconsin, St. Cloud, North Dakota and Mankato. So dominant were the Gophers that they actually outscored their opponents over that stretch by the ridiculous margin of 60-11. The streak finally came to an end against rival Duluth. It was only the team's second loss in some 33 games. They rebounded that next night, however, on Krissy Wendell's second period goal and Jody Horak's outstanding play in net to salvage a series split.

Co-captains Kelly Stephens and Krissy Wendell each tallied four points that next week against Bemidji State in the opener of the newly expanded WCHA Championships, which were held at Ridder Arena. Minnesota rolled over Ohio State in the next game, 7-1, behind Darwitz's hat-trick, which set up a date with Wisconsin in the title game. This was went down to the wire but the Gophers came out on top, 3-2, in a real thriller. After a scoreless first period, Darwitz notched her 100th point of the season to make it 1-0. Bobbi Ross then made it 2-0 when she stuffed in a rebound out front. But, with just over a minute remaining in the game, the Badgers did the unthinkable. With their goalie pulled, Wisconsin made it 2-1 with just 50 seconds to go and then got the equalizer with just 24 seconds showing on the clock. The Gophers were stunned. Down but not out, the best line in college hockey came together to score the overtime game-winner. After Wisconsin got called for two penalties in the extra session, Darwitz and Stephens set up Wendell, who put away the game winner and give the Gophers the thrilling victory and the coveted WCHA crown.

From there, the Gophers hosted an NCAA Regional game against Providence College at Ridder Arena. Down 1-0 early, the Gophers rallied with six unanswered goals to beat the Friars, 6-1, to advance on to the Frozen Four in Durham, N.H. Bobbi Ross and Kelly Stephens both scored a pair of goals in that one, while Becky Wacker and Erica McKenzie each tallied one apiece.

Minnesota scored five goals in the first period and cruised past Dartmouth in the opening round of the Frozen Four, 7-1. Darwitz set a record by scoring just 13 seconds into the game and the Gophers never looked back in this one. Darwitz scored again less than two minutes later and Wendell got into the act shortly after that. Wall and Stephens also scored in that

THE PATTY KAZMAIER MEMORIAL AWARD

In 1998 the USA Hockey Foundation created the annual Patty Kazmaier Memorial Award, which recognizes the accomplishments of the outstanding player in women's collegeiate hockey. Past recipients include: Brandy Fisher, New Hampshire (1998), A.J. Mleczko, Harvard (1999), Ali Brewer, Brown (2000), Jennifer Botterill, Harvard (2001), Brooke Whitney, Northeastern (2002), Jennifer Botterill, Harvard (2003), Angela Ruggiero, Harvard (2004) and Krissy Wendell, Minnesota (2005).

MINNESOTA'S KAZMAIER FINALISTS

1998—Nadine Muzerall	(Top 11)	
2000—Winny Brodt	(Top Ten)	
2001—Courtney Kennedy	(Top Three)	
2001—Nadine Muzerall	(Top Ten)	
2002—Ronda Curtin	(Top Three)	
2002—Laura Slominski	(Top Ten)	
2003—Natalie Darwitz	(Top Ten)	
2003—Krissy Wendell	(Top Ten)	
2004—Natalie Darwitz	(Top Ten)	
2004—Krissy Wendell	(Top Ten)	
2005—Natalie Darwitz	(Top Three)	
2005—Krissy Wendell	**(Winner — Top Three)**	

first frame, while Wendell added her second goal of the game in the third, followed by an empty netter by Jenelle Philipczyk with about a minute to go to seal the deal. With that, the Gophers found themselves back in the NCAA Finals against the Harvard Crimson. It was going to be a rematch of epic proportions between college hockey's two biggest heavyweights.

This one was all about Natalie Darwitz, who figured in all four Gophers goals and wound up ending the season with an NCAA-record 114 points. The game started out slow for the Maroon and Gold. In fact, the Gophers did not get a shot on goal until nearly six minutes had passed. They got on the board first though, when Wendell put back Darwitz's rebound out front to make it 1-0 late in the first period. The Crimson quickly tied it less than a minute into the second session, only to see Lyndsay Wall's slap-shot put the Gophers back up 2-1 about seven minutes later. Harvard tied it up again at 10:33 on a power-play goal, but Ashley Albrecht put Minnesota back up yet again about eight minutes after that on a slap-shot of her own which beat Harvard Goalie Ali Boe. Harvard would tie it up for the third and last time midway through the third period on yet another power-play goal. In fact, it was Wendell, of all people, who was called for a checking penalty with 7:32 remaining in the third period, which allowed Harvard defender Caitlin Cahow to go five-hole on Gopher Goalie Jody Horak just over a minute later. With the game tied at three apiece the game seemed destined for overtime. However, with just over a minute to go in the game, Natalie Darwitz took over. Kelly Stephens came in on Boe and fired a shot, only to have Darwitz pound home the rebound out front. The goal, which proved to be the game-winner, made it 4-3 at the 18:52 mark of the third. The Gophers hung on from there and then danced like fools when the final buzzer sounded, signifying their back-to-back NCAA National Championships.

Darwitz was a runaway pick for the tournament's Most Outstanding Player Award after breaking the Frozen Four record for points (nine) and assists (six).

"Obviously, I'm honored, but the best part is to win a national championship," said Darwitz. "That far outdoes any individual records. It's a tribute to the team."

After the game many of the players emerged from the locker room wearing T-shirts that read simply: "21 for 12." When asked what that meant, they explained that they had been wearing them since early February when, after a particularly sloppy win over St. Cloud State, Coach Halldorson put everybody through a really tough practice. Afterwards, Assistant Coach Charlie Burggraf came up with the idea in that the 21 players now had exactly 12 games left to win in order to successfully defend their NCAA title at the Frozen Four. Needless to say, the movitational tactic worked.

When it was all said and done the Gophers finished with an amazing 36-2-2 overall record. As for honors and accolades, once again it all started and stopped with Krissy Wendell and Natalie Darwitz, who had proven themselves to be the best of the very best. While both were one of the three finalists for the prestigious Patty Kazmaier Award, it was Wendell who actually wound up winning it. No matter. They were both clearly the best Division I women's hockey players in the country. As for the numbers: Darwitz wound up with 42 goals and 72 assists for an NCAA record 114 points, while Wendell tallied 43 goals and 61 assists for 104 of her own. Meanwhile, Darwitz, Wendell and Lyndsay Wall were each named as first team All-Americans, while Goalie Jody Horak earned second team honors. The trio were also named to the All-WCHA first team, while Horak and Kelly Stephens earned second team honors. Stephens, who tallied an amazing 76 points, was understandably overshadowed by her two line mates. No worries, it was probably the greatest line in the history of women's college hockey.

The 2005-06 Season and Beyond...

To say that the 2005-06 campaign would be a rebuilding year would be the understatement of the century. While the Gopher Women's roster remains locked and loaded to do serious damage in the future, the fact of the matter is that Natalie Darwitz and Krissy Wendell, arguably two of the greatest college hockey players in the history of the sport, have moved on to play in the 2006 Winter Olympics in Turin. Don't forget Kelly Stephens, she's going to Italy too. Coach Halldorson is one of the best in the business, however, and is determined to get the most out of her players and get back to the NCAA Finals. Don't bet against her, she's a proven winner.

Leading the charge this year will be Junior forward Andrea Nichols, who will take over the role as the team's captain. Meanwhile, senior defenseman Chelsey Brodt and sophomore forward Bobbi Ross will serve as the assistant captains. Other contributors up on the front line will include Erica McKenzie, who tallied 21 points as a freshman, as well as Liz Palkie, Becky Wacker, Jenelle Philipczyk and Whitney Graft. Then, along with Brodt, Ashley Albrecht and Allie Sanchez will lead the defensive corps, which appear to be solid. Also gone is All-American Goalie Jody Horak, so to replace her will be Ohio State transfer Natalie Lamme, along with a pair of freshmen in Brittony Chartier and Kim Hanlon. Finally, the team is expecting great things from its freshman class, which is headed by Gigi Marvin. Marvin tallied finished her high school career at Warroad with 425 points, ranking fifth in Minnesota state high school history.

Oh, there's one more thing to consider. Ridder Arena will be hosting both the WCHA Championship and the NCAA Frozen Four in 2006. Home ice for the Lady Gophers, hmmmm... who knows? Can you say three-peat? Stay tuned!

THE ROAD TO THE 2006 OLYMPIC WINTER GAMES IN TURIN, ITALY, GOES THROUGH GOLD COUNTRY...

Seven former Golden Gophers will compete in the 2006 Winter Games in Turin, Italy: Natalie Darwitz, Krissy Wendell, Winny Brodt, Courtney Kennedy, Lyndsay Wall and Kelly Stephens. In addition, Jenny (Schmidgall) Potter, a former Gopher who transferred to UM-Duluth after her freshman season, will also be playing in her third Winter Games.

LADY GOPHERS CAREER SCORING STATS

POINTS

246	Natalie Darwitz	(102g 144a)	2002-05
237	Krissy Wendell	(106g 131a)	2002-05
235	Nadine Muzerall	(139g 96a)	1997-01
218	Kelly Stephens	(97g 121a)	2001-05
201	Ambria Thomas	(89g 112a)	1997-01
167	Ronda Curtin	(60g 107a)	1999-03
161	Laura Slominski	(65g 96a)	1998-02
159	La Toya Clarke	(67g 92a)	2000-04
134	Winny Brodt	(41g 93a)	1998-00, 02-03
133	Kris Scholz	(45g 88a)	1997-01

GOALS

139	Nadine Muzerall	1997-01
106	Krissy Wendell	2002-05
102	Natalie Darwtiz	2002-05
97	Kelly Stephens	2001-05
89	Ambria Thomas	1997-01
67	La Toya Clarke	2000-04
65	Laura Slominski	1998-02
60	Ronda Curtin	1999-03
58	Tracy Engstrom	1998-02
45	Kris Scholz	1997-01

ASSISTS

144	Natalie Darwitz	2002-05
131	Krissy Wendell	2002-05
121	Kelly Stephens	2001-05
112	Ambria Thomas	1997-01
107	Ronda Curtin	1999-03
96	Nadine Muzerall	1997-01
96	Laura Slominski	1998-02
93	Winny Brodt	1998-03
92	La Toya Clarke	2000-04
88	Kris Scholz	1997-01

POINTS BY A DEFENSMAN

134	Winny Brodt	1998-03
112	Courtney Kennedy	1998-01
85	Ronda Curtin	1999-03
69	Lyndsay Wall	2003-05
61	Emily Buchholz	1997-01
52	Brittny Ralph	1997-99
42	Ashley Albrecht	2002-
32	Chelsey Brodt	2002-
30	Kelly Olson	1997-01
37	Melissa Coulombe	2000-04
27	Allie Sanchez	2002-

POWER-PLAY GOALS

40	Nadine Muzerall	1997-01
33	Krissy Wendell	2002-05
32	Kelly Stephens	2001-05
29	Natalie Darwitz	2002-05
25	Ronda Curtin	1999-03
20	Laura Slominski	1998-02
18	La Toya Clarke	2000-04
18	Ambria Thomas	1997-01
18	Lyndsay Wall	2003-05
12	Tracy Engstrom	1998-02

SHORT-HANDED GOALS

16	Krissy Wendell	2002-05
8	Ambria Thomas	1997-01
7	Natalie Darwitz	2002-05
6	Kelly Stephens	2001-05
4	La Toya Clarke	2000-04
4	Kris Scholz	1997-01
4	Nadine Muzerall	1997-01
3	Ronda Curtin	1999-03
3	Kristy Oonincx	2001-03

GAMES PLAYED

148	Kelly Stephens	2001-05
147	Ronda Curtin	1999-03
146	Laura Slominski	1998-02
144	NoelleSutton	2001-05
143	Melissa Coulombe	2000-04
143	Stacy Troumbly	2001-05
143	Tracy Engstrom	1998-02
140	La Toya Clarke	2000-04
138	Kris Scholz	1997-01
137	Emily Buchholz	1997-01

PLUS / MINUS

+170	Kelly Stephens	2001-05
+160	Ambria Thomas	1997-01
+156	Krissy Wendell	2002-05
+149	Nadine Muzerall	1997-01
+141	Natalie Darwitz	2002-05
+136	Courtney Kennedy	1998-01
+129	Ronda Curtin	1999-03
+123	Winny Brodt	1998-00, 03
+120	Laura Slominski	1998-02
+118	Emily Buchholz	1997-01

LADY GOPHER CAREER GOALIE STATS

SAVES
2385	Erica Killewald (199 GA)	1997-01
2213	Jody Horak (164 GA)	2001-05
1034	Brenda Reinen (73 GA)	2001-05
323	Crystal Nicholas (31 GA)	1998-00
141	Stephanie Johnson (20 GA)	2000-01
61	Sarah Harms (4 GA)	1997-98

GOALS AGAINST AVERAGE
0.80	Sarah Harms (4 GA, 299 min)	1997-98
1.25	Crystal Nicholas (31 GA, 1486 m)	1998-00
1.58	Brenda Reinen (73 GA, 2769 min)	2001-05
1.61	Jody Horak (164 GA, 6122 min)	2001-05
1.88	E. Killewald (199 GA, 6368 m)	1997-01
2.54	S. Johnson (20 GA, 473 m)	2000-01

WINS
83	Jody Horak (83-16-6)	2001-05
73	Erica Killewald (73-23-9)	1997-01
36	Brenda Reinen (36-3-5)	2001-05
25	Crystal Nicholas (25-0-0)	1998-00
6	Stephanie Johnson (6-2-0)	2000-01
3	Sarah Harms (3-2-0)	1997-98

LOSSES
23	Erica Killewald (73-23-9)	1997-01
14	Jody Horak (59-12-4)	2001-05
3	Brenda Reinen (24-3-5)	2001-05
2	Sarah Harms (3-2-0)	1997-98
2	Stephanie Johnson (6-2-0)	2000-01

TIES
9	Erica Killewald (73-23-9)	1997-01
6	Jody Horak(83-14-6)	2001-05
5	Brenda Reinen (36-3-5)	2001-05

FIRST-TEAM ALL-WCHA

2000—Winny Brodt, Nadine Muzerall
2001—Courtney Kennedy, Erica Killewald
2002—Ronda Curtin, Jody Horak
2003—Ronda Curtin, Natalie Darwitz, Jody Horak
2004—Natalie Darwitz, Krissy Wendell
2005—Natalie Darwitz, Lyndsay Wall, Krissy Wendell

SECOND-TEAM ALL-WCHA

2000—Courtney Kennedy , Crystal Nicholas, Laura Slominski, Ambria Thomas
2001—Ambria Thomas, La Toya Clarke
2002—Kelly Stephens
2003—Krissy Wendell
2005—Kelly Stephens, Jody Horak

WCHA DEFENSIVE PLAYER OF THE YEAR

2000—Winny Brodt
2001—Courtney Kennedy
2002—Ronda Curtin
2003—Ronda Curtin

WCHA ROOKIE OF THE YEAR

2003—Natalie Darwitz
2005—Bobbi Ross

WCHA ALL-ROOKIE TEAM

2003—Natalie Darwitz, Krissy Wendell
2005—Bobbi Ross

WCHA PLAYER OF THE YEAR

2001—Courtney Kennedy
2002—Ronda Curtin
2004—Krissy Wendell
2005—Krissy Wendell

WCHA STUDENT-ATHLETE OF THE YEAR

2000—Shannon Kennedy

ALL-AMERICANS

1998—Nadine Muzerall *(2nd team, Women's Hockey News)*
1998—Brittny Ralph (2nd team, *Women's Hockey News*)
1999—Courtney Kennedy, Nadine Muzerall, Jenny Schmidgall *(2nd team, AWCHA)*
2001—Courtney Kennedy *(1st team, JOFA)*
2002—Ronda Curtin *(1st team, JOFA)*
2003—Ronda Curtin, Natalie Darwitz *(1st team, JOFA)*
2003—Krissy Wendell *(2nd team, JOFA)*
2004—Krissy Wendell *(1st team, JOFA)*
2004—Natalie Darwitz *(2nd team, JOFA)*
2005—Natalie Darwitz, Lyndsay Wall, Krissy Wendell *(1st team CCM)*
2005—Jody Horak *(2nd team, CCM)*

CHAPTER 19
WHAT DOES IT MEAN FOR YOU TO BE A GOPHER?

"It is amazing, such an honor. Growing up I always hoped that I would be able to play for the Gophers, so when that happened it was really a dream come true. It is everything I thought it would be and more. The program has such a rich history now and I am so thrilled to be able to say that I am a part of that." — *Ashley Albrecht, Gopher 2003-Present*

"For me it was pretty awesome. When I came out of high school they didn't even have a Gopher Women's Hockey program. That's how old I am! So, when I was growing up I rooted for the guys because that was all there was here. My brother had played at St. Cloud State, so I was actually a Husky fan. Anyway, I wound up going to school out east initially, at New Hampshire, and then after spending a year with the U.S. National Team, followed by some time off from the game, I transferred back home. I wanted to be a part of the new program here, and just feel very fortunate and honored to have been a part of it. So, when I stepped onto the ice wearing that big 'M' for the very first time, it was really a dream come true. Being able to play college hockey in my home state with the Gophers means everything to me. I made so many great friends here and just had so much fun. We won a national championship in 2000 and really proved a lot as a team. I felt lucky to have played one year at Mariucci Arena and then, after taking some time off, coming back to play a year at the new Ridder. I just appreciate the entire experience that much more I think because of it. It was a long journey getting here, but I couldn't be happier with how it has all turned out." — *Winny Brodt, Gopher 1999-00, 2002-03*

"I can't even put that into words. I miss it so much, I really do. Being a part of that program and being a part of that community meant so much to me. The support for the Gophers in Minnesota is unmatched by anything I have ever seen. So, I was very proud to be there for four years and to represent the University of Minnesota both on and off the ice." — *La Toya Clarke, Gopher 2001-2004*

"For me it is all about pride. Growing up there was no women's hockey, so I am very proud to see how far our sport has come. I was fortunate to be in the era of girls who got to play high school hockey and it was really special to be on two state championship teams with Roseville. That experience just carried over for me and really helped me to make the transition at the next level. My four years at the University were great and I have so many wonderful memories from my time there — both on and off the ice. So, overall, it was a real honor to be able to say that I was a Gopher and to be a part of starting that amazing tradition." — *Ronda Curtin, Gopher 2000-03*

"It meant my life-long dream coming true. Growing up, I was the hugest Gopher Hockey fan ever. My brother and I watched like every single game as kids, we just loved them. I started playing hockey when I was five, with the boys, and figured that if I was going to make the team I was probably going to be the first girl ever to make it. Well, luckily for me they got their own program and everything fell into place from there. So, the Gophers have always been a big part of my life and to finally get to play for them was amazing. I still follow the program very closely and am thrilled to see just how far the program has come. It will always be a huge part of my life." — *Tracy Engstrom, Gopher 1999-02*

"It is definitely an honor to be associated with the program here. It has been a journey, that is for sure. I can remember our first season and all of the hard work that has gone into building this program into what it has become. So many good people have been a part of it, from the players to the staff to our fans, they are all a part of our success. These past eight seasons have had their share of ups and downs, but overall it has been a real dream come true for me." — *Laura Halldorson, Current Gopher Women's Hockey Coach*

"It was just an unbelievable experience. Ever since I was a little kid growing up in Blaine I dreamt of being a Gopher, so to actually be able to do that was a dream come true for me. My four years at Minnesota were great. Every team I played on was different, but each was special and unique. To end my career there with two national championships was just beyond words, I couldn't have asked for anything better." — *Jody Horak, Gopher 2002-05*

"You know, I grew up out on the East Coast and really didn't know a lot about the Gophers prior to coming there. But as soon as I got there I fell in love with the place. Minnesotans are so passionate about their hockey and that was contagious. One of the first things I learned when I got there was that every little kid wants to be a Gopher. That was so cool to me. The fans are the best in college hockey and the people there are so nice. The whole thing was just an amazing experience. Plus, I got to play with my sister, Shannon, for two years too, which was unbelievable. So, just to be a part of all that was so special to me. I lived there for a total of six years, so even though I am back out east now, I will always consider myself to be a Minnesotan." — *Courtney Kennedy, Gopher 1999-01*

"It was amazing. Even though I am not from Minnesota, I felt like I was one of you when I was going to school there. Kids there grow up playing hockey and dreaming of being Gophers. There is so much pride surrounding the program and I was just so honored to be a part of that. To put on that jersey every day, and to know what that meant was very special. I get the chills even thinking of it. It was an unbelievable program, an unbelievable school and they were the best memories of my life." — *Shannon Kennedy, Gopher 1998-2000*

"I was very proud to be a Gopher. Growing up in Michigan I never thought that I would play college hockey, so when I started getting recruited it was pretty overwhelming. I will never forget when I got there, realizing that it was the big-time. I remember going to go get fitted for all new pads, which I got to design and personalize, and I even got a brand new mask which had my nickname 'Killer' on it. It was so cool. As the Gopher goalie I felt like I was the team's backbone and the glue which held the team together. So, my time in Minnesota was just amazing and it was really an honor to be a part of that program's rich history." — *Erica Killewald, Gopher 1998-01*

"Being a Gopher was awesome. It just meant everything. Being a Gopher to me was kind of like having it be Christmas every day. To walk into that locker room and see the set-up there is amazing. To walk around Mariucci Arena and see the murals, the pictures and the names of all those great players just gave me such a sense of pride. It was jaw-dropping for me. It was also exciting because I knew that I was going to have the opportunity to be on the ground floor of building up the women's program to hopefully one day be just like that. Talk about high expectations! As for playing for the team, it was such a neat experience. People know you around campus; kids want your autograph; and you felt like a rock star at times. That respect was just incredible. I also had a little bit of added pressure in that I was the only international player there at the time for both the men's and the women's programs. It was great though and everybody made me feel so at home. You know, I don't think I even realized just how special it actually was to be a Gopher until I hung up my skates. Even now, when I tell people out east that I played hockey at the University of Minnesota, they are like 'Wow…!'. And it wasn't just the hockey, it was the friendships and the memories. Those girls are like sisters to me and will be forever. So, for me, it was a dream come true to be a part of something so unbelievable." — *Nadine Muzzerall, Gopher 1998-01*

"Anybody who grows up in the state of Minnesota follows Gopher Hockey. So, for me, to finally be a part of that amazing tradition was the thrill of a lifetime. The fact that I even got to do that was special in itself. When I was a kid if you wanted to play college hockey you had to go out east. Not anymore. So, being a Gopher is incredible and something I really appreciate." — *Kris Scholz, Gopher 1998-01*

"Like a lot of kids in Minnesota I grew up watching the Gophers on TV every Friday and Saturday night. I wanted so badly to be a part of that tradition and luckily, by the time I had graduated from high school, the program was just starting. So, for me it really was a dream come true. I was so happy just to be a part of starting a new tradition. Looking back, it was amazing. I couldn't have asked for anything more. I made so many wonderful friendships here and really had a blast." — *Laura Slominski, Gopher 1999-02*

"It was a sense of pride that I developed along the way. Coming from Seattle I never grew up dreaming of being a Gopher, the same way all of the Minnesota kids did. It didn't take me long to fall in love with the school though, and I just had a great time there being a Gopher. So, it means a great deal to me now, and I feel really proud to be a part of that awesome tradition." — *Kelly Stephens, Gopher 2002-05*

"It meant getting a chance to find myself and to find the person that I wanted to become. You know, myself, along with some of the older girls, turned down scholarships out east for the opportunity to take a chance on a brand new program with zero track record. We wanted to be the first ones, the pioneers, the building blocks of the program — and that is exactly what we were. So, I am very proud of that. To help start this program from the ground up when it was in its infancy, that was one of the most powerful experiences of my life. It has had a profound effect on my life, and where I am today It was amazing." — *Ambria Thomas, Gopher 1998-01*

"It was a tremendous honor. There is so much history and tradition behind hockey in the state of Minnesota, so to come there and be a part of that was very special. Coming from a small town in New York I was just blown away by how huge hockey is here and that has been great. I mean the fans come out to support you and every high school has its own team, it is really amazing. As Gophers, all of the girls are so close and really like sisters, which is wonderful to be around. The entire experience of being there and going to school is just great. I will never forget the rush I got when I put on my Gopher jersey for the first time. It was incredible what that represented to me. So, it is a real honor to play for the Gophers and to know that I am now going to be a part of the new history going forward." — *Lyndsay Wall, Gopher 2004-Present*

CHAPTER 20
HOW HAS GOPHER HOCKEY CHANGED OVER THE YEARS?

"I think it has evolved. You know, when I came in it was pretty much the first class of girls which had ever gone through the program. We were all so young, pretty much everybody there was either a sophomore or a freshman. So, because we didn't have any upper-classmen, or any established history, it was up to us to make our own traditions and memories along the way. It was unique that was for sure. Another thing that has changed from then to now is the fact that almost all of us older girls played with the boys growing up. That probably made the game a little bit more physical across the board I would say, whereas now a lot of the younger girls grew up playing with just girls. Playing with the boys, and being in check hockey, is just a totally different style. So, that is different too I think." — *Winny Brodt, Gopher 1999-00, 2002-03*

"One of the biggest changes that I have seen over the past several years is how much stronger the girls have gotten. They are really working hard and training in the off-season and that is translating over onto the ice. Because of that, it just raises the bar for everybody to have to get that much better." — *La Toya Clarke, Gopher 2001-2004*

"To be honest, I am jealous of what the girls have over there now. Don't get me wrong, I am really happy for their success, but we just didn't have the funding and resources back then that the girls have now. They are very lucky. For starters, they get their choice of new equipment, new skates, new sticks — and just new everything. Then, in addition to being able to play in the only women's college hockey arena in the country, they also get to do a lot of stuff in the arena besides playing hockey. There is a weight room, a conditioning room, a meeting room, a game room to relax and watch TV, and a locker room that is to die for. It is just first class all the way around and it wreaks of pride. Hey, with success comes perks, and I am just glad to see the program doing so well and that the girls are having fun." — *Tracy Engstrom, Gopher 1999-02*

"We have come a long, long way. I mean we didn't even have a league for our first two years. The level of play has improved dramatically over the past eight seasons that we have been in existence as well. When I played college hockey, those were the early days of the sport, and now it is like night and day how good it has become. The training has become so much better; the coaching has gotten better; and most importantly, the players have gotten so much better. The biggest reason for that is because the game has grown so much at the youth levels and we are now seeing the results of those young girls who grew up watching the Gophers and dreaming of one day wearing that maroon and gold jersey." — *Laura Halldorson, Current Gopher Women's Hockey Coach*

"Women's hockey has improved so much, even since I was at the 'U.' It is so great to finally see all the little girls who used to come to our games way back then, are now in high school and ready to play at the collegiate levels. The steady improvement has really narrowed the gap as far as the talent levels are concerned, and that is good for the game I think. So, the Gopher program has really evolved as the talent level has evolved around it. Now, it is the premier program in women's college hockey and that is so awesome to see." — *Shannon Kennedy, Gopher 1998-2000*

"You know, it was great to see Minnesota evolve into 'The Team.' Early on, we lost some tough games to Harvard and Duluth, when they had like four or five Olympians each on their rosters. Now though, that is us. We are the two-time defending NCAA National Champions and our rosters are full of Olympians. So, it took us a little while, but we did it and now we are on top of the women's college hockey world. I just couldn't be happier for the program." — *Nadine Muzzerall, Gopher 1998-01*

"I think in general the talent pool has increased. I mean look at last year's team which featured the 'Olympic Line' of Krissy Wendell, Natalie Darwitz and Kelly Stephens — they were incredible. The game is obviously faster paced than it was even a couple of years ago. I also think that with the team playing in the smaller rink, at Ridder, that it sped up the game too. Beyond that, just the fact that they have gotten their own rink where they can hang their own banners and make their own tradition is so huge. To be able to call a place like that home is pretty special in itself." — *Kris Scholz, Gopher 1998-01*

"Like most of the girls from my era, I grew up playing hockey with the boys. I think that those days are over for the most part though, as the girl's youth programs continually feed new talent up to the higher levels. The first high school game I ever saw was when I was in college at Minnesota, I couldn't believe it. As a result of the girls not playing with the guys, I think we may see the game evolve into more of a finesse game down the road. When they grow up not having to worry about being checked, or have any fear of getting hit, then that certainly changes the way they play. We will have to wait and see. Overall though, the popularity of the sport is really exploding and the coaching has gotten a lot better too, so that is only going to help Gopher Hockey in the future." — *Kelly Stephens, Gopher 2002-05*

CHAPTER 21
WHAT DID THE TWO RECENT NATIONAL CHAMPIONSHIPS MEAN TO YOU?

"It was amazing. I was lucky enough to win a girls state high school hockey championship when I played for South St. Paul, but this was like that times 10. Then, to win it twice in a row was almost beyond words. You just couldn't ask for anything more." — *Ashley Albrecht, Gopher 2003-Present*

"I was so excited for the team, especially because of the fact that my little sister, Chelsey, was a part of it. To see her share in what I had been through was just amazing. It was also just great to see the program doing so well. This last group of girls really put us up on the top of the women's college hockey world and that is a great place to be. It will also be great in the future too, when a whole new crop of little girls can now grow up dreaming of wearing the Maroon and Gold." — *Winny Brodt, Gopher 1999-00, 2002-03*

"I was a senior captain on the 2004 NCAA National Championship team that beat Harvard. It was amazing, probably one of the greatest moments of my life. It was just the best feeling in the world to know that I had worked so hard for four years and that I was going to get to go out on top like that. To do it with all of my friends and teammates just made it that much more special too. I was so proud of everybody. I will never forget watching everybody throw off their gloves and just hug each other out on the ice when that final buzzer sounded. It almost makes me want to cry it was so special. Then, to see the girls go back-to-back that next year, I was so proud of those guys. Even though I wasn't there, I felt like I was a part of that team too." — *La Toya Clarke, Gopher 2001-2004*

"I wish I was there and could have been a part of them to tell you the truth! Really though, they were awesome not only for the girls out on the ice, but for the entire program. That really put Minnesota on the map and will do wonders for recruiting as well as the long-term outlook of girls hockey in general. Hopefully, a whole new generation of little girls saw them and now dreams of becoming a Gopher the way I did. That would be the best thing to come out of them. Aside from that, I am just very proud to be associated with this winning program. It is great to be able to say that I was a part of starting all of this way back when, and to see how far they have come. It is just incredible." — *Ronda Curtin, Gopher 2000-03*

"It means a lot because it just shows how far the program has come. For them to go back-to-back like that has put our program on the very top of the college hockey world and that is really special to all of us who wore the 'M.' Now that I am gone, it is neat to see a little bit of our legacy continuing on with the next generations of girls. So, I am really proud of the tradition that we helped to start and the fact that the program is doing so well now means everything to me. We wanted to create a winning atmosphere in which the top girls in the country would want to come here and be a part of this. Our goal from the very beginning was to build a program that would someday rival that of the men's program next door. We have a long way to go, but I think we are well on our way." — *Tracy Engstrom, Gopher 1999-02*

"What an amazing group of athletes we had on those two teams, that was pretty special. Not only were they highly skilled players, they were also team players. They understood that talent alone wasn't going to get the job done. So, they worked hard and played together as a team.

While the first one was incredible for so many reasons, the second one was neat too in that everyone was gunning for us and the pressure was really on to try and repeat. The players came prepared though and were very consistent right up until the end. They were both unique in their own way, but equally as gratifying. I was really proud of our players and very happy for our program." — *Laura Halldorson, Current Gopher Women's Hockey Coach*

"Basically, they are indescribable. You can't really say that one is better than the other because both are so unique and both are so special. The first year we weren't really expected to win but we came together as a team and did it. It was just unbelievable the way it all happened. I still get goose bumps thinking about it. Then, to win it again the next year, you really couldn't ask for anything more. The titles meant so much to not only us, but to all the alumni and to the program as a whole. It also meant a lot to the community, which was very neat to see too." — *Jody Horak, Gopher 2002-05*

"It speaks volumes about how far this program has come. When we won the AWCHA title back in 2000 it was a big deal, but with the two recent championships being NCAA, it gives them more legitimacy maybe, with the fans. Not to take anything away from our own title, because at the time that was as high as you could go in women's college hockey, but the NCAA pedigree goes a long way I think. So, I couldn't be happier for Laura (Halldorson) and for all the players. They really made us proud." — *Courtney Kennedy, Gopher 1999-01*

"To see the program go back-to-back was so much fun. I was so proud of the girls and so proud to see the program back up on top where it belongs." — Shannon Kennedy, Gopher 1998-2000

"It is really cool that the tradition is still going strong, that means a lot to me. You know, being one of the pioneers from the program's inaugural season, I like to take credit along with the girls who came in that first year back in 1997. We took a chance to go to Minnesota, which didn't even have a team or a league to play in at the time. We all turned down scholarships elsewhere out east, where there were established programs, to try something new. We started from nothing and wound up winning the AWCHA National Championship in our third year, which really put the program on the map. I personally believe that is why a lot of the younger players like Krissy Wendell, Natalie Darwitz, Kelly Stephens and La Toya Clarke came to Minnesota. I would like to think that we laid the groundwork for those two back-to-back titles and that is why I especially take pride in them. I feel like even though I didn't step foot on the ice, that I am a still part of them in spirit. All of us older girls do, and that is what building a tradition is all about. So, to watch them having so much success, that is so gratifying and rewarding to see. I couldn't be happier for Laura (Halldorson) and for all those players who made us so proud." — *Nadine Muzzerall, Gopher 1998-01*

"I was so proud just to be a part of the program to tell you the truth. We all shared in that success and take pride in what the program accomplished. So, I was very happy for Coach Halldorson and for all the girls, they did an amazing job. One title is impressive, but two in a row, that is really special." — *Kris Scholz, Gopher 1998-01*

"It meant that the program which I helped to build up from the ground floor is now the best in the country. Wow, that is really something. I couldn't be happier for the players and for the coaches, they totally deserved everything that they worked so hard for. So, congratulations!" — *Laura Slominski, Gopher 1999-02*

"They were probably the best things that have ever happened to me. I had never experienced winning anything that big before and it was amazing. It was totally new to me and the most unreal experience. Not only did we win one, but we were able to turn around and go back-to-back, which gives me goose bumps just thinking about it. We had targets on our backs that entire next season and every team came gunning for us. So, to be able to handle that pressure and come out on top was something I will never forget. And, to be able to share that moment with my best friends, that just made it even better." — *Kelly Stephens, Gopher 2002-05*

"They make me really happy because they are the reason that I came here in the first place. My goal in coming there was to help create the foundation for a program which would become a dynasty down the road. What is so amazing is that it only took about seven years. So, I am thrilled that they were able to go back-to-back, it was amazing. I was so happy for the girls and so happy for Laura (Halldorson). I know that all of us older girls from the very beginning felt a real connection with it and were all very proud to have them as a part of our legacy." — *Ambria Thomas, Gopher 1998-01*

"What can I say? I have been so lucky to have been able to come here and be a part of two national championships in my first two years with the program. Now I am about to go to play in the Olympics too, so what a thrill it would be to come home with a gold medal on top of all that! Anyway, the first title was the most special because it was just that, my first. We had such an amazing group of girls those two years and I was so honored just to be a part of it to tell you the truth. Our top line of Darwitz, Wendell and Stephens was one that will go down in history. They definitely took the bull by the horns and were leaders on that team. I was only a freshman that year, but was thrilled just to be a part of it. We all worked hard that season and it was amazing to win it all the way that we did. To run out onto the ice when it was all over was something I will never forget. Then, to do it again the next season, that was almost indescribable. We just had a real bond, that team, and we played together so well. We all got along off the ice too, which was great. Other teams came after us pretty hard that year, but we just stayed the course and emerged as back-to-back national champions. To be the best team in the country for two straight years, that was something I will never forget. I just hope we can keep it going when I return to the team after the Olympics. I would really like to win two more titles there to tell you the truth!" — *Lyndsay Wall, Gopher 2004-Present*

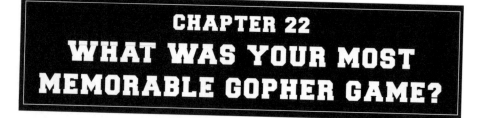

CHAPTER 22
WHAT WAS YOUR MOST MEMORABLE GOPHER GAME?

"I would have to say winning our first national championship in 2004 against Harvard. I will never forget going crazy out on the ice following the game, it was just something I will always remember. Then, to meet the President afterwards, wow, the whole experience was just so special for all of us." — *Ashley Albrecht, Gopher 2003-Present*

"I would say beating Duluth in the AWCHA Final Four in 2000. They were so tough that year and had already beaten us a few weeks earlier in the conference finals. They were up by two goals on us in that game and we rallied back to win it. It was amazing. I will never forget at one point during the game, myself, Nadine Muzzerall and Tracy Engstrom, were all in the penalty box at the same time. We thought we were done for, but we came back and won it. Then, that momentum carried us into the Finals, where we beat Brown to win the AWCHA National Championship. It was a unique situation for me because I had actually won one when I was playing out in New Hampshire. But, to do it with the Gophers was so awesome, because I felt like I was a part of starting that tradition from the ground up. It meant a lot not only to the players but also to the university and especially to our fans." — *Winny Brodt, Gopher 1999-00, 2002-03*

"Aside from winning the national championship, I would have to say that winning the semifinal game against Dartmouth just to get there was pretty special too. We were down 1-0 early on and then rallied to win it 5-1. We had never gotten past that point and were so determined.

So, once we got down early, we had a fire lit under us and we exploded for five unanswered goals. That put us into the Finals and we all know what happened from there." — *La Toya Clarke, Gopher 2001-2004*

"I would have to say beating Brown to win the AWCHA National Championship back in 2000. That was just an amazing season. Nobody expected us to win it that year but we came together as a team and made history. I think we surprised a lot of people that season, including ourselves." — *Ronda Curtin, Gopher 2000-03*

"It would have to be the 2000 semifinal game out in Boston, where we beat Duluth to get into the AWCHA championship game. Duluth was by far our biggest arch rival. We didn't like them and they certainly didn't like us. I think we had only beaten them like twice out of six times during the regular season and had just lost to them out in the WCHA Final Five a few weeks earlier. So, we headed out to Boston to play them again and wound up being down 2-0 early. We rallied back though and went on to beat them 3-2. I wound up getting the game-winner late in the third and it was so incredible. That was one of the greatest memories that I will ever have of being a Gopher. In fact, it might be the single greatest night of my entire life up to this point. Then, we just carried that excitement into our next game, where we beat Brown for the program's first ever national championship." — *Tracy Engstrom, Gopher 1999-02*

"I would have to say the 2005 National Championship. It was so dramatic the way it ended. We were tied 3-3 and thought for sure we were going into overtime, but when Natalie Darwitz scored with just over a minute to go we knew that we had it. The next thing you know we are all celebrating out on the ice for the second straight year. It was amazing." — *Jody Horak, Gopher 2002-05*

"It would have to be beating Brown to win the AWCHA National Championship back in 2000. That was definitely a big thrill for all of us. We won it in my hometown of Boston too, which made it even sweeter for me, personally, because my whole family was there. It was great though, because we were such a new program and really had very little history or tradition behind us at that point. The whole season was magical and we really came together at the end, when it mattered the most. I was so happy for my teammates and for our fans. It was just amazing and something I will never forget." — *Courtney Kennedy, Gopher 1999-01*

"It would have to be beating Brown to win the AWCHA National Championship in 2000 out in Boston. We beat UMD in the semis and from there we just cruised. It was such an incredible feeling to be able to share that with all my teammates. We played so well together that whole season and everything just came together for us at the end. It seemed like everybody contributed too, which made it even more special. I was the only senior on the team, and it was just something I will never forget. I remember at the end of the game Laura (Halldorson) asked me if I wanted to be out on the ice for the last few seconds of my Gopher career, but I decided not to so that I could dump water on everybody and start the celebration instead. What a feeling!" — *Shannon Kennedy, Gopher 1998-2000*

"It would have to be the AWCHA National Championship game over Brown in 2000. We had gotten pretty far the few years prior to that but could never get past that. So, when we finally won the title it was just amazing. Even beating Duluth in the semifinals was pretty incredible. You know, as a goaltender I actually played better under a lot of stress and pressure, and those games had it all. Luckily, I was just able to focus and give my team a chance to win it. They played hard and got it done. Looking back, it was one of the greatest moments of my life, for sure." — *Erica Killewald, Gopher 1998-01*

"While it was pretty amazing beating Brown to win the AWCHA National Championship in 2000 out in Boston, I would have to say my most memorable game was a regular season game up in Duluth my junior year. Our top two defensemen, Winny Brodt and Courtney Kennedy, were both out and we had to basically play with just two lines of players. Duluth had five Olympians at this point and were just awesome. Well, we just dug in and beat them, 4-2, and it was just a huge emotional win for us. We really pulled together that night and I will always remember that game." — *Nadine Muzzerall, Gopher 1998-01*

"It would have to be the semifinal game of the AWCHA National Championships. We beat Duluth to make it to the Finals and that was pretty big. They had beaten us in the WHCA Finals a week earlier and we wanted revenge. We got it and were able to carry that momentum into the next game where we beat Brown for the title." — *Kris Scholz, Gopher 1998-01*

"Beating Brown to win the 2000 AWCHA National Championship out in Boston was just incredible. It is hard to even put into words what it meant to me. Going into that season nobody expected too much from us, so that just made it even that much more special I think. Even getting past Duluth in the semifinal game was memorable. They were so tough that year. We wound up rallying back from two goals down to beat them and that momentum really pushed us into the Finals I think. Then, to turn around and win it all that next night was pretty amazing. It was just a true team effort and something I will never forget." — *Laura Slominski, Gopher 1999-02*

"It would have to be our first NCAA National Championship over Harvard in 2004. It was tied 2-2 going into the last period and then we exploded with four unanswered goals to win it, 6-2. Celebrating out on the ice afterwards was something I will never forget." — *Kelly Stephens, Gopher 2002-05*

"The 2000 semifinal game at Northeastern (Boston) where we beat UMD to get into the AWCHA championship game. Duluth was so good and so competitive that year and we had battled with them all season long. We had lost to them just a few weeks earlier in the WCHA Finals, so it was sweet revenge. We came from behind that game to rally back and beat them too, which was so exciting. We were just pumped that whole game, from the pre-game warm-ups until the final buzzer. It was amazing. So, to beat your biggest rival in that type of setting was special. That momentum really carried us into the next game too, which got us the title." — *Ambria Thomas, Gopher 1998-01*

"For me, it wasn't any one game that first year, 2002, it was just the whole season, collectively. From start to finish, each game was memorable for me and it all came to a peak when we beat Harvard to become NCAA National Champions. It was amazing." — *Lyndsay Wall, Gopher 2004-Present*

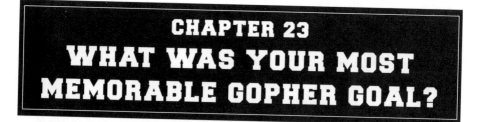

CHAPTER 23
WHAT WAS YOUR MOST MEMORABLE GOPHER GOAL?

"I scored in the national championship game and that was something I will always remember. More importantly though, it helped our team get the win and that is really all that mattered." — *Ashley Albrecht, Gopher 2003-Present*

"I would have to say scoring in the AWCHA National Championship game against Brown. I came in down the left side and faked like I was going to go around the net, but went short-side instead to beat the goalie. We won the game, 4-2, to win the program's first ever title. It was pretty special." — *Winny Brodt, Gopher 1999-00, 2002-03*

"I would have to say it was against Duluth my sophomore year when they came down to Ridder. We were ranked No. 1 and No. 2 in the nation and I got the go-ahead goal to give us the win. It was pretty memorable." — *La Toya Clarke, Gopher 2001-2004*

"I don't really remember to tell you the truth. I was not a player who was really concerned about goals, I just cared more about winning." — *Ronda Curtin, Gopher 2000-03*

"Definitely the 2000 semifinal game out in Boston where we beat Duluth to get into the AWCHA championship game. I got the game-winner late in the third and it was something I will never, ever forget for as long as I live." — *Tracy Engstrom, Gopher 1999-02*

"I scored the first goal against Brown en route to winning the 2000 AWCHA National Championship out in Boston. It was so much fun because all of my friends and family were there and they got to enjoy it with me." — *Courtney Kennedy, Gopher 1999-01*

"My most memorable goal would have to actually be the one that my younger sister, Courtney scored, because I assisted on it to make it an official 'Kennedy to Kennedy' tally. That was a pretty special moment for both of us." — *Shannon Kennedy, Gopher 1998-2000*

"It would have to be scoring the game-winning goal to beat Brown for the AWCHA National Championship in 2000 out in Boston. I came in, spun around the top of the circle and top-shelfed a snap-shot off the inside cross-bar of the net. I even impressed myself on that one! What an amazing thrill." — *Nadine Muzzerall, Gopher 1998-01*

"Nothing really amazing comes to mind to be honest. I was just happy to be out there and to have fun." — *Kris Scholz, Gopher 1998-01*

"I scored the game-tying goal in the 2000 AWCHA National Championship game against Brown. That one was pretty big and certainly memorable because it gave our team a chance to win, which is what it is all about." — *Laura Slominski, Gopher 1999-02*

"Honestly, I can't remember any one particular goal that stands out. I will just say that the ones that I scored which helped my team win on that particular night were the most special to me." — *Kelly Stephens, Gopher 2002-05*

"I didn't score that many meaningful goals, so the most memorable one for me would actually be watching Tracy Engstrom's game-winner against Duluth in the 2000 semifinal game at the AWCHA Finals. To see her expression and emotion after that was so incredible." — *Ambria Thomas, Gopher 1998-01*

"I scored against Harvard in the 2005 National Championship game and that is one I will definitely never forget." — *Lyndsay Wall, Gopher 2004-Present*

COACH HALLDORSON'S CREED...

"The foundation of our program is built on the Gopher Women's Hockey creed, which says: 'I will represent myself, the team, and the University of Minnesota with class, integrity, honesty, dependability, responsibility, a positive attitude, an unselfish and team-first attitude, accountability, a strong work ethic, loyalty, an appreciation for privileges, and an awareness of my role as a member of Gopher Women's Hockey.' Athletics is more than winning and losing. It really does have to do with how you play the game and how you conduct yourself. Our players realize that they are role models in the community and that many young eyes are often upon them. It is very important that we represent ourselves, our program, and our institution in a first-class manner at all times. Our goal is to establish and maintain a tradition of excellence that is second to none in all of college women's hockey." — *Laura Halldorson, Gopher Women's Coach*

CHAPTER 24
WHAT DOES RIDDER ARENA MEAN TO YOU?

"It is incredible. We are the only women's team in the country to have our own rink and that means so much to us and our program. It is perfect for women's hockey. I love going there and playing for our fans. We all love saying that it is 'our' rink, that means so much to us. It is a huge advantage for us too, because our fans are so loud in there and that really makes it tough for visiting teams." — *Ashley Albrecht, Gopher 2003-Present*

"What an amazing place. Playing in Mariucci was nice, but it wasn't our own. Ridder was all ours. We can hang our own banners in there and have our own traditions there. Plus, it is so much more intimate with the fans. We appreciate having it so much, it is just such a huge boost to women's hockey in Minnesota." — *Winny Brodt, Gopher 1999-00, 2002-03*

"I felt extremely privileged to be able to play there. I played two years in Mariucci and two years in Ridder, so I had a pretty good perspective on just how special it was to make that transition. We were the only women's college hockey program in the country to have our own rink, so I was so grateful to be a part of that. Our fans loved it too, which made it that much more special for us. They gave us an incredible home-ice advantage and really made the atmosphere what it was in there." — *La Toya Clarke, Gopher 2001-2004*

"I played over in Mariucci, which was great, but obviously when the girls got the new rink it was pretty special. For the program to be able to have that is just unbelievable. The smaller, more intimate atmosphere in there is perfect for girls hockey and the players love it. I mean when we played over at Mariucci we could have had a couple thousand people in there, but because it was so big it seemed like we had only a couple dozen. So, that is a big thing. It is also great for recruiting, because nobody else in the country has a facility like that." — *Ronda Curtin, Gopher 2000-03*

"Whenever I step foot in there it is all about pride for me. To know that I was one of the original girls who helped build that program up from the very beginning, it makes me feel extremely proud to see how far it has come. The arena itself is so incredible, absolutely the best ever. So, to see this place, just for women's hockey, it almost makes me want to cry it feels so good. I mean when I was growing up there were hardly any girls playing this sport. Now, to see how far the game has grown and to see all the young girls enjoying it, that is so meaningful to me. The Ridder represents a lot more than just an arena to us girls. It represents just how far we have come." — *Tracy Engstrom, Gopher 1999-02*

"It is so amazing having our own arena, we are very fortunate. It is such a positive not only for the program, but for the University and for the sport as a whole. When we have 3,000 fans in there along with the band, and we score a goal, it is just a great atmosphere. It is so loud and the kids absolutely feed off of that energy. It is intimate and really a huge home-ice advantage for us over our competition. I personally think our sport looks better on a smaller ice sheet too, which it is, versus the Olympic sized ice over at Mariucci Arena. So, we love it and our fans love it, which is the most important thing." — *Laura Halldorson, Current Gopher Women's Hockey Coach*

"It is the best. I mean to be the only program in the country with its own rink, that says a lot about what we mean to the university. We were so fortunate to be able to play there and to call that our home. It gave us a huge advantage against our opponents too. The fans were so loud in there, it was great. I think the biggest testimonial to the arena is the fact that we have led college hockey in attendance each year it has been open. So, that says a lot about your home ice advantage." — *Jody Horak, Gopher 2002-05*

"I loved playing in Mariucci Arena, it was so much fun to be in there with all of the tradition and history. Having said that, I couldn't be happier for the girls now who get to play in Ridder. What a fantastic place. That says so much about how people really care for hockey in Minnesota. I mean it is the only program in the country to have its own rink and that is a big deal. It gets so loud and crazy in there and that is what college hockey is all about. I would also say that while the rink is great for the women's program, it is also great for the men's program too. They are over there practicing on that smaller ice sheet all the time, and visa versa, with the girls going to practice on the Olympic sized ice at Mariucci. So, it is a win-win for both programs, no question." — *Courtney Kennedy, Gopher 1999-01*

"I never got to play in Ridder, I was over in Mariucci. I was so happy for the program when they got the new arena though, it is such a huge advantage for them. First of all, thanks to the Ridders for making that happen, every girl who plays hockey in Minnesota should do the same. It is an incredible facility and so unique. No other girl's program in the country has anything like that. Plus, having Mariucci next door is great too, because the team can always practice over there whenever they want to skate on the bigger, Olympic ice sheet." — *Shannon Kennedy, Gopher 1998-2000*

"I never got to play there, but was there for the ground-breaking and the whoopla surrounding the opening game. What an amazing arena, wow. The pride the girls have when they play there is almost indescribable. It represents so much not just for Gopher Hockey, but for women's hockey in general and just how far we have come. I would also add that the best thing about the arena is the fact that it was named after Bob and Kathleen Ridder, because they were our biggest supporters. Nowadays arenas and stadiums are all named after companies, so that was really special to all of us." — *Erica Killewald, Gopher 1998-01*

"I didn't get to play there, but what a facility it is. Wow. I wish I could have played there, it would have been just awesome. To me it speaks volumes about Minnesota hockey in that they would build a state-of-the-art arena like that just for the girls program. Trust me, the girls out east are jealous as heck about that. It is a really big deal and a huge recruiting tool too. Beyond that, I was just really proud to say that I knew Mr. Ridder, personally. After getting to know him, all I can say is that they couldn't have picked a better name for that hockey rink." — *Nadine Muzzerall, Gopher 1998-01*

"To be a part of this program is a real thrill. To provide opportunities to so many wonderful people is very gratifying. We are so proud of that arena and for what it means to women's hockey in Minnesota. So, hopefully our support means women now will get their fair share and will be able to compete on a level playing field. To see how far this sport has come over the years is remarkable. Girls hockey continues to grow at the youth levels and hopefully many of those girls will grow up dreaming of becoming Gophers. The recent national championships were so great to see and I couldn't be happier for Laura (Halldorson) and that entire program.

"I would also like to say that it was tough in the beginning when we were lobbying to get the arena built. A lot of people wondered why we needed our own facility when we already had Mariucci Arena right next door. Well, believe me, that arena is just as beneficial for the men's program as it is for the women's, and they lobbied for it too. The men are over there practicing on that smaller sheet of ice all the time, preparing for their opponents who don't play in Olympic sized arenas. So, it is great for both teams, a lot of people don't realize that.

"Overall, we are just very pleased to be a part of this marvelous program and to have our family's legacy be associated with such quality people." — *Kathleen Ridder, Longtime Gopher Women's Hockey Supporter; She and Her Husband, Bob, are the Chief Benefactors and Namesake of Ridder Arena*

"It shows you just how far this sport has come. Even in terms of opportunities for female athletes, it is a really big deal. For the program to have its own facility is such an advantage. I certainly have to acknowledge the Ridders too, for all that they have done for our program." — *Kris Scholz, Gopher 1998-01*

"I never got to play there, but couldn't be happier for the girls who do. It is an incredible facility and means so much for the program. It says a lot about the University of Minnesota and about how much pride they take in their student-athletes. They want to be the best in everything and certainly when it came to hockey they made a very bold statement by getting that built. It is the first and only women's-only arena in the country, which makes it pretty special in my eyes." — *Laura Slominski, Gopher 1999-02*

"It was a gift. What a blessing. I was so grateful and honored to just play there. We moved in my sophomore year, so I had played for one season at Mariucci Arena. It was like night and day. I appreciated our new home so much, it was so intimate and so special for us. What a home-ice advantage we had. I mean when Duluth came down and we packed the house, wow, what a feeling. Our fans loved it and they totally made the atmosphere in there what it was." — *Kelly Stephens, Gopher 2002-05*

"I unfortunately never got to play there, but I couldn't be happier for the girls who do. It is such an amazing facility. It has so much meaning to me too, knowing the genesis of where and how it all came together. Mr. and Mrs. Ridder were so influential in getting that whole project off the ground and without them it would never have happened. So, I am thrilled that it is their name on the outside and that they have become synonymous with women's hockey." — *Ambria Thomas, Gopher 1998-01*

"It is truly an incredible place. It is home to us and we love it. We love playing there and we love to play for our amazing fans there. To know that we are the only college program to have its own rink speaks volumes. I mean having an arena like that just shows how important women's hockey is to the University of Minnesota and just how big the sport has gotten over the past several years. I think it also means that we have stepped out of the men's program's shadow too." — *Lyndsay Wall, Gopher 2004-Present*

CHAPTER 25
HOW IS THE STATE OF THE STATE OF GIRLS HOCKEY IN MINNESOTA TODAY?

"Our sport is growing dramatically and that is really neat to see. I think it is great that women finally have the opportunity to play at different levels now. Hopefully, one day there will even be a big-time professional league similar to that of the WNBA. That would really be something." — *Ashley Albrecht, Gopher 2003-Present*

"The game is evolving, that is for sure. The hockey overall is better too. However, we are not going to see any more superstars like Natalie Darwitz and Krissy Wendell anymore, because when you play with the boys growing up you get pushed harder than you do with the girls. So, we need to step it up at the youth levels to make sure that they are playing against good competition and learning to play the game the right way. I also don't think it is healthy for girls to be playing one sport all year round either. When I was in high school I got to go to state in soccer, hockey and golf. That made me a much better all-around athlete and more importantly, I never once had to deal with burn-out or boredom. Kids need to put their skates away for a while during the Summer and do other stuff, or we are going to lose them to other sports. Parents need to be accountable for that stuff I think. Other than that, kids just need to spend more time having fun with hockey and not worry so much about playing a million games a year. They need to go to the pond and learn the game with their friends so that it is enjoyable and rewarding. That is so important. Overall though, things are going great with girls hockey and appear to be headed in a very positive direction." — *Winny Brodt, Gopher 1999-00, 2002-03*

"Ever time an Olympic year comes along the popularity really spikes. So, with this next year being another one, I fully expect the numbers to rise again afterwards. I think overall that the sport is growing, but we certainly understand that there is a lot of room for growth. The key is getting young girls interested when they are young, so that they stick with it and advance on to the next levels. That is what it is all about." — *La Toya Clarke, Gopher 2001-2004*

"I think it is great. I coach and do clinics, so I see what is going on out there. The numbers are great at the younger levels and it just seems to be growing every year. It has really carved out an identity for itself now, as a girls-only sport, and that is great to see. One of the big changes I have seen in the evolution of the game is the fact that the girls don't play with the boys anymore, and that is a big deal right there. The girls who did early on, had an advantage I think over the ones who didn't. It was much more physical and much faster too. So, the girls game has leveled out now and that is actually a good thing. We also won't probably see any more phenoms who break all the scoring records the way Natalie (Darwitz) and Krissy (Wendell) did, because teams have just gotten that much better defensively. They are much deeper too, because so many more girls are playing and they have really improved their level of play as well." — *Ronda Curtin, Gopher 2000-03*

"I coach the girls at Eastview High School, and am pretty in touch with what is going on at the youth levels. For me, I think the game is doing really well. The number of girls in the youth programs is amazing. More and more kids are starting to play and that is where it all begins. What is so neat about that too is that now, these kids have female role models that they can look up to. I never had that as a kid, it was all boys back then. I wanted to be just like Brian Bonin, who was my hockey hero as a little girl. So, that is a huge deal and really something that will go a long way in the growth of our sport. Now I see girls who want to be like Natalie Darwitz or Krissy Wendell, and that is so cool. And, the fact that people like me are coaching and giving back, that is big too, because we never had girls coaches back then who had played at a high level and could then relate that experience back to the kids. All of those things are factors in why the girls game is growing the way that it is." — *Tracy Engstrom, Gopher 1999-02*

"What I see when I watch girls high school hockey today is that the bottom has come up. There used to be a wide range of ability on most varsity teams, where there wasn't a lot of depth. Now, there are a lot more good players on the teams and most squads are two and three lines deep. A lot of that has to do with the fact that most of these kids are playing and training all year round. They just have so many more opportunities to play and to get ice time than in the past, which is great for the growth of our sport. I also think that goaltending has become much better over the years too, which has really had an impact on the game. Having said that, I don't necessarily know if the top has risen up the way the bottom has. We may not see the likes of a Krissy Wendell and Natalie Darwitz any time soon, those were just very special players who come around once in a great while. Overall though, we are doing well and I think we will only get better in the future." — *Laura Halldorson, Current Gopher Women's Hockey Coach*

"I just think it keeps getting better and better to tell you the truth. A lot more young girls are getting into it and that is what we had all hoped for way back when. Teams are getting a lot more depth and the playing field is leveling off too — which is good. High school teams don't have that one big superstar anymore, it is more of a team sport. So, overall I think it is good and can only get bigger and better in the future. I will be coaching myself next year and am excited to be able to give back and keep it all going." — *Jody Horak, Gopher 2002-05*

"I think the numbers are up and that is the right direction to be heading. More and more little girls see us and want to play hockey and that is where it all begins. This is an Olympic year this next year too, which will only help by getting us some much needed national exposure. Hopefully we can bring home the gold the way they did in 1998, and give the sport a really huge boost." — *Courtney Kennedy, Gopher 1999-01*

"I am from the East Coast and I oftentimes try to explain this to my friends out here by telling them that Minnesota hockey is just an entirely different world. The exposure we got there was amazing. We could be out shopping and people would recognize us, it was so cool. I mean we were famous to the little girls who grew up idolizing us. How great was that? The fans there are extremely smart and loyal too. The youth programs there are so organized and so cutting-edge. That is why the high school tournament is so popular and why the college teams there are so good — they all feed from that and it just keeps getting bigger and better every year. I mean the girls high school hockey tournament was just ridiculous. I couldn't believe my eyes when I saw it for the first time, it was packed! I was so jealous that I never had anything like that when I was growing up out east. You won't find that anywhere in the country either. The whole thing is so special, it really is." — *Shannon Kennedy, Gopher 1998-2000*

"Overall, women's hockey has grown tremendously over the years. We all grew up playing with the boys, and now the girls don't have to do that. So, that in itself is a huge deal in terms of just how far the game has evolved. I think that women have also built up a level of respect both for themselves as well as for their game, and that is great to see too. The biggest thing for our sport by far was the success of both the U.S. and Canada in the Olympics. The coverage that got was huge in both 1998 and 2002 and hopefully it will be even bigger this next year in 2006." — *Erica Killewald, Gopher 1998-01*

"Come on, it's the 'State of Hockey,' what more do you need to say?" — *Nadine Muzzerall, Gopher 1998-01*

"You know, when I was growing up we only had 15-and-Under and 19-and-Under, and we probably only had about six or eight teams at each level. So, it has come a long, long way. The opportunities girls have today is phenomenal. As a youth coach I can see how excited the girls are about hockey and that is so great to see." — *Kris Scholz, Gopher 1998-01*

"You know, I never even started playing hockey until I was in eighth grade, so to see the number of opportunities that kids today have is mind boggling. Minnesota is definitely leading the charge too, with more teams here than probably the rest of the country combined. I was a part of the first wave of women's hockey in the Midwest and it has really come a long way in the past 10 years. It has gotten so much stronger over that time and that is really great to see. The bottom of the pool, however, in terms of talent and skill, has risen a lot higher. The gap is closing and that is good for the game. It all just makes me really proud to be a part of it both as a player and now as a coach." — *Laura Slominski, Gopher 1999-02*

"The sport is definitely growing from the base up and Minnesota certainly has the best resources of anywhere in the country in terms of development. The talent gap has for sure narrowed over the past several years too, which is good for the game. We aren't going to see girls completely dominate at the high school levels any more because teams are too deep now to allow that. So, overall it is growing and that is great to see. I think it will continue to grow because a lot of the girls who played in college over the past several years, are now going back to their communities and are coaching at the youth levels. Their experiences and insight is so invaluable. That, maybe more than anything, will help the sport to grow and evolve for the next generation of kids." — *Kelly Stephens, Gopher 2002-05*

"I think that girl's youth hockey is growing significantly, which is great to see. It is great to see that the fundamentals of skating are being taught to younger and younger girls every year too.

These kids are getting faster; getting stronger — both mentally and physically; taking harder shots; and the development of skaters who are also play-makers has become just phenomenal." — *Ambria Thomas, Gopher 1998-01*

"I think our sport has grown and continues to grow, especially at the youth levels — which is where it all has to start. We do a lot to promote the game with young girls because we want them to not only try it, but stick with it. That is the key to success for the game to keep growing." — *Lyndsay Wall, Gopher 2004-Present*

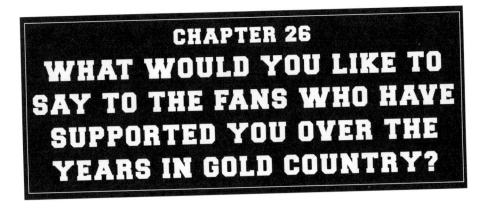

CHAPTER 26
WHAT WOULD YOU LIKE TO SAY TO THE FANS WHO HAVE SUPPORTED YOU OVER THE YEARS IN GOLD COUNTRY?

"Just thank you so much for everything. The support we get from our fans is incredible. They travel with us and they genuinely care about us. I just can't say thank you enough."— *Ashley Albrecht, Gopher 2003-Present*

"I want to thank them. They inspired me to be my best and to go out there and play every game like it was my last." — *Winny Brodt, Gopher 1999-00, 2002-03*

"I would like to offer my most heartfelt thank you to every single one of them who came out to our games to support us. Whether we were walking around campus or were out on the town, the fans were great to us and really made us feel special. They made my experience there so wonderful and I appreciate them so much." — *La Toya Clarke, Gopher 2001-2004*

"Our fans were amazing. They were so die-hard, they came to all of our games and even traveled with us on the road. So, thanks for your support, your dedication and for your encouragement." — *Ronda Curtin, Gopher 2000-03*

"Obviously, just a huge thank you, because without them we would be nowhere. They were the best. It was such a rush to run out onto the ice and hear their cheers before every game. Our fans were so loyal and so passionate about our program. They added so much energy to our games and really made the atmosphere at Ridder Arena second to none in the nation. We loved them so much and just appreciated them for everything that they did for us. They made it so fun for us, and that is what it was all about." — *Tracy Engstrom, Gopher 1999-02*

"We have a die-hard group of fans who are so loyal and have been so positive. They appreciate the skill on the ice and they appreciate the attitudes of our players. It is a very intimate relationship our players have with our fans and that is really neat to see. They stick around after games and get autographs, and that stuff goes a long way. I am proud of our players handling themselves in a first class way and I think our fans appreciate that. Our players take it personally and whenever we are playing at home in Ridder, they don't want to let them down. Our fans mean the world to us and we can't thank them enough for their support." — *Laura*

"I think our fans are great. We couldn't have asked for better fans. Believe me, I have played in a lot of hockey arenas around this country, and our fans are the best by far. They are so loyal to us and that means everything to the players and to the program as a whole. Without their support we wouldn't be where we are today, that is for sure." — *Jody Horak, Gopher 2002-05*

"They made Gopher Hockey what it is. No doubt about it. Whether they were cheering for us in the stands or hanging out with us after the games in the autograph lines, they were always there for us. We really appreciated their dedication. Their support and loyalty was just amazing, so thank you from the bottom of my heart." — *Courtney Kennedy, Gopher 1999-01*

"I honestly couldn't ask for anything more. They were so good to us as players, they really cared about us. I remember going to watch the team when they were out east last year and I saw a bunch of 'Power Play' Booster Club members. They immediately recognized me and asked me how I was doing and it was so incredible. The fans are like family, they really are. We couldn't have done it without them to tell you the truth. They were so important to us and to the success of the program. So, thank you for your love and support, it meant the world to me." — *Shannon Kennedy, Gopher 1998-2000*

"We didn't have millions of fans, but the ones that we did have were very loyal and very dedicated to following us. They were there every game, win or lose, and that just meant a lot to us. So, thank you for being there for me and for supporting me through some of the best years of my life." — *Erica Killewald, Gopher 1998-01*

"Thank you doesn't say enough. You know, we used to sign autographs after all of our home games up in the arena. Sometimes you just didn't want to do it, maybe you were tired or hurt or didn't play well, or whatever. But once you got up there and saw all of the fans waiting for you and wanting to talk to you, it was like therapy. To see the little girls who looked up to you as a role model, words can't describe what that meant. To listen to them tell you that they wear your number because you were their favorite player, stuff like that just went right to your heart. So, our fans were amazing. They kept it all in perspective for us and made us want to play harder just to please them." — *Nadine Muzzerall, Gopher 1998-01*

"Just a huge thank you. The experience wouldn't have been what it was without them. Our fans are amazing. Sometimes we had more fans in the crowd than the home team that we were playing out on the East Coast. How cool is that? So, they are amazing and I can't thank them enough for their support." — *Kris Scholz, Gopher 1998-01*

"You know, I played at Mariucci Arena during my four years in Gold Country. When we had 1,500 fans in that place it seemed like it was empty. Now you put that same number or even more in the new Ridder, and it is packed. So, our fans are terrific. It is amazing to see just how much fan support there is in Minnesota. When we used to go out to the East Coast we used to regularly have more fans at our games than the home teams we were playing did. That says so much about our fans and about how important hockey is to the state of Minnesota. Having said all of that, I guess I would just like to say thanks, your support meant the world to me." — *Laura Slominski, Gopher 1999-02*

"Thank you so much. Without our fans we would have nothing. They support us so much and we could never begin to thank them enough for what they have done for our program. They pick you up when you are down and they give you that extra boost. They made me so proud to wear that 'M,' I just wanted to play so hard for them." — *Kelly Stephens, Gopher 2002-05*

"Just a big thanks. I miss them. They supported us so well and traveled with us and everything. We played a ton of games out east where we had more fans in the crowd than the home team did. That was amazing. They are just a huge part of our program's success." — *Ambria Thomas, Gopher 1998-01*

230

"Thank you! It is unreal to see the fans that we have and to see how they follow us and support us. They have made this program what it is and without them we would be nowhere. Our sport is all word-of-mouth advertising, and our fans spread the word for us and really keep us motivated to win. They have truly defined Gopher Women's Hockey." — *Lyndsay Wall, Gopher 2004-Present*

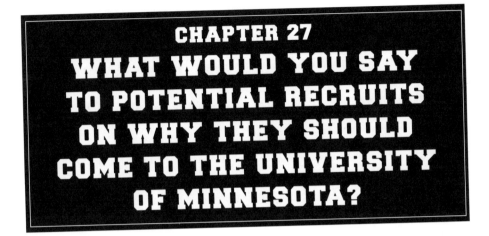

CHAPTER 27
WHAT WOULD YOU SAY TO POTENTIAL RECRUITS ON WHY THEY SHOULD COME TO THE UNIVERSITY OF MINNESOTA?

"What's not to like? The campus and university are great; we have our own state-of-the-art rink; the coaching staff is incredible; the team chemistry is fabulous and the tradition here is amazing. It truly is the best women's college hockey program in the country." — *Ashley Albrecht, Gopher 2003-Present*

"Playing here is such a unique situation. You get to play in front of your family and friends and are still able to be away from home. It is the best of both worlds. You get the best facilities and coaching; and you also get the best academics. So, it is the entire package as far as I am concerned — a real no brainer." — *Winny Brodt, Gopher 1999-00, 2002-03*

"I couldn't have chosen a better school. It was just an amazing experience. The academics were outstanding and the hockey program there is simply unmatched anywhere else in the country. The program has great support behind it and it has the finest facility in the nation. Beyond that, the coaches are great and the players genuinely like each other, so it was a really fun atmosphere to be around. I loved it." — *La Toya Clarke, Gopher 2001-2004*

"For starters, they are the only women's college hockey program in the country with its own arena. That is a pretty big deal. Then, the team is consistently good and will be competing for the national championship year in and year out. Beyond that, the team gets so much support not only from the university, but from their fans. The fans there are awesome and they are extremely loyal to the program. Last but certainly not least, it is a great place to go to college and to get your education." — *Ronda Curtin, Gopher 2000-03*

"Of course I am biased, but I would tell them that it is the best university to go to in terms of both hockey and academics. It is just a very unique and special program. The arena; the tradition; the coaches; the atmosphere; the fans — it just has it all. And it is so much more than just hockey too. It is being a part of the community, working with youth programs and being a role model to young girls. What more could you ask for? For me, it was the best four years of my life and there is no way I ever would have gone to a different school. It doesn't get any better than wearing the Maroon and Gold. The friendships and the memories are absolutely priceless.

I mean, Coach Halldorson still calls me on my birthday. The relationships that we built there, it is like family. It was just the best." — *Tracy Engstrom, Gopher 1999-02*

"I think our program is a great combination of academics and athletics. In terms of your education I tell all of our kids that they get out what they put in, because there is just so much that is offered here. From a hockey standpoint, we have had so much support and tradition and success, that I don't know why a kid wouldn't want to come play here. We have girls here now who grew up watching this team, which is just fantastic. We have fans from all over the state and they are so supportive of us and of our players. You know, recruiting has always been very important to our program's success. We got a jump-start on the other guys because we were the first Division One varsity team in the Midwest. My philosophy on recruiting has always been to get the best kids out of Minnesota, that is always our No. 1 goal. Beyond that, I don't care where they are from as long as they are good student-athletes and can contribute positively to our program." — *Laura Halldorson, Current Gopher Women's Hockey Coach*

"It is all about the experience. It is so much fun here and the friendships will last a lifetime. There is just no better place to go to school and to play hockey then at the University of Minnesota." — *Jody Horak, Gopher 2002-05*

"Whenever I see recruits out here in Boston, I tell them to go and see the campus. I tell them to take a visit and spend a weekend there being a part of the action. The entire experience there just sells itself I think. The University of Minnesota is in the hub of the Twin Cities and there is just so much to do there. Academically, it is a top notch school as well, which is why we are going there in the first place. So, between having a great academic institution and the best women's college hockey program in the country, it is really an easy sell." — *Courtney Kennedy, Gopher 1999-01*

"First, the school is unbelievable as far as academics go. The campus is great and there is so much to do there. The coaching staff is great too, and certainly a big factor in why my sister and I decided to pack up and go there from out east. The coaches could really relate to us as players and that meant a lot. They really got to know me and got to know my entire family, and that made the transition so much easier. Beyond that, look at the program. It is the best in the country, bar none. From the rink to the facilities to the fans to the tradition — it is the complete package. It is such a privilege to be able to walk into that beautiful arena and put on that jersey. They really do it up right there and they treat you like you are a star. Your opportunities are endless there both in and out of school." — *Shannon Kennedy, Gopher 1998-2000*

"For me, the biggest factor was how well I got along with Coach Halldorson. She is fantastic. When I came in for my recruiting visit I was sold on the program; I was sold on the school; and I was sold on the facilities, but she just sold me on the dream of being a part of something that was new and exciting. Looking back, it was one of the best decisions of my life." — *Erica Killewald, Gopher 1998-01*

"Just walk into Ridder Arena and then walk over to Mariucci Arena. Check out the banners and pictures hanging all over and just soak it all in. Look at the names of the Olympians, All-Americans, National Champions and the record holders. It is amazing. You can't buy pride and tradition, you earn it. We have earned it. Our fans have earned it and that is why we have the best programs in the country." — *Nadine Muzzerall, Gopher 1998-01*

"What more could you want? The University of Minnesota can offer you anything and everything. You will get treated like royalty; you will be skating in the best women's college hockey rink in the country; and you will be a part of building on an already impressive tradition that is still relatively young. Now, when people say Gopher Hockey, the pride and tradition applies to both programs." — *Kris Scholz, Gopher 1998-01*

"Well, seeing as I coach at St. Cloud State now, that is a really tough question! It is just a pride thing. If you grew up dreaming of being a Gopher, then that is the place for you. The arena, the coaches, the fans — it is just a premier college hockey program that takes very good care of its student-athletes. Overall, it was a great time and I was very proud and honored to be a part of it." — *Laura Slominski, Gopher 1999-02*

"It is the whole package. It just has everything to offer. First, it is a great school academically. Then, the fact that they have an arena specifically for women's hockey is so amazing. It shows the support and commitment that the university has for the program and for the student-athletes. If you come here you will be competing for the national championship each and every year, something most programs could never say. Beyond that, the fans here are incredible and they support us so much. It is a great atmosphere there and most importantly, it is really fun." — *Kelly Stephens, Gopher 2002-05*

"It's not why they should come, it's why shouldn't they come. Minnesota has it all; they have the coaching staff; the support system; a great educational system; the atmosphere; the facilities; and the fan support. It is just a one-of-a-kind place and if you are lucky enough to go there you should be very proud." — *Ambria Thomas, Gopher 1998-01*

"Not only is the University of Minnesota a great hockey school, it is also a great academic school. That is so important and really the reason we are all here. You will grow as a person here through both in and out of school. So, it's not just about the hockey here, it's a lot more." — *Lyndsay Wall, Gopher 2004-Present*

CHAPTER 28
HOW DO YOU WANT TO BE REMEMBERED AS A GOPHER?

"I just want to be known as a great teammate, that is the most important thing." — *Ashley Albrecht, Gopher 2003-Present*

"I would like to be remembered as a player who worked hard for everything she got. I wasn't the biggest player but I worked hard and was able to achieve success." — *Winny Brodt, Gopher 1999-00, 2002-03*

"I would hope to be remembered as a strong leader; a strong player; and somebody who made the most of her experience." — *La Toya Clarke, Gopher 2001-2004*

"I prided myself in being a team leader and wanted to be somebody who presented herself the right way so that kids could look up to her proudly. Beyond that, I would want to be remembered as somebody who helped in the building of the program from the ground up." — *Ronda Curtin, Gopher 2000-03*

"I guess I would like to be remembered as a hard working leader who was very passionate and proud to wear the 'M,' and would do anything it took to win with class and integrity. I loved every second of it and felt so fortunate to be a Gopher." — *Tracy Engstrom, Gopher 1999-02*

"My goal has always been to have a positive impact on other people's lives. Beyond that I just want to have a first class program that does things the right way, teaches the right things, emphasizes integrity, and is very positive. Having said that, I want to have all that and still be able to have my team vie for a national championship every year. If we can do that then I think

I am doing something right. So, when it is all said and done I want to be known as someone who not only prepared her players for life after college, but gave those players a lasting, positive and memorable experience as members of the Gopher Women's Hockey program.

"Beyond that, I would mention what we call our 'Gopher Women's Hockey Constitution,' which states: 1) Do the right thing the right way; 2) Be committed to continuous learning and growing; 3) Enjoy the journey. The first one is about integrity, the second one is about improving and the third is about having fun. Those three things apply both in hockey, and in life and that is what it is all about. You know, the trophies are nice, but in the end it is all about helping to foster good people who learned a lot of valuable life lessons and went on to achieve success." — *Laura Halldorson, Current Gopher Women's Hockey Coach*

"In addition to being remembered as two-time national champion, I would want to be remembered as someone who worked hard and gave her best each and every game." — *Jody Horak, Gopher 2002-05*

"I would hope to be remembered as a great teammate first, and a great defenseman second. Beyond that, I would hope to be remembered as one of the original girls who took a chance by going out there to start something special. I am so proud to be a part of that. It is amazing to see how far it has come in such a short time. And hey, I was tough. I still rank No. 2 in all-time career penalties and penalty minutes, so that should probably be in there too!" — *Courtney Kennedy, Gopher 1999-01*

"I would hope to be remembered as a leader and as a great team player. There were no individuals on our 2000 AWCHA National Championship team, so I would just like to be one of the 20 girls who got it done that year. Once a Gopher, always a Gopher...that's me!" — *Shannon Kennedy, Gopher 1998-2000*

"I guess I would like to be remembered as the first goalie in Gopher Hockey history. I made the very first save in team history and I consider that to be a real honor. Now that the program is so good, so respected and so highly thought of, that makes me even prouder to say that I was a part of it all." — *Erica Killewald, Gopher 1998-01*

"As a player I would hope to be remembered as a clutch, go-to girl, that could always be counted on. The coach used to call me a 'sniper,' so that was my role, to score goals. Then, as a teammate, I would hope to be remembered as the outgoing, eccentric, funky girl who was full of character and always tried to have fun both on and off the ice." — *Nadine Muzzerall, Gopher 1998-01*

"I would hope to be remembered as somebody who put the team first. For me it was all about the team." — *Kris Scholz, Gopher 1998-01*

"I would want to be remembered for my work ethic. Every time I went out on the ice I wanted my teammates to know that I gave it everything I had and would do anything to help my team win." — *Laura Slominski, Gopher 1999-02*

"I would hope to be remembered as someone who enjoyed the moment and never took anything for granted. I just had a smile on my face the entire time I was there because I had so much fun and loved it so much. I also hope people will remember me as a good teammate too, because I loved my teammates." — *Kelly Stephens, Gopher 2002-05*

"I would hope to be remembered as one of the original building blocks who helped create this foundation of success." — *Ambria Thomas, Gopher 1998-01*

"I would hope to be remembered as a big steady defenseman who was a leader, who contributed and who went out there and did her part for her team to win." — *Lyndsay Wall, Gopher 2004-Present*

CHAPTER 29
WHERE ARE THEY NOW?

Ashley Albrecht is a senior on the Lady Gophers Hockey team.

Winny Brodt works in sporting goods sales in the Twin Cities. In addition, she is also a member of the U.S. Women's Olympic team which will compete at the 2006 Winter Games in Turin, Italy.

La Toya Clarke presently lives in Toronto, where she is playing pro hockey with the Durham Lightning in the National Women's Hockey League.

Ronda Curtin presently lives and works in the Twin Cities and also serves as an assistant coach on the University of St. Thomas' girls hockey team.

Tracy Engstrom is a physical education teacher at Black Hawk Middle School in Eagan and also coaches the girls at Eastview High School.

Jody Horak currently lives in the Twin Cities and will be coaching girls hockey at Centennial High School in 2006.

Courtney Kennedy is a full-time hockey coach at a prep school in Boston. In addition, she is also a member of the U.S. Women's Olympic team which will compete at the 2006 Winter Games in Turin, Italy. She was a member of the 2002 squad as well.

Shannon Kennedy is presently coaching youth hockey back east and is also studying to be a nurse.

Erica Killewald is presently back in school in Michigan studying to become a certified radiologist. She is still playing between the pipes, only this time just for fun on a men's over-30 team.

Nadine Muzzerall presently teaches and coaches girls hockey at Northfield Mt. Herman, a boarding school in Western Massachusetts.

Kathleen Ridder remains involved with many charitable and philanthropic activities throughout the Twin Cities and presently resides in St. Paul.

Kris Scholz presently teaches and coaches hockey and softball at Richfield High School.

Laura Slominski presently serves as an assistant coach at St. Cloud State University.

Kelly Stephens is back in her hometown of Seattle, and is currently playing with the U.S. National Team which will compete in the 2006 Olympics in Turin, Italy.

Ambria Thomas recently moved back to Minnesota from her home state of Alaska, where she had been coaching youth hockey. She is presently going to school in Rochester, where she is studying medicine.

Lyndsay Wall is currently playing with the U.S. National Team which will compete in the 2006 Olympics in Turin, Italy. She will be a junior with the Lady Gophers upon her return to Gold Country.

CHAPTER 30
A FEW WORDS OF COACHING WISDOM FROM LAURA HALLDORSON...

Laura Halldorson grew up in Plymouth and went on to become a four-sport prep athlete at Wayzata High School, starring in volleyball, basketball and softball, as well as in hockey, where she laced em' up for the "Checkers" club team. Upon graduating in 1981, she then headed off to star at Princeton University — where the co-captain and all-conference winger led the Tigers to three Ivy League titles. Halldorson graduated from Princeton in 1985 with a degree in psychology. From there she returned home to coach volleyball, softball and basketball in the Wayzata school district from 1985-87. During that same time Halldorson led her Checkers squad to three national club championships, and even played on the 1987 U.S. National Women's Team. She then opted to head back east, to pursue her passion of coaching. After serving as an assistant at Princeton for two years, she took over at Colby College, where, after seven seasons, was named as the ECAC Co-Coach of the Year in 1996.

Then, in 1996, Halldorson got the opportunity of a lifetime when she was named as the University of Minnesota's inaugural women's hockey coach. Her job would be to literally build the program from the ground up — from scratch. A tenacious worker, Halldorson wasted little time in assembling her first team — a squad that would eventually finish fourth in the inaugural 1998 AWCHA National Championships. Halldorson then led the Gophers to an impressive 29 wins in her sophomore campaign, capped off by a third-place showing at the National Championships. In her third season, Halldorson led the Gophers to a 4-2 victory over Brown University, to claim the AWCHA National Championship — the first such coveted hardware in the history of Minnesota women's athletics. She had officially arrived!

Coach H & the Hardware...

From there, Halldorson's Gophers have risen to the top of the class in women's college hockey and have made four consecutive appearances to the NCAA Women's Frozen Four (2002, 2003, 2004 and 2005). In addition, the team won back-to-back NCAA national championships in 2004 & 2005, establishing a dynasty in the process. Among Halldorson's honors and accolades, she has been named the AHCA National Coach of the Year in 1998, 2002 and in 2004, as well as the WCHA Coach of the Year in 2001, 2002 and 2005. Since the inception of the hockey program in 1997-98, Halldorson holds a gaudy 226-44-20 record (.814 win percentage).

Today, the Lady Gophers play in Ridder Arena, the finest women's-only hockey facility in the world. And their coach, Laura Halldorson, is among the very best in the business — making for a top notch facility, coach and program as a whole. A tenacious recruiter and extremely hard worker, Coach Halldorson has earned the respect of her players and peers, and is truly a pioneer in a sport that is only going to get bigger and better in the future.

HOW WOULD YOU DESCRIBE YOUR COACHING STYLE?

"I think as a coach you just have to figure out what works best for you personally and from there you need to figure out what works best for your players. You don't want to go too far away from your personality and style that you have evolved into, but you also want to make sure that you relate to each team and each player that you coach. I think my style is unique. I am not a big yeller, but I am pretty intense because I am very competitive and I hate to lose. I also want to keep things in perspective and I don't have the philosophy of winning at all costs. So, I think it is very important how you go about things and how you conduct yourself. Beyond that I think it is important that we have a program that has class and tries to do things the right way. In terms of my actual game style, I think I just try to stay calm and interact in a positive way with my players."

IF YOU COULD MAGICALLY GO BACK IN TIME TO THE FIRST YEAR YOU WERE A HEAD COACH AND GIVE YOURSELF SOME ADVICE FOR THE FUTURE, KNOWING WHAT YOU KNOW NOW, BACK THEN, WHAT WOULD YOU SAY TO YOURSELF?

"I got into coaching because I wanted to have a positive impact on people's lives. But, sometimes you are not always going to be able to help or change people that need help. You just have to accept that are not always going to be able to have things turn out the way you want to. Sometimes there are things beyond your control and you have to accept that. I have something inside of me that wants to fix situations and problems in people, and when I see things in my players, I feel the urge to jump in and help them change. Sometimes that works and sometimes that doesn't. It is something I have gotten better at, but have had to work at over the years."

WHAT MOTIVATES YOU?

"You know I struggle with the old saying 'you win more from losing than you do from winning' because I hate to lose. It does, however, force you to push yourself to make changes and tweak what you are doing to get better. That motivates me. I am also motivated by seeing my players do well both on and off the ice."

ON THE EXPLOSIVE GROWTH OF GIRLS HOCKEY IN MINNESOTA:

"There has a been a lot of growth and positive development within our sport at all levels and that is great. Overall, Minnesota has something that no one else in the country has right now, and that is an enormous number of young girls who are playing organized hockey. The high school league is a very unique experience for these kids and it is a really wonderful thing to see happening. I mean it is such a big deal — it gets great support from the schools and so much exposure from the media. In fact, when I tell my friends out east that our state high school championship game is televised and draws about 4,000 fans, they simply can't believe it. We have truly come a long way in the evolution of the game, and I couldn't be happier to see the progress. The girls have come so far and the sky is the limit."

WHAT'S THE BIGGEST THING YOU'VE LEARNED FROM COACHING THAT YOU'VE BEEN ABLE TO APPLY TO YOUR EVERYDAY LIFE?

"I think the biggest thing is having to deal with all kinds of different situations, both good and bad. I guess the goal is to stay on an even keel emotionally and not go up and down like a roller coaster. But that is sometimes easier said than done when you get emotionally attached to your players and to your program. So, that is the challenge. You just need to continue to learn and grow and work on getting better each time out, and that is something that you can apply to your everyday life."

WHAT ARE THE KEY INGREDIENTS TO CREATING A CHAMPIONSHIP TEAM?

"Leadership is the most important thing. Beyond that people have to care about each other; they have to be on the same page; they have to buy into the system and the coaching staff; they have to work hard; they have to be unselfish and they have to be humble with no big egos. You just need to have a group of people with a positive attitude that puts the team first and works towards a common goal. All of those clichés and more are really what it is all about."

Ross Bernstein

Born and raised in Fairmont, best-selling sports author Ross Bernstein grew up loving sports. Ross went on to attend the University of Minnesota, and it was there where he first got into writing through some rather unique circumstances. You see, after a failed attempt to make it as a walk-on to the University's top-ranked Golden Gopher hockey team, he opted for the next best thing — to become the team's mascot, *"Goldy the Gopher."* His humorous accounts as a mischievous rodent then inspired the 1992 regional best-seller: *"Gopher Hockey by the Hockey Gopher."* The rest, they say... is history!

After spending the next five years in Chicago and New York working as vice president of marketing for a start-up children's entertainment company, Ross decided to take a leap of faith and come home to pursue his dream of becoming a full-time sports author. From critically acclaimed national biographies, to regional best-selling coffee-table sports history books, to inspirational children's books — he has since written some 30 books and is truly having a ball. In addition to writing for local publishers Nodin Press and Lerner Publishing, he also writes for Triumph, out of Chicago, as well as Enslow and Barnes & Noble Press on the East Coast.

Ross has been able to achieve much of his success in the world of publishing by understanding and being able to communicate his new products with the media. As a result, he has been featured as a guest on hundreds of local and national television and radio programs over his career, including: CNN, ESPN, CBS, ABC, NBC, FOX, MSG and NPR, among others. He has also been the subject of more than 1,000 written reviews in newspapers, magazines and on-line articles over the years as well.

Ross and his wife Sara, along with their three year old daughter, Campbell, and their sock-snarfing Jack Russell Terrier, Herbie, presently reside in Eagan.

I can't believe this kid just five-holed me...